OUR AMERICAN ISRAEL

OUR AMERICAN ISRAEL

THE STORY OF AN ENTANGLED ALLIANCE

Amy Kaplan

Harvard University Press

CAMBRIDGE, MASSACHUSETTS   LONDON, ENGLAND   2018

LIBRARY OF CONGRESS CATALOGING-IN-PUBLICATION DATA

Names: Kaplan, Amy, author.
Title: Our American Israel : the story of an entangled alliance /
    Amy Kaplan.
Description: Cambridge, Massachusetts : Harvard University Press,
    2018. | Includes bibliographical references and index.
Identifiers: LCCN 2018009015 | ISBN 9780674737624 (alk. paper)
Subjects: LCSH: Israel—Foreign public opinion, American. |
    National characteristics, American. | United States—Foreign
    relations—Israel. | Israel—Foreign relations—United States.
Classification: LCC E183.8.I7 K36 2018 | DDC 327.7305694—dc23
LC record available at https://lccn.loc.gov/2018009015

For Paul

CONTENTS

OUR AMERICAN ISRAEL

INTRODUCTION

IN 2009, President Barack Obama delivered a historic speech in Cairo, Egypt, where he reached out to Arabs and Muslims to repair some of the damage inflicted by the war on terror. At the same time that he was seeking common ground with the Arab world, however, Obama made a familiar and long-standing claim: "America's strong bonds with Israel are well known. This bond is unbreakable."[1]

Obama's statement was an affirmation that American presidents have routinely voiced since John F. Kennedy spoke of the "special relationship" between the United States and Israel in 1962. In Cairo, Obama's reiteration of this sentiment was clearly strategic. He had just pointed to the conflict between Israel and Palestine as a major source of tension between the Arab world and the United States. Addressing the human suffering on both sides, he needed to reassure Israel and its American supporters that this balance would not tip the scales against his primary allegiance. He was telling his audience something they already knew well, that the relationship with Israel took precedence over that with the Arab world, and in some way set its parameters. Obama's statement tapped into a vast reservoir of narratives and images, emotions and beliefs about America's special kinship with Israel. This bond, he said, "is based upon cultural and historical ties, and the recognition that the aspiration for a Jewish homeland is rooted in a tragic history that cannot be denied."[2]

Both proponents and critics have long understood the partnership between the United States and Israel as an exception to the norms of international alliances. The United States has given more monetary aid to Israel than to any other nation and has committed itself to maintaining Israel's military edge in the region. In December 2016, the Obama administration agreed to a record $38 billion package of military aid over ten years. Diplomatically as well, the relationship is in a category of its own: the United States has protected Israel from international criticism, most notably by casting many vetoes on its behalf in the Security Council of the United Nations.[3]

The fact that this political relationship is expressed as an "unbreakable bond" implies an affiliation beyond the realm of statecraft. As much a future pledge as a historical description, the phrase has a ring of consecration, like a marriage. A "bond" connotes both identification and obligation. "Unbreakable" conveys an aura of timelessness and immutability, a bedrock connection that transcends the vagaries of political alliances.

This book aims to recover the strangeness of an affinity that has come to be seen as self-evident. In 1945, it was not inevitable that a global superpower emerging victorious from World War II would come to identify with a small state for Jewish refugees, refugees who at that time were still being turned away from the United States. How did Zionism, a European movement to establish a homeland for a particular ethnoreligious group, come to resonate with citizens of a nation based on the foundation, or at least the aspiration, of civic equality amid ethnic diversity? How was the creation of a Jewish state in the Middle East translated into a narrative that reflected cherished American tales of national origins? How, in other words, did so many come to feel that the bond between the United States and Israel was historically inevitable, morally right, and a matter of common sense?

Our American Israel is the story of popular perceptions of Israel and of the ways Americans have understood this special relationship. It starts at the end of World War II, with debates about the establishment of a Jewish state in Palestine, and concludes with the war on terror, when the United States adopted a distinctively Israeli conception of homeland security. The political relationship between the two nations has always been entangled with powerful myths about their kinship and heritage, their suffering and salvation. During the seventy years since Israel's founding, certain themes have taken on the stature of hallowed beliefs: that the kinship is rooted in a common biblical heritage and shared political values, that the Holocaust created a legacy of unique moral obligations, and that the two countries face threats from common enemies.

The process by which these beliefs developed mythic status and tenacious appeal is a dynamic one. They were created, contested, and transformed over time through metaphors, analogies, and symbols that shaped popular views of political realities and imparted emotional meaning and moral value to political policy. The belief that America is an "exceptional" nation of moral force and military power underwrote and strengthened its special bond with Israel. The United States would protect and secure Israel, a moral community of both concentration camp survivors and heroic warriors. At the same time, Israel was seen as unique in its own right—a state that is both vulnerable and indomitable, an invincible victim.

Diplomatic historians have researched the strategic alliance between the United States and Israel in the international arena, scholars of Jewish history have studied the importance of Israel to the lives of American Jews, and political scientists have examined how the domestic Israel lobby influences geopolitical strategy. However, it is in the wider crucible of American culture that the diverse meanings of the "special relationship" have been forged, disputed, and remade. Looking at popular narratives about Israel, and the ways in which different individuals and groups have understood America's relationship with the Jewish state, can reveal the making of this special relationship. From a diverse array of representations and cultural expressions, patterns coalesced to form a broad consensus about America's attachment to Israel, a consensus that came to seem like common sense. The cultural alchemy that transformed the story of Israel from a particular tale about a specific ethnic state into one that resonates with the American nation as a whole has, in turn, shaped political discourse in America.[4]

Cultural perceptions, to be sure, do not dictate policies. They do, however, create a perceptual field in interaction with those policies and political ideas from which a consensus emerges about the unbreakable bond between the two nations. Cultural artifacts—whether a novel, film, newspaper article, or museum—do not work by imposing a singular and monolithic meaning on the relationship between the two nations. But they are effective precisely because they are capacious, inviting different meanings from diverse perspectives while effectively ruling out others.

The special relationship has never been just about the United States and Israel. It has included the Palestinian people from the start, even in mainstream narratives that have denied their existence, or popular images that have made them invisible to the American eye. Dominant narratives that identify Israelis with Americans have always been contested by counternarratives from both inside and outside the United States. The most popular American story of the founding of Israel is modeled on the American revolution as an anticolonial war of independence against the British, as told in the novel and film *Exodus*. A counternarrative endorses a Palestinian perspective that views the founding of the State of Israel as a colonial project bolstered by Western imperial powers. In the 1940s, American debates about the establishment of a Jewish state revolved around these conflicting interpretations, as did debates in the 1970s about Israel's occupation of territories captured in the Six-Day War. Indeed, conflicts over narratives about the founding of Israel as being an example of either colonialism or anticolonialism have reemerged with different emphases in every decade.

Parallel histories of settler colonialism expressed in biblical narratives of exceptionalism have formed the basis of American identification with Israel. Both nations have generated powerful myths of providential origins, drawing on the Old Testament notion of a chosen people destined by God to take possession of the Promised Land and blessed with a special mission to the world. Both nations were initially founded by colonists from Europe who displaced indigenous people, appropriating and transforming their land in the process of creating a new nation of immigrants. Both nations celebrate their anticolonial origins as a struggle for independence against the British Empire, and disavow their own histories of conquest.

The providential narrative has made the special relationship seem inevitable, as though it primed Christian Americans to embrace Israel long before the founding of either nation-state. In reality, it took many changes in twentieth-century America—the emergence of the idea of the Judeo-Christian tradition, post-Holocaust theology, and the politicization of evangelical Christians—to generate new stories and forge modern bonds between American Christianity and the Jewish state.[5]

Similarly, parallel conditions of settler colonialism did not alone create an American identification with Zionist pioneers. This identification came about through the development of the myth of the frontier, which found its apotheosis in the Hollywood Western, a genre that shaped how Americans viewed the founding of Israel. By the second half of the twentieth century the United States had become an imperial power itself. Stories of Israel mirroring American development arose in the context of the modern struggle for power in the Middle East, and the concurrent global movement toward decolonization.[6]

The phrase "our American Israel" comes from a Puritan expression of colonial American exceptionalism. In 1799, Abiel Abbot, a Massachusetts minister, preached a Thanksgiving sermon titled "Traits of Resemblance in the People of the United States of America to Ancient Israel." The sermon starts by noting common usage at the time: "It has been often remarked that the people of the United States come nearer to a parallel with Ancient Israel, than any other nation upon the globe. Hence, 'OUR AMERICAN ISRAEL,' is a term frequently used; and common consent allows it apt and proper."[7] This parallel with biblical Israel conferred an exceptional identity on the United States right from the start.

After World War II, similar parallels again made the modern state of Israel appear exceptional in American eyes. The phrase "our American Israel" originally used the biblical nation metaphorically to refer to the United States, yet the possessive construction also expresses how Americans have made Israel their own. This process in the twentieth century involved projection—of desires, fears, fantasies—onto the modern state of Israel. It also entailed concrete exchanges and intimate interactions fueled by the circulation of individuals and institutions between the two countries. This combination of identification, projection, and possession has contributed abundantly to ideas of American national identity, and to support for Israel as well.

Abbot's eighteenth-century sermon grounded the unstable identity of the new American nation-state in the known typology of the biblical Israel. The sermon helped to constitute the new nation as an "imagined community."[8] The word "our" conveyed a sense of national belonging to the community of white Protestant settlers, now citizens of the new nation, in part by excluding outsiders from the circle of possession. It not only distinguished the United States from "any other nation on the globe" but also effaced the memory of the Native communities that had been exterminated by warfare, disease, commerce, and agriculture to make way for the divinely chosen nation.

Viewing America in the mirror of Israel has continued to efface such memories of the settler colonial past. Yet "our American Israel" today has many more connotations: Israel can be seen through American eyes as a model of liberation from persecution, an imperial proxy doing the bidding of a superpower, a unifying object of affection, or the exclusive possession of a particular group. Israel has embodied multiple and conflicting meanings for diverse groups of Americans, and divergent interpretations have clashed during the ongoing process of creating and maintaining a special relationship between the United States and Israel.

The idea of American exceptionalism may seem ill fitting for the particular ethnoreligious identity of a Jewish state. Exceptionalism involves two components: that the United States is uniquely different from all other nations, and that, paradoxically, it also serves as a universal model for all other nations to emulate. Israel is a kind of exception that proves the rule of American exceptionalism. In the early decades of Israeli statehood, journalists and promotional material depicted the new nation as a successful replica of America—an even shinier, more robust model. It was a country built by idealistic pioneers, a haven for the persecuted, a nation of immigrants, a paragon of modernization. Israel's emulation of the United States confirmed its exemplary qualities. Americans projected onto Israel redemptive images of their own power in the world. This affinity has idealized the exercise of military force through narratives of rescue: rallying to support the besieged underdog, preventing the recurrence of genocide through humanitarian intervention, launching a war on terror to save the world from apocalypse.

Americans and Israelis alike have attributed universal meanings to Israel's founding as transcending nationalist aspirations, as a beacon to the world, a model of regeneration, an exemplar of anticolonialism. For liberals in the aftermath of World War II, Israel's U.N.-sponsored birth fulfilled internationalist ideals. Eleanor Roosevelt believed that Israel's "model state" had the potential "to promote an international New Deal."[9] In the 1958 novel *Exodus,* Leon Uris wrote of Israel's founding as "an epic in the history of man" and quoted from the 1948 Declaration of the State of Israel that the Jews had returned to their original homeland, where they had "created cultural values of national and universal significance."[10] The oft-repeated claim that Israel is the "only democracy in the Middle East" not only mirrors American values, but also renders Israel both unique and exemplary among its neighbors.

Israeli exceptionalism has its own tensions, which cannot be collapsed into a mirror of America. At the heart of Zionism was a conflict between the search for normalcy and the desire for uniqueness. A nation-state would end the persecuted status of Jews as outcasts, by making them just like other nations. Nonetheless Israel was bequeathed with a uniquely moral and uniquely vulnerable legacy from the history of Jewish suffering. This tension would take many forms from different political perspectives in debates about Israel in the United States, as to whether Israel would be held to a higher standard than other nations or would be exempted from international norms.

Key to the American understanding of Israeli uniqueness is a belief in its exceptional suffering. The paradox of vulnerability and invincibility has framed many different views of Israel, even as they have changed over time. Israelis have appeared simultaneously as innocent victims and triumphant soldiers, and Israel as both threatened with extermination and saved by its superior strength of arms. A long-standing image of Israel's uniquely humane army stemmed from popular narratives of reluctant warriors intrepidly seizing victory from the jaws of annihilation. Existentially imperiled by potential extermination, Israel's only option for survival was military preeminence, a logic that has explained the perpetual state of war forced on a peace-loving people.

The representation of America's special relationship with Israel has undergone major shifts from 1945 to the present: from the Americanization of Israel to the Israelization of America; from the admiration of Israel as a mirror of America's idealized self-image to emulation of Israel as a model for fighting America's worst nightmares. The figure of Israel as the invincible victim reflects this shift in changing narrative forms—from the heroic to the apocalyptic. Heroic narratives follow a progressive momentum in which the protagonist is the plucky underdog who fights against all odds to overcome adversity. At the end, he defeats the enemy with ingenuity and an indomitable spirit. This structure underlay the many popular stories that formed an American liberal consensus about Israel through the 1960s. In the aftermath of the Six-Day War, many Americans romanticized Israel's way of making war as a humane and muscular alternative to the American approach, which had led to the quagmire in Vietnam. As these progressive images were challenged throughout the world, Israel began to appear less as a replica of America's past than an augury of possible futures. Israel's invasion of

Lebanon in 1982 precipitated a crisis in mainstream liberal views of Israel and shattered this heroic narrative of the invincible victim.

During the 1980s, apocalyptic narratives started to supplant and reformulate heroic ones, as discourse about Israel took on a heightened moralistic and religious tenor. Apocalyptic narratives took a range of forms, many of which have continued into the twenty-first century, including those that told of the threat of a second Holocaust, and those that told of Israel's central role during the Second Coming and the end days.

After September 11, 2001, Israel's experience of terrorism offered Americans a ready-made vocabulary for articulating their own sense of unprecedented trauma. During the Cold War, the paradox of vulnerability and invincibility had already implicitly informed American perceptions of threats to national security. The paradox became even more resonant after 9/11, when the United States looked to Israel as a model for fighting the war on terror. Recasting the United States in Israel's image as existentially threatened joined the nations to each other as innocent victims of evil forces and bestowed moral righteousness on their pursuit of indomitability.

Many of these narratives and images that circulated in popular and political culture have been deployed by groups with the overt purpose of influencing U.S. policy toward Israel. More often, these narratives displayed how the story of Israel could become a generic story of relevance to all Americans, not just American Jews or Zionists. Indeed, other minorities and ethnic groups, such as African Americans, Irish Americans, and Cuban Americans, have also lobbied around foreign policy issues in South Africa, Ireland, and Cuba, all of which achieved wide political and emotional significance that captured the national imagination at particular historical and political junctures. In the case of Israel, however, what might have been the foreign policy concerns of a particular ethnic group came to have long-term symbolic associations with American national mythology. Israel became as much a domestic as a foreign issue.

The cultural work of American Jews played a major part in the development of this association. As novelists, filmmakers, journalists, intellectuals, and museum curators, they have at times been more effective than formal lobbyists in communicating their passions and ambivalences to a broader public and in shaping the way a diverse swath of Americans have made Israel their own. The American Jews discussed here were not professional advocates for Israel, nor did they identify with Israel as their major life work. Rather, they were cultural mediators who interwove their visions of Israel with compelling myths or critiques of America, and who translated their attachments or disillusionments with particular ethnic meanings into universal idioms.

In seeking to explain the strength and longevity of the myth of the unbreakable bond between the United States and Israel, it is easy to portray both countries as more homogeneous and less diverse than they are in reality. Indeed, that is in part an effect of the myth, which not only views Israel in an idealized mirror, but also projects idealized visions of American nationhood onto the image of Israel. Examining the exclusive relationship between the United States and Israel risks reproducing the myth of the exceptional relationship. Many cultural narratives and images of Israel are not unique to the United States but have been shared and elaborated in other nations that have divergent and overlapping histories in their relationship to Israel and to the United States. There are other ways to tell this story. One way would be to focus on the domestic history of the shifting alliances and divisions among different groups of Americans in relation to Israel and Palestine. Another way would be to understand how and when U.S. views of Israel dovetailed and diverged from those of other nations in different international alliances and configurations. But that is not the task here.

In his 1799 sermon, Abbot confirmed a way of speaking about the new nation that was already circulating in the public sphere. It was a matter of "common consent," he remarked, that the term "our American Israel" was an "apt and proper" one. This book explores the creation of "common consent" over the last seventy years about the "apt and proper" ways of speaking about Israel in the United States.

LANDS OF REFUGE

IN THE 1947 Oscar-winning film *Gentleman's Agreement,* a journalist played by Gregory Peck decides to pose as a Jew to gather material for a story about anti-Semitism in America. At a cocktail party he awkwardly approaches a famous Jewish physicist, played by Sam Jaffe as a thinly veiled Albert Einstein, suggesting that the two "hash over some ideas":

"What sort of ideas?"
"Palestine, for instance. Zionism."
"Which? Palestine as a refuge . . . or Zionism as a movement for a Jewish State?"
"The confusion between the two, more than anything."
"If we agree there's confusion, we can talk. We scientists love confusion."

Smiling at his earnest listener, the scientist rambles through a thicket of ideas about Jewish identity, questioning whether Jews constitute a religion, a race, or a nation. He pokes fun at the logic of each; to a secular Jew, religion seems irrelevant; to a scientist, race is unscientific; to a worldly refugee, nationalism is suspect. The confusion he sows about Jewish identity underscores the questions he first raised about the nature of Zionism.[1]

This Hollywood banter reflected serious questions that were being asked about the meaning of Zionism after World War II. Some Americans viewed the movement to settle Jews in Palestine as a humanitarian cause, one that would provide refuge for the homeless survivors of Nazi extermination camps in Europe. Others viewed Zionism as a political movement to establish a sovereign state in Palestine for Jews from around the world. Many blurred the distinction between these two ideas, while others found them irreconcilable.

It is often presumed that the revelation of the Holocaust led Americans to embrace the Zionist cause. A Jewish state, however, was by no means a universally applauded or uncontested idea in the aftermath of the war. Sympathy for the suffering of European Jews did indeed motivate many Americans to support their emigration to Palestine. But humanitarian sympathy often foundered on the political notion of a state based on an exclusive ethnoreligious identity. This notion struck some Americans as counter to their democratic values, especially in a postwar world recovering from the devastating outcome of virulent nationalism. The idea of a Jewish state in a land inhabited by an Arab majority alienated others who understood democracy as majority rule. A religious basis for national identity appeared foreign to those who believed that citizenship—irrespective of creed—should provide the basis of national belonging. Such reservations and ambivalences were widely expressed in the mainstream press, within Jewish organizations, and in government commissions.

These debates about Zionism have virtually disappeared from the American memory of the founding of Israel. Historians have focused on the political struggle between representatives of Zionist organizations and State Department diplomats for the heart of President Harry Truman, viewing it as a conflict between domestic electoral pressure and national geopolitical interests. They have also highlighted the interplay of other geopolitical and domestic factors: big power rivalries, the founding of the United Nations, Arab nationalism, oil politics, the rebuilding of Europe, and the status of Jews in the United States.[2]

But for the idea of a Jewish state in Palestine to achieve widespread acceptance, more was needed—the idea had to be Americanized. Its proponents attributed New World meanings, symbols, and mythologies to a European movement to establish a Jewish polity in the Arab Middle East. They drew parallels between *Mayflower* Pilgrims and Jewish pioneers in the familiar landscape of the biblical Promised Land, and they presented Zionist settlement as enacting American ideas of modern development. This project of Americanization took on particular urgency in the post–World War II effort to establish a Jewish state, and it had to grapple with all the ways in which Zionism appeared misaligned with American values.

In the 1940s, American liberals enthusiastically championed this project. The most powerful arguments on behalf of Zionism appeared in left-leaning publications, such as *The Nation,* the *New Republic,* and *PM*—not in the *New York Times, Commentary Magazine,* or *Life,* all of which took skeptical or noncommittal stances toward the Zionist movement. Liberal journalists, activists, and politicians fused humanitarian and political understandings to create an influential and enduring narrative of Zionism as a modern progressive force for universal good. Their way of narrating the founding of Israel was not a historical inevitability, but rather the outcome of a struggle in which the stories we are so familiar with today prevailed over others.

Contested Narratives

The United States first confronted the question of Palestine in the displaced persons camps of occupied Germany. At the end of the war, the army was holding tens of thousands of Jewish concentration camp survivors in the American sector. Haunting images of gaunt refugees behind barbed wire—some still wearing prison garb—filled newspapers and newsreels for months after the liberation of the death camps. President Truman appointed attorney Earl Harrison to lead an investigation, and his report on the crowded, unsanitary, and dismal conditions in the camps concluded chillingly: "We appear to be treating the Jews as the Nazis treated them except that we do not exterminate them." Harrison recommended that one hundred thousand displaced persons (DPs) be permitted to settle in Palestine immediately. Truman agreed and called on Great Britain to end its restrictions on Jewish immigration, which had been in effect since 1939.[3]

British foreign secretary Ernest Bevin responded by inviting Truman to convene a joint commission to investigate the impact of mass immigration on the inhabitants of Palestine and its governance. Since the fall of the Ottoman Empire in World War I, Britain had ruled Palestine under a mandate endorsed by the League of Nations in 1922. The mandate incorporated the 1917 Balfour Declaration, which expressed

British favor for "the establishment in Palestine of a national home of the Jewish people" with the caveat that "nothing shall be done which may prejudice the civil and religious rights of existing non-Jewish communities in Palestine." From the start, the meaning of the declaration had been open to interpretation and criticism—and it continues to be controversial today. The Zionist movement welcomed it as the legal foundation of the right to statehood, while Arab spokesmen denounced it as an imperial imposition with no legal standing. The British government considered that it had fulfilled its obligation by facilitating the creation of a home for those Jews who settled in Palestine, without regard to statehood.

Formation of the Anglo-American Committee of Inquiry represented a last-ditch effort by the British to maintain a foothold in their increasingly vulnerable empire in the Middle East. For its part, the United States was now, for the first time, officially participating in policymaking for Palestine. Each government appointed six members, selected for their supposed impartiality (that is, they could not be Jews, Arabs, Muslims, experts in the field, or women). Federal Judge Joseph Hutcheson, a Texas Democrat, chaired the American delegation, which included Frank Aydelotte, director of the Institute for Advanced Study; Frank Buxton, editor of the *Boston Herald;* Bartley Crum, an attorney from California; William Phillips, a career diplomat; and James G. McDonald, who was the League of Nations high commissioner for refugees from Germany in the 1930s and would later be appointed the first U.S. ambassador to Israel.[4] In the first four months of 1946, the committee held public hearings in Washington, D.C., London, Cairo, and Jerusalem, and members visited DP camps in Europe, as well as Arab capitals throughout the Middle East.

The committee focused primarily on the problem of resettling Jewish refugees, and secondarily on the consequences of this resettlement for Arab inhabitants of Palestine. The final report recommended the immediate immigration of one hundred thousand Jewish refugees on humanitarian grounds, but it rejected the political establishment of a Jewish state in Palestine.[5] The report antagonized both Arabs and Zionists, and the United States and Great Britain never agreed on its implementation. Escalating violence by Jewish militias made the British Mandate increasingly unpopular and costly to a nation recovering from

The Anglo-American Committee of Inquiry at the Jerusalem train station, 1946.

a devastating war. In 1947 the British government decided to end the mandate and to place the question of Palestine's future in the hands of the newly founded United Nations.

Although the Anglo-American Committee ultimately failed to direct policy, its proceedings remain invaluable today. They offer a kaleidoscopic perspective on the passionate debates about what the *Christian Science Monitor* called "the explosive, nettlesome, Gordian knot—call it any of these—of the Palestinian problem."[6] The committee's public hearings provided an international stage on which almost every major actor in the struggle over Palestine played a role. An avid press covered testimonies by leaders of the Zionist movement, representatives from Arab organizations, refugees in the DP camps, British officials, demographers and agricultural specialists, and celebrity intellectuals.

Two notable committee members, one American and one British, published books about their experiences. Bartley Crum, an ambitious civil rights attorney from San Francisco, wrote *Behind the Silken Curtain: A Personal Account of Anglo-American Diplomacy in Palestine and the Middle East*. Richard Crossman, a socialist Labour Party MP with an Oxford PhD, wrote *Palestine Mission: A Personal Record*. Published in 1947, the two books offer more than insider accounts of the committee's travails. Through a combination of travelogue and memoir, political meditation and polemic, both authors convey the personal reckoning that led them to champion the cause of an independent Jewish state. Crum and Crossman were the youngest and most progressive members of their national delegations. They were the only committee members to argue for Jewish statehood, although they disagreed about the impact of Zionism on the Arab inhabitants of Palestine. Written from a critical stance on the waning British Empire, Crossman's book provides a valuable contrast with the views of his American colleagues, whose nation was becoming a greater power in the Middle East. Even though their stance on statehood was a minority position within the committee, their writings presage views that would become dominant in the United Kingdom and the United States.

The last American to be appointed to the committee, Bartley Crum was promoted by David Niles, Truman's liaison with labor and minority groups and his intermediary with Zionist organizations. The State Department tried to block Crum because of his left-wing affiliations, which earned him the moniker "Comrade Crum." As an attorney, he had campaigned against discrimination toward black employees by southern railroads, and he had served as counsel at the founding of the United Nations. At the time of his appointment, he was preparing to leave for Spain to defend two members of the anti-Franco underground. While writing his book after the committee disbanded, he joined Paul Robeson and W. E. B. Du Bois in endorsing the American Crusade against Lynching.

A journalist traveling with the committee described Crum as a liberal playboy of sorts, "serious, courageous, and prepared like a trained prizefighter to battle for his convictions. He preferred drinking to eating and was so good looking that the people often turned to stare at him on the German streets." Richard Crossman eyed him as cynically angling for a political career "which could be made or marred by the attitude he adopted toward the Jewish question." Because of Crum's White House connections, committee members would avoid speaking freely in front of him, and his contacts sometimes worried that his overzealousness marred the reliability of the information he passed on to them.[7]

A story of political and spiritual awakening, *Behind the Silken Curtain* shows how an American progressive, a liberal Catholic with little knowledge of the Middle East and no experience outside the United States, confronted manifold arguments about Zionism from points of view he had never before encountered. Crum describes in detail how he listened to multiple Jewish and Arab testimonies, only to be convinced of the justice of the Zionist cause. Crum played a noteworthy role in the Americanization of Zionism precisely because he was not a government official or a Jewish member of a Zionist organization, although he interacted with major figures in both groups. His story exemplifies the synergy between an early Zionist lobby seeking to galvanize U.S. public opinion and the larger American culture in which it operated. His views can neither be reduced to pure pandering nor attributed to independent thinking alone. He understood Zionism as a liberal cause, and he made it a personal one.

In 1940, Crum had served as a close advisor to the presidential campaign of Wendell Willkie, who was running as a liberal Republican. *One World,* Willkie's 1943 runaway bestseller, became Crum's guidebook for his first trip abroad with the committee. Willkie's popular book described his world tour at the behest of President Franklin Roosevelt to muster support for the war and to counter isolationist sentiment in the

United States. Willkie's internationalist vision linked the wartime battle against fascism to the fight for social equality at home and the struggle against colonialism abroad. He tied future international stability to economic improvements in the global standard of living, which would remake the world in the image of modern, middle-class America. Crum relished Willkie's utopian ideal of ameliorating social inequality without social conflict.

Crum's "one world" ideal contrasted with the conflict-ridden worldview of his British colleague Richard Crossman. On his plane ride across the Aegean on the way to Cairo, Crossman pondered the difficulty of fulfilling the committee's charge: "We are trying to link up five different worlds in one solution: Washington, London, Vienna, Cairo, Jerusalem. It can't be done."[8] Crossman's tragic vision of the irreconcilable differences between colliding worlds was rooted in his commitment to democratic socialism and his awareness of the consequences of British colonialism.

On January 4, 1946, the Anglo-American Committee of Inquiry opened its hearings in Washington, D.C., where witnesses presented divergent and incompatible perspectives on the fate of Palestine and the desirability and feasibility of a Jewish state. From the start, Jewish organizations took center stage, though they by no means presented a united front.

At the end of World War II, the Zionist movement—founded in 1897 by Theodore Herzl in Basel, Switzerland—consisted of many organizations both inside and outside Palestine. The Jewish Agency for Palestine, headed by David Ben-Gurion since 1935, had responsibility for all aspects of Jewish settlement, including immigration and defense, and it conducted many state-like functions, including posting representatives abroad and running a press agency. Outside Palestine, the onset of World War II had shifted the center of Zionist advocacy from Europe to the United States. In 1942, in response to emerging reports of the mass murder of Jews, American Zionists held an emergency conference at the Biltmore Hotel in New York City, which became a political watershed for the movement. Rejecting the gradualist efforts of the past, delegates from around the world unanimously called for unfettered Jewish immigration to Palestine and demanded that "Palestine be established as a Jewish Commonwealth integrated in the structure of the new democratic world."[9]

The leaders of the American Zionist Emergency Council (AZEC), the group that coordinated political advocacy in the United States, distrusted the Anglo-American Committee. They regarded the establishment of a Jewish state not as a question to investigate, but as an international commitment to fulfill with all due haste.[10] Although the outspoken head of AZEC, Rabbi Abba Hillel Silver, refused to participate in the committee's Washington hearing, two well-known representatives of the group did testify. Rabbi Stephen Wise, the seventy-two-year-old veteran leader of American Zionism, moved the audience to tears. Wise, whom Crossman described as "speaking and looking like the prophet Micah," recounted the history of Zionism as a heroic response to modern anti-Semitism, from Tsarist Russia to Nazi Germany. He called on Christians worldwide to set right their historical guilt for Jewish suffering by guaranteeing that "Palestine shall be yours." Emanuel Neuman, the official representative of AZEC, argued from legal rather than moral grounds, "not to plead a favor, but to assert a right" of the Jewish people to "rebuild their national existence." To fulfill the goal of achieving a Jewish majority, Neuman proposed a population exchange that would entail transporting Jewish refugees to Palestine while transferring the Arab inhabitants of Palestine to other Arab countries.[11]

Leaders of non-Zionist Jewish organizations also testified. Without addressing the issue of statehood, the director of the American Jewish Joint Distribution Committee, Judge Joseph Proskauer, made an urgent humanitarian plea for the immediate transport of the displaced persons "to the only available haven, Palestine." The difference between the Zionists and non-Zionists, as Crum explained, was that the former "defined the Jewish case for Palestine as more fundamental than an answer to refugeeism." The political demand for a state included all of world Jewry, and "it involved the security of the position of Jews in a world composed of nationalities each with territorial centers." In the postwar world order, this view implied, only a nation-state could guarantee full human rights and freedom from oppression.[12]

To the anti-Zionist American Council for Judaism, founded in 1942, the idea of Jews as a nation—rather than a religion—was an anathema that would only provoke anti-Semitism and charges of dual loyalty. The president of the organization, Lessing Rosenwald, rejected the "Hitlerian concept of a Jewish state" and warned of the dangers of "Jewish nationalism." He proposed that the refugees languishing in DP camps emigrate to a variety of countries that were members of the newly established UN. This minority view raised such hostility at the hearing that Wise interrupted Rosenwald from the floor, and Crossman felt the "mental daggers in the audience behind him." Nonetheless, the American co-chair, Judge Hutcheson, agreed with Rosenwald that a Jewish lineage no more determined nationality than did his own Scottish heritage.[13]

In a more popular appearance, Albert Einstein took the stand with flash bulbs going off and "adoring women gazing up at him like Gandhi." The audience cheered his condemnation of British imperialism for its divide-and-conquer colonial strategy. He insisted that when freed from this yoke, Arabs and Jews could live together, and he opposed the idea of a Jewish state. "The State idea is not according to my heart," he testified. "It is connected with narrow-mindedness and economic obstacles. I believe it is bad. I have always been against it." He criticized the idea of a Jewish commonwealth as "an imitation of Europe" and said that recent history proved that "the end of Europe was brought about by nationalism." Questions of whether Jews were a nation or a religion troubled the committee throughout its deliberations, as did Einstein's warnings about the dangers of nationalism.[14]

At the hearings later that day, another famous American intellectual refuted Einstein's views. Reinhold Niebuhr, a renowned liberal Protestant theologian, represented the Christian Council on Palestine. He based his case not on the biblical covenant, as other ministers from the council did, but on the ravages of Nazism. Only national sovereignty, he argued, could protect world Jewry from persecution, as well as from the potential "racial suicide" of assimilation in the United States. As a realist, he recognized the injustice of any political solution, but he agreed with Neuman that the Arab population could be transferred to the "vast hinterland of the Middle East" in order to create a Jewish majority in Palestine.[15]

The prospect of resettlement was contested by representatives from the Institute for Arab-American Affairs who spoke before the committee. Philip Hitti, professor of Semitic literature at Princeton University, testified that the Arab claim to Palestine rested on the "very simple fact" of "continued and uninterrupted physical and cultural association between land and people." Rejecting the humanitarian argument for Jewish immigration as "an attenuated form of conquest," he added that "in the mind of the Arab, every Zionist coming in is a potential warrior." According to Crum, Hitti and his colleagues "asserted that Zionism was indefensible and unfeasible on moral, historic, and practical grounds"—that it was an "imposition on the Arabs of an alien way of life which they resented and to which they would never submit." To Crum, Hitti was substituting Arab nationalism for Zionism when he rejected the legal premise of British and international promises to the Jews as devoid of "moral validity since Palestine is inhabited by an Arab majority and therefore, ought to become an Arab state."[16]

The testimonies of Hitti and his colleagues rattled Crum. "Were the committee instructed to determine the composition and wishes of Palestine's present population," he speculated, "the Arab case might have been unanswerable." This "unanswerable" question, however, haunted the committee throughout its investigation. How could the desires of a minority—no matter how morally compelling—be imposed on a majority, other than as a form of domination? The "fair-minded Americans" on the committee became worried, wrote Crossman, when the Zionists expressed less interest in saving Jews than in establishing a state throughout the entire land of Palestine at the cost of its Arab inhabitants: "As democrats they are shocked."[17]

The idea of a Jewish state ruling a land with an Arab majority may have offended the democratic sensibilities of some of Crossman's American colleagues, but not all Americans shared this concern. On his first visit to the United States, Crossman was surprised to find widespread enthusiasm for the Zionist cause among the American public, and he attributed this sentiment to the "frontier mentality." "Zionism after all," he wrote, "is merely the attempt by the European Jew to rebuild his national life on the soil of Palestine in much the same way as the American settler developed the West. So the American will give the Jewish settler in Palestine the benefit of the doubt, and regard the Arab as the aboriginal who must go down before the march of progress." Crossman found this attitude typical of all settler societies: "The American, like the Australian and South African, has opened up a virgin country and conquered it for the white man. In so doing, he has had to fight a long battle against the aboriginal. He knows by bitter experience what such a battle means."[18]

Remarks by Crossman's committee colleague Frank Buxton, Pulitzer Prize–winning editor of the *Boston Herald,* supported Crossman's observations. In the committee's final deliberations, Buxton not only likened Jewish settlement to the American "conquest of Indians" and the "inevitable giving way of a backward people before a more modern and practical one," but he also claimed that "there was such a thing as an international law of eminent domain" and that "ultimately the worthy, the enterprising, the improvers, were bound to displace the backward folks."[19] Thus, he imagined a violent act of conquest as a step in the inevitable march of progress, in which the Arabs played the role of the "vanishing Indian."

The argument against Zionism threatened to unsettle this American narrative by awakening the possibility of an alternative past. Any proposal to halt Jewish settlement in favor of the Arab inhabitants would challenge the hallowed belief of Americans like Buxton that their nation demonstrated the unstoppable march of progress and civilization. Even though "the few surviving red Indians are now carefully protected in reserves," wrote Crossman, "America knows that if an imperial power had espoused the cause of the red Indians and argued that no settlement could be permitted, which was damaging to their rights, and that the development of the West could only be permitted according to the economic capacity of the country, half of the United States would still be virgin forest today." The same argument on behalf of the indigenous Arabs could have been made on behalf of Indians. "Because our own history conditions our political thinking," concluded Crossman, "Americans, other things being equal, will always give their sympathy to the pioneer and suspect an empire which thwarts the white settler in the name of native rights."[20] For Crum or Buxton to face seriously the "unanswerable question" of Arab self-determination was as unthinkable as it would be to espouse the original "cause of the red Indians."

After the meeting in Washington, the committee held hearings in London, where it heard similar arguments with more input from British Mandate officials. Then the members split up to visit DP camps in different European countries. The arguments in Washington and London did not prepare any of the committee members for the visceral immediacy of the suffering they witnessed in Germany and eastern Europe. On a nightmarish journey into the underworld, as Crossman described it, they "smelled the unique and unforgettable smell of huddled homeless humanity." They saw for themselves what it meant to be "the isolated survivor of a family deported to a German concentration camp or slave labor." Appalled by the squalid, overcrowded camps, they agreed that Jews had no viable present or future in eastern Europe. Unlike millions of other displaced persons, they could not be repatriated to their countries of origin; their homes and entire communities had been savagely destroyed and their property stolen, and anti-Semitism had even intensified after the war.[21]

In each camp, the committee members were greeted by DPs holding photographs of Theodor Herzl and placards reading "Open the Gates of Palestine!" In dramatic hearings, refugees of all ages expressed their fervent conviction that only in a Jewish state could they build a home free of persecution. They believed that "their one escape from Hell was Palestine," and they claimed that they would rather die fighting Arabs as "members of a Hebrew nation" than "rot away" in "assembly centers in Germany run by British and Americans who talked of humanity but shut their doors to human suffering." In a questionnaire asking for their second choice, if Palestine was unavailable, hundreds wrote "Crematorium."[22]

In the face of such emotional evidence, the committee tried to ascertain whether the DPs sincerely wanted to go to Palestine, or whether the idea was "the result of Zionist propaganda." Historians have shown that both factors were at play. Representatives from the Jewish Agency for Palestine infiltrated the camps to exert pressure on the refugees, from filling out questionnaires for them, to coaching potential witnesses, to coercing their enlistment in the Haganah, the major paramilitary organization of the Jewish settlement in Palestine. A poll showing that 96 percent of the DPs preferred Palestine over any other destination surprised even the Zionist organizers themselves.[23] Manipulated or not, many refugees did find renewed purpose by participating in Zionist activities, which gave meaning to their shattered lives and discipline to everyday chaos. Crossman and Crum both marveled at the high morale among DPs preparing for a future in Palestine, and Crossman contended that even "if there had not been a single foreign Zionist or a trace of Zionist propaganda in the camps these people would have opted for Palestine."[24]

As far as Crum was concerned, the committee could have concluded its work in Europe without setting foot in Palestine, and he lobbied unsuccessfully for an interim report demanding the immediate transport of the DPs to Palestine. Crum was especially alarmed by the evidence of resurgent anti-Semitism plaguing postwar Europe. As a practicing Catholic, he was shocked to hear bishops in Vienna voice blatant anti-Semitic views. This experience made him reflect on his own "early conditioning" and his enlightenment as a teenager by a liberal priest—who had been rejected by the Church hierarchy—that "every Catholic is spiritually a Semite." He related this religious insight to Wendell Willkie's belief that all racial or religious prejudice was a "sickness affecting civilization itself." By rescuing Jews from Europe, Crum was trying to purge his own anti-Semitic upbringing. He believed that in leading the charge to help Jews abroad, he had discovered a cure for the racism infecting the culture he had been raised in.[25]

The problem of anti-Semitism suffused the committee's debates about the establishment of a Jewish state in ways that may seem surprising today. Even advocacy for Zionism often had anti-Semitic overtones, a connection that has now been largely obscured by the mainstream story that in championing the Jewish state, Americans like Crum were rejecting anti-Semitism and trying to make amends for the Holocaust. In *Palestine Mission,* Crossman discussed this seeming paradox, calling attention to the ways that anti-Semitism could fuel pro-Zionist arguments. Although he agreed with Crum that the Jewish DPs had no place to go but Palestine, he saw this destination as a symptom of, rather than a solution to, the problem of Western anti-Semitism. "Nine months after V-E Day," he wrote, the Jews in the camps saw that "their British and American liberators made no move to accept them into their countries" and knew "they were not wanted by the Western democracies." Crossman castigated Americans as hypocrites for advocating that the gates of Palestine be opened to the same people who were barred at the gates of America. He underlined the "legitimate Arab objection that democracies should practice humanity as well as preach it to Moslems" and warned of the unseemly appearance of demanding that "one hundred thousand Jews should enter Palestine, while refusing to modify the American immigration laws."[26]

But this is exactly what the committee did demand. Crum and McDonald successfully urged Truman to upstage the report's official release by publicly accepting this single recommendation. British foreign secretary Bevin responded cynically: "Regarding the agitation in the

United States, and particularly in New York, for 100,000 to be put into Palestine. I hope it will not be misunderstood in America if I say, with the purest of motives, that that was because they do not want too many of them in New York." Bevin's remarks created a scandal, with newspapers deriding his "outright anti-Semitic outburst." Bevin did hit a raw nerve; as *Commentary* magazine put it, "the readiness of the United States to tell others what they ought to do, while doing little or nothing itself . . . had long been one of its less endearing characteristics in the eyes of other nations."[27]

Public sympathy for the DPs did not translate into welcoming them to the shores of America. When a Gallup Poll conducted in December 1945 asked whether more persons from Europe should be permitted into the country than before the war, only 5 percent agreed. In reaction to a 1947 congressional bill proposing to admit four hundred thousand DPs into the United States over four years, citizens bombarded their representatives with demands to keep out the "riffraff" and "scum of Southern and Eastern Europe." In favor of the bill, Eleanor Roosevelt warned that "every representative in Congress" told her that "the general feeling is that they wish to stop all immigration." In letters and congressional hearings, the threat of foreigners to "our way of life" merged with fears of communist infiltration. There was a widespread belief that most of the DPs were Jews, and that most of these Jews were communists. Homelessness made Jewish DPs an object of sympathy. But the degrading conditions stemming from homelessness—impoverishment, disease, the inability to work—were often attached to Jews as racialized character flaws and used as evidence of their inability to be at home in America.[28]

When Congress finally passed a DP bill in 1948, it discriminated against Jews in "callous fashion," as Truman stated upon reluctantly signing the bill. It restricted the eligibility of Jewish DPs, even as it privileged some Nazi collaborators who were refugees from communist regimes. Support for the bill was bolstered by the promise that most Jewish DPs would go to Palestine and not the United States. In 1945, when Truman had sought to make it easier for refugees to enter the United States under existing quotas, a poll found that 72 percent of respondents disapproved. A year later, when he announced his approval of the committee's recommendation to let one hundred thousand Jews immigrate to Palestine, 78 percent of those polled approved. Throughout the congressional hearings on the DP bill, Palestine cropped up as a safety valve for unwanted Jewish immigrants. Witnesses in favor of the bill repeatedly testified that only 20 percent of all DPs were Jewish and that more than 90 percent of those would rather emigrate to Palestine than to the United States. After a tour of the DP camps with the House Foreign Relations Committee, a Republican congressman declared, "If the Jewish facet of the problem could be cleared up, the solution of the remainder of the problem would be greatly facilitated. The opening of Palestine to the resettlement of Jewish displaced persons would break the log jam." Only after the conservative American Legion became convinced that most Jewish DPs in Europe would go to Palestine did the influential organization end its staunch opposition to the bill. Passage of the DP bill depended on reassuring many groups that the country wouldn't be "flooded with Jews."[29]

In contrast to conservatives, who were concerned with keeping out Jewish refugees, pro-Zionist liberals, including President Truman, did call for opening the gates of both the United States and Palestine to European Jews. Presidential candidate Henry Wallace, of the Progressive Party, declared that Palestine alone couldn't solve the refugee problem and America needed to do its part: "Once the United States was looked on as a haven of refuge for the oppressed of the world. Today we are earning a reputation as the smug center of reaction."[30]

It is easy to assume today that support for a Jewish state among non-Jews expressed philo-Semitism and that anti-Zionists harbored anti-Semitic sentiments. Indeed, at the time, advocates of Zionism did accuse their opponents of anti-Semitism, especially when criticizing those State Department members who showed sympathy to the Arab cause and had reservations about the geopolitical consequences of a Jewish state in the Middle East. Yet the reaction of those Americans who opposed Jewish immigration to the United States shows how anti-Semitism played a role in some pro-Zionist attitudes. The desire to bar Jewish immigrants from the United States was one of the factors behind support for sending those same Jews to Palestine.

The postwar period marked a turning point in the history of anti-Semitism in the United States, at the same time that Zionism became part of the American political agenda. After virulent populist campaigns against Jews before and during the war, the postwar period saw the end of discrimination in employment and housing, the abolition of quotas in higher education, deeper integration of Jews into American life, and the decline of anti-Semitic stereotypes in popular culture. But anti-Semitic attitudes did not automatically disappear as a result of their association with Nazism. While many non-Jews did accept the assimilation of Jews into the mainstream, entrenched suspicions of Jewish foreignness continued. Support for Zionism allowed some Americans to have it both ways: they could support rescuing the suffering victims of the Nazis while keeping their distance from the same people. They thus preserved an image of their own nation as a force for freedom, as the liberator of Europe. Americans could see their own values reproduced abroad in a new land of refuge that would embrace the huddled masses from Europe—without having to embrace those masses at home.

In its final report, the Anglo-American Committee respected the United States' unwillingness to take in Jewish refugees. Beyond a vague acknowledgement of common responsibility for all displaced persons, the report did not suggest that any nation alter its immigration laws. Mandate-ruled Palestine was the exception. After witnessing Jewish survivors of Nazism still languishing in stateless limbo, the twelve committee members left Europe with unanimous moral clarity. Their harmony, however, was short-lived; it did not outlast the testimonies they heard in Cairo and Jerusalem. From Europe, Palestine beckoned as a humanitarian refuge for homeless Jews. In the Middle East, the committee encountered conflicting political claims from Arabs who were already living there.

Crum responded to those claims with a narrative of Zionism as modernization. When the committee arrived at its luxury hotel in the shadow of the pyramids, Crum was horrified by the gulf between elite wealthy Egyptians and the exploited masses, who subsisted on a level of poverty he had never before witnessed. The streets of Cairo assaulted him with the sights and smells of "human degradation," where he could not free himself from the impression of being "stalked by disease." He indicted British colonialism for exacerbating class divisions by bolstering the power of a feudal aristocracy, and he believed that Zionism, as a model of modern development, offered the solution to poverty and backwardness throughout the region. When he heard Egyptian protesters chanting, "We want Egypt for the Egyptians and not for the British," he thought they wouldn't mind having the Jews stay in Palestine, because the Jews had done more to improve the Arab standard of living than the British had.[31]

At the committee hearings in Cairo, which took place at the Mena House Hotel on the outskirts of the city, Crum faced a powerful challenge to this view in the testimony of Abdul Rahman Hassan Azzam. The Egyptian secretary-general of the eight-month-old Arab League, Azzam addressed the committee while flanked by representatives from Syria, Saudi Arabia, and Yemen. Both Crum and Crossman were moved to quote at length from his speech in their books. Azzam Pasha, as he was called, referred to Jews in familial terms, as "our brothers" and "our cousins," and he rejected the tarring of Arab opposition to Zionism as anti-Semitic. He told a story of Jews abandoning their kinship with Arabs by becoming European and then returning to the Middle East to implant Western ideas of imperialism. They were supported first by British and then by American pressure, enabled by their own "terrorism." According to Azzam Pasha,

> The Zionist, the new Jew, wants to dominate and he pretends that he has got a particular civilizing mission with which he returns to a backward, degenerate race in order to put the elements of progress into an area which has no progress. Well, that has been the pretension of every power that wanted to colonize and aimed at domination. The excuse has always been that the people are backward and that he has got a human mission to put them forward. . . . The Arabs simply stand and say "NO." We are not reactionary and we are not backward. . . . We have a heritage of civilization and of spiritual life. We are not going to allow ourselves to be controlled either by great nations or small nations or dispersed nations.

Rejecting the establishment of an exclusively Jewish state, he proposed instead an autonomous Palestine that would respect the will of the Arab majority and safeguard the equality of Christians, Jews, and Muslims.[32]

Crum and Crossman offered radically different interpretations of this speech. No matter how deeply Crossman came to believe in the justice of Zionism, he understood the opposing perspective that "Jewish colonial settlement in Palestine from the Arab point of view is simply another variant of the Western imperialism which they are determined to discard." In the testimonies that followed, Crossman heard Arabs speaking the language of the Four Freedoms for which World War II had been fought, and making universal claims based on the Atlantic Charter, which promised the right to self-determination for all.[33]

Crum, on the other hand, adamantly rejected Azzam Pasha's answer to the "unanswerable" question he had first heard in Washington. He voiced his rebuttal using the exact discourse of the civilizing mission that Azzam Pasha decried. Crum's version of this discourse might be described as Orientalist progressivism. Crum found the basic tragedy of the Middle East to be that Arabs' "antipathy was toward Westernism," which he defined as progress rather than domination—"opening the door to some measure of freedom and happiness to the forgotten men and women of this area." Arab nationalism was only skin deep, as Crum saw it—it was a sentiment manipulated by representatives of a feudal aristocracy to maintain their power over the toiling Arab masses. Crum could not imagine Arab leaders truly representing their benighted people, and so he spoke on their behalf: "I felt there could be no real conflict between the deepest aspirations of the Jew, as expressed in Palestine, and those of the Arab peoples. The Jewish ideal based upon the philosophy of the European West seeks a way of life in which man achieves dignity and a measure of fulfillment of his deepest needs." Western ideas promised to cure the social evils of the East by offering a "chance for a decent life as free as possible from squalor, disease, corruption, exploitation." Crum defended these values by quoting from the U.S. Declaration of Independence: "'life, liberty and the pursuit of happiness,' which we hold as the inalienable rights of every man—surely these Western ideals are not evil." Crum saw Zionism as a form of Westernism and painted both in distinctly American hues, as following a universal model of social progress.[34]

Crum thus viewed Arab nationalism not only as opposing Zionism but also as rejecting modernity itself. Even though Azzam Pasha explicitly rejected the stereotype of Arab backwardness, Crum saw Arab society though an Orientalist lens, as mired in an ancient past where the ideals of the French and American revolutions "had not penetrated the citadels of Islamic authoritarianism." Why, he asked, "had this entire area, only one day by plane from London and two from New York, simply dropped out of existence as far as modern man was concerned?" Crum concluded that young Arab intellectuals longed for liberation, to throw off "the veil, the fez, the sickness, the filth, the lack of education," but that their "wily" elders deluded them into identifying Zionism as "foreign domination." They did not yet realize that "Zionism was probably the only force within sight which would help to release them." Crum rendered Zionism as an American-style rescue mission that could liberate Arabs from the twin evils of Islamic backwardness and British colonialism.[35]

Crum eagerly embarked on the train from Cairo to Jerusalem. He described the changing geography as a kind of time travel—from decaying past to burgeoning modernity. He felt himself liberated from Egypt's "desert scenes—the mud hovels; the faceless children, or so they appeared wrapped up in the same nondescript robes as their parents: the slow, painful miserable existence." As soon as the train reached the Jewish settlements in Palestine, he wrote, "the tempo and color of life changes sharply. Things seemed to quicken, to become more alive; children suddenly were no longer tiny bundles of rags, but youngsters, wearing shorts, with sturdy arms and legs and open smiling faces and bright eyes—alert and human again." Crum's choice of words says more about his own point of view than about different costumes: he saw Arab children as foreign objects, and Jewish children as familiar human subjects. The landscape echoed this contrast: "After the vast expanse of desert and mud flats, it was a treat to see man's order upon earth again: green field, regularly plowed, brown trees and green foliage. That was my first impression of the Holy Land." His first panoramic view of Palestine offered an antidote to the disorder and decay that repelled him in Egypt. Even though this was his first visit, his use of the word "again" expressed his sense of returning home to a familiar environment.[36]

Like many American travelers to Palestine since the nineteenth century, Crum and his colleagues approached the landscape through two mental guidebooks: the Bible and images of the American west. As the train rolled through Gaza, Crum recalled the story of Samson, while the landscape reminded him of "country between San Francisco and Los Angeles." Judge Hutcheson, the American committee cochairman, was relieved to find: "This is Texas." Crossman made note of these responses, wondering why "Americans feel at home here whereas we feel ourselves utterly remote from England."[37]

Why did Palestine feel so familiar to the American visitors? It had to be more than geographical formations. Americans viewed geography through the lenses of biblical and national narratives that made the land appear at once ancient and modern. They projected onto Jewish settlements mythic images of a pioneering past and nostalgia for the dawn of their own modernity. Marveling at Tel Aviv as "the youngest metropolis of the world," Crum exclaimed: *"Here before your eyes is proof that Palestine Jewry is bringing civilization to the Middle East."* The city stood out against the backdrop of generic Arab backwardness. In the "overgrown Arab village" of Jaffa—a major port city that had been at the center of trade and cultural exchange for centuries—Crum only saw "streets of squalor and a population diseased and beaten by life." In the "thoroughly civilized community" of Tel Aviv, by contrast, Crum marveled at the "tree-shaded boulevards, with opera and theaters, with playgrounds and modern schools, with busses and apartment houses." Everywhere in the city, "you could stand on the street corner and say: 'this might be any American town.'"[38]

If Tel Aviv resembled contemporary America, the kibbutz—a collective agricultural community central to the history of Jewish settlement and to the Zionist imagination—evoked idealized images of America's pioneer past. A settler from New Jersey expressed to Crum a feeling "akin to what the early settlers in the Western states must have felt: a sense of ever-expanding horizons, a challenge of worlds to conquer." Crum applauded the kibbutz as a "striking contribution to modern life" through its social and agricultural experimentation, and he saw its members as reliving the past of "genuine pioneers." Crum described his New England colleague, Frank Buxton, welling up with tears after visiting a kibbutz. "I felt like getting down on my knees before these people," Buxton exclaimed. "I've always been proud of my own ancestors who made farms out of the virgin forest. But these people are raising crops out of rocks!" In their adoration of the kibbutz, these Americans merged collectivism and individualism in the recovery of a mythic frontier past.[39]

Crum repeated a central tenet of Zionism, that working the land would bring forth the New Jew. By reclaiming the land from "desert and swamp," Jews were redeeming themselves from their Old World past. This creed resonated with American narratives of the frontier's transformative power. Shedding memories of Hitler's Europe and "the

Children from Kibbutz Hulda, Israel, 1948.

ancient story of Jewish persecution," wrote Crum, the pioneers became "a new generation of Jews rising free from the stigma of the ghetto, free from the self-consciousness of 'differentness.'" Working the land in Palestine stripped away the New Jews' European otherness and made them appear more like Americans.[40]

Crum found evidence for this transformation of eastern European Jews in a "strange phenomenon" that made their offspring raised in Palestine not only stronger from working the land, but also whiter and more Western than their parents:

> Many of the Jewish children I saw were blond and blue-eyed, a mass mutation that, I was told, is yet to be adequately explained. It is the more remarkable because the majority of the Jews of Palestine are of east European Jewish stock, traditionally dark-haired and dark-eyed. One might almost assert that a new Jewish folk is being created in Palestine: the vast majority almost a head taller than their parents, a sturdy people more a throwback to the farmers and fishermen of Jesus' day than products of the sons and daughters of the cities of eastern and central Europe.[41]

Crum offered a Christian point of reference for the New Jew in Palestine, who paradoxically reverted to biblical prototype and evolved into a type of white Westerner. By returning to the ancient homeland, the stooped ghetto Jews, bowed by exile, were restored to their roots as brawny and muscular workers of the land. At the same time, they came to look more like white Americans.

Crum was not the only one to remark upon this "mutation." In 1948, James McDonald, one of the members of the Anglo-American Committee, visited an Orthodox synagogue in Jerusalem. While listening to the prayers of two hundred young boys, he was "struck once more by the variety of the faces of the boys. Had I not know where I was, or heard the Hebrew words, I would have sworn that most of them were of Irish, Scandinavian or Scotch stock, or at any rate of the ordinary mixture of the American middle west. Only here and there was there a face even remotely resembling the 'Jewish type.'" He concluded that "Israel's young Jews had no distinctive 'racial attributes.'" In 1951, journalist Kenneth Bilby described a parade of kibbutz children in similar terms: "They were even featured, sturdy, bleached by the sun. I would have defied any anthropologist to mix these children with a crowd of British, American, German and Scandinavian youngsters and then weed out the Jews." He viewed them as becoming less like "their Semitic cousin in the Arab world." In the eyes of these visitors, as European Jews in Palestine became whiter—and more civilized—the Arabs among whom they settled appeared darker and more primitive.[42]

Whiteness was a familiar sign that helped Crum cognitively navigate a land populated by approximately 1,300,000 Arabs and 600,000 Jews. As he and his colleagues traveled through Palestine and listened to hours of hearings, they would not have been able to maintain the myth that the land had been empty or uncultivated before Jewish settlement. Crum argued that Jewish settlements were not encroaching on Arab lands and villages, and that if left alone by imperial powers, Jews and Arabs would live together harmoniously with the aid of Jewish improvements. He saw the kibbutz not as a foreign outpost or a land grab, but as blending harmoniously into the landscape. In one location, he noted "how smoothly Palestine Jewry fits into the life of Palestine. Nearby was a monastery, and not far was an Arab village." When Crum asked kibbutz members if they had "experienced any trouble with the Arabs," they answered that neighboring Arabs were the first to draw water from the kibbutz's newly drilled well. He witnessed one kibbutz member, a former Berlin lawyer, adjudicating a dispute between two Arabs. At the end of his travels through Palestine, Crum found "no conflict of interests" and concluded that Jews had nothing but good to offer local Arabs: "*the basic truth of Arab-Jewish life in Palestine*" was that "*political conflict on high levels does not affect the relations among the men on the street.*" Only Arab "kings, sheiks, and effendis" considered "Zionism's social and technical innovations" to be a threat, "because they mean lifting the masses from their ignorance."[43]

Crum's vision of harmony is set into sharp relief when contrasted with Crossman's view of the conflict at the heart of Jewish expansion into Arab lands. The socialist ethos of the kibbutz movement captivated Crossman, and he deeply admired the Labor Zionist movement as "something which will develop into the finest piece of Western socialism since Vienna." Yet, he added, "no one suggested that the Vienna socialists should go out and occupy the mountain homes of the Greeks in the Peloponnesus." He similarly debunked the idea that Palestine was a despoiled land suffering from centuries of neglect. The stony hillsides near Nablus reminded him of Greece and southern Italy, "with white bare rock tops, partly terraced from top to bottom with olive groves, vineyards and crazy cornfields [wheat fields] six yards across." In rural Arab communities, Crossman saw not a barren landscape, but one created by human cultivation and shaped by ongoing habitation. Nor did he see a relic of times past, for "everywhere there is astonishing evidence of increased cultivation and better cultivation." The local Arabs, according to Crossman, suspected Jewish land purchase was "penetrating like an advanced guard . . . to break up a mountain way of life, in which a man has the right to leave a hillside full of stones if he wants to." Crossman concluded: "If I was a mountain Arab I would want to shoot any Jew who came to Nablus."[44]

After traveling throughout Palestine, the committee convened hearings at the Jerusalem YMCA under armed guard and amid mounting violence by Zionist militias against the British army. Here Jewish and Arab leaders made their most impassioned arguments about immigration and statehood in Palestine. The first witness was seventy-four-year-old Chaim Weizmann, the venerated head of the World Zionist Organization who would become Israel's first president. His four-hour testimony both alarmed and reassured the committee members. As reported in the *New York Times,* his advocacy of a Jewish state relied on the influx of one million Jews over ten years, in order to secure a Jewish majority. Instead of offering a compromise with the Arabs, he made an eloquent appeal for the Jewish Agency's proposal "to transfer to Palestine from Europe, the Orient, and other parts of the world, the largest possible number of Jews in the shortest space of time."[45] Weizmann viewed immigration as a political vehicle for state building.

Although Weizmann went beyond the humanitarian argument for refugee resettlement, he nonetheless impressed some committee members with his moderation and honesty. Crossman, for one, was relieved by Weizmann's admission that the issue was "not between right and wrong but between greater and lesser injustice. Injustice is unavoidable and we have to decide whether it is better to be unjust to the Arabs of Palestine or to the Jews." For Crossman, this question presented a moral dilemma, but for Crum it offered moral clarity. The "least injustice in determining the fate of Palestine" was clear to him: "European Jewry cannot be expected to resettle on soil drenched with Jewish blood. Their only hope for survival lies in the creation of a Jewish state in Palestine." To emphasize the comparison with America, he quoted Weizmann's resonant analogy: "the leaky boats in which our refugees come to Palestine are their *Mayflowers,* the *Mayflowers* of a whole generation."[46]

At the hearing in London, Crum had raised the issue of nationalism with Weizmann: "We've had many difficulties with the words 'Jewish state,'" Crum observed, adding that "Judge Hutcheson feels it suggests a narrow nationalism, which he and, I think, many of us find abhorrent." In the immediate aftermath of World War II, "narrow nationalism" evoked the specter of parading brown shirts and fascist salutes. Weizmann responded with a rhetorical question: "Surely the world does not think that the Jewish people, who have suffered so much from narrow nationalism, would themselves succumb to it?" Crum ultimately rejected the idea that a Jewish state would be chauvinistic or racially biased. In support of this view, he quoted the assertion of Golda Myerson (later Golda Meir) that "we don't want to be a master race."[47] Crum agreed with her and Weizmann that the experience of persecution inoculated Jews from the darker associations of nationalism. Yet the committee's final report expressed concern about the efflorescence of Jewish nationalism in Palestine, finding "many signs that fanaticism and nationalist propaganda are beginning to affect detrimentally the Jewish educational system."[48]

Nationalism was also rejected by one of the most moving witnesses, Judah Magnes, the American-born president of the Hebrew University of Jerusalem. During World War I, his pacifism had led him to renounce his pulpit as a rabbi in New York and move to Palestine. Magnes had long advocated a binational state; he proposed limiting Jewish immigration so as to equalize the population between Arabs and Jews, and he called for equal representation in government and civic society. He was one of a small group of intellectuals who testified before the committee, including the philosopher Martin Buber. Magnes's ideas had a strong moral appeal for the committee members, who were "visibly stirred" by his quiet rhetoric and his ethical commitment to fair play, cooperation, and self-determination for both Arabs and Jews.[49]

While some committee members harbored doubts about a Jewish state, they were even more skeptical of the idea of an Arab state in Palestine. The Arab movement for independence did not seem to meet the bar of legitimate national aspirations. Crum discredited Arab nationalism as an elitist ploy. He ridiculed the pan-Arab movement and the very idea that Muslims and Arabs from as far away as Iraq would have an interest in the fate of Palestine (though Jewish attachment to Palestine from as far away as the United States did not seem strange to him). The greatest weapon Crum wielded against Arab nationalism was his belief that the leader of the Palestinian Arabs had been allied with Hitler. The grand mufti of Jerusalem, Haj Amin al-Husseini, had taken refuge from the British in Berlin during the war and supported Hitler's policy to exterminate Jews. Crossman, too, expressed concerns; he created a sensation in the Jerusalem hearings when he displayed a photograph of al-Husseini saluting S.S. troops and demanded an explanation for this "unholy alliance." Crossman nevertheless acknowledged that there might be reasons why an "Arab patriot could not help being indifferent" to the British war cause and might hedge his bets, in case the Germans won. Crum's view was uncompromising; for him, the mufti's wartime alliance invalidated Arabs' claims and proved that their objections to Zionism were anti-Semitic.[50]

There was one Arab witness, however, whom Crum could not so easily dismiss. Albert Hourani, director of the Arab Office in Jerusalem, had served in the British intelligence service during the war and studied at Oxford; later, he would become a renowned historian. Hourani argued for the "establishment of Palestine as a self-governing state with an Arab majority, but with full rights for its Jewish citizens." He rejected the charge that Arab nationalists were anti-Semitic, explaining that if "the Palestinian state is to be an Arab state, that is not because of racial prejudice or fanaticism, but because of two inescapable facts: the first that Palestine has an Arab indigenous population, and the second that Palestine by geography and history is an essential part of the Arab world."[51]

Hourani challenged the fundamental assumptions on which the Anglo-American Committee was constituted. He argued against treating the question of immigration "simply on humanitarian grounds" because it could not be divorced from "its general political framework." Not only did he expose the hypocrisy of Western nations, which were forcing Arabs to take in the same refugees that they would not accept into their own countries—he also claimed that Zionists were not aiming to "solve the refugee problem for its own sake, but to secure political domination in Palestine," and that "their demand for immigration is only a step towards dominating Palestine." As evidence, Hourani cited Ben-Gurion's testimony to the committee: "he was asked whether he would save the lives of 100,000 German Jews at the cost of giving up his ideal of a Jewish state, and he said no."[52]

Hourani claimed that the humanitarian argument was connected with the imperialistic outlook that the United States and Great Britain shared. Rather than adjudicating the "conflict of two races and two nationalisms," they were instead imposing a foreign state on Palestine, and thereby denying its people their homes and the right to self-determination. Hourani charged that the two governments were deluding themselves in thinking that they were operating as "impartial peacemakers and judges in no way involved in the conflict, but holding the two antagonists apart and doing justice between them." Hourani predicted that "there can be no settlement" in Palestine "until the Zionists realize that they can never hope to obtain in London or Washington what is denied them in Jerusalem."[53] That is, the existence of the committee itself revealed that a Jewish state in Palestine could only be established by force under the aegis of imperial power.

In the final deliberations in Lausanne, Switzerland, the committee rejected Hourani's argument and recommended that "100,000 certificates be authorized immediately for the admission into Palestine of Jews who have been the victims of Nazi and Fascist persecution." It did not, however, recommend the establishment of a Jewish state. The American co-chairman, Judge Hutcheson, expressed the strongest reservations about the compatibility of an ethnoreligious state with the practice of democracy. From the outset, his opinions worried a representative of the Jewish Agency who was monitoring the committee. He described Hutcheson in a memo as "a man with a heart of gold, simple, solid, and of great common sense. The chief difficulty—his formalistic conception of liberal democracy." This conception made Hutcheson suspicious of the plan to establish a state only after a Jewish majority had been achieved. It appeared to him like a rigged vote. He asked why religious identity rather than territory should determine the nature of the state: "Why then in Palestine should we have a Jewish state? Why don't you have a Palestinian state?" Hutcheson wanted to know how any group could "expect to come into a land which they do not populate in anything like the majority (in fact, it was begun in a very small minority) and demand that their characteristic and their point of view shall be enforced upon the others." Ultimately Hutcheson could not agree to a plan to "import people into a country for the deliberate purpose of creating there a majority in order to dominate the country and take control away from its inhabitants. . . . We could not have made ourselves parties to such a scheme of creeping conquest by colonization."[54]

Thus in the final report, the Anglo-American Committee rejected the political establishment of a Jewish state in Palestine on the grounds that "Jew shall not dominate Arab and Arab shall not dominate Jew in Palestine," and that "Palestine shall be neither a Jewish state nor an Arab state."[55] But the committee could not recommend a sovereign structure in which this non-domination would materialize. Instead it recommended deferring the question of Palestine's independence by continuing the British mandate as a UN Trusteeship.

Crum and Crossman were the only two members to argue for the partition of Palestine into separate Jewish and Arab states. The books they published in 1947 constituted a kind of minority report. Their political solution would eventually triumph in the momentous United Nations vote for partition at the end of 1947. In making the case for an autonomous Jewish state, both Crum and Crossman resolved the tension between the political and the humanitarian by representing the Zionist cause as transcending politics, as something nobler than nationalism and less heavy-handed than colonialism. They each asserted that the establishment of a Jewish state in Palestine would ultimately not harm its Arab inhabitants.

Both men concluded their books by describing the personal appeal of Zionism to their progressive ethos. Expressing reservations all the way through, Crossman wrote that he might not have endorsed the partition of Palestine "if the national home [for Jews] had merely been a national home." Instead, "in Palestine I had come to realize that it was something more, a socialist commonwealth, intensely democratic, intensely collectivist." He believed that "no Western colonist in any other country had done so little harm, or disturbed so little the life of the indigenous people," and he hoped that "Jews had set going revolutionary forces in the Middle East, which in the long run, would benefit the Arabs."[56]

Crum described his embrace of Zionism as the culmination of a spiritual journey. In his final walk through the Old City of Jerusalem, he came face to face with the principles of Jesus Christ, which conjoined his religious and political beliefs. "The brotherhood of man, the community of work by all for the good of all" he found practiced "by the Jews of Palestine." Crum dedicated his book to the memory of Wendell Willkie, and he had no doubt that the Zionists had already created "'one world' in microcosm"—"a new and valid civilization . . . in which the hopes of the Jews and the rights of the Arabs will be reconciled."[57]

Crum approached Zionism in the same spirit as he did other causes advocating liberation from oppression; he also worked against racial discrimination and lynching in the United States, against Franco's fascism in Spain, and for fair employment and the UN charter. He did not see the Jewish claim to Palestine as a matter of "special pleading," but as part of an international struggle for freedom with a distinctly American cast:

> I have written this book because I believe so strongly, and because I want my fellow Americans to share my belief, that Palestine is an essential part of this stand for freedom. If you are a Catholic, perhaps Irish by background, you need only to read County Mayo

for Rehovoth; if you are a Negro, you need only substitute for the concentration camps of Cyprus and Eritrea a county in Mississippi; if you are Protestant, or an "Okie," you will understand the struggle. What our American forebears fought for in the eighteenth century, the Jewish pioneers are fighting for today.[58]

The Liberal Consensus

Behind the Silken Curtain articulated the manifold appeal that made Zionism a popular cause for American liberals in the aftermath of World War II. Crum joined forces with a diverse group of journalists, politicians, and intellectuals, some of whom had begun advocating for a Jewish state before the war ended. They crafted narratives that merged the humanitarian idea of a haven for refugees with the political goal of national sovereignty, and they championed Zionism as one among a number of progressive movements for liberation and social justice. Although they were aware of Arab objections, they found various ways of imagining that a Jewish state in Palestine would do more good than harm to the Arabs living there.

During a time of disillusionment and disarray that beset many left-leaning liberals at the end of World War II, Zionism promised to renew their faith in progressive American values. With the death of Roosevelt, they mourned the end of the New Deal's commitment to social equality. As internationalists, they welcomed the formation of the United Nations but feared that the developing Cold War would hijack global cooperation, and some criticized Truman for propping up British imperialism. As they fought among themselves about the power of communism at home and abroad, some saw reactionary forces in the United States as a greater threat than communism, and many were targeted by anti-communist campaigns. The struggle for a Jewish state restored moral clarity. It revived the fight against fascism when shifting alliances made it appear that the United States was eager to rehabilitate former Nazis. In the Zionist experiment in collective agriculture, liberals imagined New Deal–style public projects bringing social equality to the Middle East. The UN's vote for partition upheld the internationalist ethos of this new yet fragile experiment in international governance. And in defending the Jewish armed struggle against the British Empire, some leftists rode the wave of contemporary anticolonialism and harked back to the United States' own revolutionary heritage.

Freda Kirchwey, editor of *The Nation*, fiercely championed Zionism. The iconoclastic journalist I. F. Stone wrote pro-Zionist articles in the *New York Post, The Nation*, and *PM*, the progressive New York newspaper (which Crum purchased before it folded), and he published two books about his experiences in Palestine. Kirchwey and Stone both visited Palestine, as did Henry Wallace, the 1948 presidential candidate for the Progressive Party and editor of the *New Republic*. Other well-known progressives who spoke out on behalf of Zionism included Eleanor Roosevelt, Reinhold Niebuhr, W. E. B. Du Bois, Sumner Welles, and Dorothy Thompson.[59]

These journalists and activists constituted an informal network rather than an organized group. They shared ideas, citing one another and writing prefaces and reviews of one another's books, and crossed paths not only in Palestine, but also in progressive venues in the United States. Some were aided directly by the Jewish Agency and the American Zionist Emergency Council, organizations that invited journalists to Palestine and helped fund and publicize their research and books. *The Nation*, for instance, received a $50,000 grant from the Jewish Agency for "conducting research and publishing articles and reports, and promoting the Zionist cause among American liberals and foreign delegates to the United Nations." Fueled by this support and her own political enthusiasm, Kirchwey worked closely with the Jewish Agency to lobby for partition, and she submitted a 130-page memorandum to the United Nations on behalf of *The Nation*.[60]

The mainstream press was less enthusiastic about the Zionist movement. The *New York Times* expressed the most skepticism, and its publisher, Arthur Sulzberger, was a member of the anti-Zionist American Council for Judaism. Henry Luce, editor of *Life,* as well as influential commentators such as Walter Lippmann, James Reston, and Joseph Alsop, urged caution about supporting a Jewish state out of concerns that the United States could be drawn to intervene militarily and would alienate the Arab nations, a source of oil and anticommunist sentiment. Many left-leaning pro-Zionist writers would come under attack by anti-communist campaigns, and officials of the new state would heartily welcome their visits after they were marginalized at home. But that would come later. In the late 1940s, progressive politics aligned with

Zionism to create a powerful narrative about Israel as a liberal project, one that would capture the American imagination for decades to come.

For Freda Kirchwey, a secular intellectual from a Protestant background, advocating for a Jewish homeland renewed her wartime crusade against fascism and anti-Semitism as part of a broader struggle against racism and prejudice. During the war, writers at *The Nation* and the *New Republic* had been among the first to publish the horrifying news about the Nazi extermination camps. Kirchwey reversed *The Nation*'s long-standing commitment to pacifism to lobby President Roosevelt to enter the war. The liberation of Europe, however, appeared incomplete as long as displaced persons remained behind barbed wire. Nor did the defeat of Hitler spell the end of fascism, which remained alive in Franco's Spain, in Latin American dictatorships, and in right-wing tendencies in the United States. Kirchwey feared that fighting fascism would take a back seat to rivalry between superpowers.

For Americans like Kirchwey, who viewed fascism as the main enemy of freedom in the postwar world, supporting the victims of fascism became paramount. As a matter of justice, those Jews who had survived the Nazi effort to exterminate them had a right to a state of their own. Kirchwey thought that Zionism was immune to the pitfalls of nationalism because she saw the Jewish victims of Nazi atrocities in universal terms, as a "flaming symbol to all the world of humanity and freedom." They represented everything the fascists were trying to annihilate: "the spirit of humanity, of free inquiry and tolerance, of reason as opposed to blind will. . . . The values the Jewish people symbolize belong in the end to all men and women of good will everywhere." By extension, a Jewish state represented more than the national aspirations of a particular religious group. Reporting on her 1946 visit to Palestine, she wrote that Jewish settlements taught "a lesson in cooperative democracy planning . . . a lesson not for the Jewish people alone but for the world." The issue was "not simply justice for the Jews, but that justice for the Jews means peace in the Middle East and a more democratic development in that whole area." Democracy did not refer to the practice of majority rule, as it did for Judge Hutcheson. For Kirchwey, a democratic ethos attached to Jews because they embodied those political values that Nazism had failed to defeat.[61]

In Kirchwey's mental map of Palestine as the front line in the postwar fight against fascism, opponents of Zionism stood squarely on the other side. She dismissed Arab claims to Palestine as contaminated by Nazi collaboration. In her memorandum to the UN, the longest of the twenty-eight chapters is titled "The Role of the Grand Mufti in World War II." She was determined to prove that the mufti did not merely join an alliance of convenience against the British, but was an anti-Semite and a fascist both before and after the war. Quoting several pages from Crum's book, she accused the mufti of being "responsible in large part for the Nazi program of extermination of the Jews." Kirchwey's vastly exaggerated narrative of the mufti's responsibility for the Final Solution would grow in importance decades later when the Holocaust came to play a greater role in America's relationship with Israel.[62]

Not all left-wing journalists who traveled to Palestine vilified Arabs as Nazis. On his first visit in 1945, I. F. Stone, a secular Jew, felt "immensely attracted" to the "one place in the world" where the "Jews seemed completely unafraid," and he thrilled to the experiments in socialism and the "exhilarating atmosphere of a great common effort." Nevertheless, he understood the Arab opposition to Zionism as a political response and not an expression of anti-Semitism. "The Arab does not hate the Jew," he concluded, "but he fears being dominated by him." He worried that Jewry was stuck in a "blind alley" as long as it demanded an exclusive Jewish state. To illustrate this blindness, Stone used a common American analogy, but with an uncommonly negative twist: "The closest parallel in American experience is Puritanism, and Palestine is indeed much like the frontier in our own country, both in colonial times and the West." He decried the defects in both settler societies, reflected in the Zionist "failure to take into account the feelings and aspirations of the Palestinian Arab." Exhorting Jews not to be the beneficiaries of British imperialism, Stone endorsed Judah Magnes's binational proposal for Jews and Arabs to "live together on an equal basis," a "nobler and politically sounder goal than any narrow Jewish nationalism."[63]

Despite their different views of Arab opposition to Zionism, Kirchwey and Stone shared the perspective of Orientalist progressivism. Most American liberals who wrote about Palestine were enthralled by one development plan in particular, a proposal to create an irrigation project in the Jordan River Valley. Walter Clay Lowdermilk, a soil conservation specialist in the Department of Agriculture, had first come up with the plan. In 1939, Lowdermilk led an expedition to survey land use in the Near East, North Africa, and Europe, to glean knowledge that could help Americans reverse the calamitous effects of the Dust Bowl. A Methodist from North Carolina, he wrote of his automobile trek across the Egyptian desert as a modern two-day reenactment of the forty-year journey of the ancient Jews wandering in the wilderness. In Palestine, he discovered a depleted land in decline from its fertile condition in biblical times and in antiquity, when it functioned as the breadbasket of the Roman Empire. To his delight, he discovered that Jewish colonists were applying scientific agricultural methods to restore these wasted lands. Lowdermilk proposed to exponentially increase the availability of arable land by means of a large-scale project called the Jordan Valley Authority (JVA), which was modeled on the Tennessee Valley Authority, the signature New Deal public works project. Lowdermilk confidently predicted that his design would develop the entire region on both sides of the Jordan River; it would thus serve indigenous Arabs as well as making room for at least four million more Jewish immigrants.[64]

The American Zionist Emergency Council was thrilled to discover in Lowdermilk an "objective, scientific, non-Jewish observer," and they helped publish his 1944 book *Palestine: Land of Promise*. Filled with biblical and American tropes, the book grafts a scientific story of soil reclamation onto a racialized story of Arab degeneration and Jewish regeneration. Lowdermilk dates the beginning of the land's decline in fertility to the seventh-century Arab invasion, claiming that "nowhere has the interrelation between the deterioration of a land and the degradation of its people been so clear as in Palestine." The image of a desolate Holy Land had a long pedigree among Western travelers. Lowdermilk refurbished this image in his invention of what he called the Eleventh Commandment, which he broadcast on the radio in Jerusalem and used as the epigraph to his book: "Thou shalt inherit the holy earth as a faithful steward conserving its resources and productivity from generation to generation." He praised Jewish settlers for fulfilling precepts to protect the land from erosion, overgrazing, and deforestation, and he warned that those who failed in this stewardship doomed their descendants to "live in poverty or perish from off the face of the earth."[65]

Lowdermilk's book offered a technocratic fantasy that American progressives heartily embraced. The JVA project would use the American tools of scientific engineering to create new land to accommodate millions of Jews without disrupting Arab inhabitants, and it would quell resistance by providing the Arabs with the capacity for modern development. The Lowdermilk plan promised to resolve a contradiction at the heart of Zionist claims about indigenous Arabs: Jewish settlement would not interfere with the Arab way of life, even as it would modernize Arab society. It would allow development without domination.

Lowdermilk's writing re-created Palestine in the image of the American wilderness. "Colonization in America was like the colonization of Palestine," he wrote, with one key difference. Settlers in Palestine had to cultivate old and impoverished soil rather than the "virgin land" of the New World. The combination of advanced methods already employed by enterprising Jewish colonists with New Deal–style public works would transform Palestine into a "new and bountiful land."[66]

The JVA appealed as a socioeconomic resolution to the intractable political conflict between Zionists and Arabs, mitigating liberals' concerns about colonial dispossession. Henry Wallace credited Lowdermilk with introducing him to the justice of the Zionist cause. Lowdermilk had presented the scientific case for Palestine's "absorptive capacity" before the Anglo-American Committee, and I. F. Stone concluded his *Nation* review of the committee report by locating the "key to the future" in the large-scale rehabilitation of the Jordan Valley to "benefit both Jews and Arabs." Although the final report mentioned the JVA only briefly, as a remote possibility, Crum wrote an enthusiastic chapter about it in his book, in which he chastised the British members for skipping a meeting in Jerusalem with two American engineers who had worked on the TVA and the Boulder Dam. For him, American engineering promised to elevate Zionism beyond petty political conflicts between Jews and Arabs to a grand project of modernization. Kirchwey also showcased the JVA proposal in her memorandum to the United Nation in favor of partition.[67]

At a time when America's large-scale rebuilding efforts were shifting to the Marshall Plan in Europe, the Zionist project offered a potential reprise of the New Deal ethos. It reanimated the dream that public works could alleviate the misery of the "common man." In the liberal version of Israel's early development, Americans' dreams of modernization doubled as nostalgia for their own recent past. As Eleanor Roosevelt put it in 1953, "the democratic socialism of the labor-Zionists might indeed become the model state that would promote an international New Deal."[68]

Most liberals who embraced Zionism as a New Deal for the Middle East were internationalists who enthusiastically welcomed the founding of the United Nations. Their lofty hopes deflated, however, as the organization threatened to become a forum for managing big power rivalries rather than a more comprehensive world government. The UN vote on the partition of Palestine renewed their faith in the young organization as a symbol of international cooperation, despite the complicated process that went on behind the scenes. The lobbying was intense, the close vote had no legal binding, the outcome was contested, and the plan was ultimately unworkable without military force. None of these conditions detracted from the moral luster of internationalism, however. The fact that both the United States and the Soviet Union voted for partition buoyed the faith of some liberals in international cooperation across hardening Cold War lines. The memorandum Kirchwey submitted to the General Assembly linked the fate of Palestine to the "honor of the United Nations, its capacity to maintain peace, and its willingness to extend the area of human rights and dignity."[69]

The UN partition plan bestowed on the Jewish state an internationalist imprimatur. Even though the Arab nations vehemently opposed partition and condemned what they saw as an unfair process, Americans could feel that they had supported a fair compromise that gave both Arabs and Jews less territory than they had demanded. Eleanor Roosevelt, who had once harbored reservations about the undemocratic nature of a Jewish state, believed that "the integrity of the United Nations and its internationalist principles" were at stake in upholding the decision. As a UN delegate, she later became annoyed with Truman for sidestepping the organization to recognize the State of Israel directly instead of going through the delegation. Henry Wallace wrote that partition would "strengthen the UN and increase the hopes of those who work for world peace" and that it would give stateless Jews representation in the world assembly, where they were outnumbered by Arab nations. Without correcting this imbalance, the UN, he warned, would fall into "moral bankruptcy." On the day after the partition vote, the editors of the *New York Times* declared that the UN vote erased their long-standing "doubts concerning the wisdom of erecting a political state on a basis of religious faith." The UN shifted this basis to a kind of international democratic process, which seemed a more legitimate grounding than religious identity.[70]

The vote for partition on November 29, 1947, ignited widespread violence in Palestine between Arabs and Jews. In response, the following March, the United States introduced a proposal to rescind partition. Zionist supporters denounced this proposal, rallying around the imperative of upholding the authority of the UN. Sumner Welles, former undersecretary of state, wrote an entire book, *We Need Not Fail* (1948), to make this point. In high-flown rhetoric he warned that not only would the UN determine the future of Palestine, but the fate of Palestine would determine the future viability of the UN: "To those who believe that the future of humanity depends upon the achievement of collective security as envisaged in the Charter of the United Nations, the imposition of a just and lasting solution of the Palestine problem has long since seemed an imperative necessity."[71] Those who defended the integrity of the UN, however, felt no compunction about criticizing decisions that went against the new State of Israel's most extreme demands. In September 1948, when the UN mediator in Palestine, Count Folke Bernadotte, called for the right of Arab refugees to return to their homes, *The Nation* criticized him for betraying the principles of the United Nations itself.[72]

American liberal narratives of Israel's founding matched praise for the UN's internationalism with denunciations of British imperialism. In this context, they understood Jewish paramilitary organizations to be fighting a revolutionary war against colonial rule in Palestine, akin to the one fought by Americans in 1776. "Just as the British stirred up the Iroquois to fight the colonists," wrote Henry Wallace, "so today they are stirring up the Arabs." At the same time, headlines from Palestine told of bombings and assassinations by underground Zionist militias, and editorials in U.S. newspapers raised concerns that Jewish terrorism was plunging Palestine into a spiral of escalating violence. Indeed, the figure of the terrorist threatened to overshadow that of the refugee in the international Zionist campaign for public opinion. In the United States, references to 1776 served to differentiate legitimate from illegitimate violence. In a *Nation* article, "Gangsters or Patriots," I. F. Stone lambasted a *New York Times* characterization of the Haganah, the oldest and major military arm of the Jewish settlement, as "vigilante" in origin and as an "underground gangster group . . . which prides itself on its conservative terrorism." Stone described the Haganah as "a democratic militia"—the "People's Army of Palestine Jewry." He praised the Haganah for its limited military objectives: to defy the British restriction on immigration and to "settle on forbidden land." Stone distinguished this group from two right-wing paramilitary groups, the Irgun and the Stern Gang, which were affiliated with the extremist Revisionist faction of the Zionist movement. To Stone, these groups were aberrations, not Zionists but "quasi-fascist terrorists," even though they banded together with the Haganah to form the Jewish Resistance Movement. To distinguish anticolonial resistance from terrorism, Stone concluded that members of the Haganah "are no more gangsters than were the men of Concord or Lexington," those iconic sites of the American Revolution.[73]

In 1946, at the invitation of the Haganah, Stone became the first American journalist to accompany a ship that was transporting Jewish refugees from Europe to Palestine, in defiance of British Mandate restrictions. He wrote a popular series for the newspaper *PM*, filled with lively tales of cloak-and-dagger intrigue, wrenching portraits of loss and survival, and inspiring testimonies to the zeal for *Eretz* (the Hebrew term for the land of Israel). Stone vividly humanized the "displaced persons," a term he rejected, describing it as a "model of detached and frigid understatement." Later he gathered the popular series together into a well-received book, *Underground to Palestine*.

Stone's book included the major tropes of the narrative that progressive Americans told about Zionism in the years following World War II. His personal discovery of kinship with the Jews of Europe added poignancy: he realized that if his parents hadn't emigrated from Russia to America, he might have gone to the gas chambers or ended up a "ragged and homeless" refugee. As he drew closer to his Jewish "brothers," he recorded their plaintive Yiddish songs, which expressed longing for a world lost to catastrophic violence. At the same time, he narrated their journey in resolutely American tones, as a story of rebirth in the transformative voyage from Old World to New. In contrast to the "defeatist spirit" hovering over a shattered Europe, he was amazed by the "tremendous vitality" of the refugees and by their determination to build a new life in a new land.[74] In his book, Stone focused on the journey and not the arrival, chronicling the dream of a Jewish homeland uncluttered by Arab realities that disrupted these dreams—realities that he had noted in his earlier reports from Palestine.

American analogies abound in his story. The chapter title "The Underground Railroad" linked the illegal immigration to the struggle against slavery. The society formed on board the ship mirrored the American melting pot, reminding Stone of the riotous diversity of people found at "Orchard Beach or Coney Island on a hot Sunday . . . packed with people in every possible costume." As a microcosm of the new Jewish society, "linguistically the ship was a floating Babel." The only common language that transcended national differences was the voyagers' fervent desire to reach Palestine and start anew. As they severed their ties to a defeated Europe that had violently rejected them, Stone saw them not as representing an ancient birthright but as creating a modern identity in a land of immigrants. He drew parallels with the capacious vision of the New World frontier as an open space of freedom, where Europeans of different cultures had been transformed into independent Americans. In his epilogue, Stone called on Jews and Christians alike to support the "so-called illegal immigration" to Palestine as a moral obligation. "And if those ships are illegal," he concluded, "so was the Boston Tea Party."[75]

Stone presented the immigrants not as helpless victims, nor as people reclaiming a biblical heritage, but as revolutionaries in the American mold, fighting against the British Empire. In an enthusiastic review in *The Nation,* Bartley Crum wrote that support for a Jewish national home would "restore the moral prestige which the Western democracies have forfeited" in their association with imperialism, "for colonial peoples everywhere in the world are on the march toward freedom. In the vanguard of that march are the Jewish pioneers." Even though Stone and Crum disagreed about binationalism, to both of them, Zionism promised more than a particular national homeland; it was an essential step in the global struggle for freedom.[76]

Stone's initial articles in *PM* about his clandestine voyage made him a darling of the Zionist movement, which showered him with invitations to speak and called on him to persuade unconvinced Jews of the justice of the cause. But his acclaim was short-lived, according to an essay he would publish thirty years later in the *New York Review of Books,* "Confessions of a Jewish Dissident." As Stone recalled in that 1978 essay, while he was thinking about turning his *PM* articles into a book, friends in the Zionist movement, including "a partner in one of the topmost advertising firms in America," took him out to lunch and "outlined a $25,000 advertising campaign to put the book across." This proposal, however, had strings attached, as he remembered: "But then came the awkward moment. There was one sentence, I was told, just a sentence or so, that had to come out. I asked what it was. It was the sentence in which I suggested a bi-national solution, a state whose constitution would recognize, irrespective of shifting majorities, the presence of two peoples, two nations, Arab and Jewish." Stone refused to take out the offending passage, and "that ended the luncheon, and in a way, the book. It was in effect boycotted."[77] Stone did go on to publish *Underground to Palestine,* choosing the progressive publishing company Boni and Gaer, which advertised it with a ringing endorsement from Albert Einstein.

Stone's views of Israel went through many changes in those thirty years. At the time of his trip to Palestine, his attachment to binationalism did not quench his enthusiasm for the Zionist project. A firmer commitment to a just solution for two peoples would emerge more strongly after 1967. But in 1948, neither he nor his fellow liberals predicted that the UN vote to partition Palestine would create a violent and irreparable rupture. They had imbued a nationalist movement with the moral urgency of a humanitarian mission, and they imagined that a Jewish state—whether alone or in federation with an Arab state in Palestine—would benefit and not dominate the Arabs living there. These liberal narratives blinded them to the violent dispossession that created a new refugee crisis and would lead to the revival of the Palestinian nationalist movement.

The Presence of Absence

In 1948, I. F. Stone and Freda Kirchwey both took trips to the new State of Israel while it was still at war. They expected to find a nation like the one they imagined, one that fulfilled their progressive visions of Zionism as antifascist, anti-imperialist, and internationalist. They were not prepared, however, for the massive displacement they witnessed as hundreds of thousands of Arabs fled from their homes. The UN partition vote in November 1947 ignited war between Jews and Arabs in Palestine five months before Israel declared its statehood in May 1948.

Stone and Kirchwey visited the country at an early stage of nation-building and national myth-making, before dominant narratives about the war congealed. In Israeli—and American—collective memory, this period would become known as the War of Independence—a war fought by the young country of Israel against hostile Arab nations backed by the British Empire. Palestinians would collectively remember the same period as the Nakba, the Arabic word for "catastrophe," when at least three-quarters of a million Palestinians fled or were expelled from their homes. Stone and Kirchwey celebrated the new Jewish state in their journalism, but their accounts of the war were somewhat conflicted. Writing about the struggle that transformed Palestine into Israel, they built their reports to fit the preconceived liberal frameworks they brought with them. Their writing naturalized the absence of Arabs from the new nation, but the ghostly presence of Arabs in flight from Palestine haunted their prose.

References to binationalism or even to "the presence of two peoples, two nations, Arab and Jewish" disappeared from I. F. Stone's writing in 1948. He traveled to Israel in May to report for *PM* on Israel's declaration of sovereignty and its ensuing war against the invading Arab armies. He was surprised to discover that the war was over in a sense before it even began, because the goal of establishing a state had been achieved. "From a military point of view" he wrote, "the Jewish State was fully in existence the day it was declared. Partition was an accomplished fact." By the time the Jews declared the establishment of their state on May 14, he added, "of some 350,000 Arabs in the Jewish area, 300,000 had fled." Stone's story is less about a battle between two armies than about a moral confrontation in which Jews held their ground, despite their meager arms, and Arabs ran away, without provocation.[78]

Stone's account would not quite square with the later, dominant narrative that Israel's War of Independence did not start until it declared independence, after which it defended its fragile borders from the onslaught of overwhelming numbers of Arab armies. Nor would it fit the Israeli story that Palestinian Arabs ran away at the dictate of their leaders. By the end of January, Stone wrote, Palestinian Arab leaders had grown so alarmed by the departure of twenty thousand people from the country that they asked the neighboring nations "to refuse visas to these refugees and seal the borders against them." But what caused them to leave? Although Stone reported on Jewish militias committing violence, and he also recorded the massive numbers of Arabs abandoning every major city, he did not present the two as being connected with each other. In Jaffa, he vividly described Irgun and Haganah fighters attacking neighborhoods throughout the city with armored cars and mortars, but as for the fifty thousand inhabitants, he wrote: "The city was encircled and its people began to flee. Jaffa became a ghost town." In Jerusalem, he described Haganah men risking their lives block by block, but concluded: "In the meantime, virtually the entire Arab population of the city had fled." In the north, "the Arabs began to flee. . . . So Safad fell to the Jews." The closest he came to venturing an explanation was to speculate about the "unwillingness of the Palestinian population to put up a last-ditch fight." Stone acknowledged that in the fighting after May 14, an additional "350,000 Palestinian Arabs fled eastward and northward from the Israeli armies, in many cases abandoning homes and fields out of sheer fright without attack." Yet he made no effort to understand what might have frightened them, if not an attack or the threat of one.[79]

Stone collected his war reports into an attractive coffee-table book, *This Is Israel*, with photographs by the famed Robert Capa (and a preface by Bartley Crum), published in 1948. The overarching narrative of the book is about the birth of a nation, which overshadows its references to the Arab flight. Chapter titles form a sequence from "The Pains of Birth," to "The Lusty Baby," to "Wicked Midwives," to "Israel Is Born." Stone presents Israel as the rightful first-born child of the United Nations. The drama opens neither with the partition vote of 1947, nor with Israel's Declaration of Independence in May 1948, but with diplomatic efforts to rescind partition on a "Black Friday" in March. The "wicked midwives" who threatened "to bring about a stillbirth" are the British Foreign Office, feudal Arab regimes, and the U.S. State Department, which was catering to oil companies, bankers, and anti-Soviet rivalry. The "lusty baby" thus had to give birth to itself, making its way against a world of reactionary forces composed of millions of Arabs and Muslims, the British Empire, and American capitalism. Stone does not show the Jews in Palestine primarily doing battle with the Arabs living there. It is the absence of these Arabs that makes possible the narrative of self-birth, "in which the Jews implement partition for themselves." According to Stone, the Arabs who did fight played only a halfhearted

Palestinian residents evacuating from Jaffa in the face of advances by Israeli forces, May 7, 1948.

supporting role for the British, who seemed "as unsuccessful in using the Arabs against the Jews as they were 150 years before in stirring up the Indians against the American colonies." Stone furthermore evokes his prewar belief in anticolonial solidarity to posit that "many Arabs, like almost all the Jews, felt that this was a British War." He attributes the vastly different outcomes for Jews and Arabs not to direct confrontation or to military advantage, but to the virile dedication of one and apathy of the other: "the Jews held and the Arabs failed because one people cared enough to die and the other didn't."[80]

Stone concludes the book with a progressive vision of the new nation as both a sanctuary for the survival of the Jewish people and a global "laboratory in the building of a new society." He depicts Israel as the "little man" of nations, aligned with other "small powers strengthening the UN as their own protection against the division of the world into contending groups moving toward common catastrophe." Israel demonstrated the possibility of transcending the antinomies of the Cold War. Its "mixed economy, voluntary farm collectives, [and] network of cooperatives" all proved that "socialist devices and democratic method could be combined, social justice achieved without sacrifice of individual freedom." Yet Stone's harmonious vision of coexistence excluded the Arabs of Palestine. *This Is Israel* symbolically emptied the land of Palestinians and repopulated it with photographs of new Israelis creating a brave new world.[81]

Stone did not write about the Arab refugees until he returned to Israel in 1956. Throughout the war of 1948, however, a number of American journalists did link the plight of the Arab refugees to that of the Jewish refugees on common humanitarian grounds. In May, a *New York Times* headline read "Palestine Strife Creates DP Issue," and in August, *Time* magazine called Arab refugees the "new D.P.s." Journalists reported that the Arab refugees in makeshift camps in Lebanon, Syria, Gaza, and Jordan were living in even more dire conditions than were the refugees in Europe, that they were much more numerous than the Jewish DPs after World War II, and that fewer facilities and organizations were in place to aid them. In addition to comparing Arab refugees with the Jewish DPs, journalists also noted the irony that the solution to one crisis was creating the problem of the other, and they reported that Jewish refugees were moving into homes abandoned by those Arabs now living in refugee camps. The U.S. Congress debated whether to include Arab refugees in its deliberations on the immigration bill for displaced persons and rejected the idea. The United Nations called for their repatriation, which the U.S. government supported. But Israel made an early decision not to allow refugees to return, a decision the government would enact through a series of laws as well as by destroying more than four hundred Arab villages. This decision had to be explained to a world that had just supported the political establishment of the Jewish state on the humanitarian basis of creating a homeland for homeless refugees. One pro-Zionist American journalist bluntly expressed this dilemma in a letter to an Israeli diplomat: "In preventing Arab refugees from returning to their native land, the Jews may be subject to the same kind of criticism for which I and others have criticized intolerant Gentiles. . . . Now we have a situation in which the Jews have done to others what Hitler, in a sense, did to them!" On these grounds, some Americans urged Israel to accept the return of at least a portion of the Arab refugees.[82]

At the same time, others were working to discredit any parallels between the two groups. For these journalists, including Freda Kirchwey, this meant treating the stories of Jewish DPs and Arab refugees as essentially different in kind and denying them any shared moral or political significance. At the end of 1948, Kirchwey wrote a five-part series for *The Nation* titled "Israel at First Glance." She described her trip from the airport this way: "We drove to Tel Aviv through sharp moonlight that revealed plainly the little Arab villages by the roadside. Many had been shattered by gunfight. All were deserted." She did not comment on this emptiness, but she reassured her liberal readers that although she was traveling with a government representative, that arrangement would not compromise her reports; rather, it would give her access to a "freely functioning intelligent information service run by people who respect the virtue of facts."[83]

Kirchwey visited the "silent and deserted" city of Jaffa to address the question "Why did the Arabs run?" She registered the momentousness of more than fifty thousand people fleeing from Palestine's largest Arab city. And she briefly noted the attack and siege by the combined forces of the Irgun and Haganah at the end of April. Yet she did not mention the impact of this attack on the population. Instead, she claimed that the mass flight from Jaffa, and other Palestinian cities and villages, seemed "to have little to do with the fighting itself."[84] She drew a picture of the neighboring towns of Jaffa and Tel Aviv as "hostile Siamese twins," sharing the poisoned blood of mutual hatred that had naturally exploded into war. During her visit, she witnessed the damage to one district in particular, where the houses were riddled with bullet and mortar holes and their interiors had been trashed by Israeli soldiers. But the destruction in Jaffa appeared to her to be an aberration; her press guide told her that although individual soldiers occasionally looted in defiance of orders, the authorities disciplined them. At stake for Kirchwey in the image of the humane soldier was her investment in the Jewish refugee as a universal symbol of noble suffering and the creation of the Jewish state as a moral triumph for civilization over fascism.

By the time Kirchwey started considering answers to the question of why the Arabs fled, she had already ruled out Jewish soldiers as a cause. She ran through a list of possible motivations that drew on Orientalist images of Arab backwardness. And she portrayed Arab civilians as behaving differently from most civilians throughout world history, who supposedly stuck to their land while waiting for troubles to end. All her speculations led to the same implication, that Arab roots in the land were shallow; they must not have felt very attached to their homes if they willingly abandoned them. Kirchwey concluded that "a dozen reasons probably combined to create the vast epidemic of fear that drove some 500,000 Arabs out of Jewish Palestine into the already overcrowded ranks of homeless, penniless 'displaced persons.'" Characterizing fear as an epidemic turns attention away from the violent external sources of that fear, instead imagining it as an internal phenomenon by which an invisible agent infects individuals of the community.[85]

By severing humanitarian needs from political rights in the case of Arab refugees, many liberals who had fused these together in their argument for a Jewish state came to view the refugees neither as collective victims of political processes—of violent expulsion or ethnic cleansing—nor as war refugees with an internationally mandated right to return home. Labeling displacement as individual hardship, rather than as an assault on a community, had the effect of denying Palestinian Arabs a claim to a collective solution. Kirchwey presented the Israeli case against repatriation during the same month that the UN General Assembly passed Resolution 194, resolving that "refugees wishing to return to their homes and live at peace with their neighbors should be permitted to do so at the earliest practicable date." Kirchwey reported that most Israelis felt no obligation to help the refugees return, because repatriation would saddle the new country with a "big and unassimilable minority." She recorded a change of heart expressed by "one of the wisest men in Israel" (whom she doesn't name). Although this man once had an "intimate association with Arabs," he now believed that they had "forfeited all claim on us" by fleeing at the behest of their leaders. He advocated the resettlement of refugees in Arab nations, possibly through an "exchange of populations," in which Israel would "take all the Jews now in the Arab states." Kirchwey acknowledged that some Israeli officials believed that "when peace comes, the refugee Arabs should be readmitted after careful screening," but she came to agree with the other group, "who look upon the Arab exodus as an unexpected and enormous favor conferred upon Israel by its enemies," a favor it had no obligation to return by readmitting the refugees.[86]

Although Kirchwey rejected Israeli responsibility for the flight of the Arabs, she could not quite lay the question to rest during her travels.

Like a Freudian return of the repressed, it came up indirectly in her visit to the village of Ein Karem in the hills outside Jerusalem, a trip she made with two Israeli press officers and Bartley Crum. Like many visitors, she was struck by the beauty of the village, where most of the buildings remained intact, including an old Franciscan church, even though its population had fled. She happily reported that a Spanish priest confirmed to Crum that the Jewish soldiers had behaved properly, protecting the holy sites as well as the abandoned and locked houses and the handful of remaining villagers living in the courtyard of an old church. This idyllic scene was suddenly interrupted by an agitated older Arab woman who ran up to the Arabic-speaking press officer and, "shaking her fist and gesturing toward the door," dragged him upstairs. There they saw a young woman shouting a complaint against an Israeli soldier. From the look of "fierce indignation" on her face, Kirchwey "could imagine nothing less serious than rape." Hence, she expressed astonishment to hear that the women were only accusing the Israeli soldiers of stealing the lid of their Primus stove. The press officer explained that because of their poverty, "it means something to them. Besides, they probably feel uneasy here."[87]

Kirchwey did not probe the uneasiness of the Arab women any further, or her own. The story ostensibly showed how the worst that Israeli soldiers were capable of was petty theft. But the fact that Kirchwey herself brought up rape, even if only to dismiss it, means that it must have been on her mind. Traveling in Israel at the time, even with a press officer translating, she might well have heard stories from other journalists about rape and looting and the demolition of villages by Israeli soldiers.[88] An event she could not have missed hearing about was the massacre at Deir Yassin, a village in sight of the hilltop of Ein Karem. On April 9, 1948, troops from the Irgun and the Stern Gang murdered over one hundred villagers, including many women and children. There were also cases of rape and mutilation. Every major American newspaper reported the massacre.[89] In Palestine, it instilled terror and panic in surrounding villages and beyond, and the news provoked many villagers to flee. When Supreme Court Justice William O. Douglas visited Ein Karem in 1949, he inquired of two old women living there why three thousand inhabitants had abandoned their beautiful ancestral home during the war, even though the Israeli army had never attacked it. One of the women responded that right after Deir Yassin, "some thought all of us in Ein Karem might also be killed some night."[90]

Around the same time that Kirchwey visited Ein Karem, in December 1948, the massacre at Deir Yassin featured prominently in a letter to the *New York Times* by Albert Einstein, Hannah Arendt, and twenty-five other intellectuals, protesting a visit by Menachem Begin, former commander of the Irgun. The letter denounced the new political party he had founded as "closely akin in its organization, methods, political philosophy and social appeal to the Nazi and Fascist parties." Deir Yassin provided their chief evidence. The letter accused "terrorist bands" of attacking a peaceful village with no military objective, murdering civilians, and then forcing survivors "to parade as captives through the streets of Jerusalem." In contrast to the outrage expressed by Jewish and Arab leaders, Begin's "terrorists" proudly publicized the massacre and invited foreign correspondents to view the corpses. The letter states: "It is inconceivable that those who oppose fascism throughout the world, if correctly informed of Mr. Begin's political record, could add their names and support to the movement he represents."[91]

Kirchwey's "Israel at First Glance" series for *The Nation* did not take note of Deir Yassin as possibly contributing to the "epidemic of fear" that made the Arabs flee. And Stone did not mention the massacre as one of the causes of the Arab flight underlying the fait accompli of statehood. This omission was not likely due to lack of knowledge, but to a discordance. The story of Deir Yassin clashed with their deeply held belief in the moral significance of the new Jewish state as a universal symbol of social justice.

These preconceived narratives barred them from seeing the haunted landscape of the new nation, as another American journalist described it: "In holiday drives through the country, people saw whole Arab villages razed to the ground—insurance against the owners' return. . . . True, they saw new immigrant cities. . . . But always in the background, ghostlike, was the crumbled Arab village, . . . a visual reminder that the Arabs, too, had a Diaspora."[92]

2

FOUNDING ISRAEL IN AMERICA

Dan Wakefield's review of the bestselling novel *Exodus* appeared in *The Nation* in April 1959. It began this way: "A friend recently told me about an elementary school class in East Harlem, composed mainly of Negro and Puerto Rican children, who were asked by their teacher to vote for their 'favorite country.' The results of the voting were Ghana, first; Israel, second." Kwame Nkrumah, president of the newly independent nation of Ghana, had recently visited Harlem to cheering crowds. Wakefield noted a comparable "fascination with the birth and growth of the new Israel" around the globe that "has crossed about every line of age, race, creed, color, language, culture and character—with the exception of Arabic—and, ironically, that violent exception is one of the prime contributing factors in the strength of the fascination." Although the Jewish state may have been an anomaly in the Middle East, it was the Arabs whom Wakefield labeled as anomalous—the "violent exception" to the worldwide enthusiasm for Israel. It was the "fact of eight million surrounding enemies" that made Israel such a popular "underdog." With its victory in 1948, Israel took its place in the rank of modern democratic movements, including African nations throwing off the yoke of European colonialism, and the youth of East Harlem overcoming racial discrimination.[1]

Israel was "the stuff of fiction," wrote Wakefield, who had spent six months there in 1956 as a correspondent. It had "every conceivable element of drama—'conquest of the desert,' 'return to the soil,' 'ingathering of exiles,' 'conflict of cultures,' 'the Promise and Fulfillment' of Biblical prophecy." Yet no novelist—not even an Israeli one—had really captured this drama until Leon Uris, a "war-hardened, bestseller-proved

American author," wrote his blockbuster novel about "Israel's war of statehood." Despite some reservations about the literary merit of *Exodus,* Wakefield applauded Uris's "skillful rendering of the furiously complex history of modern Israel" in popular form. Reviewers and readers alike embraced *Exodus* as "a brilliant history of the dreaming of, the founding of, and the making of Israel."[2]

To tell his story of Israel, Uris built on the progressive narratives of the Zionist project told earlier by Bartley Crum and his liberal colleagues. This, too, had been a story of liberation, but Uris showed less interest in their humanitarian vision of Israel as a social experiment, and he shared none of their occasional moral qualms. Starting with the origins of Zionism in eastern Europe, Uris penned a nationalist saga for Cold War America. The novel extolls a militant Israel founded by tough Jewish warriors fighting for a righteous cause. In an epic struggle between good and evil, a persecuted minority heroically overcomes crushingly powerful foes to restore its ancient birthright in the triumph of a modern state.

Exodus fits into a type of foundational fiction that nations tell about themselves. Such popular novels do for nations what Virgil's *Aeneid* did for Rome: they yoke the state to the land in a mystical eternal unity, and they narrate the birth of the nation as the apex of an inevitable historical trajectory. *Exodus* has often been compared in its epic scope and massive sales to *Gone with the Wind,* which transformed the history of the Civil War into a shared national past. But *Exodus* is different in that it is not a story told by Israelis about their own country, but one told by an American author for American readers. Uris saw himself as writing "for the average American who shares a tremendous moral heritage with the Jews of Israel."[3] Millions of Americans would not have known of this shared heritage until they had read a novel about Israel's founding that resonated with myths of American origins. *Exodus* converted a foreign history set in Europe and the Middle East into a familiar narrative of settling the frontier and rebelling against a tyrannical Old World empire. As its title proclaimed, the novel grounded its modern narrative of revolution in the equally familiar biblical story of the Promised Land.

One cannot overestimate the influence of *Exodus* in Americanizing the Zionist narrative of Israel's origins. Its publication was a benchmark event in mass-market publishing, breaking records in print runs and sales. The fastest-selling work ever published by Bantam, it stayed on the *New York Times* bestseller list for more than a year, sold more than twenty million copies in the next twenty years, and has never gone out of print.[4] Otto Preminger directed an equally popular star-studded film, based on the novel, in 1960. Critics lauded its "dazzling, eye-filling, nerve-tingling" power as "a fine reflection of experience that rips the heart." Like the novel, the film struck many as "living, documented history" and as a "powerful instrument of contemporary truth."[5]

Exodus had an enormous impact on shaping the mainstream historical narrative—and the attendant moral lessons—of Israel's birth. Across the political spectrum, scholars, journalists, and activists agree that it provided "the primary source of knowledge about the Jews and Israel that most Americans had."[6] By transmuting history into the timelessness of myth on a grand scale, *Exodus* achieved great staying power. It forged the popular American identification with Israel for decades to come, in the face of alternative narratives that told different versions of that history. Both the novel and the film conveyed a double image of Israel, as a symbol of social justice through the rebirth of an ancient land, and as a source of redress for particular injustices through the rejuvenation of Jewish masculinity. *Exodus* had such a profound impact on the Americanization of Israel's origins because it seamlessly interwove seemingly contradictory stories: of a universal mission with a particular national triumph, and of the redemption of humanity with ethnic regeneration through violence.

Remaking the *Exodus*, 1947–1960

Exodus transformed a historical failure into a fictional success. The novel opens in 1947, a time of international debate and violent conflict about the plight of Jewish refugees and the future of Palestine. Uris based his story on the SS *Exodus,* a ship carrying 4,500 illegal immigrants, mostly from displaced persons (DP) camps, that tried to breach the British blockade of Palestine. Before the ship neared the coast, six Royal Navy destroyers surrounded and rammed it. Sailors forced their way on board with live ammunition, killing three crew members while unarmed passengers resisted with little more than tin cans and bottles. After towing the damaged ship to Haifa, the British forcibly transferred

SS *Exodus* with Jewish immigrants on board in the port of Haifa, 1947.

the refugees to three dilapidated prison-like vessels and deported them back to Europe. When the refugees refused to disembark at their French point of origin, the British transported them to occupied Germany. An international outcry arose against returning Jews to the country that had tried to exterminate them.

The organizers of the expedition did not aim to land thousands of refugees surreptitiously on the moonlit shores of Palestine. Rather, they aspired to shine light on the inhumane restrictions of the British quota system, which limited Jewish immigration into Palestine. They succeeded in turning the plight of the *Exodus* into a much-needed public relations coup for the Zionist cause. Newspaper headlines from Palestine had been filled with reports of bloody terrorist raids, sabotage, and assassinations by Jewish militias against the British. The most notorious was the bombing of the King David Hotel in Jerusalem, which killed ninety-one people in July 1946. In American editorials at the time, antipathy toward Jewish terrorism vied with sympathy for illegal Jewish immigration. When news of the *Exodus* reached the front pages, however, the Zionist cause captured the moral high ground, as journalists turned their gaze from Jewish terrorism to British brutality.

The journey of the SS *Exodus* directed public attention away from Jews wielding guns and dynamite. It showcased instead the long-suffering refugees, desperate for a homeland and resolute about not returning to Europe, armed with nothing but food tins and bitter taunts to toss at British sailors, and singing spirited rounds of "Hatikvah." International reporters were already on-site in Haifa to report on the investigation of the United Nations Special Committee on Palestine (UNSCOP), which would soon recommend partition to the General Assembly. One of those journalists was Ruth Gruber, who had accompanied the Anglo-American Committee to the DP camps the year before. Her shocking photographs of the damaged ship and dazed refugees were published in *Life,* and she would later gather her reports in a book with an introduction by Bartley Crum. The *Exodus* affair is credited with swaying some of the UNSCOP members to vote in favor of partition.[7]

In 1947, the story of the *Exodus* played a key role in a contest for the public face of Zionism in the international arena. Who would become its emblematic figure—the refugee or the terrorist? American liberals identified these figures with opposing Zionist organizations and political strategies. I. F. Stone, for one, praised the Haganah for its struggle to lead clandestine immigration to Palestine, but he joined other liberals in condemning the right-wing paramilitary groups the Irgun and the Stern Gang for perpetrating acts of terror that betrayed Zionist ideals.

In fictionalizing this story, Uris merged the image of the suffering refugee with that of the ruthless terrorist, interwove the process of illegal immigration with that of armed struggle, and united the Haganah and the Irgun in a common narrative of anticolonial revolt. The novel deviates dramatically from the historical record by landing the passengers safely ashore in Palestine. The mastermind of the ship exploit, Ari Ben Canaan, the ruggedly handsome Jewish protagonist, leads the refugees out of a DP camp in Cyprus under the watchful eyes of the modern pharaoh, the British high commissioner. Ari succeeds in delivering them to the Promised Land, fulfilling the cry, "Let my people go!"

Unlike the historical ship, which carried mostly adults, Uris's fictional ship is full of orphans, who commit themselves to a hunger strike until they are permitted to sail for Palestine. Every hour, unconscious youngsters weakened by starvation are laid out on the deck, as newspapers around the world cry out for the British to relent. At the fortieth hour of the strike, when Ari's lieutenants confront him with their doubts about watching children starve to death, he responds gruffly that children this age are "already fighters" in Palestine and that "this is only another way of fighting." His zealous lieutenant contrasts their public deaths with that of the "six million Jews" who "died in the gas chambers not knowing why," proclaiming that "if three hundred of us on the *Exodus* die we will certainly know why. The world will know too."[8] Starving children might not have gone over well on the screen, so in the film version, Preminger included feisty adults on board. The moral authority of innocent children, though, does inform a powerful opening scene, when two mothers holding their babies refuse to obey Ari's orders to leave the ship. They defiantly choose death over returning to a life behind barbed wire. Children play major roles in the novel and film as both innocent victims and dedicated fighters.

Uris invented his child warriors as a rebuke to the most famous Jewish child of the 1950s, Anne Frank, whose bestselling diary became a prizewinning Broadway play that Uris attended. Her story repelled him with its focus on Jews hiding in attics. He insisted that there was "something far more decent about dying in dignity which is, of course the choice that every Jew had. They did this in the Warsaw Ghetto." Uris resented the Frank family for showing no anger toward the Nazis, and he hoped "this type of Jew has ceased to exist forever."[9] A strong motivation for writing *Exodus* was to dislodge the image of Jews as passive victims. Uris wanted to believe that the Jews of Europe did indeed have the "choice" to die fighting.

Uris was convinced that Israelis disliked Anne Frank as much as he did, because of their "strong feelings about Jews who will not fight back."[10] In creating his young protagonists, he rejected the figure of the Jewish child as a universal symbol of peace and humanistic forgiveness. He remade Anne Frank in the character of the idealistic Karen Hansen Clement, daughter of a professor from Berlin who sends her to Denmark to be raised by a Christian family during the war. Escaping assimilation into European society, Karen feels drawn to Palestine to search for her Jewish identity. With rifle in hand, she dies defending a dangerous outpost of the new nation at the end of the novel. But first, she falls in love with the hard-bitten Dov Landeau, a child veteran of the

Warsaw Ghetto. He grudgingly boards the *Exodus* only for the purpose of exacting revenge by joining the terrorists in Palestine. In creating these characters, Uris managed to let his readers have it both ways. Karen's gentle innocence invites the kind of sympathy accorded to the adolescent Anne Frank, while Dov's vengefulness evokes the righteous anger Uris found disturbingly lacking in the Frank family.

Uris made another revealing change in the historical record by expunging the central role that American Jews played in the 1947 saga. "The *Exodus* story had begun in America," wrote Ruth Gruber, "for the ship was an American excursion boat and the crew were GIs and sailors and Merchant Marine men."[11] American Friends of the Haganah purchased the original ship in Baltimore, and they met at I. F. Stone's house for one of their planning meetings.[12] Most of the crew were Jewish veterans, and a young Protestant minister with a New England accent became the media spokesman for the ship after the British attack.

Given Uris's desire to reach a broad American audience, it might have made sense to highlight the fighting spirit of American volunteers to create a bridge of identification for his readers. But excluding American Jews from Israel's founding epic had the canny effect of presenting its origins as a universal struggle for freedom and not as the special interest of a particular ethnic group. By kicking American Jews off the *Exodus,* Uris made his Zionist characters appear both more and less familiar—less like stereotypical Jews and more like archetypical Americans.

In place of the American Jews who had actually been on the *Exodus,* Uris invented a non-Jewish romantic heroine, a nurse named Kitty Fremont—"one of those great American traditions like Mom's apple pie, hot dogs, and the Brooklyn Dodgers."[13] Having lost her husband to war and a young daughter to polio, Kitty feels no purpose in life until she grows attached to Karen and follows her to Palestine, intending to adopt her. Kitty then falls in love with the irresistible Ari. She learns to overcome her genteel anti-Semitism and commits herself to living with him and, in a sense, to adopting the entire new nation.

In the film, Preminger enhanced Israel's American qualities by casting the main characters with actors whose whiteness stood out luminously on the screen. Ari Ben Canaan was played by the blue-eyed Paul Newman, one of the hottest young male stars of the decade, whose father was Jewish. Ari's sister, Jordana, was played by Alexandra Stewart, a statuesque blue-eyed blond. Karen, played by Jill Haworth, appeared blonder and fairer than her potential adoptive Protestant mother Kitty, the willowy Eva Marie Saint. On screen Karen's whiteness has an aura that casts light on the darkest Jewish character, Dov, played by a brooding Sal Mineo, looking like he just walked off the set of *Rebel without a Cause*. The film paints in Technicolor what earlier visitors, like Crum, described as a "mutation" to the physical features of Jews in Palestine, making them fairer and less stereotypically Jewish than their eastern European parents. The main characters in the film, because of their whiteness, are easily seen as Euro-Americans. Meanwhile, when this film appeared in 1960, the majority of Jewish immigrants coming to Israel were from Arab and North African countries.[14]

In Americanizing the founding of Israel, *Exodus* also added a Christian dimension. Kitty represents the American who discovers in Zionism the mystical qualities of the Holy Land that she heard about in Sunday school. "I have learned that it is impossible to be a Christian without being a Jew in spirit," she tells Karen in a settlement in Galilee on Christmas Day. Kitty speaks the language of the recently invented Judeo-Christian tradition, which embraced Catholics, Protestants, and Jews in a shared American identity and, during the Cold War, united them in faith against "godless communism." In *Exodus,* it also unites them against Arabs. The novel's copious Old Testament references with particular Zionist meanings took on broader significance to readers in this Judeo-Christian context.

The Christian appeal of *Exodus* resulted in the famous lyrics of the movie's soundtrack. *Exodus* won an Oscar for best original score in 1960, but the sonorous instrumentals did not have lyrics until Pat Boone wrote the refrain that would become inseparable from the memory of the film: "This land is mine, God gave this land to me." Boone was one of the most popular white rock-and-roll crooners of the 1950s, and his recording of the *Exodus* song topped the charts. A clean-cut alternative to Elvis Presley, Boone was a born-again Christian. His lyrics would not have raised eyebrows in an America that had undergone a religious revival in the 1950s, the decade when "one nation under God" was added to the Pledge of Allegiance. The song resonated with a Cold War American identity by evoking a God-given land where children play freely and dedicated pioneers bravely sacrifice their lives to defend it.[15]

Although Uris was the driving force behind what became the *Exodus* phenomenon, the idea for the novel did not originate with him but in Hollywood, with the vice president of MGM, Dore Schary. A political progressive and an observant Jew, Schary did not hide his affiliations in an industry where many Jewish executives were secretive about their religion and shied away from screening Jewish subjects. Schary thought the time had come to tell Israel's story. He selected Uris, who was not particularly knowledgeable about Israel or dedicated to Jewish causes, because of his reputation as a bestselling novelist and screenwriter. Uris appreciated Schary as "the one man who will gamble on 'message pictures'" at a time when Joseph McCarthy's witch hunts had made political films risky. The subject of Israel could breach this taboo without seeming un-American. Uris negotiated two lucrative contracts, one with MGM for a screenplay, and the other with Random House for a novel, and in 1956 he headed to Israel to do research for both.[16]

For Israel's tenth anniversary in 1958, Uris hoped to re-create the public relations sensation that the original *Exodus* voyage had generated in 1947. The Israeli government eagerly welcomed the promise of positive publicity. The Foreign Ministry worried about its cool reception from the Eisenhower administration, which did not have the personal and sentimental connections to the Zionist movement that had existed under President Truman. The government feared negative public opinion about the controversial and unresolved issues of the Palestinian refugees and the internationalization of Jerusalem. It was also receiving widespread condemnation for making military raids across its borders, where reprisals against Palestinian infiltrators struck many as disproportionately violent against civilians. In 1954, the Foreign Ministry launched concerted campaigns to improve Israel's image in the media, churches, schools, and businesses, and in the halls of Congress. When Uris contacted the Israeli consulate in Los Angeles to prepare for his trip, he received a hearty welcome, a hefty stack of recommended books to read, and offers of assistance.[17]

In Israel, officials treated him as a minor celebrity. They gave him a guide, a car, a hotel room, and "unlimited access into all places and to all people." He believed the Israeli government embraced this opportunity to "get perhaps their best book on Israel." He also hoped the arrival of a major film company would boost the economy and broadcast Israel's message "to a billion people around the world on film." A well-connected Foreign Ministry official, Ilan Hartuv, served as his guide and introduced him to veterans of the 1948 war and to high-level members of the government and the military, including Yigal Allon, Teddy Kollek, Moshe Dayan, Golda Meir, and Yigal Yadin. Hartuv accompanied Uris to battle sites from 1948 and included him on a patrol through the Negev Desert with a squad of paratroopers. He arranged a tour of a DP camp on Cyprus and passage on a secret flight to Iraq to bring back Jewish immigrants.[18]

Three years later, Israel greeted Otto Preminger with even more fanfare when he arrived to direct the first major American film shot entirely on location in Israel. Preminger was at the peak of his career as an independent director and producer of popular serious films, and though he had never been involved with the Zionist movement, his upper-class Viennese Jewish background gave him connections to the Zionist elite. Hartuv again served as the liaison to a government that was eager to help Preminger turn the country into a stage set. The army transported cast and crew, the navy lent three destroyers, and twenty thousand extras appeared on the streets of Jerusalem for the filming of the UN vote. The Israeli government rightfully anticipated that the Hollywood film would generate more publicity and tourism on the heels of the novel's runaway success.[19]

In 1956, Uris had not been in Israel long before he developed a pretty clear picture of the story he wanted to tell. As he wrote to his father from a hotel room in Tel Aviv, "I am writing a book for Americans . . . Gentiles . . . not for Jews." Nor was he writing for those New Deal liberals who idealized Zionism's humanitarian mission: "I must show her as a human place and not as an ultra-glorious utopia." Uris was captivated by Israel's military prowess. "The real Israel," he wrote, "is a nation of young marines. . . . This is Israel . . . the fighter who spits in the eye of the Arab hordes and dares him."[20]

Uris had been a young marine himself. Joining up at seventeen immediately after the attack on Pearl Harbor, he served as a radio operator in the South Pacific. The war provided an escape from a desultory adolescence shuffling between his divorced working-class parents in Philadelphia and Baltimore. Uris's father, William, had gone to Palestine in 1920, leaving Poland with his brother to join a socialist youth group. But he found the environment too harsh, the ideology too nationalistic, and the employment opportunities too scarce. Disillusioned, he left and joined his large family in Pittsburgh. In the United States, he worked as an editor and organizer for several Jewish socialist organizations, but never with much success. His son Leon, raised in a secular and radical household, wanted to make it in America rather than change the world. In a letter from Israel in 1956, Leon warned his father that he would not comprehend its youthful warrior spirit: "Israel was won by a gun and it will be saved by a gun. If you think this spirit was gained here by old scholars, you are sadly mistaken. The spirit of Israel is the strength of her fighters."[21]

Uris had first written about American fighters in *Battle Cry*, a novel about his experience in the Marine Corps. Published in 1953, the book competed against a formidable list of World War II bestsellers: Norman Mailer's *The Naked and the Dead* (1948), James Jones's *From Here to Eternity* (1951), and Herman Wouk's *The Caine Mutiny* (1951). Uris despised these authors' negative portrait of war and military authority. He rejected "the degradation and slime of Mailer, Jones, Wouk the 'ain't war hell' school of writers" by writing a gung-ho novel "about an outfit of men who loved each other and believed in what they were fighting for."[22] *Battle Cry* became a bestseller, and Uris wrote the screenplay for an equally popular film, thus launching a successful career as a Hollywood screenwriter. In his second novel, *The Angry Hills* (1955), Uris first broached the topic of fighting Jews in the Middle East. He based the novel on the memoir of an uncle who had fought in the Palestine Brigade—a unit of Jewish soldiers in the British army in World War II. The novel was not well received, and soon afterward Uris turned to the popular genre of the Western. He wrote the screenplay for the box-office hit *Gunfight at the O.K. Corral* (1957), where lawman Wyatt Earp (Kirk Douglas) kills a gang of outlaws on the main street of Tombstone, Arizona. Based on a true story, this was the most frequently filmed showdown during the golden age of the Hollywood Western.

The American marine and the Western gunslinger would provide the prototypes for the Zionist protagonist of *Exodus*. And the heroic narrative of Israel's War of Independence would provide an antidote to the cynicism of modern war novels. Uris described his work on *Exodus* in the mold of the tough soldiers he extolled. He spoke of his research trip as though it were a military campaign, boasting of his intense physical and mental preparation, and relishing the dangers of being shot at and trekking across the desert.[23] His main publicity photo displays his mil-

LEON URIS

WITH A PATROL IN
THE NEGEV DESERT

Leon Uris "with a patrol in the Negev Desert," author jacket photo from the first edition of *Exodus*.

itary ideal: dressed in battle fatigues and boots, he holds a machine gun and leans cockily on an army jeep, staring confidently into the camera against the blinding desert background.

One of the unexpected highlights of Uris's journey was a relatively young kibbutz at the border of Gaza, Nahal Oz, founded by soldiers and joined by civilians to farm land previously owned by Palestinians. Expelled in 1949, many of the families resettled in Shejaiya, Gaza, close enough to look over at their land across the border. Nahal Oz was a prized dateline for foreign journalists. With its proximity to a dangerous border and its photogenic young soldiers, who had left behind comfortable lives in modern Tel Aviv to found a kibbutz, it was the quintessential frontier town. Edward R. Murrow compared it to a "stockade," or American army barracks, on an episode of the acclaimed television news magazine *See It Now*. Uris viewed this episode, called "Egypt-Israel," while writing his novel.

"Egypt-Israel," which aired in 1956, offered a daring exploration of the conflict between Israel and Egypt from both sides of the border. The first half starts with Howard K. Smith interviewing Egyptian president Gamal Abdel Nasser. It ends in Gaza with interviews of Palestinians—aided by a translator—in a crowded refugee camp. Of different ages and backgrounds, each man, pointing across the border, describes where in Israel his ancestral lands were. Angrily shaking fists in the air, the refugees express their determination to fight to return to their homes. The second section starts across the border, with Murrow's visit to Nahal Oz. Visually it appears to American viewers as though they are returning home from a foreign country. The camera enters the modest apartments and scans bookshelves filled with titles in English, a radio playing classical music in the background. Murrow then climbs a watchtower in the dead of night to interview an Israeli guard. A handsome young soldier with an informal slouch, he answers Murrow's questions in halting English: no, he doesn't want to take anyone's land, and he doesn't understand politics; he just wants to live in peace as a farmer, yet he has no choice but to defend innocent lives. Murrow was justly proud of "Egypt-Israel" as a rare example of balanced broadcast journalism. But the episode ends with the Israeli perspective on the dark, menacing frontier, beyond the well-lit perimeters of the settlement.[24]

Uris happened to arrive in Nahal Oz at an important moment in Israeli history and national mythmaking. There he heard Moshe Dayan, chief of staff of the Israel Defense Forces, deliver a memorable graveside eulogy for a slain kibbutz member. On April 29, 1956, Roi Rothberg, a kibbutz security officer, was killed and mutilated by Palestinians from Gaza while he was patrolling the fields. His murder followed a long chain of violent events, in which Palestinian infiltration across the border was met by severe Israeli reprisals, culminating in the killing of fifty-eight Arab civilians during shelling of Gaza City on April 5.[25]

Dayan's oration became an immediate national classic; broadcast and reprinted frequently, it achieved an iconic status in Israeli national memory similar to that of the Gettysburg Address in the United States. Dayan's eloquent lament elevated the loss of the "lean blond youth" into a symbol of collective mourning. Rothberg's ultimate sacrifice obligated the community to sanctify him with a renewed call to arms. A main trope of the eulogy is the failure of vision. Blinded by his desire for peace, "by the quiet of a spring morning," Rothberg—and by extension all of Israel—did not see the severity of the threat right in front of him. Dayan called on the mourners to see themselves through the eyes of the Palestinian refugees: "Why should we complain at their fierce hatred of us? For eight years they have been dwelling in refugee camps in Gaza, and before their very eyes we are turning the land and the villages where their forefathers dwelt into our home." Israeli commentators have noted the unusual candor of this statement, which acknowledged the claims of Palestinians forced from their land. What is so striking now is the apparent contradiction between Dayan's understanding of the refugees' situation and the militant conclusion of the eulogy. For Dayan, acknowledging Palestinian grievances demanded acting with vigilance and force: "Without the steel helmet and the cannon's mouth, we cannot plant a tree nor build a house." To no longer "shrink from seeing this enmity" meant to be "ready and armed, strong and hardy, for if the sword slips from our fists—our lives will be cut short." The headline of the story in the *Jerusalem Post* read, "We Must Not Be Lulled by Peace Talk—Dayan."[26]

The funeral made an impression on Uris, who wrote admiringly to his father of the mourners' fortitude: "Not one tear, not one word of revenge against the poor ignorant Arabs. Such tragedies only strengthen the young Israelis in their determination to defend and settle their land." He emphasized the bravery and innocence of Rothberg, claiming that he had been killed defending the children's house, and comparing him to the biblical Samson, who, because of his gentleness, failed to bring down the gates of the Philistines. Though Uris attended the funeral and read the translation of Dayan's eulogy in the *Jerusalem Post,* he disregarded the references to Arab refugees. Similarly, in his comments on the Murrow show "Egypt-Israel," he referred only to the Nahal Oz section.[27]

In *Exodus*, Uris drew on a reservoir of cultural images from Nahal Oz for the climactic scene of Karen's murder in a fictional border settlement he called Nahal Bidbar. Uris relied especially on material from a photo essay in the magazine *The Coronet*. Founded on "barren desert" in 1953, Naha Oz was, according to the magazine, threatened by over two hundred thousand Arab refugees who were lingering in "filthy tent camps, unwanted by their host country," where they spent their time "in resentful reverie." Their idleness produced hatred, and "the energetic settlers of Nahal Oz are the closest objects of their hatred." Photographs of young Israeli farmers toiling on the land with smiles on their faces and rifles on their shoulders are accompanied by the caption, "On the explosive Gaza strip, where Arabs and Jews are separated by inches of land and chasms of hatred, Israel's potent defense weapon is the spirit of its youthful kibbutz pioneers who defy infiltrating marauders, bombings and even ambush, and refuse to be bullied off their land."[28]

The narrative of Israeli innocence and self-defense precluded viewing Arab refugees as motivated by a desire to recover their homes. In *Exodus,* this narrative framed Uris's entire history of Zionist settlement, from flashbacks about Ari's family arriving from Russia in the 1890s, to the War of 1948, through Karen's murder in 1956.

The New Jew on the American Frontier

Building a new nation entailed creating a new man. In his protagonist, Ari Ben Canaan, Uris fashioned the prototype of the "tough Jew" as an amalgam of American and Israeli masculine archetypes.[29] One such Israeli type appeared in Dayan's eulogy: the warrior-farmer risking his life to defend his land, with one hand on the plow and the other on his gun. In choosing the name Ari, which means "lion" in Hebrew, Uris alludes to one of the earliest examples of this figure in Zionist mythology, the Roaring Lion Monument at Tel Hai, which Uris visited in 1956. In the novel, Ari's father and uncle enter Palestine through Tel Hai in the northern Galilee. A hallowed site in Zionist historiography, Tel Hai was an isolated outpost of young Jewish settlers that fell to an Arab attack in 1920. Its celebrated military leader, Joseph Trumpledor, left a legacy of final words, crafted to instruct future generations: "It is good to die for your country." The story of Tel Hai represented a symbolic break from the theme of Exile, a central myth of Israeli national origins that presented the Jews as having been exiled from their original homeland. The repudiation of Exile fueled Zionist ideology, which rejected the image of the weak Jew of the Diaspora as a long-suffering victim submissively entrusting his fate to God. The heroic fighters of Tel Hai represented "the antithesis of the exilic Jew."[30]

This Zionist credo has striking parallels with the myth of the American frontier as a crucible of rebirth, where pioneers merge with the land to strip themselves of the garments of Old World oppression. Whereas the myth of the New World frontier entails a rejection of the past, Zionism imagines rebirth as the return to an ancient land, to a time that preceded the Diaspora. The New Jew—a term intended to distinguish the Zionist pioneer from the European Jew—not only renewed the land as a biblical birthright, but revived the muscular body of the ancient Hebrew warrior through his martial skills. This lineage extends from the biblical conquest of Canaan—hence Ari's surname, Ben Canaan, meaning son of Canaan. In *Exodus,* Old World victims of pogroms and extermination camps cast off their identity as persecuted subjects and transform themselves into New Jews by mastering the land and fighting the British and Arabs.

For Ari to become an American hero, he had to shed the stereotypes of Jewish masculinity. Kitty finds herself magnetically attracted to this "big Palestinian," a "gorgeous man" with a "hard handsome face," who does not "act like any Jew I've ever met." As a "strapping six-footer with black hair and ice-blue eyes," Ari "could be mistaken for a movie leading man." In the movie, a glistening, bare-chested Ari emerges godlike from the Mediterranean in the night to carry out his secret mission. When wounded in battle, he stoically bears the pain that "could have killed an ordinary human being." His emotional toughness matches his robust physique, so unlike a typical man of the Diaspora. A "scorner of sentiment," he has bemused tolerance for the biblical idealism of his comrades. "We have no Joshua to make the sun stand still or the walls to come tumbling down," he reminds them, and he works with "superhuman stamina" because "he does not believe in miracles." Of the prayers of Orthodox Jews, he says dismissively, "They don't quite realize that the only Messiah that will deliver them is a bayonet on the end of a rifle."[31]

Ari may not have resembled the Jews Kitty met at home, but readers would have recognized a typical American hero from a Hollywood Western—with his extreme individualism and preference for action over words. Reviewers wrote of "the Jewish Western," in which "glorification of courage in Jews" looked like "Shane turning on his tormentors and winning." (In *Shane* [1953], a lone gunslinger protects struggling farmers from a ruthless cattle baron.) Uris knew the genre well from writing the screenplay for *Gunfight at the O.K. Corral,* and one of his favorite reviews of the film was titled "When Men Were Men—and Killers." In 1976, he would claim that "You can write westerns in any

Poster for the film *Exodus,* 1960, starring Paul Newman as Ari Ben Canaan.

part of the world," and in 1958, he transposed the western frontier onto Palestine and mapped its terrain through the symbolic geography of the border between civilization and savagery.[32] On the screen, the setting of *Exodus* nostalgically revived the grandeur of sweeping panoramic landscapes, wide open for heroic pioneers—a view that was already receding from the Hollywood screen.

Exodus reenacted the primal myth of the American frontier as a tale of "regeneration through violence."[33] The hero in a Western ventures across the border of the civilized world to the wilderness in order to colonize dark, chaotic regions and learn the way of the Indians, thereby ridding himself—and the society he represents—of darkness. It is the barbarism of the Other—whether Indian or Arab—that forces the hero to become violent; he adopts their methods in order to defeat them, and to establish a border between legitimate and illegitimate violence. Ari forges his character in his encounter with Arabs, in the same way as an Indian fighter in the typical Western. Living among the Arabs when young, he learns to speak fluent Arabic and to scout the land from his "adopted brother," Taha, the son of the friendly local mukhtar, who has voluntarily sold his land to Ari's father to help civilize his own people. In later military exploits against the British, Ari easily disguises himself as an Arab. His familiarity with Arabs allows him to better enforce the hierarchy between himself and them. Fighting Arabs is an essential rite of passage for Ari as he comes of age in a hardscrabble new settlement. After a group of Arab youth ambushes Ari with stones, his father blames himself for naïvely believing in the possibility of coexistence with his Arab neighbors. He teaches Ari how to use a bullwhip, the same one he used to subdue the first Arab merchant who tried to cheat him. When Ari confronts his youthful tormentors, he expertly throws the whip "with a lightning flick" around the neck of the leader; the lash "snapped so sharply it tore his foe's flesh apart." The boys of the village never attack him again.[34]

Ari, though, never becomes enamored of violence for its own sake, and he follows his father's advice to use his whip judiciously: "You hold in your hand a weapon of justice. Never use it in anger or revenge. Only in defense." This early lesson in violence against Arabs forms the crucible for Ari's individualism. As Kitty explains, when she feels rebuffed by his steely cool, he "comes from a breed of supermen whose stock in trade is their self-reliance. Ari Ben Canaan hasn't needed anyone since the day he cut his teeth on his father's bull whip."[35]

In this morality tale, Uris portrays Arabs less as noble savages than as uncivilized hordes who exist outside the realm of law and must be kept in line by frontiersmen wielding the "weapon of justice." Indeed, it is impossible to read *Exodus* today without taking offense at its overtly racist stereotypes. Uris's depictions came from a vast menu of Orientalism and colonialism. He portrays indigenous Arabs as squalid remnants of an ancient Islamic civilization and blames them for despoiling the Promised Land, turning it into "festering stagnated swamps and eroded hills and rock-filled fields and unfertile earth." Arab neglect made it necessary for Zionist settlers, like Ari's father, to laboriously drain the swamps of the Huleh Valley and redeem "a land that had lain neglected and unwanted for a thousand years in fruitless despair until Jews rebuilt it."[36]

In contrast to Ari's fierce individualism, Uris lumps Arabs together as "mobs" and "gangs." Jews exercise violence with restraint; Arab violence is irrational, excessive, and vengeful. Unscrupulous Arab leaders ignobly whip up their followers into shrieking frenzies by promising them "easy victories, loot, and rape." Throughout the novel Uris transforms political resistance on the part of Arabs into irrational sexual violence. Ari's formative trauma was the rape and murder of his thirteen-year-old girlfriend during the Arab Revolt of 1936–1939. His erstwhile Arabic "brother," Taha, turns against the Jews in 1948 only because Ari forbids him to marry his sister. Such a union would threaten the sexual boundary between Arabs and Jews, a boundary that is as vigilantly policed as that between American frontiersmen and Indians. This recurring theme of sexual violence and vengeance makes it impossible for Ari—or the reader—to imagine Arab opposition to a Jewish state as politically motivated. Exhibiting the contradictions of most stereotypes, the Arabs of *Exodus* are both aggressive and spineless; they do not wield arms for a higher cause but rather revel in violence for its own sake, and Uris blames their refusal to defend their own homes in 1948 on their cowardice.[37]

Furthermore, Uris projects onto his Arab figures the stereotypes of Jewish timidity that he was trying to undo. By exaggerating Arab cowardice, he purges from the brave New Jew the taint of those submissive Jews who "chose" not to fight their Nazi persecutors. In the character of Dov, Uris turns the concentration camp survivor into a hardened warrior. As a child in the Warsaw Ghetto Uprising, Dov shot a German soldier point-blank and was then captured and sent to Auschwitz. In Zionist mythology, the exceptional Diaspora Jews of the Warsaw Ghetto Uprising took their place in the pantheon of Jewish rebels, and Israelis celebrated the story of valiant resistance at a time when survivors of the camps were shunned for their powerlessness. *Exodus* dramatizes this contrast between the New Jew as fighter and the Diaspora Jew as victim when Karen finds her father in a mental institution. He had survived a concentration camp but is too debilitated to recognize her; he had doomed himself by naïvely believing that Jews could assimilate into German society. Karen's future lies with Dov, the youngest incarnation of the fighting Jew, who joins a terrorist organization that Uris calls the Maccabees, after the ancient Jewish rebels who liberated Judea from Syrian rule. To dramatize this contrast in the film, Preminger compresses the order of historical events so that smoke is seen billowing from the King David Hotel explosion just as Karen unsteadily walks out the door of the mental hospital. (The actual bombing had occurred a year before the *Exodus* incident.)

By focusing on retribution rather than suffering, *Exodus* diverged from the liberal arguments for a Jewish state as a safe haven and as moral reparation for fascism, which would redeem Western civilization as a whole. The novel presents the violent struggle for a state as vengeance for Nazi atrocities and retribution for a long history of Jewish persecution, including Arab brutality in Palestine. In the words of Ari's uncle, "Nothing we do, right or wrong, can ever compare to what has been done to the Jewish people. Nothing the Maccabees do can even be considered an injustice in comparison to two thousand years of murder."[38]

In its depiction of Jewish masculinity, the film version of *Exodus* takes a different course from one of the few earlier films about refugees in Israel, *The Juggler* (1953), directed by Stanley Kramer. In that film, Kirk Douglas plays a former entertainer from Munich, a concentration camp survivor who has been psychologically traumatized by the loss of his home and family. Paranoid and distrustful, he flees from every effort to make a home in the new state. Israel does finally rescue him, through the love of a blonde, buxom Israeli who carries a rifle and dances the hora with him. The viewer is left, however, with the overall impression of the juggler's irrevocable psychic damage that a new nation cannot fully repair.

When Dov arrives in Palestine, a scarred and brooding soul, he also bears deep psychological scars, yet he is healed by his commitment to take up arms in a harsh masculine communion. In an emotionally searing scene of initiation, Dov descends into a dimly lit basement to undergo a ritual induction into the Maccabees. Surrounded by his elders, he breaks down when confessing that he was repeatedly raped by Nazis in Auschwitz: "They used me like you use a woman!" After this admission of shame, a candlelit ceremony purifies him. Holding a Bible in one hand and a rifle in the other, he swears to sacrifice his life for the cause. Dov's renewed masculinity thrusts aside his feminized victimhood, and he emerges into the Palestine sunlight as a toughened New Jew.

Uris freely adapted Zionist myths of national origins for his American audience. His personal rejection of the Diaspora mentality, so central to Zionist beliefs, targeted contemporary American Jewish writers. He despised what he saw as the self-absorption of Jewish writers, who psychoanalyzed their personal neuroses and whined about their parents in print. "I'm made ill by those beatnik writers who degrade the Jews," he said to an interviewer, and by beatnik, he meant Jewish. He hoped the publication of *Exodus* would be a literary turning point, when "Jewish writers would stop apologizing for their Jewishness" and "stop with the neurotic ghetto characters." It would be "like a breath of spring air for the American people to meet Mr. Ari Ben Canaan," he wrote in a letter to his father—"the fighting Jew who won't take shit from nobody . . . who fears nobody. He will be a departure from the Mailer . . . [Marjorie] Morningstar apologetics. He will be a revelation for America and I believe America will love Ari Ben Canaan just as they loved the Marines in *Battle Cry*."[39]

Zionist mythology created the New Jew by repudiating his Diaspora predecessors. In his own brand of American Zionism, Uris created the "fighting Jew" and a "nation of marines" to expunge the images of contemporary Jews in the cultural repertoire of American Jewish writers. The subject of Israel allowed Uris to treat his writing as a virile art and to promote himself as novelist to the rank of his tough Israeli fighters.

The theme of toughness was not just a personal obsession of Leon Uris; it had broad cultural resonance at the time. In 1958, the year *Ex-*

odus was published, the editors of *Look* titled a special edition "The Decline of Masculinity." That November, Arthur Schlesinger Jr. published "The Crisis of American Masculinity" in *Esquire*. Ten years earlier, he had sounded an early warning about "flabby" American political thought in *The Vital Center*. Postwar American men were "soft," complained critics throughout the decade. Former war heroes were surrendering their individualism en masse to the pressure of conformity, the routine of office work, the seduction of affluence, and the apron strings of suburban domesticity. The "crisis of masculinity" bundled many social and political anxieties into an overall fear of softness.[40]

As an antidote to this malaise, Schlesinger called for "a new virility in public life." "Tough-minded" realism would serve as a bulwark against "the utopian sentimentality of left-wing progressivism." The cult of toughness soared to rhetorical heights in a young senator's clarion call to the New Frontier. John F. Kennedy, a model of masculinity, rallied modern Americans to emulate "the pioneers of old" who stoically "gave up their safety, their comfort and sometimes their lives to build a new world here in the West."[41]

For Uris, the Israeli hero perfectly embodied this new virility, and the land of Israel epitomized the New Frontier. Uris joined the liberal Cold Warriors who rejected the soft idealism of progressives in the name of realism. His Israel was not an "ultra-glorious utopia" that would model a New Deal for the world, as Eleanor Roosevelt had hoped. The kibbutz in *Exodus* is a military outpost, not the socialist experiment that thrilled I. F. Stone and Bartley Crum. Ari tends his private farm with no aspiration to start a Jordan Valley Authority, a project that had delighted liberals a decade before. In *Exodus,* the UN partition vote creates an "abortion of a state," and it does not imbue Israel with the higher authority of internationalism claimed by Freda Kirchwey and Sumner Welles. The international community, in Uris's view, had betrayed the Jews, who "stood alone and with blood and guts won for themselves what had legally been given them by the conscience of the world."[42]

Uris did share with progressives the view of Zionism as an anticolonial struggle. For him, though, that opposition to colonial exploitation was not an opportunity for an alliance between Jews and Arabs. Instead, he portrayed the revolt against empire as a heroic vehicle for Jewish nationalism.

Zionism as Anticolonialism

"It's the story of our own Revolutionary War against the British, transposed to Palestine." That's how a reviewer for the *Los Angeles Times*
explained the "extraordinary success" of *Exodus,* which had been read
by "millions of Americans" and had "enormous appeal for non-Jewish
readers."[43] That appeal stemmed from the familiarity of this national
narrative.

The slogan "It's 1776 in Palestine" had been used to muster American support for Zionism since World War II. In the 1950s, Israel's
American advocates revived the 1776 analogy to encourage the United
States to sell arms to the new nation. Uris kept in his scrapbook an editorial from the 1956 *Congressional Record* that likened "the courage
and stamina of the Israelis to that of the courageous Americans who
declared their independence in 1776"; it concluded that "to help Israel
today is to help ourselves."[44] In 1958, Israel's tenth anniversary was
celebrated at Independence Hall in Philadelphia, where the U.S. Declaration of Independence had been signed. Many luminaries who attended, including former president Truman, called attention to the
location's symbolism.

The image of Britain as the evil empire was relatively new in Hollywood. When the first American movie about Israel, *The Sword in the
Desert,* came out in 1949, its unsympathetic portrayal of the British offended some viewers who honored the alliance of World War II. The
New York Times reviewer criticized the portrayal of the British as "pip-
pip old chaps, killers, unmerciful policemen."[45] A decade later, the
British Empire was losing its luster in a rapidly decolonizing world. The
trailer for Preminger's *Exodus* included a signature scene in which Kitty
worriedly exclaims to Ari, as they look out over a magnificent landscape, "You can't fight the whole British Empire with six hundred
people. It isn't possible." He responds with a question: "How many
Minute Men did you have in Concord, the day they fired the shot heard
around the world?" She doesn't know the answer, but he does. Viewing
Israel's founding as a revolt against empire, Americans could look in a
mirror to imagine their own heroic past writ large.

The "Israeli Minutemen" of *Exodus,* as one reviewer called them,
were given a revolutionary lineage in the novel that predated 1776.[46]
"Right in the same place we fought the Roman Empire we now fight

the British Empire two thousand years later," proclaims one of these fighters.[47] The British Empire in *Exodus* appears as an amalgam of ancient Rome and biblical Egypt. *Exodus* maps Jewish liberation onto the biblical narrative of freedom from slavery in the scene where Ari leads the displaced persons out of British camps in Cyprus. At the same time, this liberation replays the shot heard round the world. In Uris's history, the plot of Jewish revolution moves inexorably from the pharaohs to the Roman Empire, to culminate in the struggle against the British Mandate.

These far-flung connections would have come easily to an American audience schooled in the popular Roman and biblical epics of the late 1950s, such as *The Ten Commandments, Ben-Hur,* and *Spartacus.* Dalton Trumbo started working on *Exodus* while finishing the screenplay for *Spartacus,* Stanley Kubrick's Oscar-winning epic about a slave revolt in ancient Rome. Both films follow a similar plot about the struggle for freedom against a decadent empire. In the Cold War milieu, the Egyptian or Roman movie sets loom above the actors like twentieth-century totalitarian architecture. What's more, the Roman and Egyptian overlords speak with British accents. The revolutionary heroes in each case—Moses, Judah Ben-Hur, Spartacus—all speak with American accents as they fight for independence from tyranny. Sharing the epic dimensions of these films, *Exodus* presented a Jewish revolt against the British Empire that was identifiably American.

Viewed in an American mirror, a nation founded in revolt against empire could not be regarded either as a conquering power or as one rooted in colonialism. The word "conquest" appears in Uris's novel only in reference to the Zionist idea of "national land and the conquest of self-labor." Working the land precludes the subjugation of others: "The Haganah would not try to conquer the Palestine Arabs. 'Palestine will be conquered with our sweat.' It was an army of restraint."[48] The idea of restraint implies that Jews use violence only defensively, to protect their work on the land, and allows them to disavow any violence previously committed against Arab denizens of that same land.

The narrative of revolt rhetorically displaces those inhabitants and replaces them with Jewish settlers, who are now seen as the indigenous population. In a ten-page statement that Uris wrote, titled "Outstanding Action of the Jewish Underground," he applauded the Irgun's 1944 declaration that "the real enemy facing the Jews in this struggle of a Jewish state were not the local gangs of Palestine Arabs, but Great Britain. Not a battle between warring tribes, but a full scale revolt." According to this logic, Jewish settlers play the role of colonized subjects rising up against foreign rule. "Here for the first time in centuries," wrote Uris, "a race of so-called 'natives' had dared to face the British ruler with the same medicine which British colonial rule had applied to others." This narrative made Jewish resistance the prototype of modern anti-colonial rebellion. At the same time, it erased the history of Zionist settlement under the aegis of the British Empire. In the same account, Uris described the 1948 attack on Jaffa, which decimated the population of the largest Arab city in Palestine, as a military operation against the British: "The Irgun demolished houses to create rubble to block British tanks, and attack gangs in their base." By "gangs" he meant "the 100,000-odd inhabitants reinforced by Arab troops."[49] Uris's narrative elevated the Jewish struggle above ethnic tribalism to the universal politics of revolution, while it relegated the resistance of Palestinian Arabs to apolitical criminal activity.

While Uris adopted this version of Israeli history as a revolt against a venal empire allied with local bandits, Preminger and Trumbo wished to portray a more liberal view of Israel. They found Uris too unsympathetic to the British and the Arabs. As Preminger explained in an interview, *Exodus* is "an American picture, after all, that tries to tell the story, giving both sides a chance to plead their side."[50] For ex-marine Uris, the scrappy fight for Jewish liberty made *Exodus* an American tale. For the cosmopolitan Preminger, it was the liberal tolerance of opposing viewpoints that gave the film its American character. When Preminger hired Dalton Trumbo to write the final screenplay, Trumbo was one of the Hollywood Ten, blacklisted for refusing to testify before the House Un-American Activities Committee in 1947. (Bartley Crum was one of their attorneys.) Trumbo and other blacklisted writers had continued to work under pseudonyms, but Preminger garnered attention when he openly named Trumbo in a *New York Times* interview as the screenwriter for the film.

Trumbo was aware that Preminger's profession of fairness to both sides nevertheless served to reinforce a partisan perspective on historical events and cast Israel in a positive light. In a note to the director about the final screenplay, Trumbo described how this perspective informed his drafting of the climactic scene, in which twenty thousand extras in Jerusalem tensely await the results of the UN vote on the partition of Palestine:

> By their willingness to compromise and to accept partition the Jews persuaded the world of their reasonableness as opposed to the unreasonableness of the Arab claims. This is regardless of the fact that actually the Jews, too, wanted the whole land for themselves. I choose to dramatize their perhaps reluctant acceptance of partition as a *desire* for it. It is better dramatically and better for Israel that it be that way, rather than to dramatize their desire for *all* of it (which would place them on the level of the Arabs in the audience's mind).[51]

Concerned, however, about appearing "unjust historically," even while acknowledging the dramatic and political need to elevate the Israelis above the Arabs, Trumbo pressed Preminger to include speeches about the need for justice for both Arabs and Jews.

The film combines Uris's hard-core nationalism with Preminger's and Dalton's more liberal concerns. It showcases the internationalism of the UN vote to legitimate the quest for Jewish sovereignty. But the film's most exciting action scenes center on the breakout from Britain's Acre Prison, the Irgun's "greatest feat," as Uris described it. As in most historical fiction, tensions between family members represent broader social conflicts. Through his masterminding of this feat, Ari reconciles his right-wing uncle of the Irgun with his labor-Zionist father of the Haganah, whose opposing positions on terrorism had been keeping them apart. In their version of this prison escape, Uris and Preminger did not simply give credit to the Haganah that duly belonged to the Irgun, as detractors complained. *Exodus* resolved the internal Zionist rivalry in a vision of national harmony, even as it Americanized the narrative of Jewish revolt against colonialism as the mainstream story of Israel's founding.

Both film and novel effaced the violent dispossession of Palestinians, with a glorified interpretation of Israel's founding as an event "unparalleled in human history." In addition to recounting the particular history of Jewish persecution and national restoration, *Exodus* presents the establishment of Israel as a universal good—as the embodiment of human aspiration and the fulfillment of the noblest impulses of mankind. The novel quotes from the 1948 Declaration of the State of Israel, which intertwines the particular and the universal: "the Land of Israel . . . was the birthplace of the Jewish people. Here their spiritual, religious, and national identity was formed. Here they achieved independence and created a culture of national and universal significance. Here they wrote and gave the Bible to the world." In the novel, Uris proclaims, "Young Israel stood out as a lighthouse for all mankind." The story of a particular nation becomes "an epic in the history of man."[52]

Karen is the character in *Exodus* who best articulates the universal significance of Israel. She decides not to go to America with Kitty, rejecting a soft life of suburban comfort in favor of a tougher idealistic path. Karen explains that "this little land was chosen for us because it is the crossroads of the world, on the edge of man's wilderness. This is where God wants His people to be . . . on the frontiers, to stand and guard His laws which are the cornerstones of man's moral existence." Kitty at first responds despairingly that the new nation is surrounded by "savages trying to destroy you." But she then feels uplifted by Karen's insistence that "Israel is the bridge between darkness and light."[53] Even though Karen remains in Israel, Uris translates her reasoning into the American idiom of the frontier. In this mythology, the frontier marks not only the geographic border between nations, but also a Manichean opposition between civilization and savagery.

Jewish children in *Exodus* represent the progress of civilization, from the orphans aboard the ship to the young people who are successfully evacuated from Gan Dafna in a dangerous mission during the war. When Kitty compares this youthful colony to the neighboring Arab village, Abu Yesha, she laments, "How pathetic the dirty little Arab children were beside the robust youngsters of Gan Dafna. How futile their lives seemed in contrast. . . . There seemed to be no laughter or songs or games or purpose among the Arab children. It was a static existence—a new generation born on an eternal caravan in an endless desert."[54] This passage does the rhetorical work of displacement, transporting the Arab children from their homes to a metaphorical desert. The portrayal of their existence as both static and nomadic removes them from the progressive arc of history and thus from a future rooted in the land.

If, according to the exceptionalist logic of *Exodus,* the Jews revolted against the British to establish not only earthly boundaries but also a moral frontier, then the Palestinian Arabs who claimed their own land could only embody the forces of darkness. In describing the UN partition vote in the novel, Uris writes that universal "truth" supported the cause of the Jewish State: "It was the truth that the neutral UNSCOP [United Nations Special Committee on Palestine] had found in Palestine: the truth that Palestine was a tyranny-ridden police state; the truth, seen through the thin veil of Arab deception, of the Arab failure to advance culturally, economically, and socially from the Dark Ages; the truth apparent in the Jewish cities that had sprung from the sand and the Jewish fields that had been made to grow from desolation; the truth of industry and ingenuity; the truth—implicit in the DP camps—of the humanity of the Jewish case."[55] The concept of "truth" here works as a weapon. It expunges Arabs from the map of modern nations by driving them across the frontier between civilization and barbarism. They are identified as antiquated—in their authoritarian rule—and stunted—in their "failure to advance"—and thus not worthy of political measure. The weapon of truth transforms an exclusive story of a particular people into a narrative of humanity that equates Israel with the inexorable march of progress.

As the antithesis of enlightenment, the Arabs in *Exodus* bear the major responsibility for their own destruction, as though their backwardness inevitably caused them to give way before progress. In the novel, the village of Abu Yesha invites "occupation" by an invading Iraqi army. Taha, who rules the village after his father's death, allows the Iraqi forces to operate freely, even though his villagers would rather live in a benevolent Jewish state. In the logic of the novel, Taha's refusal to side with the Jews—with the universal forces of humanity and modernity—gives Ari no choice but to forcibly evacuate the village and expel its inhabitants, and then level it to the ground house by house. This destruction is represented not as a choice made by the novel's hero, but as an act forced upon him by the refusal of his "adopted brother" to accept Zionism as a means for Arabs to liberate themselves from their own darkness.

In the movie, in contrast, Taha behaves like a "good Indian," and he does make the enlightened choice to side with the Jews. Preminger added a stock Hollywood Nazi to lead the reluctant local Arab resistance, thinking, apparently, that this would make the Arabs appear less villainous than they do in the novel because they are being forced to follow an evil outsider rather than developing animus to Jews by themselves. Wittingly or not, Preminger associates the Arabs with Nazis and denies them a political will of their own. In a shocking scene that evokes an American lynching, Ari finds Taha's corpse hanging from a noose, with a Jewish star branded on his chest and a swastika painted on the wall. This iconography makes Taha, who is killed for collaborating with the Jews, a Judaized victim of Nazism rather than a victim of Jewish violence in Palestine. Ari buries Taha alongside Karen in the same grave, in a gesture to a future when Jews and Arabs will be able to live side by side. After Ari speaks the film's final word, *shalom* (peace), in his eulogy, the camera follows the armed mourners—including Kitty—as they board a convoy of trucks going off to fight Israel's War of Independence.

In the longer time frame of the novel, Uris includes a fictionalized reference to the 1948 Deir Yassin massacre, even while he shows irrational violence as almost always being committed by Arabs. Although he makes a reference to the "unforgivable massacre of innocent people," Uris was primarily concerned that the story of Deir Yassin might tarnish Israel's humane reputation, so he presents it as an aberration on the part of otherwise restrained Jewish fighters. He uses the grammatical indirection of the passive construction to imply that Jewish troops did not intentionally target their victims: "In a strange and inexplicable sequence of events panic broke out among Maccabee troops and they opened up a wild and unnecessary firing. Once started it could not be stopped. More than two hundred Arab civilians were massacred." The narrator regrets that this event, "the blackest blot on the Jewish record," had "fixed a stigma on the young nation that it would take decades to erase." Uris tries to hasten this erasure by framing the massacre as an exception and arguing that it had nothing to do with the fear that drove Palestinian Arabs to flee. Other than this one exceptional episode, the "Arabs who remained in Palestine were completely unmolested," and the Arab leaders bore full responsibility for forcing their people from their homes. To reassert the exceptional nature of Jewish suffering, he writes, "This one example of Jewish excess—in the heat of war, one must remember—pales beside the record of scores of Arab-led massacres in over three decades."[56] Israel may have vanquished the British Empire, but its identity relies on this ongoing narrative of victimization.

In the novel, Uris ends his account of the 1948 war at the Suez Canal not with a confrontation between Israel and Egypt, but with the Israeli

Air Force shooting down six British fighter planes: "It only seemed fitting somehow that the last shots of the War of Liberation were against the British."[57] Fitting, because it fit an Americanized narrative of Israelis refighting the 1776 American Revolution, eliminating Arabs from the political landscape as historical actors either in their resistance against Zionist settlement or in their own revolt against the British Empire.

"Lots of people around the world have decided they want to run their own lives," explains an American reporter in the opening of the novel. "Colonies are going out of vogue this century."[58] *Exodus* placed Israel at the vanguard of this global trend. As a historical novel, it reveals as much about the time of its production as about the history it recounts. In the late 1950s, Asian and African countries were rapidly declaring their independence from European colonial rule. In the context of the Cold War, Americans viewed these struggles for decolonization with admiration, but also with ambivalence and paranoia in cases where they feared that communists were backing independence movements. The story of Israel's revolutionary origins offered a reassuring image of stability amid these bewildering changes.

Israel's anticolonial origins grew all the more important after it had joined forces with its former colonial overlord, Great Britain. When Egyptian president Gamal Nasser nationalized the Suez Canal in 1956, Israel secretly colluded with Britain and France to launch a massive invasion of Egypt. The Sinai-Suez War represented the nadir of Israel's early diplomatic relationship with the United States. President Dwight D. Eisenhower, with UN support, pressured Great Britain and France to halt their occupation of the Canal Zone. Soon after, he forced Israel to withdraw from the Sinai and Gaza, under threat of sanctions.

America's global image as an opponent of colonialism was one of the many strategic concerns at stake for the administration during this crisis. Defending Egypt's sovereignty was not Eisenhower's primary goal; in fact, he feared that Nasser's nationalization of the canal would inspire similar moves in the oil fields of the region. A more important consideration was that the United States was engaged in a Cold War struggle for the allegiance of newly decolonized nations in Africa and Asia. These nations had rallied behind Nasser, and the United States was eager to resist the Soviet Union's labeling of America as imperialist. "Vice President Calls It Declaration of Independence from Colonialism," proclaimed a headline in the *Washington Post*. "For the first time in history," stated Vice President Richard Nixon, "we have shown independence of Anglo-French policies toward Asia and Africa which seemed to us to reflect the colonial tradition. That declaration of independence has had an electrifying effect throughout the world."[59]

Nixon's hyperbole expressed a wish to share in, if not appropriate, the limelight shining on Nasser, whose actions in standing up to colonialism did indeed have an electrifying effect on the new nations of Africa and Asia. Nixon evoked the Declaration of Independence at a time when it was being deployed by national movements across the globe and the political spectrum. In 1945, Ho Chi Minh modeled the Vietnamese Declaration of Independence on the American one, seeking American support to no avail. In 1951, *Time* named Mohammad Mossadegh, the democratically elected prime minister of Iran, Man of the Year, and in his U.S. tour, he identified Iran's independence with the 1776 struggle for freedom from "the chains of British Imperialism."[60] In 1960, the "Year of Africa," an article in *Life* compared Ghana's formation of a new government to the "first perilous steps taken by the American colonies."[61] In 1965, the white minority government of South Rhodesia patterned its Unilateral Declaration of Independence on the American declaration of 1776.

For Americans during the Cold War, their own revolution became a rhetorical touchstone for evaluating national independence movements, and for distinguishing anticolonialist uprisings from nationalist revolutions that posed a communist threat. When nonaligned nations met in Bandung, Indonesia, in 1955, Eisenhower tried to cast the conference in American terms as bearing witness to Emerson's vision of the 1776 shot heard round the world.[62] When Hungarian demonstrators stood up to Soviet tanks in 1956, he compared them to the Minutemen repelling the British.[63] The spectacle of British paratroopers landing in the Canal Zone, though, pulled global attention away from the Soviet incursion into Hungary. The Eisenhower administration hoped that once the invasion of Egypt had been halted, Afro-Asian support for Nasser would turn toward condemnation of the Soviet "imperialism by the bayonet." The tension between supporting American-style independence and opposing radical revolution was expressed by Secretary of State John Foster Dulles as the problem of "how to guide the new nations from colonialism to independence in an orderly way. . . . We must have evolution not revolution."[64]

Israel appeared to fit this model to a tee. While *Exodus* was enter-
taining readers and viewers with its story of Israeli independence, the
American press was heralding Israel's foreign aid policy as a nonimperial
model for encouraging development in Africa. Israel was not invited to
Bandung, but it did actively cultivate relationships, through economic
and military aid, with newly independent African nations such as Ghana.
Newspapers reported on Africans studying in Israeli universities and
kibbutzim, and Israeli technicians "going out to assist the newly independent Africans, who find in Israel a welcome alternative to the great
powers of East and West."[65] Articles portrayed Israel as a paradigm for
decolonization; as one journalist put it, Israel was "the strongest link
between the white nations and the chaotic African situation."[66] These
stories characterized Israel as a force for orderly modern development,
firmly inside the Western world but opposed to European colonialism.
This image of Israel as a developmental bridge between East and West
offered a Cold War version of Theodore Herzl's 1896 idea that a
Jewish state in Palestine could serve the West as "part of a wall of defense for Europe in Asia, an outpost of civilization against barbarism."[67] Although this bulwark may have turned into a bridge during
the era of decolonization, Israel was still seen as policing the same
border—fostering American theories of development while guarding
against both communism and revolution.

Exodus did not directly address policy dilemmas, but on a popular
level, it offered a symbolic resolution of the American ambivalence
toward decolonizing nations. Israel's "War of Liberation," as Uris called
it, was connected with emancipation from European colonial rule, while
Israel's enemies, especially Egypt, were associated with revolution as
anarchy or communism. Arab revolutions are unthinkable in *Exodus*
except as irrational violence stemming from an inferiority complex, a
resentment of modernity, and hatred of Jews. In the Sinai-Suez War,
Israel may have chosen the wrong side of history by colluding with European colonialism. But by 1958, *Exodus* was offering a vision of the
nation as an anticolonial exemplar, one that sought what Dulles had
referred to as "independence in an orderly way." *Exodus* aligned Israel
with America not by treaty or formal alliance but by telling a story
that reflected America's view of itself as a champion of national independence. The novel contributed to the mystique of Israel's anticolonial founding and helped to obscure its colonial origins.

Exodus ends in 1956 with Israel on the verge of war with Egypt, in a final scene at a Passover Seder commemorating the exodus from Egypt. By means of this biblical trope, Uris presents modern Egypt not in terms of its twentieth-century struggle against colonialism, but as the modern incarnation of ancient tyranny: "The Egyptians, the original oppressors, had become the symbol of all the oppressors of all the Jews throughout all the ages." The Seder takes place right after news arrives that Karen has been murdered "by a gang of *fedayeen* from Gaza."[68] In Uris's fictionalized border town, based on Nahal Oz, he renders Palestinian fighters who crossed the border from refugee camps as criminal agents of the modern pharaoh through a narrative that sanctifies Israel's birth as anticolonialist, while erasing the Arab struggle for self-determination.

The Other Exodus

Exodus succeeded in bringing Americans to the Promised Land. "As a piece of propaganda, it's the greatest thing ever written about Israel," opined Israel's prime minister, David Ben-Gurion. The head of Israel's Ministry of Tourism said that "we could have thrown away all promotional literature we printed in the last two years and just circulated *Exodus*." In 1959, El Al Airlines sponsored a twelve-day "Exodus Tour of Israel," which paired scenes from the novel with sites from antiquity or Israeli history. Fiction supplanted history, as tourists would ask to visit places where events from the novel occurred. Tourist guides reported that *Exodus* rivaled the Bible as background reading for visiting the Holy Land: one visitor, for example, asked to see the Galilee, a place he "read about in *Exodus*." If *Exodus* replaced the Bible as the onsite guide to the contemporary Israeli landscape, it served a similar function for millions of Americans who stayed at home.[69]

Exodus did have its detractors, though. In a 1961 essay, the young Philip Roth delivered a scathing attack on its historical amnesia, suggesting that the popularity of the book and film among Americans had to do with the focus on the tough Jewish fighter in an attempt to remove "from the nation's consciousness . . . nothing less than the memory of the holocaust itself, the murder of six million Jews in all its raw, senseless, fiendish horror." Roth compared *Exodus* to the inane prospect of a popular movie that would "enable us to dispose of that other troublesome horror, the murder of the citizens of Hiroshima." Such a movie celebrating "the beautiful modern city that has risen from the ashes of atomic annihilation" would serve to exonerate Americans of their guilt.[70]

Exodus teaches that "you don't have to worry about Jewish vulnerability and victimization after all, the Jews can take care of themselves." If *Life* magazine presents Adolf Eichmann on the cover one week, and a few weeks later a picture of Sal Mineo as a Jewish freedom fighter, writes Roth, then "the scales appear at last to begin to balance, [and] there cannot but be a sigh of relief." Roth believed that Uris's portrayal of the founding of Israel as violent retribution for Nazi extermination meant relinquishing the moral authority of the Jew: "The Jew is no longer looking out from the wings on the violence of our age, nor is he its favorite victim; now he is a participant." To Roth, *Exodus* demonstrated not exceptionalism but a nationalistic norm, because "a man with a gun and a hand grenade, a man who kills for his God-given rights (in this case, as the song informs us, God-given *land*) cannot sit so easily in judgment of another man when he kills for what God has given *him*."[71] The tough Jews of *Exodus* represented to Roth the ultimate form of assimilation into American society. No longer outsiders or victims burdened with moral insight, the Jews of *Exodus* have been Americanized through a call to arms that effaces their history of suffering, and their nation's responsibility for the suffering of others.

In his critique of "new Jewish stereotypes," Roth showed no interest in the old Arab stereotypes that pervade the novel and film. To Arab readers, though, *Exodus* represented what Aziz S. Sahwell called a "distortion of truth." In a pamphlet published by the Arab Information Center in 1960, Sahwell detailed the prejudiced portrayal of Arabs and their way of life, and he judged the novel to be propaganda masquerading as history. One of the only critics to point out that the novel ends in 1956 with a "justification of aggression against Egypt," Sahwell interprets *Exodus* as not only narrating retrospectively the history of Israel's birth, but also predicting the future of Israel's strategy of preemptive war.[72]

Many American Jews have testified that *Exodus* inspired them, motivating some to feel pride in their Jewish identity, some to fight for social justice, and some even to imitate the tough Ari Ben Canaan and enlist in the Israeli army.[73] It is less common, however, to read of reactions to *Exodus* by Arab Americans. To convey one response, I draw on personal correspondence with Albert Hazbun, the father of a colleague, Professor Waleed Hazbun, who remembers as a child wondering about *Exodus* after finding it on his father's bookshelf.

In 1959, as a young Palestinian from Bethlehem, Albert Hazbun moved from the American University of Beirut to San Francisco to work as an engineer-in-training at the Bechtel Corporation. A few days after his arrival he bought a copy of *Exodus*. Having heard about the book in Beirut, he wanted to read it himself to be able to respond to its claims. He recognized its similarity to other popular American genres with tough-guy heroes: "I read the book quite carefully and managed to do it by isolating my thoughts from the politics and read it as an adventure story same as a Mickey Spillane or Perry Mason." But this familiarity did not dampen his indignation: "The events in the book were so false and outrageous to me that I thought that intelligent people would see through that and not accept it at face value. There were several sentences in the book that were so outrageous to me that they stayed with me many years to come."

When the film came out a few months later, Hazbun followed the reviews avidly and was shocked when the Bechtel employee social group put up a large poster announcing, "Bechtel Evening at *Exodus*"—an exclusive engagement for the company at the San Francisco theater that was screening the movie before its wide distribution. Hazbun contacted the Bechtel manager in charge to protest: "I was surprised that Bechtel, the company with so much work in the Arab countries, which should have known better, was allowing such blatant Israeli propaganda for the employees instead of educating them to the true facts and events. He actually agreed with me, but said that it was too late for him to cancel the event. He then suggested that I was free to provide the employees with better facts." Hazbun printed copies of a review that criticized the novel for its distortion of history, and he posted it on all the bulletin boards in his building next to the announcement regarding *Exodus*.

"Next morning I noticed that all my papers were missing. So I made it my task to show up early every morning to inspect all bulletin boards and replace any missing revue papers. I did this every day until the day the movie was shown." Hazbun and his wife attended the movie with the other Bechtel employees. "It was hard not to feel with and support

Ari Ben Canaan, but the viciously anti-Palestinian message was diffi-cult to watch. I have never forgiven Paul Newman or Eva Marie Saint."[74]

The review Hazbun posted on the bulletin boards came from the journal *Issues,* published by the American Council for Judaism (AJC), an anti-Zionist organization headed by Rabbi Elmer Berger. The ACJ had shrunk in numbers and influence after Israel's establishment had stilled the debates about Zionism in the 1940s. But the organization decided to publish a slim volume called "*Exodus*—Unhistorical Novel," containing two essays on Uris's novel, reprinted from *Issues.* Addressing the portrayal of both Jews and Arabs, the essays objected to the excep-tionalism championed by this popular narrative. "*Exodus* distorts" concluded one review, "because it separates Jews out of the stream of history, establishes them as virtually the only victims of mankind's abysmal side, and then projects this role of perpetual scapegoat into the future. Except that Israel is now created to serve as a savior of the Jews." Irwin Hermann's "A Historical Appraisal" opened with the claim that "the inadequacy of the book (and of the Zionist interpre-tation of these events) lies in the refusal to recognize the integrity of the fundamental Arab grievance." He saw parallels between Zionist land and labor policies and those of other settler colonial projects. Using a word that may sound jarring because of today's debates, he blamed the "thoroughness of the Zionist colonial 'apartheid'" for pre-venting "a peaceful solution of all the problems." Condemning the novel's "glorification of Jewish terrorist activity," the review concluded that the novel "is not a book of hope but of despair, not one of asser-tion but resignation; for its principal theme that a Jew cannot live an honorable life except in Israel is nihilism of the worst sort."[75]

These were indubitably minority views at the time, for they criticized, in different ways, the exceptionalist narrative of Israel's revolutionary origins. That foundational story achieved authority as history by mir-roring the anticolonial image of the American nation in a decolonizing world. For the *Exodus* story to hold sway for so long as the dominant narrative of Israel's founding, it would have to do battle with alterna-tive narratives that placed Israel and the United States within a history of colonial settlement and imperial power. But when war erupted in the Middle East in 1967, the popularity of *Exodus* provided a ready-made template for journalists to use in their portrayals of Israel's fighting Jews.

3

INVINCIBLE VICTIM

On June 8, 1967, three days into what Israel would later dub the Six-Day War, the *New York Times* published a feature on the chief of staff of the Israel Defense Forces, Yitzhak Rabin, with the headline "Hero of the Israelis." Recounting Rabin's rout of the Egyptian army from the Sinai Peninsula, the article identified him as the "prototype of a fictional hero," the inspiration for Ari Ben Canaan in Leon Uris's novel *Exodus*. Two weeks later, *Life* magazine repeated this claim in an article that included a photograph of Rabin in military uniform, his shirt unbuttoned at the neck, gazing upward at the recently captured Western Wall in Jerusalem.[1]

Rabin did not, in fact, serve as the model for Uris's fictional hero, even though journalists may have thought the "blue-eyed, sandy-haired and rugged" commander looked the part.[2] Fiction, though, did provide journalists with a prototype for their heroic portrayal of the Israeli soldier in the 1967 war. The *Exodus* reference rendered the descriptor "hero of the Israelis" immediately legible as a deadly if reluctant warrior, equal parts muscle and morality. A popular and enduring narrative of the war followed the equally familiar plot of plucky David trouncing a lumbering Goliath, in the form of the Israel Defense Forces overcoming the threat of annihilation from surrounding Arab armies.

The Six-Day War is commonly considered the turning point in the special relationship between the United States and Israel. The small nation's lightning victory and righteous cause appealed to a nation embroiled in the Vietnam War, and Americans en masse fell in love with Israel. The enthusiastic media found "a measure of relief in the switch from Vietnam to the Mideast," wrote *Variety* magazine. "Heroes and villains seemed easier to come by," and "colorful characters" abounded, "right out of central casting." Tapping into nostalgia for the moral clarity and decisive outcome of World War II, the Arab-Israeli conflict fulfilled the dreams of those who "yearn wistfully for wars that were," and "Israel's blitz tactics doubtless produced the desired catharsis."[3]

The Israeli heroes of the June war may have leapt from the silver screen of *Exodus* to distract Americans from their own quagmire in Southeast Asia. But the war's final outcome did not mesh with the view of Israel's founding as an anticolonial act. On June 5, 1967, after a tense three-week standoff with Egypt, Israel launched an attack that obliterated the Egyptian air force and in a few hours essentially decided the course of the war. That day, even as Israel's leaders announced that the country would not seek to expand its territory, its army hurtled forward on three fronts.[4] Israel conquered the Sinai Peninsula and Gaza Strip from Egypt, the West Bank and East Jerusalem from Jordan, and the Golan Heights from Syria. One million Palestinians came under Israel's military rule, as it quadrupled the extent of the territory under its control.

The belief that Israel had narrowly snatched victory out of the jaws of defeat became the common-sense understanding not only of the war's chronology but also of the nation's existential state. Yet in the years immediately following the war, as Israel tightened its control over the lands and people it had conquered, a global counternarrative emerged about Israeli colonialism, a narrative that framed the rise of Palestinian nationalism as a Third World revolutionary movement and linked Israel not with anticolonial struggles but with American imperial power in Vietnam. Mainstream commentators across the political spectrum, not just on the radical left, expressed unease with Israel as an occupying power. Israel's old-fashioned military triumph, which seemed so appealing at first, occurred at a moment in history when territorial expansion conflicted with the global trend toward decolonization. This, too, is one of the enduring legacies of the Six-Day War.

After Palestinian resistance groups turned to violent acts of international terrorism in the 1970s, and the Cold War intensified the conflict between the United States and Third World nations, a new narrative gained currency that united Israel and America as leaders in a global war of civilization against barbarism. It came to displace the counternarratives of Israeli colonialism in the U.S. press and mainstream discourse.

Ten years after the Six-Day War, "pro-Israel" narratives did not simply supplant critical ones; rather, the paradoxical—and heroic—image of Israel as an invincible victim became hegemonic in the United States—precisely when Israel came to offer Americans a mirror in which to understand their post-Vietnam role in the world.

Romancing the Israeli Soldier

In the narrative that emerged from the Six-Day War, Israel came to appear both vulnerable and invincible at the same time, at risk of destruction yet militarily indomitable. Its Arab enemies were portrayed as the inverse: formidable enough to obliterate an entire nation, yet incapable of matching Israel's military forces on the battlefield. That story begins with Egypt, aligned with Syria, threatening Israel's existence by closing the Straits of Tiran to Israeli shipping, ousting UN peacekeeping forces, moving troops to the border, and signing a defense pact with Jordan. After three weeks of impotent international diplomacy, during which no one comes to its aid, Israel launches a preemptive attack in self-defense, crushes the menacing armies, and seizes vast swaths of territory for its own protection. The story ends with Israel's military forces miraculously achieving victory against all odds.

Evidence of Israel's military preeminence did not influence the impression of extreme vulnerability presented in this narrative. On May 24, 1967, *New York Times* correspondent James Reston reported that Egypt's army could not match Israel's armed forces in quality or preparedness. Two days before the war, he reported from Cairo that Egypt, under President Gamal Nasser, "does not want war and it is certainly not ready for war." Reporting from Tel Aviv on the second day of the war, Reston noted the exhilaration over the initial defeat of Egypt, and he wrote that the Israelis "had to fight to save the existence of their country. This is clear on any objective analysis of Nasser's political and military moves."[5] The perception of Israel's existential peril grew even more amplified after its total triumph. A week after the war's end, *Life* magazine editorialized that only the word "astonishing" could describe how "tiny Israel stood in the role of victor over the surrounding Arab nations that had vowed to exterminate her." The same editorial stated that "the tremendous discrepancy between the competence of

Israeli and Arab armies is the most obvious fact from the start." The "fact" of military imbalance did not make Israel's victory any less "astonishing" in the American press.[6]

During the tense three weeks leading up to the war, however, apprehension about the possibility of Israel's extermination did not appear in most media reports. Editorials unanimously condemned Egyptian aggression, but they did not express concern that its troops might decimate the Israeli military, let alone the entire nation. Although journalists reported Nasser's fervent speeches rallying the Egyptian masses to destroy the Jewish state, few believed that Egypt's military capacity matched its saber rattling. Editorials urged the United States to lead a naval convoy to reopen the Straits of Tiran in order to uphold international law, not to rescue Israel from destruction.[7] The Jewish American press did show concern for Israel's safety. But most of its reports and commentaries expressed confidence that Israel's steely determination and military capability would safeguard it. References to Nazi extermination appeared in some of these articles, less as warning of a potential recurrence than as providing an object lesson that Israelis had learned to avert by becoming ace fighters.[8]

The press echoed the assessment shared by Israeli military leaders, U.S. government officials, and the intelligence agencies of both countries. In the buildup to war, newspapers ran articles with headlines like this one from the *Los Angeles Times*: "Odds in Battle Favor Israel, Experts Declare." On June 4, Defense Minister Moshe Dayan assured the media that Israel would win the war without outside help. And when war broke out a day later, newspapers concurred that Israel would win an easy victory. They showed little worry about an Israeli defeat, let alone the country's extermination, questioning only how many days it would take Israel to win and at what cost. When news of Israel's early morning attack reached the White House, Walt Rostow, President Johnson's special assistant on security, announced the beginning of "the first day's turkey shoot."[9]

The narrative that Israel had narrowly averted an apocalypse in June 1967 was largely a retrospective one. It gained greater currency after Israel's stunning triumph and has shaped popular memory of the war and Israel's image as a nation. The story of a rapid and extreme reversal of fortune did make for dramatic reporting. Israel's military feat appeared all the more astonishing and even "miraculous"—an oft-used word—and it elicited wild enthusiasm from the American public.

To call attention to this retrospective narrative is not to deny the genuine fear experienced by Israelis before the war. It arose from many sources. Murderous rhetoric broadcast on Egyptian radio was heightened by fears fanned by the Israeli government. Traumatic memories of the Holocaust had recently been evoked by the trial of Adolf Eichmann in Jerusalem in 1962. Even during the heady elation that followed the war, the experience of military dominance did not banish fears of defenselessness. *Life* reported that Israelis still lived with the nightmare that history could just as easily have cast them as victims instead of victors.[10] This fear also affected American Jews, who, after the war, expressed as much dread of Israel's vulnerability as pride in its army's robust heroism. Amid victory celebrations, according to journalist J. J. Goldberg, "what the American Jewish community learned from the war" was that "Israel might be destroyed at any moment." A newfound attachment to Israel brought forth guilty memories of the Holocaust for some American Jews, who, in an outpouring of emotion and frenzy of fundraising, demonstrated their determination to protect the Jewish state from what they believed could have been another genocide. Pride in Israel's victory and identification with its vulnerability, in addition, helped revive a sense of Jewish identity that Jewish leaders feared was imperiled not by Arab armies, but by assimilation into mainstream American society. Whatever the psychological and sociological roots, the belief that Israel had been threatened by annihilation did not abate over time but became memorialized as history.[11]

In the arena of international diplomacy, Israel raised the specter of annihilation to refute accusations that it had provoked the hostilities and to make its case for keeping the captured territories in the interest of national security. On June 19, Israeli foreign minister Abba Eban, "one of the television heroes of the United Nations," stated to the UN General Assembly with signature eloquence that the "true origin" of the conflict was the Arab threat to Israel's "very right to exist," a threat that persisted after the war's end. Refuting Soviet premier Alexei Kosygin's charges of aggression, Eban proclaimed Israel's deployment of arms to be a "righteous" cause: "As righteous as the defenders at Valley Forge, as just as the expulsion of Hitler's bombers from British skies; as noble as the protection of Stalingrad from the Nazi hordes, so was the defense and security of Israel's existence against those who sought our nation's destruction." Arab aggression, stated Eban, provoked Israel at the "lowest ebb of its fortunes," and in response, its army re-enacted the "uprising of our battered remnant in the Warsaw ghetto as a triumphant assertion of human freedom." In this narrative, besieged Israelis did more than mount a defensive war against hostile neighbors: they refought World War II, this time smashing Nazi surrogates in the Middle East.[12]

"Valley Forge" invoked the familiar American trope of Israel's anti-colonial origins at a time when the image of Israel as conqueror seemed too close to colonialism for some. On the day of Eban's UN speech, a New York Times editorial implored the "lightning conqueror, to show magnanimity to her victims" and not to rush to annex Arab Jerusalem—or expel Arabs in another "human tragedy." Approximately two hundred thousand Palestinians crossed into Jordan during the war, many fleeing for the second time, as refugee camps that had been established in 1948 came under Israeli control in Gaza and the West Bank.[13] A Washington Post editorial wrote of Israel's "public relations woes," which started when, at the end of the war, the army demolished scores of houses in East Jerusalem to create an open plaza by the Western Wall, expelling the residents and raising the "accusation of forced expulsion" of Palestinians to Jordan. Israel had an "image problem as a tough victor," wrote the New York Times, for an "army of occupation cannot maintain the admiration showered on a victorious army" when "the pre-war David has become the post-war Goliath."[14] The postwar portrait of Israel as existentially vulnerable and forever subject to extinction by powerful enemies restored its role as David and countered the rival image of Israel as a heartless conqueror and colonial power.

The paradoxical narrative of a militarily supreme nation that is under grave threat would have resonated with many Americans during the Cold War. In the build-up to the Six-Day War, editorials across the country expressed more concern for the safety of the United States than for Israel because of the political alignment of the Soviet Union with Egypt, and Syria and the United States with Israel. A war in the Middle East, it was feared, could provoke a superpower confrontation and result in a nuclear conflagration. "The threat of war between Israel and the Arab states," warned the Los Angeles Times "has brought us closer to nuclear conflict than any post–World War II crisis—including the

Cuban missiles incident."[15] Ever since the dropping of the atomic bomb, Americans had held a double-edged image of their nation as the triumphant leader of the free world—but one living under the shadow of nuclear holocaust.[16] The "domino theory" justifying the war in Vietnam—the idea that the fall of one communist country as far away as Southeast Asia would trigger others to fall—added to the sense that there were omnipresent, but vague, forces menacing the United States.

In 1967, Israel appeared under threat of the kind of annihilation that had stalked the United States for over two decades. Israel magnificently vanquished this threat in six days by crushing the same enemies—Soviet-backed forces—that the United States had not been able to defeat even after years of fighting in Vietnam. Israel's defense minister, Moshe Dayan, "wasn't playing dominos," wrote Bill Mauldin in the *New Republic*. "His back was to the sea. On all other sides he was eyeball to eyeball with a vicious enemy who meant to exterminate the Israeli soldiers' families, homes and country."[17] The dramatic action of Israeli soldiers averting apocalypse had a cathartic effect. In Israel's swift victory over Soviet allies, Americans could vicariously experience both the dread of vulnerability and the thrill of invincibility, the irrefutable victory that was eluding them in Vietnam.

American portraits of Israeli soldiers conveyed this paradox of invincibility and vulnerability on a human level, one that reinforced the image of them as reluctant conquerors rather than consorts of colonialism. The combined qualities of martial prowess and aversion to violence, brazen determination and youthful insouciance, toughness in battle and touching humanity together created his romantic appeal. Photographs of rugged, handsome Israeli soldiers filled *Life* magazine's special edition, "Israel's Swift Victory," which was rushed to newsstands at the end of June. The Associated Press and United Press International soon followed with book-length compilations, *Lightning out of Israel* and *Swift Sword,* and CBS broadcast a special report, "How Israel Won the War." As their titles indicate, these celebratory accounts portrayed the war from the standpoint of the victor. Together these media reviews consolidated an overarching narrative of the Six-Day War that interwove images of muscular strength matched by humane innocence as a hallmark of the Israel's armed forces and its identity as a nation.[18]

"Israel's Swift Victory" told the standard paired stories: one of an overwhelming military operation wreaking destruction; the other of a small endangered nation defended by its citizen-soldiers. The volume opened with a two-page photograph of a burning truck and a dead Egyptian soldier face down on the sand with a "fist-sized hole punched through his tunic." The war started, according to *Life,* when "Israel launched its offensive" and "struck with devastating surprise at two dozen Arab airbases in Egypt, Syria, Jordan, and Iraq." Black-and-white photographs showed rows of exploded fighter-bombers. Within hours, "Israel had sealed its victory" by destroying the entire air force of each nation.[19] Bellicose language described the ground wars that followed. In Israel's "savage attack on four fronts," its tanks "thrust" into Egypt; "slashing into the Egyptian-held Gaza Strip" and "stabbing into the Sinai desert," they "smashed ahead day and night." Jordan suffered a "savage Israeli onslaught" as Israeli planes blasted positions with "napalm canisters which exploded with lurid flames." In a thrust into the hills of Syria, Israeli troops "smashed through each successive line" and knocked out tanks in a "fury of phosphorous."[20]

Photojournalists were enchanted by the Sinai desert's wide-open terrain. Israeli tanks dashed across it practically unimpeded to the Suez Canal, leaving a trail of burnt corpses and damaged materiel. On the cover of "Israel's Swift Victory," a black-and-white panorama of the sand-swept desert provides the background for a close-up color photo of an unshaven, dust-covered Israeli commander squinting in the sun, holding binoculars and dangling a cigarette. Looking relaxed and masterful, he surveys the quiet desert, recently a battlefield and now dotted with tiny figures carrying bundles on their heads, as through straggling through an earlier nomadic age.

The desert landscape of the war in the Middle East contrasted starkly with images of the war in Vietnam. In articles comparing the two wars, journalists portrayed the blazingly bright background for Israel's military achievement as matching the clarity of its cause, while the jungles of Vietnam symbolized the murkiness of America's goals. American soldiers persistently complained about the invisibility of enemy combatants, who hid in tunnels and bunkers throughout the dark jungle. They came to view the Vietnamese landscape itself as the enemy, as *Time* reported: "U.S. forces are fighting not only Communist troops in Viet Nam but also the vegetation that conceals and feeds them." Newsreels showed U.S. bombers flying in orderly formation dropping tons of bombs on heavily forested terrain that concealed the targets. In contrast,

Israel's rapid air war was shockingly well documented from above, with photographs showing exploded fighter planes smoldering while still neatly lined up in their desert bases. Israel's military power was illustrated by panoramas of destruction: mangled tanks strewn for miles throughout the desert, burnt corpses fallen in the sand, and masses of prisoners baking in the sun behind barbed wire.[21]

Humane portraits of Israeli soldiers tempered the ferocity of these images. Photographs of military preparation in "Israel's Swift Victory" show bare-chested soldiers cheerfully taking "an open air shower . . . after a day of waiting in the Negev desert near the Egyptian-held Gaza Strip." Crowded together under the streaming water, buff young men scrub themselves vigorously, brawny torsos glistening in the sun. At the center a handsome youth with shampoo in his hair smiles directly at the camera, inviting, friendly, and confident. The men's nakedness conveys tough virility along with a touch of vulnerability in their endearing boyish innocence. The title reads: "Israel's cool readiness."[22]

This image contrasts markedly with a photograph on a prior page of Egyptians clamoring for war, under the title "The buildup of fervor as Nasser casts the die." A crowd of angry protesters in Cairo are chanting and pumping their fists in the air. At the center, a man hoisted on someone's shoulders faces the camera directly with hands raised and mouth open, as though he is yelling at the viewer. An adjacent photograph shows uniformed soldiers carrying banners with Arabic writing and skulls and crossbones, calling for "the defeat of Israel and death of Jews." In counterpoint, the next page shows the prime minister of Israel alongside text reproducing his words: "The Jewish people has had to fight unceasingly to keep itself alive. . . . We acted from an instinct to save the soul of a people." The images set up a disparity between men motivated by a just cause to fight for life, and maniacs motivated by extreme ideology in the pursuit of death.[23]

Half-naked Israelis standing in water appear in two more striking photographs in this special edition. In the first, a well-built bearded man wearing only underpants, a hat, and glasses wades in the Gulf of Aqaba, holding a machine gun across his waist, demonstrating easy mastery in a cocky, casual pose.[24] The second reproduces a photo that appeared on the cover of *Life* magazine's June 23, 1967, issue and became an icon of Israel's victory. A tanned, lanky soldier stands in the Suez Canal with water up to his chest. His face grimy from battle and

LIFE

WRAP-UP OF THE ASTOUNDING WAR

Israeli soldier cools off in the Suez Canal

JUNE 23 · 1967 · 35¢

Cover of *Life* magazine, June 23, 1967.

black curls tousled, he wears a wet shirt that shows off his muscular physique and hoists his rifle into the air. He looks skyward into the bright sun, white teeth shining, his eyes matching the deep blue water that fills the frame with no shore or horizon. It is a picture of military triumph and virile sexual appeal.[25]

These water scenes convey an aura of purification and rebirth, in stark contrast to the parched desert landscape strewn with Arab corpses. In a caption under a picture of Israeli soldiers surveying dead Egyptians, *Life* noted that "besides those killed in combat, countless Egyptians perished of thirst and starvation."[26] A photo of Egyptian prisoners of war shows them in undershirts, stripped of their uniforms with hands tied behind their backs. If Israeli nakedness reveals the tough and tender human body beneath the uniform, the nakedness of these soldiers exposes their humiliation in defeat.

Robust Israeli soldiers who mastered the desert terrain made a contrast not only with Egyptians, but also with American soldiers trapped in Vietnam. Mike Wallace hosted two CBS specials soon after the Six-Day War, one called "How Israel Won the War," and the other, about a hilltop outpost near the demilitarized zone in South Vietnam, "The Ordeal of Con Thien." In the first, Wallace interviews five young Israeli pilots who are lounging informally in their flight suits around the wing of their jet fighter. Bashful and boastful, they speak of "making something for history." In contrast to the Israelis' quiet invincibility, the American marines in Con Thien appear painfully vulnerable. Two barechested young men resting against sandbags talk of being "boxed in" and shot at like a "bull's eye." Against footage of wounded men in the background, another marine resignedly says, "There isn't much you can do," adding, "You can't be saved you can only be lucky."[27] Three months after the Six-Day War, Con Thien became a symbol of American impotence. The cover of *Time* on October 6 featured a photograph of a young American soldier curled up in a fetal position inside a trench, clutching his helmet with his bare arms. The banner reads "Rising Doubt about the War."

The confident insouciance of Israeli soldiers delighted American reporters. They expressed surprise that even in uniform, the troops did not look like conventional forces. Wallace noted with a smile that the Israeli soldiers "look like a rag-tag group," walking around "unkempt and unshaven" in the most "extraordinary group of uniforms or nonuniforms that I have ever seen."[28] James Reston marveled that although "modern armies do not sing," Israel's was a "singing army, not polished but rumpled . . . young and middle-aged waving to the youngsters at the side of the road and smoking and singing like Hemingway's heroes at the start of the Spanish Civil War."[29] In *Harper's Magazine,* Marshall

Frady later observed that "for all its legendary deadly precision, the Israeli Army, from the youths at the front to its somewhat rumpled officers at headquarters, still seemed to have the informal quality of a guerrilla force, existing in an easy cohabitation with civilian society."[30] This oft-noted disregard for military decorum made Israeli soldiers appear more like rebels than conquerors.

The distinguished literary critic Alfred Kazin visited Israel during the summer of 1967 and wrote a long piece about his experience for *Harper's*. Like many liberal Jewish intellectuals, his enthusiasm for Israel in the wake of the Six-Day War replaced his former skepticism about the Jewish state. He was especially taken by the combination of "militant self-confidence" and anti-authoritarianism of the young Israelis, who did not appear to conform to military standards. He described Israeli soldiers as looking like "young actors waiting to get into a TV Western." His guide, the Israeli novelist Haim Gouri, responded with delight, "The Jordanian army *looks* like an army, but ours?" The lack of uniformity among Israeli soldiers underlined their resistance to military regimen and their natural toughness. On a Friday night in Jerusalem, Kazin relished the sight of "Greenwich Village looking soldiers, in hippie beards and camouflage pants . . . flirting with girl soldiers who in their neat outfits looked delicious," fusing the counterculture and militarism. For Kazin, these modern soldiers marked the distance Jews had come from their long-suffering ancestors in the Diaspora. He was one of many Jewish intellectuals who took pride in Israel's astounding military success, yet found reassurance that its street life appeared more like Greenwich Village with its peace symbols than the militarized society he criticized in America.[31]

The presence of women soldiers enhanced the modern appeal of the Israeli army. As the nation mobilized for war, *Time* reported, "girls in khaki miniskirts and pertly cocked overseas caps were on round-the-clock duty at sandbagged gun positions."[32] Journalists rarely described women soldiers without mentioning their miniskirts, finding their youthful sexuality channeled wholesomely into a "folksy army." Girls of eighteen, noted Theodore White in *Life*'s special issue on the war, are "ushered forth by families as if to wedding or nunnery." In the military, he added, boys and girls meet and marry, and the army provides the rabbi and wedding banquet. The armed forces ensured the survival of the nation by procreation as well as military defense.[33]

The most celebrated Israeli hero of the Six-Day War was General Moshe Dayan, the charismatic defense minister. Pictures of his chiseled face crossed by a black eye patch adorned the covers of news magazines, and he appeared almost nightly on television news shows. Comedians and politicians joked about hiring Dayan to teach the Viet Cong a lesson.[34] Descriptions of his irresistible charm accompanied analyses of his military expertise. A *New York Times* portrait of the "hawk of Israel" equated his military daring with his earthy sexuality, and his identity as a modern, Israeli-born sabra was contrasted with the older, militarily cautious—and prudish—generation of leaders born in Europe. In a feature article in *Look* magazine, his novelist daughter, Yael Dayan, even commented on the large number of women who fell in love with her father.[35] Military and sexual power merged to create the masculine mystique of this cult-like figure.

Dayan also represented the egalitarian and unifying qualities of Israel's "people's army," which, enthused *The Nation*, had "no visible or material distinctions between officers and regulars." In a photograph of Dayan in "Israel's Swift Victory," he sits cross-legged on the ground, holding an orange soda, as he listens to an animated group of officers in motley attire. This photo abuts a close-up of a beautiful young boy intently observing a machine gun being prepared by a reservist. Together these images conveyed a spirit of national unity in the "citizen army," where everyone, from school-age youngsters to the highest-ranking generals, rallied together. In the *New Republic*, Bill Mauldin shunned the hero worship of generals to locate Israel's military strength in the "farmers, homebuilders and merchants who have had a long and gaunt struggle for survival." Mauldin was well known from World War II for his popular cartoon strip about ordinary GIs, published while he served as an infantryman. To him, Israelis reincarnated the American spirit of the citizen-soldier that had disappeared in Vietnam.[36]

Israel's total mobilization of civilians for war was presented in the American press as evidence not of a militaristic society but of its peace-loving values. The antimilitarism of the Israeli soldier went beyond his casual appearance to his inner moral fiber. Kazin quoted an officer saying that his men in the Sinai "fought without hatred" but with "terrible rage at the waste" of lives. He reported that his guide, Gouri, noted with great pride that there had not been a single instance of an Israeli soldier raping an Arab woman. As evidence of Israel's peaceful inten-

Israeli defense minister Moshe Dayan with a group of officers just before the outbreak of the Six-Day War, from "Israel's Swift Victory," special edition of *Life* magazine, June 1967, p. 11.

tions, Gouri took Kazin to visit a middle-class Palestinian couple in Ramallah in order to return their confiscated car and to expound on the need for cooperation between Arabs and Israelis. Kazin noticed that the hospitable but skeptical couple did not warm to the protestations of Israeli gallantry, and they quietly let their visitors know that they hailed from Jaffa before 1948.[37]

In an article in the *Atlantic*, famed military historian Barbara Tuchman wrote that "a recurrent mention in the post-war talk is of weeping." An officer confessed to her, "I was fighting and crying, . . . because I was shooting and killing." She did meet a soldier who was happy "killing as many Arabs as he could," but she presented him as an exception to the rule that "these lions fought with tears." With their reluctance to kill, Israelis were disinclined as a nation to adopt the role of conqueror, for in too short a time "the Jews have come from persecution to rule over others." She quoted General Rabin as the first to recognize this burden in his victory speech: "The Jewish people are not accustomed to conquest, and we receive it with mixed feelings."[38]

The portrayal of conquest as inimical to Jewish identity peaked in accounts of the capture of East Jerusalem from Jordan. After three days of fierce fighting, wrote *Life*, the Israeli army's entry into the Old City "seemed as much pilgrimage as conquest," and the magazine quoted Dayan as saying, "We have returned to the holiest of our places never to depart from it again."[39] Replicating the primal Zionist narrative, Dayan rendered the conquest of foreign land as the return to a biblical homeland. The capture of East Jerusalem yielded some of the most enduring emotional photographs of the Israeli soldier: fresh-faced and battle-tested, youthful soldiers gazed upward at the Western Wall in solemn awe and exultation.[40] Helmeted soldiers embraced the stones, weeping; while toting Uzis, they danced with bearded Hasidim in black coats and hats. One especially striking image from United Press International shows a soldier from behind, wearing a skull cap while praying at the wall, and in place of a prayer shawl his shoulders are draped with an ammunition belt.[41] The capture of Jerusalem added a mystical aura to the image of the sharpshooting but innocent Israeli warrior restored to his ancient roots.

The portrayal of Israeli soldiers as hesitant conquerors in 1967 drew on the anticolonial founding narrative as told in *Exodus*. The liberal press especially emphasized that the Israelis did not want to repeat the

Israeli soldier with bullets as prayer shawl praying at the Western Wall in Jerusalem, June 1967.

errors of Western imperialism. As Stanley Wolpert asserted in *The Nation*, "they express no wish to maintain martial rule over the more than one million Arabs living in borderland regions their armies have overrun."[42] Six months after the war, the *New Republic* acknowledged that Israeli attitudes were hardening about keeping the occupied territories and that Palestinians desired independence from both Israel and Jordan. Yet the same article found hope in Dayan's assertion that "we are not colonialists," and that "we don't aim to impose a Pax Hebraica."[43]

Writers applauded this anticolonial attitude in ordinary soldiers. On a trip to Bethlehem and Hebron, for instance, a *New Republic* reporter saw few signs of military occupation and instead more of a "county fair," with Israeli soldiers and civilians buying ice cream and taking donkey rides. He followed a group of Orthodox soldiers to a "holy place where Abraham and other Elders of Zion are entombed." After the soldiers knocked and requested entry, the door was shut in their faces. The soldiers made "no effort to press further for the entry denied them to a Jewish holy place by a vanquished Moslem guardian." The reporter might not have realized that this holy place was also the hallowed Ibrahimi Mosque—vanquished or not—and he praised the soldiers' polite refusal to take what was rightfully theirs: "Strange conquerors!"[44]

This narrative of a reluctant conquest made the Six-Day War seem the opposite of America's experience in Vietnam. The Israeli soldier appealed to hawks and doves alike, as a military model and a moral exemplar. The "lightning" victory shone brightly against the deepening quagmire facing the U.S. military. The Israeli air force accomplished in hours what Operation Rolling Thunder, the massive bombing campaign in North Vietnam, could not do in two years. Israel's unified nation of citizen-soldiers was a reproach to a divided America of draft resisters and antiwar protestors. A "people's army," where generals and privates fought side by side, highlighted the gaps between the grunt's experience on the ground in Vietnam and the official pronouncements of the generals in charge. Moreover, a nation threatened by annihilation could not have imperial aims, and an army fighting for survival made mockery of the domino theory and the idea of defending American honor in a distant land.

Global Counternarratives

"Israel is not Vietnam," argued antiwar liberals Michael Walzer and Martin Peretz in an essay published in *Ramparts,* a leading organ of the New Left, a month after Israel's 1967 victory. The essay was part of a special issue on the "Israeli-Arab Crisis." Walzer and Peretz wrote that they had been in favor of the United States taking military action in response to the Egyptian blockade of the Straits of Tiran. Since then, they had faced criticism from both right and left:

> We have been asked: "How can you demand unilateral military action in the Middle East and oppose it in Vietnam?"; "Why should the 'national liberation' of the Arabs be resisted and that of the Vietnamese not resisted?"

In other words, wasn't it hypocritical to oppose one war and support the other? Not at all, they answered. To the right, they explained that Israel was not like South Vietnam, where the United States was illegally intervening in a civil war to prop up an artificial state of its own creation. To the left, they answered that Israel was not like America, which was fighting an imperialist war against a national liberation movement. Israel, they claimed, was neither a colonizer itself nor an outpost of imperial power; it was an imperiled democratic nation struggling for survival.[45]

Walzer and Peretz's argument for Israeli exceptionalism aimed to refute an emerging counternarrative that portrayed the Six-Day War as a war of colonial expansion. This narrative located Israel and Palestine on a global map where crosscurrents of U.S. imperialism, European colonialism, Third World revolutions, and black liberation movements in America and Africa intersected and collided. In this transnational context, Israel's uniqueness took on a different meaning entirely: it could be viewed as a colonial power resisting the global movement toward decolonization. Today we might assume that in the late 1960s and early 1970s, only those on the radical left would identify Israel with colonialism. Yet in the mainstream media at the time, both liberal critics of the Vietnam War and staunch Cold Warriors expressed concern about Israel's territorial expansion and its military rule over civilians, and they shared a lexicon of analogues with the radical left that linked Israel and Palestine to sites of colonial power struggles around the world.

In their *Ramparts* essay, Walzer and Peretz rejected the argument that both Israel and the United States were "bastions of imperialism, on guard against the rise of the Third World." To counter the characterization of Jewish settlers in Israel as European colonizers, they argued for the nation's anticolonial pedigree, reviving the narrative of Zionism as a movement for emancipation. They contrasted Israel's history with that of other colonial powers: "The Jewish colonization of Palestine," they wrote, "differs from other colonizations in Africa and Asia in that the immigrant community"—that is, Zionist settlers—"was committed to do its own work" and did not "exploit the Arab population." This self-sufficiency prevented the development of the social hierarchies that existed between French settlers and Arabs in Algeria, or between whites and blacks in Rhodesia and South Africa. They found Israel more authentically socialist than many Third World regimes, like Nasser's Egypt, pointing out that "the typical Jewish agricultural unit was not the plantation but the *kibbutz*." Furthermore, they claimed that imperial powers were not responsible for establishing the Jewish state. Quoting from a 1948 article by I. F. Stone, they contended that British and American diplomats and oilmen had sided with the Arabs and opposed the new state. Dissociating Israel from the taint of colonialism, they concluded that the source of the Middle East conflict was the refusal of Third World and communist governments to "recognize the threat posed by the present Arab rulers to the very survival of Israel."[46]

The same issue of *Ramparts* included an essay by I. F. Stone, "The Future of Israel," that demonstrates how radically his political views had changed since 1948. The greatest threat to Israel's survival, as he saw it, arose from its jingoism and chauvinism, which intensified the state of belligerence with its neighbors. Stone called on Israel to relinquish conquered territories and take responsibility for the Palestinian refugees, since its sovereignty over all of historical Palestine now forced the nation to confront a long-slumbering moral crisis. He insisted that Israelis must finally recognize what he too had ignored in the euphoria of 1948—"that a kindred people was made homeless in the task of finding new homes for the remnants of the Hitler holocaust." The Palestinian refugees, he wrote, "lost their farms, their villages, their offices, their cities and their country." Recalling his argument from the 1940s that Jews and Arabs should band together against British imperialism, Stone warned Israel not to "remain a Western outpost in an Afro-Asian world casting off Western domination." In order to survive, it must "join the Third World."[47]

Stone was widely denounced when he elaborated these arguments in the *New York Review of Books* three months later in an essay, "Holy War," that opened provocatively: "Stripped of propaganda and sentiment, the Palestine problem is, simply, the struggle of two different peoples for the same strip of land." Stone viewed the conflict between Arabs and Jews as a tragic narrative that was, at its essence, "a struggle of right against right." It was incumbent upon Israel from its position of strength, he believed, to do justice to the Palestinians. Arguing against Walzer—and indeed his own earlier position—he wrote that "the fact that the Jewish community in Palestine afterward fought the British is no more evidence of its not being a colonial implantation than similar wars of British colonists against the mother country, from the American Revolution to Rhodesia."[48]

In the same year, 1967, the Black Power movement also included the Middle East conflict in a global context that pointed to the United States and Rhodesia as sites where colonialism and racism converged. In their influential book *Black Power: The Politics of Liberation,* Stokely Carmichael and Charles Hamilton chose as an epigraph a sentence from an essay by Stone that had been published a year earlier: "In an age of decolonization, it may be fruitful to regard the problem of the American Negro as a unique case of colonialism, an instance of internal imperialism, an underdeveloped people in our very midst." The authors contended that "institutional racism has another name: colonialism."[49] Advancing the Black Power movement meant seeing the struggle for liberation in the United States in relation to anticolonial insurgencies around the world. In the United States, just as in Rhodesia and South Africa, they argued, colonialism inheres in the relationship between blacks and whites living next to each other, not in distant lands.

When war broke out in the Middle East in June 1967, radicals in the Student Nonviolent Coordinating Committee (SNCC) and the Black Panther Party were already finding links between resistance to American racism and a transnational anti-imperialist movement that was taking place throughout the Third World. They encountered the Middle East through the teachings of Malcolm X and the writings of Frantz Fanon on the Algerian Revolution, and through the travels of leaders like James Forman and Stokely Carmichael to Hanoi, Algiers, and Havana.[50]

In this spirit, the SNCC newsletter started a new series, "Third World Round Up." The editors announced that since "we Afro-Americans are an integral part of The Third World," it was important to "understand what our brothers are doing in their homelands," and they chose Palestine as the topic for the first article in the series.[51] The article analyzed the history of Zionist settlement, starting with its inception as a colonial force that violently subjugated an indigenous people and seized Arab homes and land "through terror, force, and massacres."[52] Graphics accompanying the article provocatively portrayed both contemporary Israel and the United States as racist and imperialist. The article, however, made specious anti-Semitic claims about Jewish dominance of global finance, and it offended many by accusing Israel of committing massacres and comparing them to the mass murders at Dachau. The controversy that erupted was such that it reached the front page of the *New York Times.* Jewish organizations excoriated the article's "hate-filled" rhetoric and "racism," claiming that it took a pro-Arab and Soviet position that "smacks of anti-Semitism." Well-known civil rights leaders joined in condemning anti-Semitism as detrimental to the goal of fighting against all forms of discrimination.[53] An editorial in *The Movement,* a small magazine affiliated with SNCC, rejected the label of anti-Semitism and, reasserting SNCC's alliance with "revolutionary aspirations of the third world," claimed that "Israel, as characterized by the actions of its statesmen and military men, is opposed to these aspirations." The editorial also raised the issue of hypocrisy that Walzer and Peretz had rejected, questioning the motives of those liberals who "oppose American militarism and support Israeli militarism," who denounce Lyndon Johnson but acclaim Moshe Dayan.[54]

At the same time the Black Panther Party was developing a transnational analysis of the relationship between black freedom struggles and Palestinian resistance. These connections deepened over time through personal contacts in Algiers between Black Panthers and members of the Palestine Liberation Organization (PLO). In 1968, the critique of American imperialism provided the fundamental tie between Palestinians and black Americans. The Panthers condemned Israel as "an imperialist, expansionist power in Palestine" and posited that blacks and Arabs both suffered from racial oppression, although it took different forms: "Zionism in Palestine and fascism here in America—but the cause is the same: it's U.S. imperialism." They drew special attention to the political imprisonment of Palestinian and black revolutionaries, framed as dangerous criminals or terrorists by Israel and the United States, both of which they characterized as police states. At a press conference in 1970, Huey Newton, head of the party, claimed that Israel was "created by Western imperialism and maintained by Western firepower."[55]

For the most part, established African American civil rights leaders rejected these radical positions toward both Israel and the United States; instead, they upheld the story of Israel as a liberal beacon of emancipation and an imperiled democracy. Members from the A. Philip Randolph Institute, a black labor organization, including Randolph and Bayard Rustin, formed a new organization, Black Americans in Support of Israel Committee. In 1970, the committee sponsored a full-page ad in the *New York Times,* "An Appeal by Black Americans for United States Support for Israel," signed by over two dozen influential figures. It called Israel "the most democratic country in the Middle East" and implored the U.S. government to guarantee Israel's security and "right to exist" through arms sales, so that the nation could freely implement its ideals of social justice.[56]

A few months later, a counter ad appeared that addressed an issue first raised by the Black Power movement in the late 1960s and later embraced by many African American organizations in the anti-apartheid movement: Israel's military and economic alliance with South Africa. The ad, "An Appeal by Black Americans against United States Support for the Zionist Government of Israel," was signed by fifty-six black activists, artists, and intellectuals. It expressed Afro-American solidarity with Palestinians, both engaged in the same struggle "for self-determination and an end to racist oppression," and it related both struggles to the anticolonial revolution "in places such as Vietnam, Mozambique, Angola, Brazil, Laos, South Africa, and Zimbabwe." The appeal focused on Israel's close relationship with apartheid South Africa, referring to the two nations as "privileged white settler-states" that exchanged arms and military training.[57]

Israel's American supporters grew concerned about its reputation among African Americans, and in 1969 the Israeli government invited a delegation of black journalists to tour the country. In a seven-part series in the *New York Amsterdam News*, correspondent Dick Edwards described his Israeli hosts' emphasis on their humanitarian and anti-imperialist commitments both in the newly occupied territories and in Africa. Israeli officials, reported Edwards, described projects in the West Bank to improve the lives of Palestinians and rejected the possibility of annexation. Foreign Minister Abba Eban spoke to the group about Israel's aid to black African nations, explaining that the Israelis were uniquely suited to help other emergent states. When asked about the fraught subject of the white-ruled African states, Eban stated that Israel had severed relations with Rhodesia at great economic cost and rejected the South Africans' offer to upgrade its diplomatic status in Pretoria. He cited the memory of "gas chambers in Auschwitz" as the reason why Israel chose justice over friendship with these states.[58]

South Africa's noted affinity for Israel, however, complicated Israel's efforts to distance itself from that apartheid nation. The *Los Angeles Times* reported that the South African government regarded Israel as playing the same role as white South Africa: "defending an outpost of western, white civilization in a sea of uncivilized hordes." In the *New*

York Times, foreign correspondent C. L. Sulzberger wrote of the growing economic and political ties between the two countries and explained why, from the Afrikaner perspective, they were natural allies, with Israel sharing an "apartheid problem—how to handle its Arab inhabitants." In one of several incensed letters to the editor responding to this article, Martin Peretz rejected any parallels between the control of a "huge landmass of a black majority by a wholly alien white minority" and a people's return to a "small and ancient homeland." Israel, in his view, was not South Africa, just as it was not Vietnam.[59]

The euphoria that had initially seized the media during the Six-Day War, focused on images of Israel's existential vulnerability and humane military, vied with unsettling images of its domination over others. As soon as the war ended, the U.S. war in Vietnam began to be used as a cautionary tale and not just as a contrast with Israel's heady triumph. "Military victory will be no solution in the Middle East," warned the *New York Times,* "any more than the military victory the United States is seeking in Vietnam would be in South East Asia." The *Washington Post* anticipated that as more stories of napalm injuries to civilians emerged from the Jordanian front, the conscience of Israelis would be touched, just as "this country has been touched by the photographic record of injury" to civilians in Vietnam. These parallels became more pronounced when reporters turned their attention to Israel's efforts to quell Palestinian resistance in the newly occupied territories. *Time* reported that Israel was using American counterinsurgency tactics: building electronic barriers to deter infiltrators and retaliating against guerrilla raids by razing the fighters' homes. The Vietnam experience became a warning that "a retaliation raid in massive force" only steels the will of the resistance and brings in new allies.[60]

Commentators expressed concern about the damage that colonialism could do to Israel's character. "Conquering peoples are never very attractive," wrote columnist Joseph Kraft about his travels through the West Bank, and "the Jews, or perhaps I should say we Jews, are no exception." Using an American analogy, he criticized the "abundant quotation of Scriptures as title deeds, asserting as a kind of manifest destiny, Israel's right to the newly conquered lands." A *Washington Post* editorial chastised the Israeli government for failing to recognize that "colonialism, however benevolent, doesn't work." Although syndicated columnist Flora Lewis blamed Arab aggression for Israel's expansion, she saw no point in "denying that it was colonialism in the old fashion sense." She predicted that Israel "did not seek this peculiar little empire, but it is likely to prove harder to give up than it was to acquire."[61]

One of the most outspoken critics of Israel's occupation in the mainstream press was also a great admirer of the country. Joseph Alsop, an influential syndicated columnist for the *Washington Post* and the *Los Angeles Times*, was a fervent anticommunist and an early advocate of U.S. intervention in Vietnam. He believed that Israel was just like South Vietnam, a Cold War ally in need of U.S. support against Soviet client states. Alsop visited Israel in the fall of 1967 on his way to South Vietnam. At first, he savored the romance of the victory of a "magnificently brave people," exemplified by his "generous-hearted" military guide, "a model officer, a burning patriot, a deeply moral man," who made Alsop feel like he was traveling in a time machine back to the heroic revolutionary age of America's founding fathers.[62]

Nonetheless, Alsop found it alarming that the majority of Israelis, from leaders to ordinary citizens—his guide included—were "passionately determined never to give back the more important conquered territories, especially the Gaza Strip and above all the West Bank of the Jordan." Throughout his travels—from an Arab-run restaurant in East Jerusalem to apparently pacified villages on the West Bank—he noted that the "basic problem of the occupied and occupiers" was "starkly posed." Alsop venerated Moshe Dayan, whom he had cited as a military authority on Vietnam. But he doubted the viability of Dayan's plan to contain Palestinian dissent by combining tough measures, such as demolishing houses and exiling leaders, with the benign formula of "occupation without administration." Alsop repeatedly demanded of the Israelis he met, "Do you really believe this can go on forever? Do you really believe you can avoid using an iron fist to hold this land?"[63]

The analogy Alsop used for Israel's "iron fist" was not Vietnam but Rhodesia. In 1965, Rhodesia's white-dominated government had declared independence from Great Britain and instituted rule over a vast majority-black population. "Holding down a huge Arab population," warned Alsop, "with no rights except the right of local self-government will create in Israel—it must be squarely, brutally faced—something perilously like the relations between the races in Rhodesia." Alsop referred to a study predicting that the population of Arabs would outnumber that of Jews in Israel in a decade, a shift that would place Jews in the role of white Rhodesians.

Alsop's analogy connected to his fears of racial uprisings at home. In the summer of 1967, black insurrections erupted in Detroit and Newark and were brutally suppressed by the police. Though Alsop derided all radical groups as Soviet stooges, his language reflected the Black Power movement's comparison of domestic racial violence with Third World struggles. He warned of the grave risk of America "declining into a continent-sized South Africa" and asked the same questions he would pose to Israelis about the dangers of occupation: "Is America's white majority to find safety only by repression and by force? Are we to live forever with a deprived minority held down only at gun-point?"[64] In Alsop's vision of the world, the situation in Rhodesia and South Africa provided a harbinger of the threat facing both the United States and Israel. Maintaining racial hierarchies and holding occupied territories would lead to mass insurrection and violent state repression, which would in turn destroy the claims of both nations to represent democracy, freedom, and progress in the struggle against communism.

In a striking inversion of Israel's image in the West as a paragon of modernity, Alsop decried what he called the "non-modernism" of Israel. He criticized Israeli leaders for their "antimodern" delusion that a "protectorate can be maintained without brutality and even with benefit to the protected population." Though he sympathized with Israel's desire for security, he worried that a prolonged occupation would turn it into an atavistic garrison state. Ultimately, Alsop wished to protect an ideal vision of Israel from the morally corrosive impact of occupation, which "year after weary, angry year, will cause all Israel's shining courage, noble self-denial and richly creative intelligence to go for naught in the final verdict." This romantic sentiment meshed with what Alsop believed was a realist Cold War imperative to prevent the emergence of Soviet proxies from resistance movements such as the Palestinians, and it echoed idealizations of American freedom as the opposite of communist oppression.[65]

For a brief time following the Six-Day War, journalists were intrigued by the rise of Palestinian resistance, and they presented Palestinian guerrillas in a romantic revolutionary narrative, though it was one that offered little competition to the more intimate romance with the Israeli soldier. The PLO presented itself on the world stage as an anti-imperialist movement against the colonial occupation of Palestinian land, and it modeled its international image on the successful Algerian resistance against French colonialism and the Vietnamese struggle against the United States.[66] After the humiliating defeat of 1967, a younger generation of Palestinian leaders took their struggle into their own hands, abandoning the hope that Arab nations would liberate them. They organized new cadres of Palestinian fedayeen—Arabic for "men of sacrifice"—to conduct guerrilla raids into Israel, first from Jordan and then from Lebanon. Yasser Arafat led the largest organization, Fatah, and headed a coalition of militant groups under the umbrella of the PLO. Israel launched severe reprisals against fedayeen positions and their civilian supporters in towns and refugee camps on both sides of the Jordan River. In a significant battle in March 1968, Fatah inflicted heavy casualties on Israeli troops in the Jordanian village of Karameh. Although Israel declared victory, Fatah's brazen resistance made it wildly popular throughout the Arab world. The battle took on mythical proportions in which a heroic defeat became a rallying cry and a founding narrative of national liberation. As *Time* explained in terms Americans would understand, "Karamah became the fedayeen Alamo."[67]

Curious about this new force in the region, journalists flocked to clandestine training outposts, refugee camps, and PLO headquarters. In December 1968, *Time* featured Yasser Arafat on its cover in the style of a political poster. Wearing dark glasses, a black and white keffiyeh, and a denim shirt open at the neck, he looked handsome and confident. A line drawing above his head depicted a shrouded commando shooting a machine gun, under a banner reading "The Arab Commandos: Defiant New Force in the Middle East." The cover article opened with a quote from a Voice of Fatah radio broadcast: "The revolution of Fatah exists! It exists here, there, and everywhere. It is a storm, a storm in every house and village." To Israelis, the "raiders" were "terrorists and thugs," but to Arabs, "they were freedom fighters in the best guerrilla tradition." For members of the "Palestinian Diaspora" in refugee camps and Arab capitals, the fedayeen "awakened a sense of pride" by taking "the destiny of the Palestinians into their own hands." In the process, Arabs "have come to idolize" Arafat.[68]

The Palestinian movement appealed to the international revolutionary spirit of 1968. As youth around the world took to the streets to protest American imperialism in Vietnam, many discovered inspiration

Yasser Arafat, cover of *Time* magazine, December 13, 1968.

for radical social change in Third World leaders like Che Guevara, Fidel Castro, Mao Tse-tung, and Ho Chi Minh. Young men toting guns and shouting revolutionary slogans, whether Cuban revolutionaries, Vietnamese guerrillas, or American Black Panthers, had an allure for the New Left and the counterculture. Journalists compared Amman, Jordan, to Hanoi and described refugee camps as a "protective jungle" that "any kind of resistance movement needs."[69] They noted posters of Ho Chi Minh, Mao, and Che on walls in refugee camps, and reported that the Black Panthers were receiving training at a Fatah base in Algiers.[70] The fedayeen, reported *Time,* took their inspiration from the "apostle" of the Algerian revolution, Frantz Fanon, "the late Martinique-born Negro psychiatrist who preached in *The Wretched of the Earth* that for the oppressed and the colonized people of the world 'violence is a cleansing force.'"[71] After Fanon's death in 1961, his book achieved a global reach that extended from Palestine to Third World liberation movements to black militants and student radicals in the United States.

The revolutionary style of the fedayeen presented a masculine mystique that appealed to foreign correspondents, who wrote vividly about their dangerous treks to locate secret training camps or to interview a commander in the back alleys of Amman. Journalists who had reported from Vietnam, Cuba, Yemen, and other revolutionary hotspots encountered a familiar scene in Jordan: "armed men in khaki and basketball sneakers slowly climbing back to the base camp in tents in the rocks . . . the backslapping, the smiles of relief, fatigue, and pride of the kind one sees on the faces of returning astronauts."[72] This incongruous metaphor represented the fedayeen as modern heroes, triumphantly returning from feats comparable to mastering outer space. Images of youthful rebels, however, were often tempered by darker depictions of the refugee camps they came from, described by one journalist as "the spawning ground for the militant Palestinian commandos," where "everything tends to fester" and where commandos "infected" the inhabitants with discontent.[73]

Despite this gloomy image of the camps, the modernity of the Palestinians became a recurrent theme among journalists. The worldliness of a young generation stood out against the nostalgia of their refugee parents and defeated Arab leaders. The press attributed the humiliating rout of Arab armies in 1967 to their feudal backwardness and their preference for rhetoric to action. In an interview with Arafat published in the *New York Times,* Dana Adams Schmidt contrasted the ineffective bombast of his elders with Arafat's "restrained eloquence, sentimentality and humanism," noting his "personal modesty and devotion to action." The liberation of women from traditional constraints offered further evidence of Palestinian modernity. *Time* described young women in refugee camps trained in first aid and weaponry, chanting "I have broken my chains. I am a daughter of Fatah!" In a visit to a group of "militia girls," Marshall Frady interviewed young women who extolled the opportunity to abandon their conservative upbringing for a wider perspective.[74] Schmidt, reporting on the Popular Front for the Liberation of Palestine (PFLP), interviewed a spokesman who "wanted the world to know that the whole Palestinian community, women and children, as well as men, is imbued with revolutionary fervor." The spokesman, wanting to "break the Hollywood stereotype of the stock-character

Arab, the idea of the Bedouin with a knife in his teeth," insisted that the Palestinians are "modern men, women, and children."[75]

Palestinian modernity was also reflected in the achievements of an educated cosmopolitan elite. In "The Palestinian Refugees: A New Breed: Smart, Skilled, Fanatical" in *The New Republic,* Georgie Anne Geyer debunked the image of impoverished, uneducated, "hangdog" refugees "without land and without future." In contrast, Palestinians were "the most advanced people in the Arab world" with "one of the highest percentages of university people of any national group in the world." One was hard pressed to find a leader of the fedayeen who was not a "doctor, lawyer or literary person." She contrasted this future-oriented generation of "cosmopolites" with their nostalgic parents stuck in refugee camps, mired in "memory, without hope, without work, without future" and "without the security of the timeless Moslem village hierarchy." While their worldly sons and daughters shared no memory of life in Palestine, education and political ideology taught them that "a terrible injustice was done, and they yearn to correct it."[76]

This radical separation from their parents made Palestinians appear remarkably similar to early Zionists. The idea of Palestinians as "the Jews of the Arab world" was repeated among journalists. In their cerebral idealism, wrote Schmidt, Palestinians resembled their Jewish "cousins" as an "equally extraordinary people."[77] Palestinians appeared as a "mirror image of American Jews" for their commitment to education and industriousness, and the way that assimilated Palestinians "now dominate many areas of Arab life."[78] The combination of modern deracination with longing for a lost homeland uncannily echoed the Jewish experience and made Palestinians more recognizable to an American readership. Partisans of both Palestinians and Israelis drew parallels between their deployment of violence in a nationalist struggle. In a *New York Times* feature, "The Middle East Is Potentially More Dangerous than Vietnam," Walter Laqueur, a renowned historian of Zionism, expressed doubt about Dayan's contention that Palestinians find it "easy to live under occupation and difficult to undermine it." No matter how many economic improvements Israelis brought to the occupied lands, opined Laqueur, "a young Arab patriot will support the guerrillas in the same way a young Jew in Mandatory Palestine joined the Haganah, the Jewish military organization during the British mandate."[79] George Habash, leader of the PFLP, drew a similar analogy in an interview in the *New York Times.* He related his group's attacks on civilians to the assaults he had observed as a schoolboy in Jerusalem in the last years of the British Mandate. He recalled the violent methods of "such Jewish groups as Stern and Irgun Zvai Leumi as they fought the British and early Arab nationalist organizations." In 1948, Habash had arrived home from his medical studies in Beirut "to accompany an exodus of women, children and old men—through searing heat with a minimum of food and water—to the Jordanian lines at Ramallah. Some died on the way." Habash objected to the Western press labeling the PFLP as a terrorist group, claiming that "terrorism . . . is what made of us refugees—what drove our people to the camps."[80]

In a dichotomy reminiscent of the depiction of Jews in Palestine after World War II, the media often fell back on a dualistic image of Palestinians as either refugees or terrorists. In an unusual departure from this pattern, Peter Jennings presented a television news special, "Palestine—a New State of Mind," that focused on educated, middle-class Palestinians in Beirut, where Jennings was bureau chief for WABC. Filmed in discussions around the dinner table and on a university campus, bankers and engineers, housewives and shopkeepers, professors and students articulated their desire to return to their homeland and described their plans for building a modern secular state. They asserted their sense of national solidarity with refugees in camps and their pride in the fedayeen. As they argued over political strategies, they laughed at the accusation that they were planning to push Jews into the sea and expressed puzzlement about the lack of understanding they encountered in trips to America.[81]

Jennings's perspective was rare at the time on American television. He described the Israel-Palestine conflict as a "fundamental tragedy" between "two cultures, Arab and Jewish," who both "have proper claims to this small but special strip" of land. Similarly, a 1970 *Time* article, "Palestine: A Case of Right v. Right," which took its title from I. F. Stone's controversial 1967 essay, quoted an Israeli labor leader stating a minority view that "the first thing we have to do is recognize that the Palestinian Arabs exist as an infant nation."[82] This narrative of two competing nationalisms would not gain currency in the United States again until the Palestinian intifada of the late 1980s.

In the late 1960s and early 1970s, the outlines of Palestinian nationalism were slowly and faintly becoming visible through global analogies with contemporary liberation struggles, and through comparisons of the aspirations of a new generation of Arabs with those of the New

Jews who founded Israel. This emergent narrative, however, remained a fragile construct that would disappear from mainstream American culture for many reasons, including the ongoing romance with the Israeli soldier, the staying power of Western stereotypes of Arabs' Cold War alignments, the Palestinian turn to international acts of terrorism, and the easy access of the media to Israeli perspectives.

Another factor that worked against the image of Palestinians in America was the overt effort by Israeli spokesmen and sympathetic journalists to undermine the revolutionary appeal of Palestinian resistance. Abba Eban protested that the guerrillas were not "fighting for freedom" but were in fact "fighters against freedom." He explained that "the image that world opinion should have of them is not the image of Maquis, or resistance fighters, but the image of the S.S., the image of the guards at Auschwitz and at Bergen Belsen."[83] When the prime minister of Israel, Golda Meir, was asked about the significance of the new Palestinian fighting forces in the region, she responded dismissively that "there were no such thing as Palestinians" and that historically, "It was not as though there was a Palestinian people in Palestine considering itself as a Palestinian people and we came and threw them out and took their country away from them. They did not exist."[84] Meir acknowledged that the fedayeen were a new factor, but did not consider them important diplomatically as part of a representative body of the Palestinian people. Between Eban and Meir, the Palestinian resistance was represented as both Nazi-like in its violent capacity and negligible in its political importance.

Israeli government spokesmen used Vietnam analogies to belittle the competence of the fedayeen. *Time* quoted an Israeli officer dismissing Palestinians as amateurs, even though he grudgingly conceded that Arafat had eluded capture several times. "We cannot dignify them with the name guerrilla or commando," he claimed, for "the Arabs who cross over show no daring. In that respect they are nowhere near Viet Cong standards."[85] Even Palestinian terrorism had paltry effects compared with attacks by the Viet Cong, as it took over a year for Palestinians to perpetrate the same number of attacks in Israel that Saigon had experienced in a few days.

In an inverted mirror image of invincible yet vulnerable Israelis, Palestinian guerrillas appeared as both threatening and impotent. Although they had Nazi-like power to endanger Israel's existence, they acted too ineffectually to breach Israel's defenses or dampen its fortitude. "Anti-Israeli Guerrillas Are Mostly a Nuisance," declared the headline of a story by Alfred Friendly, who won a Pulitzer Prize for his articles on the Six-Day War in the *Washington Post*. He cited an Israeli intelligence report that Palestinians broke down under interrogation faster than members of any other resistance movement in history. Palestinians, in his view, did not present a modern alternative to the defeated Arab states. Instead, the fedayeen operated with the same degree of impotence and "opium dream" delusions, abetted by the "purple prose of the Western press." Indeed, he deemed that Arabs from Baghdad to Algiers were gullible enough to believe that the fedayeen were "making Israeli soldiers bite the dust like Indians in a cowboy movie."[86] What better way to highlight this delusion for American readers than to reverse the frontier roles of cowboys and Indians.

"Israel is not Vietnam" meant to some American antiwar liberals that Palestinians were not struggling for self-determination as the Vietnamese were. Nothing annoyed Israelis more, wrote Philip Ben in the *New Republic,* than the "vague suggestion by foreigners" that Israel's conquered territories were "akin to Vietnam, where bombs and ambushes are daily routine, and where the Israeli hold is shaky." Israel succeeded in pacifying resistance, where Americans had failed. In contrast to Americans, who did not belong in Vietnam, Israelis believed that "if they wanted to stay alive in Tel Aviv, Haifa and West Jerusalem they had to conquer East Jerusalem, Jenin and Hebron. Now they have no alternative but to stay there."[87] Rejecting analogies to Vietnam had the effect of recasting Israeli conquests as a struggle for survival. This narrative of the invincible victim prevailed over global counternarratives about colonial expansion, as did the wholesome image of the Israeli soldier fighting expertly—and with moral angst—for the survival of a tiny beleaguered nation.

Barbarism versus Civilization

The inverted mirror images contrasting Israeli heroism with Palestinian treachery became even more diametrically opposed when Palestinian terrorists began hijacking passenger jets. "Skyjacking" seized media headlines and shifted the geographical terrain of the Middle East conflict to a new global arena. The narrative of Palestinians as freedom fighters struggling against Israel's anachronistic colonial occupation was soon eclipsed by a new narrative, one that evoked earlier images of Israel as a modernizing force in a backward region. The media recast the struggle between Palestinians and Israelis as an epic conflict between barbarism and civilization. As the 1970s progressed, Palestinian nationalism became inseparable from international terrorism in the media, which represented the Palestinian terrorist, driven by murderous ideology, as the dark other of the idealized Israeli soldier, motivated by the will to survive. Israel was portrayed as both the ultimate victim and the vanguard of defense against the forces of barbarism. Together with the United States, it safeguarded Western values from a hostile world composed of Third World and communist nations.

The PFLP shifted its armed struggle from local ground raids to the global arena of air travel in 1968, when it launched several attacks against flights operated by El Al, the Israeli national airline. Leaders of the group believed that these spectacular feats would draw the world's attention to the cause of the Palestinians and would demonstrate their modernity by disrupting technologically advanced transportation and communication networks. As long as they attacked only the Israeli airline and released passengers alive, the American reaction was somewhat muted, for airline hijackings occurred frequently throughout the 1960s in the name of a variety of political and personal causes. This changed dramatically with the targeting of the first American jet plane.

On September 6, 1970, members of the PFLP commandeered a TWA flight en route from Frankfurt to New York—forcing it to land with three other aircraft on an abandoned airfield in Jordan. The media was riveted on the desert scene. After six days, the hijackers evacuated the passengers and, in the words of *Time* magazine, "blew up $25 million worth of aircraft, in many ways the symbols of wealth and advanced technology." The headline of the cover story in *Time* reveals the symbolism of this shocking episode: "The U.S. and the Skyjackers: Where Power Is Vulnerable." The story emphasizes the impotence of advanced nations against a handful of lightly armed fanatics. Called "pirates of the sky," they appear as though from an older era to force civilization into a "retrograde time machine." What made the desert scene so threatening was the "oddly terrifying juxtaposition of technology and barbarism," and it generated nostalgia for the time when civilization could retaliate against barbarous acts with impunity. In an interconnected nuclear world, wrote *Time*, President Nixon could no longer follow the lead of Thomas Jefferson, who once dispatched freighters "to clean out the Barbary pirates who menaced American trade in the Mediterranean." Ronald Reagan, then governor of California, wanted the United States to return to an imaginary time of omnipotent power, when "an American could simply pin a little American flag on him and be safe even in the midst of a revolution in some other country, because the world knew that this country would go any place in the world to get back any citizen of ours."[88]

Skyjacking also ominously linked foreign terrorists to militants at home. The international revolutionary connections that inspired young radicals became bogeymen for law-and-order politicians. "The Palestinians' tactics," opined *Time,* "are analogous to the methods of radical bombers in the U.S. in the sense that both abandon law for what they regard as the higher authority of their revolution." Both groups, "acting out of a sense of despair and powerlessness," were willing to "wreck 'the system'" in any way, even if it meant sacrificing the lives of bystanders. *Time* quoted an editorial from the *Berkeley Tribe,* an underground newspaper of the counterculture: "We are all the new barbarians. We are closer to the Palestinians than some like to admit. We are the people without the power in the world. Maybe soon, planes carrying very prominent international pigs like him [Reagan] will be hijacked from the U.S. to parts unknown. By, say, freaks."[89]

The image of barbarians confronting the civilized world burst onto prime-time TV during the 1972 Summer Olympics in Munich, West Germany. On June 5, five Palestinian guerrillas from the Black September Organization invaded the dormitory housing Israeli athletes and coaches, killing two and taking nine others hostage. With dozens of sportscasters and journalists on the scene for the games, the nerve-wracking events were broadcast to millions of viewers as they unfolded in real time. Again and again, viewers watched a Palestinian terrorist peer over the apartment balcony with a ski mask covering his head and dark holes cut out for his eyes, like a death mask. His silent appearance punctuated wrenching human interest stories about the lives and families of each Israeli hostage. A day of tense negotiations culminated in an airport shootout after a botched rescue attempt. The guerrillas executed the remaining hostages by shooting some and throwing a grenade under a helicopter holding others, and the German police killed five of the guerrillas.

The Munich Massacre, as it became known, took on great symbolic power. This was the first time the Olympic Games had been held in Germany since Hitler hosted them in 1936. To overcome this dark history, the organizers had emphasized harmonious international cooperation over political conflict. They also aspired to efface the memory of the political controversy that had arisen during the 1968 Olympics in Mexico City, when African American athletes had raised their fists in a Black Power salute during the medal ceremony as the U.S. national anthem played. The terrorist attack undermined the universal message of civilized competition among nations, and the German location evoked the particular history of Jewish extermination.

Newspaper editorials denounced the killing of the Israelis as an attack on civilization itself. The murder at the Olympics plumbed "new depths of criminality," wrote the *New York Times:* "Arab terrorists made it plain that their real target was civilized conduct among nations, not merely Israel." The border between civilization and barbarism remained ambiguous for certain other American commentators, however, who drew parallels between the carnage at the Olympics and violence being perpetrated in Vietnam. For some, the horror in full view in Munich was a reminder of the suffering that was hidden from view in Southeast Asia. "To condemn the obvious face of terror in Munich," wrote Stephen Rosenfeld in the *Washington Post,* is to "blur the less conspicuous face of terror in Vietnam." He found "scant moral difference between throwing a hand grenade into a helicopter carrying athletes and dropping a 30-ton load of bomb on a half mile-long swath of Vietnamese soil where peasants happen to live." Only by halting its own terror in Vietnam, he opined, could America redeem its moral authority "to use its great but now-hobbled influence to limit terror elsewhere." Another columnist called on Americans who felt "the horror the Israeli athletes must have felt" to "identify themselves with those on whom the American bombs are falling."[90]

This counternarrative connecting American imperialism to violence in the Middle East did not gain much purchase. More compelling for most Americans was the narrative of the existential threat to the Jewish people and the State of Israel, as exemplified by the murder of innocent athletes on German soil. Expressing the paradox of vulnerability and invincibility on a global scale, Prime Minister Golda Meir pro-claimed Israel's resolve to fight on a "farflung, dangerous and vital front-line" beyond its own borders, "to carry the war of terrorism back to the Arabs—guerrillas and host countries alike—and to strike at times and places of Israel's own choosing."[91] The fierceness of Israeli reprisals briefly threatened again to blur the boundary between civili-zation and barbarism. In "Israel's New War," *Time* wrote that the Israeli air force extracted "savage revenge" for Munich, in raids on suspected guerrilla hideouts in which at least two hundred civilians were killed.[92] In the United Nations, the Security Council voted to condemn Israel's military actions, without mentioning Palestinian terrorism. But the United States vetoed the resolution, exercising its second veto in UN history, the first of many to follow on behalf of Israel. At stake, according to Ambassador to the UN George H. W. Bush, was something "much broader than that of the question of Is-rael and the Jews. What is involved is the problem of terrorism, a matter that goes right to the heart of our civilized life."[93] The U.S. veto once again reinforced the contested boundary, with America leading the civilized world by defending Israel against the barbarism that was manifested not only by terrorism but also by the votes condemning Israel in the United Nations.

In the aftermath of 1972, the interwoven image of Israel as both in-domitable and vulnerable began to fray—once again and not for the last time. Israel's aura of invincibility suffered a tremendous blow during the Yom Kippur War of October 1973, when Egypt and Syria success-fully coordinated surprise attacks on the territories Israel had conquered in 1967. Israel succeeded in beating back the offensive, but not without a massive airlift of fighter jets and weapons from the United States. The cost of victory to Israel was a high number of casualties and a disillu-sioned public with low morale. The aftermath of the war brought Is-rael and the United States closer together in policy and perception, as President Nixon and his secretary of state Henry Kissinger committed the United States to maintaining Israel's military edge in the region and dramatically increased the level of military, financial, and diplomatic support. At the same time, Israel faced growing international isolation, especially among Third World nations at the United Nations, which in-vited Yasser Arafat, leader of the PLO, to address the General As-sembly in 1974.

During the same period, Americans were undergoing their own crisis of confidence as the divisive war in Vietnam staggered to an ignominious end, and the Watergate scandal forced out a president and revealed deep layers of government corruption. Both events challenged a core belief in American authority as a force for moral good at home and abroad. Some Americans resented the loss of this certitude and blamed it on the upheavals of the protest movements and the counterculture. Others pointed to the creed of American exceptionalism as the cause behind the devastation wreaked on millions of people in Southeast Asia. The image that best symbolized the mood of national humiliation was a chaotic helicopter evacuation from a rooftop in Saigon on April 28, 1975, while victorious North Vietnamese tanks rolled through the gates of the U.S. embassy.

Conservative American intellectuals blamed the resulting spirit of defeatism not on the prosecution of an unjust and unwinnable war, but on cowardly acquiescence to criticism—criticism by the New Left at home, and by Third World nations in the United Nations. Pledging to resist the Third World in the international body, President Ford appointed as UN ambassador an outspoken Democrat and one of the original voices of neoconservatism: the pugnacious Daniel Patrick Moynihan.[94]

On November 10, 1975, the General Assembly adopted a highly controversial resolution that declared Zionism to be "a form of racism and racial discrimination" and linked Israel with the pariah states of Rhodesia and South Africa for their "common imperialist origin" and "racist structure." The vote split around Cold War and postcolonial lines, with 72 in favor, 35 against, and 32 abstaining. Americans were overwhelmingly opposed to the resolution, and editorials across the nation unanimously condemned it as an anti-Semitic attack on the Jewish state. The resolution was also decried as an attack on the United States by Third World nations and their communist supporters.

Ambassador Moynihan rose to the defense of Israel and simultaneously fortified the American values that appeared to be under fire. In a fiery speech to the General Assembly, Moynihan proclaimed that "this day will live in infamy," quoting Franklin D. Roosevelt's iconic phrase about the attack on Pearl Harbor. Such references to World War II served to tie America and Israel together as morally innocent victims besieged by evil forces. Moynihan called the resolution an "abomination of anti-Semitism" and declared that its intent was to grant "symbolic amnesty—and more—to the murderers of six million European Jews." His fundamental argument was that Jews do not constitute a race, and the Jewish state includes non-Jewish citizens; therefore the Zionist movement that founded this state could not be racist. Moynihan's speech restored the anticolonial narrative of Zionism as part of the modern "upsurge of national consciousness and aspiration" from nineteenth-century eastern Europe to contemporary Africa and Asia. Zionism "was to those persons of the Jewish religion a Jewish form of what today is called a national liberation movement." Of all national movements, Zionism was "unique" and "singular," claimed Moynihan, because it "defined its members not in terms of birth but of belief." He concluded that only racists who consider Jews to be a race could consider Zionism to be racist.[95]

To Moynihan the UN resolution represented nothing less than the decline of civilization. No "civilized person" could accept the equation of Zionism with racism, he declared, so "to think that it is an idea now endorsed by the United Nations is to reflect on what civilization has come to." In opposition to this barbarism, his impassioned defense of Israel stood up for "civilized values that are or should be precious to all mankind."[96] Moynihan not only revived the image of Israel as the invincible victim; he also advocated that America start seeing itself in the same light. In response to blatant anti-Semitic remarks by Idi Amin, president of Uganda, he impugned all African states with the charge of racism. He claimed that they had attacked Zionism only as a cover for their hatred for democratic states, of which Israel was one of a dwindling minority in the world. Moynihan similarly decried self-hating liberals at home, who "believe that our assailants are motivated by what is wrong about us." On the contrary, Americans, just like Israelis, "are assailed because of what is right about us. We are assailed because we are [a] democracy."[97]

While campaigning for the U.S. Senate a year later, Moynihan pointed to Israel as "a metaphor for the condition of democracy in the world today." Israel's vulnerability to annihilation exemplified the existential danger to all democracies "under siege" worldwide. Like the proverbial canary in the coal mine, Israel had long recognized this peril, which other democracies were only beginning to realize. Thus, he concluded that "to defend Israel is to defend liberty and democracy and therefore also to defend the United States." He implied, in addition, that the United States should follow Israel's lead in making itself militarily indomitable.[98]

Moynihan's UN speech was widely lauded for reviving American self-confidence. One television commentator explained that "the country is simply tired of feeling self-disgust," accounting for the "joyous response to Moynihan's passion and candor at the UN." According to another, Moynihan proved that America would "no longer accept 'moral lectures from moral inferiors.'" *People* magazine described his appeal as that of a quintessentially American type, a "fighting Irishman" who talks tough.[99] Moynihan tried to buoy America's battered self-image with his strong defense of Israel. He exhorted Americans to see themselves in Israel's image, as a bulwark of civilization that was perpetually imperiled by and victorious over the forces of barbarism—an amalgam of Third World bullies, terrorists, totalitarians, and self-doubting leftists at home.

Eight months after the speech, Israel dramatically enacted the role that Moynihan had praised it for with its astonishing foray to rescue hostages from Entebbe, Uganda. Enthusiastic media coverage revitalized the portrait of Israel as an indomitable and righteous military power, defending beleaguered innocents and striking a blow for civilization. Americans basked in Israel's glory, which struck some as a gift, coming as it did during lackluster bicentennial celebrations on July 4, 1976.

On June 27, four hijackers, including members of West German and Palestinian radical groups, commandeered an Air France jet en route from Tel Aviv to Paris and forced it to fly to Uganda, where they were welcomed by dictator Idi Amin and joined by more guerrillas. The hijackers separated out the Israeli and Jewish passengers and held them in the airport terminal as hostages, releasing the others. After a week of frustrating negotiations, Israeli commandos surreptitiously flew three cargo planes to the Entebbe airport. Landing under cover of darkness, they stormed the terminal and shepherded over one hundred Israeli hostages onto the planes. In less than two hours, captives and commandos were on their way home, having lost only three hostages and one Israeli soldier, Jonathan Netanyahu, the young strike force commander who was the brother of future prime minister Benjamin Netanyahu. The Israelis left in their wake seven slain terrorists, forty-five dead

"An Israeli Superman Saves His People in Entebbe," 1976. Cartoon by Tony Auth, *Philadelphia Inquirer*.

Ugandan soldiers, and eleven exploded Russian MiGs, a quarter of Amin's air force.

The "spectacular rescue mission," dubbed Operation Thunderbolt, electrified the American media. Journalists called it "extraordinarily daring," a "courageous lightning raid," and a "brilliant and heart-lifting victory over terrorism" that became an instant legend. News specials reconstructed blow-by-blow accounts that took on mythic dimensions and became etched in American popular culture. Bantam published William Stevenson's *90 Minutes at Entebbe* in record time, and half a dozen more books followed within a year. Within weeks the press was abuzz with the "Entebbe Derby," the rush to create films and TV specials. In addition to two American movies, an Israeli film was released in the United States by the director who would later make *The Delta Force* (1986), which featured a rescue scene based on Entebbe.[100]

Accounts of Operation Thunderbolt reprised the glory of Israel's victory in the Six-Day War, telling a similar story with the same vocabulary, such as "lightning strike" and "miracle." In both cases, action trumped diplomacy. Going it alone with a surprise strike once again proved the impotence of international negotiations. Virile and sensitive Israeli soldiers were said to have sung haunting songs and read poetry in the belly of the cargo jet transporting them to Africa. The book *90 Minutes at Entebbe* painted a picture of Israel's people's army: "soldiers with civilian jobs, pilots who were also university students; politicians with a taste for philosophy or archaeology." And the enemy was presented in as contradictory a manner as in 1967. The German-led hijackers raised the specter of extermination by separating Jewish passengers from the others, yet along with the Ugandan armed forces, they appeared risibly incompetent. The depiction of young Jonathan Netanyahu as a martyr, sacrificing his life for others, and the loss of so few hostages demonstrated the exceptional value Israelis placed on human life.[101]

In 1967, after the Six-Day War, the conservative columnist William F. Buckley had applauded Israel for rescuing America from the antiwar movement, turning "our doviest doves into tiger sharks." In 1976, commentators discovered in Operation Thunderbolt an antidote to the post-Vietnam malaise that clouded America's bicentennial celebrations. Governor Ronald Reagan exclaimed that the Israelis "were acting like America used to act." Editorials seized on the fact that the raid had occurred on the Fourth of July to reignite pride in the revolutionary heritage Israel shared with America—the plot of *Exodus*. Now terrorism took the place of the British Empire as the tyrant, and the Israelis showed the world "both why and how one must resist it." In this spirit, an editorial in the *New York Times* called the raid an "effective declaration of independence from international blackmail, to which the ordinary rules of international law simply cannot apply."[102]

"The Israeli Commando Force: Faceless, Swift, Deadly," read a *Washington Post* headline. Israeli commandos had furtively crossed international borders to turn the tactics of terrorists against them in a spectacular act of salvation on a global stage. In flouting international law in the name of a higher cause and violating airspace beyond their borders, Israeli soldiers might have looked much like the very terrorists they were fighting. But they played the guerrilla in a redemptive register, validating the necessity, as the *Post* article put it, for "the afflicted [to] take the law into their own hands." The drama of the stealthy sharp-shooting Israeli commando appropriated the glamour that had for a short time been associated with defiant Palestinian fedayeen and Third World revolutionaries.[103]

By 1976, the regional conflict of June 1967 had become globalized. Many Americans saw Israel's mission in Africa as symbolizing the defeat, in the name of Western civilization, of a nightmare coalition of threats against America. Student radicals, Third World revolutionaries, terrorists, African dictators, all armed by the Soviets, represented the barbaric forces that threatened America as well as Israel, both at home and abroad. The introduction to *90 Minutes at Entebbe* barely mentions Palestinians or Arabs. The book begins: "During the first hour of Sunday, July 4, 1976, a raiding party escaped from the heart of Africa with more than a hundred hostages held by a black dictator." In most accounts, Amin becomes inseparable from the terrorists and is described as a "petty tyrant," a "half-thug, half-buffoon," standing in the way of freedom. Israeli soldiers did not simply rescue their own from Palestinian terrorists and European radicals. They saved white civilians, citizens of the civilized world, from the African heart of darkness.[104]

The spectacle of victory over the Third World—of Israelis blowing up Soviet jet fighters before soaring out of Africa with freed captives—contrasted dramatically with the images of Americans fleeing in helicopters from the rooftops of Saigon. The efficiency and righteousness of the raid epitomized a just alternative to America's bumbling and brutal violence in Vietnam. Israeli commandos did more than free hostages held captive by terrorists in Uganda. Operation Thunderbolt also rescued America's romance with the Israel Defense Forces.

4

"NOT THE ISRAEL WE HAVE SEEN IN THE PAST"

"THE ISRAEL WE SAW yesterday is not the Israel we have seen in the past." So concluded a dismayed John Chancellor of NBC news, in his commentary from a rooftop in West Beirut on August 2, 1982, with smoke billowing in the background. Anyone watching the nightly news after Israel invaded Lebanon in June of that year would have agreed, but they would not have agreed on the reason. Some believed that Israel's militarism was ruining its reputation. Others pinned the blame on journalists like Chancellor, claiming that media bias was tarnishing Israel's image.

Chancellor decried the "savage Israeli attack on one of the world's big cities." The "stench of terror all across the city" raised questions about Israel's stated military goal of stopping terrorist incursions into northern Israel by the Palestine Liberation Organization (PLO). Shaking his head, Chancellor asked, "What in the world is going on?" If Israel's security problem was fifty miles to the south, "what's an Israeli army doing here in Beirut?" He then answered his own rhetorical question: "We are now dealing with an imperial Israel, which is solving its problems in someone else's country, world opinion be damned."[1]

"Much of what you have read in the newspapers and newsmagazines about the war in Lebanon—and even more of what you have seen and heard on television—is simply not true." So claimed Martin Peretz in the *New Republic* that same week. Peretz had visited southern Lebanon in June at the invitation of the Israeli government. In "Lebanon Eyewitness," he accused journalists of exaggerating civilian casualties and ignoring the true story of Israel liberating the Lebanese people from the PLO stranglehold.[2]

The invasion of Lebanon precipitated a crisis in American perceptions of Israel. The nightly spectacle of jets bombing a densely packed city, vistas of collapsed apartment buildings, close-ups of maimed and traumatized civilians, all shocked an American audience. How could— or should—one frame these events? Some framed the Lebanon War in terms of the continued efforts of a small, beleaguered country to defend its fragile security and sovereignty. These voices invoked familiar, heroic stories of Israel's past military conflicts: the swift victory over vast armies bent on its annihilation in 1967, the relief of repelling the surprise attack that made it appear so vulnerable in 1973, and the celebration of the daring rescue mission in Entebbe in 1976. Other commentators highlighted the parallels with America's recent quagmire in Southeast Asia. They began calling Lebanon "Israel's Vietnam," noting the common features: burnt-out villages, high civilian casualties, "rolling thunder," and an antiwar movement at home. Shock at day-to-day violence turned to moral outrage in September, after the massacre of civilians in refugee camps.

The Lebanon War dealt a blow to the popular consensus that had crystallized in 1967, one that appealed to liberals and conservatives alike. The invasion appeared to shatter the narrative of Israel as the beleaguered underdog, wielding force only to defend itself from extermination. The siege of Beirut, when Lebanese and Palestinian civilians became visible as victims of Israel's bludgeoning force, severely tainted Israel's image as the invincible victim. Israel had, of course, faced international condemnation before. But in 1982, for the first time, criticism rang out from the center of American society, from mainstream media, politicians, intellectuals, and leaders of Jewish organizations. Israel would now face such criticism again and again, especially during the eruption of the first intifada in 1987.

What was different about the response to the 1982 invasion of Lebanon was not only the startling vision of what Chancellor called "imperial Israel." Equally important, and possibly more enduring, was the vociferous and well-organized reaction to the criticism—exemplified by Peretz's articles. The fierce backlash aimed to counter disillusionment with Israel by monitoring and censuring the media for anti-Israeli bias. Pro-Israel organizations stepped up their lobbying for direct U.S. aid

Israeli shelling of West Beirut, August 2, 1982.

to enhance Israel's security and simultaneously attempted to secure the narrative of Israel's existential vulnerability in the face of Palestinian resistance.

The 1980s witnessed more polarization in American public discourse about Israel than ever before. At the same time, the Reagan administration significantly increased U.S. financial aid, military cooperation, and diplomatic allegiance, presenting Israel as a "strategic asset" in a reheated Cold War. The public battles over the legitimacy of Israel's use of force and of Palestinian grievances were waged not over policy alone, but over the stories and images deployed to represent Israelis and Palestinians, over what literary critic Edward Said called the "permission to narrate."[3] By the end of the decade a new consensus was taking shape among American liberals, who started to acknowledge Palestinian narratives and national aspirations. This recognition, they believed, was necessary for resuscitating Israel's moral health and guaranteeing its political survival—in addition to being an imperative of social justice. At the same time, conservatives increasingly condemned all criticism of Israel as anti-Semitic and denied the legitimacy of Palestinian nationalism or even the existence of the Palestinians as a people. The Lebanon

War has receded from American popular memory, but the battle over the media portrayal of that war drew the major dividing lines that would frame debates about Israel and Palestine into the present.

Crisis

On June 6, 1982, Israeli defense minister Ariel Sharon launched an invasion into southern Lebanon, under the command of Prime Minister Menachem Begin. In a campaign dubbed Operation Peace for Galilee, troops from the Israel Defense Forces (IDF) crossed the border, with the stated self-defensive purpose of destroying the PLO's capacity to attack the population of northern Israel. Within days, the IDF had moved past the stated goal of establishing a twenty-five-mile buffer zone; Israeli forces destroyed Syrian planes and missiles in eastern Lebanon and advanced to the outskirts of Beirut. During a nine-week siege of Beirut, Sharon ordered intensive air, naval, and artillery bombardment of Palestinian strongholds, pummeling civilian neighborhoods and refugee camps in West Beirut and the city's southern outskirts. In August, the United States brokered a truce that required the PLO to abandon Lebanon and installed an international peacekeeping force—including U.S. troops—to protect the Palestinian civilians in refugee camps. By September 1, Palestinian forces had left Beirut for other Arab countries, and President Reagan withdrew the American troops. When the Israeli-backed president-elect and Maronite leader Bashir Gemayel was assassinated, Sharon ordered Israeli troops back into West Beirut, which set the scene for massacres in the Sabra and Shatila refugee camps. Israeli troops withdrew to a buffer zone in southern Lebanon in 1985, where they remained until withdrawing from the country completely in 2000. Although estimates of casualties from the Israeli invasion through the subsequent occupation vary widely, the numbers of Lebanese and Palestinian dead and wounded—the vast majority civilians—far outpaced those of Israeli soldiers. Fatality figures range as high as 19,000 Lebanese and Palestinians, and close to 700 Israeli soldiers.[4]

In the first days of the invasion, the U.S. media hewed closely to the Israeli government's narrative of retaliation, defense, and liberation. Palestinian terrorism, reporters duly explained, had triggered Israeli strikes. Newscasts displayed caches of captured PLO weapons. When

Israeli tanks swiftly barreled to the outskirts of Beirut in mid-June, reporters faithfully conveyed Israel's account of its larger goals: to liberate Lebanon from the chaos of civil war and the stranglehold of "foreign forces," including the PLO and Syria, and to install a friendly government led by Israel's Christian allies. Television reports showed Lebanese civilians welcoming Israeli troops with flowers and songs.[5]

The official Israeli framing of the war was quickly belied by evidence on the ground. Within days of the invasion, news outlets began to report harrowing scenes of civilian suffering in areas beyond clear-cut military targets. In ABC's June 10 broadcast from the coastal city of Sidon, the camera surveyed flattened neighborhood blocks, while the correspondent stated that "in destroying PLO infrastructure," Israel had "destroyed in the process the infrastructure of all civilian life in cities where the PLO was based." Other stories told of a mass burial of over eighty Lebanese civilians, and hospitals where Israeli troops had arrested doctors and nurses on the suspicion that they were terrorists. Images of homeless and terrified civilians soon supplanted those of Lebanese warmly greeting Israelis. As *Newsweek* reported, while "some Lebanese welcomed the defeat of the PLO, they also regarded Israelis with suspicion, if not fury."[6]

The Israeli press office pushed back in response to these stories, accusing the press of exaggerating causalities and blaming the PLO for jeopardizing civilians by embedding military installations among noncombatants. In turn, correspondents juxtaposed official government statements with the scenes they had witnessed. David Shipler, Jerusalem bureau chief of the *New York Times*, quoted an Israeli reporter stating that "dozens of journalists physically present on the scene and witness to the disparity between the official announcement and the truth no longer believe what they are officially told." Israeli soldiers, he added, often listen to Lebanese radio stations for more credible news of the war.[7]

In early July, at a time when the government was accusing news organizations of exaggerating the destruction, Shipler visited southern Lebanon and witnessed Israel's methodical demolition of Palestinian homes in refugee camps. Noting that the IDF had barred the press from seeing the more extensive damage in the camps, he explained that the connotation of "camp" as a collection of makeshift dwellings did not adequately describe the "sprawling towns of narrow streets and jumbled concrete houses, built gradually over the years since the refugees from Palestine were driven here by the fighting in Israel's 1948 war of independence." The Israelis were now razing these towns, he explained, because the PLO had been "integrating military installations in the camps' civilian settlements," thereby "exposing the Palestinian civilians to Israeli attack." Shipler then compared the Israeli demolitions to U.S. tactics in Vietnam, where he had served as a correspondent: "The Israelis want to deny any future guerrillas use of the shelters and the camps for military purposes, much as the American troops in Vietnam obliterated villages to deny their use to the Vietcong." This analogy might have raised alarms for Americans who remembered the strategy of "destroying a village in order to save it," especially when Shipler compared the psychology of Israeli and American soldiers, both of whom failed to distinguish between fighters and noncombatants on the grounds that "they are all terrorists."[8]

Among international correspondents, the Vietnam War had left a legacy of skepticism toward official press briefings and wariness about government censorship. Stories on Israeli censorship became a recurring news item. Newspaper dispatches were at times headed with notices indicating Israeli or Syrian censorship, and television broadcasts used more dramatic means to notify viewers. On June 26, NBC gave a harrowing account from West Beirut of an intensive day of shelling, in which U.S.-made weapons had hit neighborhoods and killed or injured two thousand people. Against a darkened background appeared the words "Casualty Pictures Removed by Israel Censors." Israel attempted to prohibit the transmission of an ABC News interview with PLO leader Yasser Arafat. When ABC defied the ban, its struggle with the Israeli censors received at least as much media attention as the interview itself.[9]

The media's focus on Israeli censorship highlighted the fact that Israel had a particular point of view, and that, like any other nation, its perspective on events was partial, self-interested, and politically motivated. Israel had lost the claim to innocence that it had maintained during prior wars. Its messaging was no longer unassailable, and its worldview no longer smoothly nor automatically reflected that of the American news audience.

For the first time in an Israeli-Arab conflict, journalists experienced the war from the perspective of an Arab country alongside that of Israel.

In contrast to the situation in 1967, when Egypt threw out foreign journalists before the outbreak of war, all the major news outlets had correspondents in Beirut, the long-standing nerve center for the international press in the Middle East. Some correspondents had been covering the Lebanese civil war for several years, so they knew the terrain well and would arrive at the site of a bombing before the ambulances and local police. Many experienced the bombardment of the city first hand, since the majority of reporters lived in West Beirut, home to PLO headquarters and leftist Lebanese factions.[10]

Anchors on nightly network news programs would routinely introduce the day's fighting in two separate segments from different points of view. Audiences could watch Israeli tanks firing from the heights of East Beirut, and then see close-ups of shells hitting neighborhoods in West Beirut. On July 2, NBC Evening News reported on Sharon's visit to East Beirut, where he vehemently announced to reporters that Israel's goal was to "destroy"—a word he used three times—the "terrorist PLO Palestinian organizations." The next segment interviewed a physician in a West Beirut hospital and showed children who had been injured by shrapnel.[11]

In addition to contrasting images, access to different sides of the conflict provided correspondents with competing narratives. On June 9, Thomas Friedman, Beirut bureau chief for the New York Times, interviewed Rashid Khalidi, whom he identified as a spokesman for the PLO. The Israeli goal to "crush the P.L.O." in Lebanon, claimed Khalidi, was a step toward the ultimate aim of controlling Palestinians in the West Bank and Gaza and destroying their "idea of an independent Palestinian state." The Israelis hoped, he said, that in the absence of PLO leadership, they would be able to quash resistance to their rule in the occupied territories and to establish a quiescent leadership there that would agree to some form of limited autonomy allied with Jordan.[12]

During the first few weeks of the invasion, correspondents challenged the Israeli government's credibility in its official accounts of specific incidents. The impact of reporting on the devastating nine-week siege of Beirut put cracks in Israel's image as a vulnerable nation deploying military power with humane restraint. As reports depicted civilian suffering under daily aerial strikes and artillery barrages, the media foregrounded the human cost of "Israel's war machine." Cameras surveyed "whole neighborhoods reduced to rubble," where there was "no time to find bodies before the next bomb fell." Reporters described the physical experience of the bombardments that "touched all the senses," the "terrifying sounds," the persistent "stench of death," and the pervasive feeling that "nowhere is safe." Showing piles of garbage between collapsed apartment buildings, reporters told of Israel cutting off electricity, water, and food to the entire population of West Beirut. In a telling linguistic reversal, correspondents repeatedly used the word "terror," a label long identified with Palestinian violence, to describe life under siege. "West Beirutis," wrote a reporter in the *Washington Post* on July 18, "consider the Israelis masters of terrorism." After fourteen hours of continuous bombing on August 11, an NBC correspondent concluded that "every day has its moment of terror."[13]

The modern urban setting of Beirut brought the war close to home for American viewers. John Chancellor described Beirut as half the length of Manhattan, and the *New York Times* referred to a neighborhood of Beirut as its "Gramercy Park," now a "sunlit horror of dazed people." Images of Israel's previous conflicts had focused on tanks crossing the desert or soldiers moving single file through Jerusalem's ancient passageways. Beirut presented a radically different setting, where viewers now witnessed a city "shelled to death from without and within." In "Beirut: A City in Agony," *Newsweek* described how "at times the once grand city of Beirut simply disappeared in the smoke of its own devastation." After waves of bombing shook the capital, "15-story buildings crumpled like cereal boxes. The streets became skating rinks of broken glass and the splash of phosphorous bombs spread a scalding blaze of orange." Since 1975, the ongoing Lebanese civil war had shattered the image of Beirut as the Paris of the Middle East. In 1982, journalists compared Beirut to other European cities ravaged by military assaults, such as Madrid during the Spanish Civil War, and Stalingrad and Berlin during World War II.[14]

The urban setting shifted American perceptions of Lebanese and Palestinians in particular, and of Arabs more generally. On the television screen, viewers saw middle-class city-dwellers wearing Western-style clothing, working as teachers or bankers, walking through rubble to thinly stocked grocery stores. Amid the wreckage, they were holding together fragments of everyday life that would look familiar to the average American viewer. Reporters told the life stories of ordinary Arab citizens, and in interviews they tallied their personal losses and inveighed against the violence. These images did not fit stereotypes of Arabs as murderous terrorists, nomadic shepherds, or wealthy robed sheiks. On July 9, for example, NBC aired a news segment titled "One Family's Tragedy" that featured a family named the Kasiers, whose apartment building was bombed in the middle of a family reunion, killing the grandmother and a seven-year-old child. And that was not their only loss. Sitting with his wife in the ruins of a modest living room, the father, an interior designer, related in English the chilling story of searching through hospitals and morgues for his sister, only to find her body in six pieces. Separating the human story from the political context, the reporter concluded, "the Kasiers are Lebanese, not Palestinian. They weren't really involved in this conflict—until—a family reunion."[15]

Although "Palestinian" was still used by Israelis and Americans as a synonym for terrorist, this equation began to come apart. Palestinian victims of Israeli violence increasingly took the stage as sympathetic characters in the American media. As it became clear that the Israelis aimed not only to oust the PLO but to destroy the refugee camps and disperse their inhabitants, correspondents put together reports on Palestinian homelessness. On July 15, an ABC reporter interviewed Palestinians who had been trapped by the invasion. They described their support for the PLO, their fear of Lebanese reprisals, and their concern for their young sons, who were armed to fight. "Where am I to go?" cried a woman who had come to Beirut thirty-four years ago from the Galilee.[16]

"The Palestinians: Where Do They Go From Here?" read the cover of *Newsweek* on August 16. The stories in this issue conveyed an image of a Palestinian community that was united by a shared sense of nationhood but diverse in terms of class, religion, politics, citizenship, and history. The issue included interviews with refugees in camps, professionals in the Palestinian diaspora, a PLO spokesman, and an outspoken journalist on the West Bank. To humanize the Palestinians, these articles used a strategy, common in press coverage at this time, of comparing Palestinians to Jews: to their heroic resistance at Masada and in the Warsaw Ghetto, to their experience as refugees after World War II, to their longing for a nation, and to their professional successes. These comparisons made Palestinians appear less foreign and more familiar, emphasizing their similarity with Israelis rather than their enmity.[17]

The question "Where do they go from here?" conjured a historical shadow: the issue of how the Palestinians got to Lebanon to begin with. Reports on destroyed refugee camps invariably pointed back to the Palestinian Nakba of 1948, to the story of dispossession and exile that led to these camps. American correspondents often repeated the Israeli narrative that blamed the Arab nations for not "taking in" the Palestinians in order to make Israel "look bad."[18] Nonetheless, the sight of Palestinians losing their homes in Lebanon at least raised the question of where they belonged today. The *Newsweek* issue highlighted several aspects of the Palestinian experience that suggested answers: that Palestinians from Beirut to Detroit maintained a deep attachment to the homes they had lost in 1948; that they supported the PLO in its stand against Israel; and that moderates wanted to see a Palestinian state alongside the State of Israel. In short, a war that set out to destroy Palestinian nationalism had the ironic effect of introducing the idea of a Palestinian homeland to an American audience.

Another influential aspect of the media coverage was the portrayal of the PLO in a more sympathetic light. Journalists reported on the political and familial ties between ordinary Palestinians and PLO members, and described the organization's establishment of social institutions such as schools, hospitals, and libraries. By the second week of the war, journalists had started calling PLO combatants "fighters" rather than "guerrillas," and occasionally interviewed armed young men who did not conform to the stereotype of a hate-filled terrorist.[19] On July 1, CBS interviewed a handsome nineteen-year-old PLO member who had studied mathematics in school and read a poem on camera. On August 13, NBC interviewed Palestinians in the Shatila refugee camp as they rummaged through the ruins of their homes. A PLO fighter spoke quietly in halting English: "Israel cannot destroy all the Palestinian people—they can destroy home and building—but they cannot destroy the people—and we are still here." By the time the PLO fighters left Beirut at the end of August, their narrative of resistance had gained more credibility in the American media, which showed Palestinians heralding them, even in defeat, for surviving the onslaught of a more powerful army.[20]

Overall, the media coverage of the invasion widened the lens on Palestinians to hint at fragments of a new narrative for an American audience. As Philip Geyelin of the *Washington Post* wrote, "There's more to the 'Palestinian cause' than a PLO covenant with clauses calling for Israel's extinction, more to it than the person of Yasser Arafat. There's a grievance and a goal—an independent homeland—that most of the nations of the world (and many Americans) think is reasonable."[21]

"War Has Cost Israel Its Underdog Image," read a headline in the *Los Angeles Times* on June 30, 1982. As Palestinian suffering became more visible, Israel's reputation suffered, too. When the IDF captured over six thousand prisoners, it faced international criticism for refusing to grant them the status of prisoner of war, as required under the Geneva Convention. "Israelis are sensitive to world public opinion," explained an article in the *Washington Post*, "and the presence of thousands of Palestinians in internment camps creates a distasteful image"—particularly, it noted, for a country with many citizens who had themselves been in concentration camps. Americans were also sensitive to world opinion, and an editorial in the same paper expressed concern that "high civilian losses challenge the widely held belief in this country that Israel is a special nation with a moral mission, deserving of its special relationship with the United States and the massive military and economic aid it receives." Commentators repeatedly expressed disappointment at the diminishment of Israel's moral stature. Alfred Friendly, who won a Pulitzer Prize for his coverage of the Six-Day War, expressed his disappointment with Israel, noting the decline of the nation he had once admired: "Perhaps it was expecting more than was possible—that Israel should remain the country with a conscience, a home for honor, a treasury for the values of mind and soul. At any rate it is no longer." Friendly mourned the loss of a romantic image that journalists like himself had had a hand in creating.[22]

As it had in 1967, the Vietnam War provided a reference point for understanding Israel's military conduct, but this time journalists pointed out the similarities rather than the differences. The Israeli military no longer stood out as a sterling alternative to the American way of war. Israel was "paying the price in damage to its international image," wrote David Lamb in the *Los Angeles Times*, for using "overwhelming military power against an outgunned guerrilla army." In the Middle East, as in Southeast Asia, he wrote, television brought home the horrors of war; and just as the United States had done, Israel denounced the coverage rather than its army's destruction of civilian lives.[23]

Soon after the June invasion, a burgeoning antiwar movement, Peace Now, brought thousands of Israelis into the streets in protest. These demonstrations also evoked parallels with the American experience. In "Some Israelis Fear Their Vietnam Is Lebanon," David Shipler described the protesters' concern that this war "would stain the national honor, obliterating recent boasts of having the world's most humane army."[24] Israel appeared to be sinking in a quagmire of its own making. This analogy with Vietnam, however, also cast Israeli disillusionment in a familiar mold. Comparing Israel's peace movement to America's antiwar movement burst one romantic bubble at the same time that it inflated another one—that of the moral integrity of Israel's citizenry, which resonated with those liberal Americans who were reckoning with the legacy of Vietnam.

The invasion of Lebanon provoked strong responses from American Jews, some of whom began to break the traditional taboo against criticizing Israel in public. While the major organizations pledged verbal and financial support for Begin's war effort, especially at the outset, progressive journalists and liberal leaders increasingly broke ranks to voice their dissent out loud. In "The Silence of American Jews," published in the *Village Voice*, Nat Hentoff lambasted a Jewish congressman who "kvelled over the brilliant success of the Israeli Defense Force" while ignoring news that dozens of bodies had been dumped in a pit in Sidon. Stories about discord among Jews became a news item. The *New York Times* described the "disgust" and "shame" Jews felt about Israel's callousness toward civilian lives, and their recoil at seeing the Israeli flag flying in a suburb of Beirut.[25] Opposition to the war occasionally crossed political lines; I. F. Stone noted that defenders of Israel who used to call him and Noam Chomsky "stooges of the P.L.O." were now signing the same petitions. On July 4, sixty-six prominent American Jews, including seven rabbis, published a full-page advertisement in the *New York Times* in support of Israel's Peace Now movement. The ad condemned the fighting as "contrary to the original Zionist vision," and it advocated "self-determination" for the Palestinians. Signatories included well-known intellectuals with varied political approaches to domestic issues, including authors Saul Bellow and E. L. Doctorow, critics Alfred Kazin and Irving Howe, political theorist Michael Walzer, and the sociologists Nathan Glazer and Seymour Martin Lipset, who had penned an op-ed in the *New York Times* strongly opposing the war.[26] These self-identified Zionists rejected Israel's military aggression because it did not fit their understanding of the nation as engaging only in just wars of self-defense.

Jewish critics of the war often brought a sense of personal and communal betrayal to the narrative of Israel's declining morality. Some expressed fear that Israel was "losing its soul" as well as its position as a counter to American imperialism. Columnist Richard Cohen compared Israel's lies about its war aims in Lebanon to America's secret bombing of Cambodia and its covert support for the coup in Chile that toppled Salvador Allende. The "widespread slaughter of civilians," he wrote, "has undermined Israel's claim to moral superiority, once its richest political asset in the West." He also felt personally deceived: "Maybe it was just me—naïve me—but Israel was supposed to be the place where the truth was told, where idealism thrived, where things were different from other countries. The country was founded not on some lust for gold or for territory, but for moral reasons."[27] In expressions of disillusionment, both Jews and non-Jews attested to the moral exceptionalism that lay at the heart of their vision of Israel. Their focus on Israel's betrayal of its own values often overshadowed their attention to the damage it did to others.

This sense of disillusionment, however, did not fundamentally challenge these critics' support for Israel or make them rethink its history. Indeed, the sense of betrayal provoked by the war provided the foundation upon which to rebuild the idea of Israel's exceptional morality. Lamenting the loss of Israeli idealism in Lebanon made it possible to rejuvenate the founding myth of Israel's virtuous origins. Commentators treated the regime of Sharon and Begin as an aberration that temporarily sullied the essential "good name of Israel, built by sacrifice, restraint and principles of justice." In this context, critics praised Israeli protesters as the guardians of the nation's enduring ethical values. Hentoff called attention to a soldier, interviewed on Israeli TV, who asked whether "we have some kind of double standard for our own suffering and those of other people." This soldier, in Hentoff's view, represented the true Zionist ethos, as it had been articulated by David Ben-Gurion, that the nation could only survive if "Israelis maintain their moral, spiritual and intellectual standards." For many liberals, an idealized vision of Israel's past and essential identity was still salvageable from the rubble of Beirut, even if it had been veiled for a time by the smoldering ruins.[28]

This recuperation even managed to survive the horrific events that occurred three months into the war, when over eight hundred Palestinian civilians in the Sabra and Shatila refugee camps were massacred between September 15 and 18. Following the assassination of Bashir Gemayel, the Israeli-supported present-elect of Lebanon and leader of the Phalange party, Sharon directed his army to reoccupy West Beirut in violation of an international agreement to withdraw. Israeli troops that were surrounding the refugee camps permitted their right-wing allies from the Phalange to send more than one hundred well-armed militia members into the camps for the stated purpose of rounding up remaining terrorists. In a three-day rampage, the militia butchered and mutilated defenseless Palestinians, including women, children, and the elderly. Israeli soldiers lit the way at night with flares, and Israeli guards on surrounding rooftops were close enough to observe the slaughter. The encircling Israeli troops made no effort to stop the massacre, which their commanders knew of within hours, and they blocked screaming women from fleeing the camps. The atrocities provoked worldwide condemnation, as did Begin's self-righteous refusal to accept any responsibility. International denunciation and domestic protests led Begin reluctantly to appoint a limited commission of investigation.[29]

Israel's involvement in this depravity unsettled the strict moral hierarchy that provided the basis for an American identification with the Jewish state. "Palestinians have now had their Babi Yar," wrote conservative columnist George Will. The very possibility of comparing the massacre of Palestinians to the Nazi massacre of tens of thousands of Russian Jews in World War II "has altered the moral algebra of the Middle East, producing a new symmetry of suffering." The idea of equivalency between Palestinians and Jews upset Will's belief "that Israel incarnates the response—the reproach—of intelligence to animalism." He identified this moral superiority with American principles of democracy and decency.[30]

The focus of the American media quickly shifted from the suffering of Palestinians to the anguish of the Israelis. The cover of the September 27 issue of *Time* shows a chilling black-and-white photograph of huddled corpses in bloodied everyday clothes, strewn across a narrow alley. The banner reads in large black letters: "Massacre in Lebanon: Palestinian Civilians Are Slaughtered." A week later, *Newsweek* featured a very different cover. Under the banners "Israel in Torment," and "The

LEFT: Aftermath of massacre in the Sabra and Shatila refugee camps, cover of *Time* magazine, September 27, 1982.   RIGHT: Cover of *Newsweek*, October 4, 1982.

Anguish of American Jews," a blue-and-white Star of David on an Is-raeli flag frames a dead dove lying upside down with a blood-flecked breast and an olive branch in its mouth.[31]

A new narrative of the massacre had taken hold: Israel's innocence may have died in the refugee camps of Lebanon, but national soul-searching led to moral rebirth, and self-scrutiny reaffirmed Jewish values. To be sure, American journalists did join their international col-leagues in painstakingly reconstructing the details of the massacre, combing through bulldozed evidence and interviewing traumatized wit-nesses. Inside the *Newsweek* issue, readers found detailed reportage from Beirut, as well as U.S. opinion polls that showed support for Is-rael plummeting to a record low.[32] The *Newsweek* cover pictured the death of Israel's innocence as the narrative framework for piecing to-gether the fragments of this gruesome tale.

In an astonishing turnabout, the massacre became widely known as Israel's tragedy because it dealt a near-death blow to its hallowed image as invincible victim, an image that had been unraveling throughout the war. The massacre threatened to turn upside down the reigning paradigm of vicious terrorists and innocent victims. In the *Jerusalem Post*, Wolf Blitzer called the massacre a "disaster for Israel in Washington—indeed throughout the United States. It will take many years—if ever—to regain its once very high moral image in America."[33] Like Deir Yassin in 1948, Sabra and Shatila in 1982 became a public relations problem, but one that offered the opportunity for a cathartic expression of moral reprobation. Just as Labor Zionists once distanced themselves from the Irgun's savagery, portraying its violence as an aberration, so Israel's liberal supporters in 1982 distanced themselves from both Begin's craven leadership and the Phalangists' heinous acts. The sincere outpouring of moral revulsion had the double-edged effect of isolating the massacre from other incidents of civilian casualties throughout the war and redeeming faith in the nation's moral character.

In the weeks following the massacre, the media focused on Israel's "crisis of faith" and its soul-searching to recover its moral bearings. "The best proof that morality is still alive in a people is the sense of shame," wrote Anthony Lewis, and journalists did their best to find evidence of Israel's shame. Even Martin Peretz, who blamed media lies for Israel's declining prestige, ended an editorial in the *New Republic* that week—while reasserting support for the war—"not in praise of Israel, but in praise of its shame." This story of shame distinguished the nation's citizens in torment from its leaders in denial, and Israel's introspection reestablished its ethical superiority to its Arab allies and enemies. Palestinian anguish dropped out of this story, except as an object of compassion that enabled Israel's moral growth.[34]

Jews and non-Jews alike contributed to the narrative of ethical rejuvenation. For Rabbi Arthur Hertzberg, leader of the Conservative movement and a respected scholar, this meant purging the leadership that had led Israel astray. In his widely circulated *New York Times* op-ed "Begin Must Go," he denounced Sharon for having "sullied" Israel's principled armed forces and reaffirmed the belief that Israel essentially "is not a militaristic country." He claimed that the majority of its citizen-soldiers sympathized with protesters against the war and opposed "the handful who obeyed Sharon's orders to close their eyes last week in Beirut." Hertzberg stirred up controversy by attacking Israeli leaders, but at the same time, he salvaged a treasured image of Israel's humane military.[35]

Editorials similarly rediscovered Israel's antimilitary nature in the turmoil on its streets, in the "agitated, demanding protesters in Tel Aviv" who became "the true 'defenders of Israel.'" The *Christian Science Monitor* viewed the Peace Now demonstrations as evidence of "regeneration" in a nation built on the principles of "political democracy and humane religion." Israeli "anguish," opined the *New York Times,* gave the lie to "the charge that militant Zionism, as exemplified in Israel's expansionist moves, has destroyed the traditional moral conscience of the Jews."[36]

An additional fear had been that Israel's moral stance had degenerated to the level of the surrounding "Arab" culture, viewed as primitively brutal. "Maybe the ultimate tragedy of the seemingly nonstop war in the Middle East," lamented Richard Cohen, "is that Israel has adopted the morality of its hostile neighbors." Meg Greenfield warned that Israel's moral failure in Sabra and Shatila might be the PLO's best revenge, "measured as much by whatever success they have in corrupting Israeli sensibilities and emotions as in killing Israeli citizens and friends." For Israelis to act inhumanely meant that the nation had succumbed to the low ethical standards of its enemies. This similarity with its enemies, rather than its own military aggression, threatened to make Israel unworthy of the "moral claim it makes to nationhood and survival."[37]

The American press breathed a collective sigh of relief when Begin agreed to appoint a commission to investigate the massacre. The intention alone eased the moral conscience of Israel's liberal supporters and confirmed that the nation had not sunk to the level of its neighbors. In its lead editorial on September 29, entitled "Israel Finds Its Voice," the *New York Times* asked rhetorically, "Are there people of comparable honor and courage in the Arab world who can appreciate Israel's revulsion?" The formation of a commission of inquiry showed that Israel's better nature had prevailed and lifted it above the moral swamp of the surrounding Middle East. For the *Washington Post,* the commission had a cathartic value that would prove Israelis to be "true to their deepest impulse of compassion for people as innocent and defenseless as once—many times—they were themselves." Israelis would restore their exceptional morality by reclaiming the legacy of Jewish persecution. The same editorial agreed with President Reagan's assessment that the Israelis are "proving with their reaction to the massacre that there's no change in the spirit of Israel."[38]

Backlash

Israel's anguish helped to restore its moral luster for liberals. But conservative supporters had a different response—they believed that Israel had done nothing to be ashamed of in Lebanon and blamed the media for the negative images of Israel's military conduct. "For sheer intensity and breadth," wrote Roger Morris in the *Columbia Journalism Review*, "the controversy fueled by coverage of the Israeli invasion seems to have few parallels in recent journalistic history."[39] Although American Jews were divided about the war, mainstream Jewish organizations closed ranks with right-wing supporters of the Likud Party and neoconservative intellectuals to criticize what they saw as media bias and to defend Israel's damaged reputation. New watchdog organizations emerged during the conflict and would continue to monitor coverage of Israel long after the war's end.

As the war raged, critics bombarded news outlets with letters, protests, and angry delegations. They did not target editorial opinions alone, but also sought to discredit the reporting by correspondents on the ground. They blamed television news for inflicting more damage on Israel than its enemies' militaries had. News executives took unprecedented measures to respond. NBC Nightly News aired letters reacting to John Chancellor's commentary, and the *Washington Post* invited a representative of the Jewish community to observe its foreign desk for a week. Soon after the fighting ended, the Anti-Defamation League of B'nai B'rith (ADL) released a study of the nightly news on all three networks. The study charged that the news coverage contained many inaccuracies, especially about casualty figures, and that it lacked balance and objectivity, as evidenced by the focus on graphic scenes of suffering to the exclusion of broader political and historical context. The study concluded that television news stories had unfairly generated "revulsion at the war's violence among viewers—violence that was implicitly and explicitly associated with Israel."[40]

A year after the invasion, the American Jewish Congress convened a conference in Jerusalem called "*Hasbara*: Israel's Public Image:

Problems and Remedies." The Hebrew word *hasbara*, which means "explanation," is widely used to refer to public information efforts designed to promote a positive image of Israel. At this meeting, chaired by an American advertising executive, participants from the United States and Israel treated the invasion of Lebanon as a public relations disaster of major proportions, one with possible long-term repercussions. Their discussion focused on how best to repair the damage to Israel's reputation, and what could be learned from this fiasco about how to better market Israel's image in the future.[41]

"The world has changed since 1967," observed one participant, Ehud Olmert, a parliament member from the Likud Party and future prime minister, who trenchantly diagnosed the problem: "We now appear to the rest of the world to be a military superpower." And that view, he acknowledged, "is not totally incorrect." As evidence, he pointed to Israel's destruction of an atomic reactor in Iraq in 1981 and of Russian missiles in Syria during the Lebanon War. Americans, he joked, wish they could have sent Israelis to Tehran in 1979 to save the hostages taken during the Iranian Revolution. But Israel's power presented a dilemma: it led the world to expect "certain political concessions—as is deemed appropriate for a military power." Olmert was referring to concessions to the Palestinians proposed by Reagan, which included relinquishing occupied territories and halting the construction of settlements there. "The tragedy is," Olmert explained, "that while we are strong, we are also weak and vulnerable in ways that no other country in the world is vulnerable. Hasbara's main challenge is to reconcile these two extremes, to present our weakness to the world realistically."[42] After the Lebanon War, this was indeed a challenge for those rallying to Israel's defense—how to represent to the world an image of Israel's special vulnerability in the face of its demonstrable power.

The imperative to reclaim this view of Israel lay at the heart of the attack on news coverage in 1982. The media, according to its critics, was unfairly brandishing images and words against a vulnerable nation. In "Lebanon Eyewitness," Martin Peretz wrote that seasoned journalists had become dupes of PLO manipulation. After a quick tour of southern Lebanon sponsored by the Israeli Army, he repeated the claims of Ze'ev Chafets, American-born director of Israel's Government Press Office, who labeled the foreign press corps in Beirut

"Chairman Yasser's Best Battalion." Western journalists were gullible prey, adduced Peretz, because of their romantic images of Third World guerrillas as freedom fighters, a delusion they had picked up in Vietnam.[43]

Anti-Semitism offered some critics a deeper explanation of media bias. Thus argued Norman Podhoretz, neoconservative editor of *Commentary Magazine*, in his widely circulated essay "J'Accuse" (a title he borrowed from Émile Zola's impassioned defense of the Jewish French army officer Alfred Dreyfus, who had been unjustly accused of treason in 1898). His article advances the idea of the "new anti-Semitism," a term that had been developed by the ADL in the 1970s to explain what the group believed was undue condemnation of Israel's occupation of Palestinian territories. Leaders of the organization believed that bigotry against Jewish people, traditionally associated with the right, was generally on the wane in America. Yet they saw a resurgence of prejudice on the left, which unfairly targeted Israel as the "Jew among the nations." In the wake of Lebanon, Israel's defenders in the United States had to explain how this anti-Semitism of the left had infected mainstream newspapers and broadcast networks, which included many Jewish journalists.[44]

In "J'Accuse," Podhoretz renders political critique as thinly veiled anti-Semitism by invoking Israel's unique status as a persecuted state. Although Israel may have triumphed militarily, he argues, the unprecedented "explosion of invective" triggered by the war proves its existential vulnerability. "Vilification of Israel," he writes, "is the phenomenon to be addressed, and not the Israeli behavior that supposedly provoked it." Words, rather than armies, now offer the greatest threat to Israel's security, and to defend Israel means to police the boundary of acceptable public discourse.[45]

Podhoretz narrates the history of Israel's invasion in a way that reestablishes its role as victim. He denounces those liberals who profess concern for Israel's soul in order to exaggerate "the evils Israel was committing against others" and to blame "Israeli intransigence and/or aggressiveness and/or expansionism" for causing the conflict. Podhoretz positions the Lebanon War as the most recent chapter in a continuous narrative of Arab aggression and Israeli innocence that started in 1948. As in 1967 and 1973, Arab attacks forced Israel to defend itself—this time against PLO raids—and Israel once again reacted with restraint and utmost regard for human life. Thus, the word "invasion," he claims, is actually a misnomer for a war of self-defense and liberation.[46]

Podhoretz excoriates commentators for their choice of language as much as the content of their writings. He condemns author John le Carré for claiming, "It is the most savage irony that Begin and his generals cannot see how close they are to inflicting upon another people the disgraceful criteria once inflicted upon themselves." Edward Said outrages him by accusing Israel, in its massive bombing of Sidon and Tyre, of pursuing "an apocalyptic logic of exterminism." And Anthony Lewis, of the *New York Times,* comes in for attack for writing that Israeli's goal in Lebanon was "to exterminate Palestinian nationalism" in a bid to annex the West Bank. Podhoretz criticizes their selection of words that connote parallels between the Israeli invasion and Nazi genocide. He uses a similar idiom himself, however, in calling for the "elimination of the radical rejectionist Palestinians—whether or not they call themselves the PLO."[47]

It is not only Holocaust references that Podhoretz objects to, but also most other historical and political analogies. He ridicules writers who compare Israeli militarism to Sparta, its generals to Caribbean dictators, its bombing of Beirut to a "blitzkrieg," or its expansionist goals to those of communist Vietnam. He rebuffs the very possibility of analogizing Israel to any other nation. Israel, he implies, is incomparable. Only anti-Semitism could account for the inflated language of such irrational critiques, he claims; but first, he provides a broader definition of the term. Anti-Semitism is at work, he writes, when people apply a "double standard" whereby Jews as a people, or Israel as a Jewish state, "are condemned when they claim or exercise the right to do things that all other people are accorded an unchallengeable right to do." Thus, all states are considered to have the right to protect their borders or pursue self-determination, but when Israel does so, it is accused of "committing the crimes of racism and imperialism."[48]

This new definition of anti-Semitism casts a wide net that includes those Jews who hold Israel to a higher standard than other nations. Such utopianism, he claims, imposes on Israel a suicidal yardstick of perfection and betrays a misunderstanding of Zionism, which aims to "*normalize* the Jewish people, not to perfect them." The "refusal of the Arab world" to accept the Jewish state presents the only obstacle to this "normal and peaceful life" and forces Israel to "live in a constant state of siege." In such conditions, Podhoretz finds it remarkable that Israel has not become "a garrison state or a military dictatorship." Instead he celebrates its vital democracy, "the only one in the Middle East and one of the few on the face of the earth." Ironically, as Podhoretz himself admits, "Israel *has* become a light unto the nations." In striving to be normal, Israel has indeed became exceptional.[49]

The neoconservative defense of Israel's operations in Lebanon contributed to the argument for reviving American power during the Reagan presidency. Podhoretz had just published the book *Why We Were in Vietnam,* in which he endorsed Reagan's interpretation of the Vietnam War as a "noble cause." Israel's action in Lebanon epitomized the same noble commitment to fight for a cause and refuse to back down under criticism. Israel's democracy, in his view, was a shining rebuke to surrounding Third World nations, and its military commitment acted as a reproach to the anemic antiwar sentiment that had held sway over Americans since Vietnam. In the "glare of *that* light, the current political complexion of the Western democracies takes on a sickly, sallow, even decadent look." The war in Lebanon repulsed only the faint-hearted, according to Podhoretz, who exhorted Americans to be ashamed not of Israel's brutality but of their own failure of nerve.[50]

"J'Accuse" brands critics of Israel as anti-American. The same journalists, charges Podhoretz, who had hysterically opposed the war in Vietnam were now opposing the American fight against communism in Central America and were advocating appeasement of the Soviet Union. They did not appreciate the service Israel was providing in destroying the Soviet Union's proxies in the Middle East. For neoconservatives, Israel became an exemplar to follow. "We in the West confront in the Soviet Union a deadly enemy sworn to our destruction," Podhoretz declaims with a key analogy, "just as Israel does in the Arab world." The essay concludes by accusing critics of Israel "not merely of anti-Semitism but of the broader sin of faithlessness to the interests of the United States and indeed to the values of Western civilization as a whole."[51]

It was not just neoconservatives, however, who agreed with Podhoretz's premise that "vilification of Israel" was the main problem unleashed by the war in Lebanon. New organizations sprouted up to defend Israel from criticism and repair the damage done to its reputation. Mainstream Jewish American organizations also stepped up their public relations efforts to influence public opinion, expanded their surveillance of Israel's critics on college campuses, and developed new strategies to control the narrative about Israel's relationship with the Palestinians.

The Committee for Accuracy in Middle East Reporting in America led the charge. CAMERA was founded in 1982 "to respond to the *Washington Post*'s coverage of Israel's Lebanon incursion, and to the paper's general anti-Israel bias." After the war, it opened chapters in major American cities, spawned new organizations, and expanded its surveillance to all forms of media, including newspapers, TV networks, the wire services, radio, film, and the Public Broadcasting Service, a favorite target. It pressured media outlets not to air advertisements, documentaries, or news segments, warning them to monitor themselves in advance in order to avoid criticism. Publishing a relentless parade of what the group saw as falsehoods from mainstream news sources also worked to affirm Israel's beleaguered status in the war over representation.[52]

As Podhoretz's rhetoric demonstrates, criticism of the media and support for Israel's military activities did not take place in a vacuum, but in the intensifying Cold War atmosphere under Reagan. Conservatives attacked media bias against Israel as part of a broader critique of the "liberal media." Since the Vietnam War, their argument ran, the media had been overly critical of the use of force. Open societies, like Israel and the United States, had their hands tied unfairly in military maneuvers because of the kind of media scrutiny that totalitarian societies did not allow. They accused journalists of exaggerating the violence against civilians of American-supported dictators in Central America and of romanticizing the guerrillas, just as they did the PLO. CAMERA took cues from Accuracy in Media, a conservative organization that in 1982 had attacked the credibility of journalists who exposed the massacre of civilians in El Mozote, El Salvador.[53]

In addition to CAMERA, two well-established organizations, the American Israel Public Affairs Committee (AIPAC) and the ADL, expanded their own efforts to monitor Israel's critics and to counter the damning narratives that had emerged from the Lebanon invasion with pro-Israel narratives. Although AIPAC is a lobbying organization focused on foreign relations and U.S. governmental support for Israel, and the ADL's mission is to combat prejudice in America, their interests in defending Israel from criticism started to converge in the 1970s, and they took similar steps to dampen support for Palestinian perspectives that had begun to emerge in reaction to the Lebanon War.

AIPAC shifted gears in the 1980s, both institutionally and strategically. In addition to enlisting greater grassroots participation, its leadership developed a new emphasis on generating authoritative narratives about Israel: policy narratives to shape the way Washington insiders understood Israel's importance to the United States, and cultural narratives to mold public opinion. Public discord over the invasion of Lebanon intensified the discomfort that many American supporters of Israel had felt when the right-wing government of Begin came into power in 1977. In the face of his belligerent policies, lobbyists could no longer appeal to the old consensus about a movement of democratic pioneers seeking a new life in a homeland free from persecution, and a nation that only wanted peace with those seeking to destroy it. During the Reagan administration, AIPAC emphasized the idea that Israel was America's "strategic asset," a politically stable and technologically advanced bulwark against Soviet aggression in the region. This concept offered a policy-oriented version of Podhoretz's image of Israel as the savior of Western civilization.[54]

Promoting Israel's strategic value, however, was not enough to undo the damage that the Lebanon War had inflicted on Israel's reputation. Both AIPAC and the ADL published pamphlets designed to counter criticism of Israel and warn against what they saw as pro-Arab propaganda: *The Campaign to Discredit Israel* and the *AIPAC College Guide: Exposing the Anti-Israel Campaign* (AIPAC), and *Pro-Arab Propaganda in America: Vehicles and Voices* (ADL).[55] Both organizations had been monitoring pro-Palestinian and Arab-American groups since the 1970s, and the invasion of Lebanon gave these projects new urgency in the arena of public opinion.

All three publications opened with the war in Lebanon, announcing that it had left Israel newly vulnerable to pro-Arab propaganda in the United States. They warned that after the PLO lost its base in Beirut, its supporters had shifted their propaganda war to focus on America. Arab supporters, they charged, exploited the distorted media coverage to characterize Israel as a "militaristic," "brutal," and "oppressive" nation and to promote the "myth of an 'aggressive' and 'imperialistic' Israel." The pamphlets described a well-funded anti-Israel network consisting of Arab nations, Arab-American organizations, PLO representatives, foreign students, former American ambassadors, radical activists, and Arab and Jewish intellectuals. More than half the pages in these pamphlets consist of the names of individuals and organizations, along with detailed accounts of their publications, activities, connections, and speeches. The criterion for inclusion in the lists was any conceivable contact with the PLO. The authors justified the publication of names on the grounds that it would help pro-Israel activists to thwart the network's long-range goal of "destroying Israel's positive image" and causing the United States to recognize the PLO and curtail military and economic aid to Israel.[56]

The pamphlets expressed concern about the growing sophistication of anti-Israel propaganda, pointing out that its aim was to represent Israel not as David, but as Goliath, to show that Israel is "the aggressor, not the defender; the executioner, not the victim; the superpower, not the underdog." This view would in turn support a dangerous new perception of the conflict as between "an aggressive and powerful Zionist state" and "the weak Palestinian Arabs."[57]

The "Palestinian problem," countered one of the AIPAC pamphlets, had no basis in reality. It existed only as an "effective public relations weapon, and the attention given to it is probably the greatest single achievement of anti-Israeli propaganda to date."[58] To turn attention away from the Israel-Palestine axis, the pamphlet insisted that Arab aggression had created the refugee problem in 1948, and that Israel had since then been besieged by the Arab states, "supported by the Communist bloc and the Islamic world." In its lobbying efforts, AIPAC worked to hold the U.S. government to the 1975 pledge, made by Secretary of State Henry Kissinger, not to recognize the PLO or to speak with its representatives. These pamphlets explain why any acknowledgment of the Palestinians seemed so damaging to Israel's public image.

Both AIPAC and the ADL feared that anti-Israel propaganda was making headway on college campuses, but they conveyed a contradictory sense of the power of pro-Palestinian groups. The *AIPAC College Guide* warned that pro-Palestinian speakers had succeeded in "defining the parameters within which much of the campus debate about Israel and the Middle East takes place," even though they were failing to sway the hearts and minds of most American students. AIPAC claimed victory but called for continued vigilance. A program with Hillel, the organization for Jewish students, trained students to monitor and create files on speakers, and—if they couldn't cancel the events outright—to interrupt, challenge, and write negative reviews in student newspapers. Most important, students should learn to "restore balance" and correct the erroneous description of the conflict as "one between Israel and the *Palestinian Arabs*" and to reject the idea that the roots of the conflict lay in the "refusal of Israel to grant Palestinians their rights."[59]

A number of academics and journalists criticized AIPAC and the ADL for tactics that they said smacked of McCarthyism. The Middle East Studies Association, the main organization of scholars and educators in the field, voted unanimously to condemn what they called "blacklisting." In two *New York Times* columns, Anthony Lewis admonished both organizations for underhanded attacks on Professor Walid Khalidi, a political scientist at the American University of Beirut and visiting fellow at Harvard, who, in 1978, had written an article in *Foreign Affairs* that advocated for a Palestinian state alongside Israel. The head of ADL, Kenneth Bialkin, refused to back down, claiming that Khalidi could not be a true "moderate" because he had not publicly disavowed the PLO. By declaring that Khalidi, like everyone else on the list, was not a moderate, the ADL claimed the right to define acceptable discourse and reasserted the image of Israel as a victim. Even if it was no longer besieged by powerful Arab armies, it was being threatened by people uttering—or refusing to utter—specific words.[60]

The monitoring and blacklisting of critics of Israel did indeed have chilling effects on individuals and institutions, but these strategies alone were not sufficient to restore the story of Israel as the underdog or to erase the new images of Palestinians that Americans had glimpsed in the Lebanon War. The events of 1982 had posed a severe challenge to the standard narratives about Israel's founding in 1948 and its triumph in 1967. Israel's conservative supporters now found it necessary to create a new account of an old story of the founding of Israel, one that would actually make the Palestinians disappear.

In 1984, a book appeared seemingly out of nowhere to perform this magic act: *From Time Immemorial: The Origins of the Arab-Jewish Conflict over Palestine,* by the little-known journalist Joan Peters. After the Lebanon War, it took a heavily documented six-hundred-page tome to argue what Prime Minister Golda Meir had remarked in 1969, that "there were no such thing as Palestinians." Peters claimed to have proven that the Arabs known as "Palestinians" were in fact not native to Palestine. Based on demographic data, she argued that Palestine had been thinly populated when Jewish settlers first arrived, and that Arabs had migrated into the area only after these settlers had cultivated the land, developed industries, and raised the standard of living. The founders of Israel, according to Peters, did not expel a people from their homeland—they merely displaced some recent economic migrants.[61] The book was eventually exposed as error-filled and fraudulent, but it was at first warmly received and has had a lasting impact.

From Time Immemorial aimed to restore the foundational narratives of Israel's origins that the war in Lebanon had severely undermined. The invasion had unsettled more than the humane image of Israel's military; it had also reopened thorny questions about history, especially as they bore on the present. About 1948: How did the Palestinians end up in refugee camps in Lebanon? Where did they come from and where did they belong? And about 1967: Who would rule the occupied territories in the West Bank and Gaza? In Israel, in response to these questions, historians had begun reexamining the archival record and debunking the myths of Zionist historiography. These "new historians," a loosely knit group, revised the account of 1948 to include the Palestinian history of the Nakba. They revealed that the nascent Jewish state at the time of partition was less vulnerable, militarily and diplomatically, than commonly thought; that it bore some responsibility for the expulsion of Palestinians and the subsequent refugee problem; and that the new state had resisted international efforts at peace-making, a failure traditionally blamed on Arab intransigence.[62]

Peters reinvigorated the very myths that these Israeli historians were unraveling. In the introduction to the book, she cast herself in the role of a scholarly David wielding unpopular truths against an Arab Goliath who had usurped the historical record. In a nod to George Orwell, she coined the term "turnspeak" to describe the "cynical inverting or distorting of facts, which for example, makes the victim appear as the culprit." The most egregious inversion, she claimed, was the one that had turned Palestinians into the dispossessed casualties of Zionism. To set the historical record straight, Peters returned Jews to their rightful role as victims, and Arabs to theirs as culprits.[63] She restored the image of Palestine as an uninhabited wasteland until Jewish pioneers regenerated the land. In asserting that Arab migrants were drawn to the economic opportunities created by Zionist settlement, she revived the narrative of Jewish colonization as modernization that had been so important to the liberal supporters of Zionism in the 1940s and 1950s. She shored up Podhoretz's claim that all conflict stemmed from the Arabs' violent rejection of Israel. And she expanded this narrative back in time to the Ottoman Empire, to undo the "turnspeak" about Jews living peaceably in a Muslim world that tolerated and protected them. She claimed, on the contrary, that Arab countries had always mistreated Jews because of Islam's inherent anti-Semitism. She endorsed the right-wing belief that Jews who had been expelled from Arab lands were the real refugees of 1948, not Palestinians. She thus described the events of 1948 as a "population exchange" rather than a violent displacement of Palestinians from their homes. Peters revived the founding narrative of the Jewish national revolt against the British Empire, which *Exodus* had enshrined in the American imagination. She came close to blaming the British for complicity with the Holocaust, asserting that they had encouraged Arab immigration into Palestine in order to keep out those Jews fleeing from the Nazis. Peters's book breathed new life into myths that have persisted into the present.[64]

Before publication, Harper and Row secured testimonials from many respected Jewish intellectuals; the jacket featured encomiums by Barbara Tuchman, Saul Bellow, Elie Wiesel, Lucy Dawidowicz, and others. A blurb by journalist Paul Cowan stated bluntly, "I can never again think of the Arabs as the Palestinians. If readers take it as seriously as they should, it would literally reformulate the terms of debate on the Middle East." American reviewers for the most part applauded Peters for what they described as historical truths that she had uncovered through detailed demographic and historical research. "This book is the intellectual equivalent of the Six-Day War," enthused the *National Review*. "If the pen is mightier than the sword, Joan Peters has done more to destroy Arab claims to Palestine than all the derring-do of the Israeli Army since—well if not from time immemorial, then at least from 1948 to the foreseeable future."[65]

But serious concerns about Peters's scholarship soon emerged. Norman Finkelstein, a graduate student at Princeton University, painstakingly exposed the book's numerous errors, from misinterpretation of sources to outright plagiarism, and his findings were corroborated by other historians. British scholars panned the book's shoddy scholarship, and

Israeli historian Yehoshua Porath described it as "sheer forgery," noting that Israelis dismissed it as a "propaganda weapon." In the *New York Review of Books,* Porath wrote, "What is surprising is that Joan Peters still writes as if the Zionist myths were wholly true and relevant, notwithstanding all the historical work that modifies or discredits them." Critics showed, most damningly, that her major conclusions about the population of Palestine in the early twentieth century were based on faulty interpretation of demographic data. Edward Said described the book's reception as "a case of orchestrated compliance by which the history and actuality of an entire people are consigned to non-existence." Harper and Row nevertheless reprinted the book several times without requiring Peters to correct the errors. In "There Were No Indians," Anthony Lewis summarized the outrage of the books' critics: "neither Miss Peters nor any of her supporters has answered a single one of the charges of distortion and fraud made against it."[66]

It is not surprising that Leon Uris at the same time returned to the history of Palestine in his 1984 novel *The Haj.* He felt compelled to revisit the founding tale of *Exodus* from what he considered to be "the Arab perspective." The novel's first-person narrator, Ishmael, tells his family's dark story of social and psychological degeneration, against the background of Zionism's progressive ascent. Uris's goal in fiction was similar to Peters's history. He used a kind of ventriloquism to acknowledge Palestinians in order to erase them from the landscape as historical actors. Uris portrayed Arabs living in Palestine as recently settled nomads, and he blamed their displacement in 1948 on the backwardness and venality of Islamic culture, not on dispossession by Jewish settlers, who only tried to uplift them. The book musters every imaginable Orientalist stereotype. It represents Arabs as driven by fanaticism, mutual mistrust, and sexual derangement, and it depicts their irrational hatred of Jews as inherent to Islam's warring creed.[67]

Reviewers roundly panned *The Haj* as a literary failure and as offensively prejudiced. Though it spent thirty weeks on the bestseller list, it had less impact on public discourse than *From Time Immemorial.* Both works are instructive failures. They sprang to the defense of Israel in the aftermath of the Lebanon War, which dealt a blow to the reigning *Exodus* narrative. After Lebanon, neither author could ignore the presence of Palestinians, and each felt compelled to represent Palestinians in order to make them disappear. Peters and Uris expressed in historical and fictional form the backlash against the media portrayal of Israel's invasion of Lebanon. They incorporated the arguments of Podhoretz, AIPAC, the ADL, and the Hasbara conference, which held that the plight of the Palestinian refugees was nothing but propaganda, and that in reality Israel continued to be the innocent victim of Arab violence. Despite the combined strength of these campaigns to sway public opinion, their shared narrative of Israel as the invincible victim could not entirely erase the searing images from Lebanon or efface Palestinians from the political landscape.

New Liberal Consensus

The war in Lebanon provoked a new awareness of Palestinians among American liberals, in spite of the intense backlash from the right. Even liberals with strong attachments to Israel felt the need for stories that could account for Palestinians as a people with political grievances and national aspirations. A new narrative became even more urgent with the eruption of the first intifada at the end of 1987, when Palestinians in the West Bank and the Gaza Strip began to protest the Israeli occupation in collective acts of civil disobedience that continued for five years. Television again brought the crisis home to Americans. This time, viewers were not seeing bombs dropped from a distance on a foreign city or dazed victims digging through the rubble. They had close-up views of Palestinians demonstrating in the streets of their own towns, coming face to face with Israeli soldiers. They watched men, women, and children marching, chanting, throwing stones, and raising Palestinian flags. The anxiety of conservatives that the media had turned Israel into Goliath became a graphic reality on the screen. Palestinian youths wearing jeans and keffiyehs threw stones at heavily armed Israeli soldiers, who responded with live ammunition, severe beatings, mass arrests, and deportations. Minister of Defense Yitzhak Rabin, a hero of 1967, now was calling for "force, might and beatings."[68] American reactions to coverage of the intifada echoed those that had followed the Lebanon War, with outrage at the violence, cries of media bias, and anguish about Israel's soul. But in the intifada, viewers encountered images of Palestinians not only as victims, but as political actors protesting oppression and advocating for a nation of their own.

Children throwing stones at Israeli soldiers during the first intifada, Am'ari refugee camp near Ramallah, February 1, 1988.

A liberal consensus emerged in the 1980s around a narrative of two peoples fighting over one land, and a belief that only mutual recognition could resolve the conflict between them. This narrative could lead to a variety of political conclusions, and it would undergird proposals for the peace process and a two-state solution through the end of the twentieth century. Proponents of this focus on two sides believed that including Palestinians would not result in distancing the United States from Israel, as conservatives feared; rather, it would repair the damage done to Israel's reputation in Lebanon and reaffirm Israel's affinity with America.

Two major contributions to this narrative were made by journalists who had covered the invasion of Lebanon for the *New York Times*. In 1986, David Shipler received a Pulitzer Prize for *Arab and Jew: Wounded Spirits in the Promised Land*. Three years later, Thomas Friedman's *From Beirut to Jerusalem* won the National Book Award. Their titles announced that they had two intertwined stories to tell—a tale of two cities, and a tale of two peoples. A seasoned correspondent who had reported from Moscow and Vietnam, Shipler served as the *Times* Jerusalem bureau chief from 1979 to 1984. Friedman arrived in Beirut in 1979 for his first assignment and in 1982 became the *Times* bureau chief there. In 1984, he replaced Shipler in Jerusalem. The two shared a George Polk Award in Journalism for their reporting on the invasion of Lebanon. Friedman received two Pulitzers, one for his detailed account of the Sabra and Shatila massacre, and a second for his reporting on the first intifada. Shipler's reissued *Arab and Jew* became the basis of two well-regarded PBS documentaries, in 1989 and 2001. *From Beirut to Jerusalem* launched Friedman's career as a Middle East expert and one of the best-known U.S. columnists on global affairs.[69]

Both books are travel narratives with an American reporter as protagonist. Shipler introduces himself as "neither Arab nor Jew," but an outsider living in Jerusalem, who has come to care about the suffering of both groups and to feel frustrated by their intolerance toward one another. Explicitly abjuring politics, he maps the psychological landscape where Jews and Arabs encounter one another with stereotypes, prejudice, and misunderstanding, stemming from a history of mutually inflicted traumas. At the heart of the matter, Shipler sees "a clash between two nationalisms, each coveting the same land." The chapters toggle back and forth to treat every topic from the perspective of both Arabs and Jews. Shipler eloquently portrays the histories and dreams that propel both, and does not shy away from discussing the terrorism and atrocities that each have committed against the other. The conflict, he avers, cannot be resolved by treaties alone, but only when the two peoples are willing to recognize both their mutual mistrust and their interdependence "by looking into each other's eyes."[70]

Friedman is a more ebullient main character in his tale of a fall from innocence into experience. He starts with his disillusionment as a young American Jew infatuated with an idealized image of Israel after the Six-Day War. He frames his reportage from Lebanon and Syria within his personal odyssey of reimagining his relationship with Israel. In contrast to Shipler's insistence on the distance of the objective observer, Friedman introduces himself as an avowedly interested party and makes his confessional honesty a source of authority. He describes how his frankness about Israeli brutality in Lebanon led to a public fight with his editor, who deleted the word "indiscriminate" from his account of Israeli bombing, and how it also got him into trouble with Jews at home, to his parents' dismay. He reacts to the massacre in Sabra and Shatila as a "personal crisis," a blow to the image of "the heroic Israel I had been taught to identify with." Anger at the IDF's betrayal ("How could you do this to *me*," he asks) motivates his prizewinning articles detailing the Israeli involvement in the massacre.[71]

Both authors attempt to debunk myths about Israelis and Palestinians for American readers. They ridicule as equally outdated the Arab opposition to Israel's existence and the Jewish denial of Palestinian nationalism. Both portray the Israeli looting of the PLO Research Center in Beirut in September 1982 as a powerful symbol of this denial. Breaking into what looked like a nondescript office building but was in fact an academic research center, Israeli troops carted off thousands of books and irreplaceable archival records, leaving behind only broken furniture and offensive graffiti. The Israelis faced something "more dangerous" than ammunition there, writes Friedman: the center contained "books about Palestine, old records and land deeds belonging to Palestinian families, photographs about Arab life in Palestine . . . and, most important, maps—maps of pre-1948 Palestine with every Arab village before the state of Israel came into being and erased many of them." The center was "like an ark containing Palestinians' heritage . . . their credentials as a nation." To Shipler, this effort to "steal the Palestinians' past and identity" was part of a larger effort that included outlawing the Palestinian flag and any expression of support for the PLO, including most uses of the word "Palestine."[72]

Shipler relates this suppression of Palestinian identity to the stereotypes and prejudices that have become deeply ingrained in Israeli language, culture, and everyday life, and are matched in kind by Arab denigration of Jews. Friedman focuses on the dehumanizing impact of war and occupation. In response to the Shatila massacre, he writes, Israeli soldiers "did not see innocent civilians being massacred and they did not hear the screams of innocent children going to their graves." Instead, they saw a "'terrorist infestation' being 'mopped up' and 'terrorist nurses' scurrying about and 'terrorist teenagers' trying to defend them." In the Israeli psyche, he explains, you "don't come to the rescue of 'terrorists,'" for "there is no such thing as 'terrorists' being massacred."[73]

The idea of symmetry frames both books, which strive to represent Palestinians as equal to Israelis and to juxtapose parallel stories from both sides of the conflict. Symmetry offered a powerful corrective to the dehumanization of Palestinians and to the predominance of Israeli perspectives in American discourse. Shipler's was one of the few American books at the time to include lengthy interviews with "Israeli Arabs" (Palestinians with Israeli citizenship). He empathically depicted the widespread discrimination they faced from government laws and everyday interactions. Friedman focused on Palestinians in the occupied territories and sympathetically portrayed their expression of national identity during the intifada.

Symmetry, however, also worked to obfuscate the underlying power dynamics that structured interactions between Israelis and Palestinians. To be sure, both Shipler and Friedman understood the monopoly of power that the Israeli state wielded over Palestinian lives. They wrote of symmetry primarily in terms of group psychology and culture; but as a result, they relegated institutional hierarchies to the margins. They conveyed the impression of Israelis and Palestinians as equally vulnerable and equally threatening to one another.

Shipler writes that "much of the everyday friction at the points of Arab-Jewish contact is cultural, a conflict of East and West, a bad chemistry of mixed styles." Examples range from hospitality codes, to shopping styles, to "the bureaucratic encounter" for Arabs crossing the Allenby Bridge between the West Bank and Jordan after 1967. He reports that members of the local aristocracy felt insulted by being strip-searched at that crossing, especially by having their shoes dumped in a pile with those of mere commoners. This resentment he attributes to a "clash of values" between "the Arabs' sense of honor and class consciousness" and the "Israeli Jews' egalitarianism," which has bureaucrats treating everyone alike. Focusing on the contrast between Arab traditionalism and Israeli modernity, he overlooks the obvious control that Israeli border guards wield over Arab bodies and mobility.[74]

By exploring psychological and cultural landscapes, Shipler is able to ignore political geography. In a chapter on the stereotype of the "alien, superior Jew," which follows one on the "primitive, exotic Arab," he visits a small village in the West Bank whose inhabitants believe this stereotype even though they have had no direct contact with Jews. Although Shipler acknowledges the villagers' fear of the settlements encroaching on the surrounding countryside, he then proceeds to show how the image of the Jew as alien arose from theological and historical sources in the textbooks and newspapers of the wider Arab world. Power drops out of his analysis.[75]

In Friedman's book, too, symmetry obscures relations of domination. In a poignant tale of two funerals, he shows how the conflict has effaced the boundary between soldiers and civilians on both sides. In one case, an unarmed Israeli woman settler on her way to buy groceries was killed by Palestinians, who view all settlers as soldiers of the military occupation. In the other case, an unarmed Palestinian student demonstrating at his university was shot by Israeli soldiers, who see protesters not as students, but as a lethal threat to their security. At a state funeral for the Israeli, Friedman describes a government minister eulogizing the woman as a soldier who died to defend her country. He notes that Palestinian leaders similarly extolled the dead student as a national martyr, at a funeral that resembled a political festival. Both groups suffer, he contends, when mourning transforms the death of individuals into political symbols.

Yet Friedman also describes how much more difficult it was for the Palestinian student's family to bury him. To prevent political gatherings, the Israeli army was impounding slain Palestinian bodies and compelling the families to bury their loved ones alone at midnight. In this case, Friedman tells an adventurous tale of friends sneaking the body out from under Israeli guard. His main point is a symmetrical one, to show how both groups manipulate mourning for nationalist ends. Yet he does not comment on the vast asymmetry of power evident in these funerals. The Israeli government officially sanctioned a state funeral for a settler in occupied territory. The same state prohibited the Palestinian family from burying their dead on their own time and on their own lands.[76]

Symmetry is also fundamental to Friedman's account of the intifada, which he narrates as a war of rage on both sides. Palestinian protests against the occupation "set off an equally intense explosion of rage on the Israeli side of the fault line," writes Friedman, and "just as a rage began to simmer and bubble to the surface among Palestinians vis-à-vis the Israelis, who never let them feel at home, a similar rage grew inside Israelis vis-à-vis Palestinians, who never let them relax and enjoy their country." In a representative confrontation, Friedman reports Palestinian youths and Israeli soldiers hurling the same vulgar curses at one another. The Israeli soldiers, explains Friedman, felt as much frustration as the Palestinian youths, not because of physical danger, but because Palestinians made Israelis feel insecure, as though they did not belong in their own homes. What's more, uncomfortable in the role of policeman, the Israeli soldiers felt stymied by being restrained from deploying the full military force at their disposal. Even though the fatality figures dramatically belie this depiction of symmetry and restraint, Friedman considers Israeli feelings of insecurity to be as significant as their physical assaults on Palestinians.[77]

This narrative of equivalence relies on potent analogies with America that kept Palestinians from capturing the moral high ground in the battle for representation. At the beginning of the uprising, when the Israeli army faced criticism for firing live ammunition at protestors, Friedman instructed television viewers on how to view the violence. They were not watching the "equivalent of Birmingham in 1960 or Berkeley in 1968," he wrote, but the "equivalent of Bull Run in 1861." It would no more occur to them "to use rubber bullets against the Palestinians than it would have occurred to the North to use rubber bullets against the South in the Civil War." The civil rights analogy compares Palestinians to black Americans fighting for equal rights against violent police power. The Civil War analogy, in contrast, conveys the impression of two matched military forces capable of doing equal harm to each other.[78]

Friedman, to be sure, acknowledges the "asymmetry in firepower in the clashes between Israeli soldiers and Palestinian youths," noting that "Israelis had vastly superior weapons compared to the Palestinians." Nonetheless, "there was not an asymmetry in the stakes," he insists. Friedman finds equivalence in group psychology, averring that "Israelis felt just as deeply as Palestinians that their communal survival was at stake in what was happening in the streets." He recognizes the brutal record of Israel rage "in the X-rays of the hundreds of Palestinians who had their arms or legs or ribs broken by Israeli soldiers." Yet he wants his readers to understand the "real fear behind the Israeli clubs," the fear of never feeling truly at home in a land claimed by others.[79]

For Friedman, the acknowledgment of two sides at war foregrounds Israeli vulnerability as a physical and psychological reality—an ancient wound as painful as Palestinian deaths, and a grievance as valid as Palestinian protests. Conservative reviewers criticized Friedman for eschewing the older narrative of Israel menaced by the entire Arab world. But his new narrative of symmetrical rage and equal insecurity restored the perception of Israelis as victims, even as their clubs and bullets told a contrary tale.

Friedman draws on the paradox of vulnerability and invincibility to explain Israeli reluctance to negotiate with the Palestinians. At the end of 1988, in response to the intifada, Yasser Arafat publicly recognized Israel's right to exist and stated that the PLO "renounced all forms of terrorism."[80] Most Israelis, claimed Freidman, experienced themselves as either too weak or too strong to take advantage of this historic announcement. On the one hand, they felt too insecure to negotiate away a single parcel of territory. On the other hand, they felt too powerful to have an incentive to concede any land. Friedman places the burden of reassurance on the Palestinians in the occupied territories. Only in "their original method of civil disobedience," he declares, could they make themselves "so indigestible to the Israelis that they want to disgorge them into their own state, while at the same time reassuring the Israelis that they can disgorge them without committing suicide." Without acknowledging Israel's vigorous repression of the many acts of civil disobedience at the heart of the intifada, Friedman attributes to Palestinians the ultimate power both to force the hand of the Israelis and to assuage their existential angst.[81]

Friedman's attention to both sides—to Beirut and Jerusalem, Palestinians and Israelis—ultimately teaches him to "identify with and feel affection toward an imperfect Israel." This is his journey's destination: after weathering his disillusionment in Lebanon, and putting the intifada in perspective, he concludes: "Well, she ain't perfect. I'll always want her to be the country I imagined in my youth, But what the hell, she's mine, and for a forty-year-old, she ain't too shabby." Although he riled some readers by drawing parallels between the governments in Beirut and Jerusalem, he confirmed his belief in Israel's exceptional character: "The day when going from Beirut to Jerusalem means not going anywhere at all is a day Israel will rue forever." Symmetry yielded to hierarchy. Friedman's personal narrative of disenchantment and reconnection demonstrated how other Jews, and Americans in general, could move beyond their disappointment and lingering shame about Israel's behavior in Lebanon and during the intifada. They, too, could adopt Friedman's mature understanding of Israel's superior—albeit flawed—position in the Middle East and thus restore their special relationship.[82]

Although Shipler had less invested in this romance, he, too, searched for symmetry and discovered moral hierarchy. With equal interest in the psychology of both Arabs and Jews, he discovered more depth in the Israeli Jewish psyche. Both groups have terrorists, he explains, but Israelis punish theirs, while Palestinians hail theirs as heroes. Both groups have religious fundamentalists, but only Jews agonize over the relationship between religion and nationalism. Neither group understands the historical traumas of the other. Israel does not accept that "some of its finest heroes expelled Arabs" in 1948 or committed massacres after the state was founded, but he accuses Palestinians of inflating their suffering to make it "parallel with the Jewish suffering at the hands of the Nazis." In a rare expression of personal outrage, he excoriates them for chanting "Ansar is Auschwitz" to protest conditions in a notorious prison camp in southern Lebanon.[83]

Shipler extolls the Israeli response to Sabra and Shatila, when "the citizenry itself mobilized into an explosion of conscience unparalleled in the modern history of Western democracy. Nothing like it ever happened in the United States after American soldiers massacred Vietnamese at My Lai." Even though this response soon gave way in the general population to a hardening of racist attitudes toward Arabs, he values the Israeli conscience that is being preserved by a flourishing community of writers and artists. In contrast, he notes, "One can look in vain for comparable writing on the Arab side. What theater and literature exists among the Palestinians in Israel, the West Bank, and Gaza is rarely self-critical, usually polemical within the limits of Israeli censorship, and never—that I could find—touched with that fine sense of decency around which the dissenting Jews spin their works." Even the Arab theater he admires is "shallower than the search for ethics you see in Jewish theater." Although he mentions censorship, his comparative framework excludes the question of how state power limits artistic production, including the resources to translate literature and disseminate it internationally.[84]

Both authors aimed to establish a kinship between their American readers and the Israelis they portray. To Shipler, Israel resembled the America that was trying to right its own history of racial oppression. As one reviewer wrote, "Like so many of his countrymen—gentile or Jew—who have spent time in Israel, Mr. Shipler clearly has been attracted by the openness, energy and often cantankerous individualism of this brash little democracy that can often seem a far-flung extension of America itself, so redolent of both its virtues and its faults." In an interview, Shipler mentioned receiving angry letters about his criticism of Israeli racism. He replied that Americans had to relinquish their idealized images and understand the traumatic meaning of 1948 for Palestinians. "It's a bit like us and the Indians. It's only recently that we came to grips with what the white men did to the Indians." Shipler also compared Israeli racial attitudes with those of whites toward blacks in the United States, viewing the solution to discrimination against Israeli Arabs in the light of an American model of desegregation.[85]

Shipler concludes his book with a chapter melding American and Israeli ideals, starting with an epigraph from Theodore Herzl, Zionism's founder: "If you will it, it is not a dream." The chapter focuses on rare, innovative programs that bring together Arab and Jewish youth to confront their own prejudices and foster mutual understanding. Most of these groups were organized by idealistic American Jews. Though Shipler explicitly avoids political proposals to resolve the conflicts he explores in such depth, he implicitly posits a mediating role for Americans—whether in the role of these young idealists or in his own role as objective observer—who can imagine a bridge that the two parties cannot create on their own.

Friedman expresses skepticism about these same young idealists. In the face of outright conflict during the intifada, he saw Jewish Americans in Israel, like everyone else in the Middle East, falling back on their primary tribal allegiance. Friedman does, however, advocate a strong role for the U.S. government in resolving the conflict, a role that would replicate on a national scale his own position as a dispassionate observer of both sides and a passionate advocate for Israel.

His journey from Beirut to Jerusalem ends in Washington, where he implores the United States to take the lead as a tough peacemaker. But the toughness should be tempered by respect for Israel's vulnerability, he advises, because confronting Israel in public or threatening to withdraw aid would be counterproductive. Friedman writes that Washington has "too many strategic, emotional and religious interests" not to take the lead, and that it could "still bring Arabs and Israelis the best of America's outlook, without being devoured by the feuds and passions that consume them." American optimism conveys the message that the "past is dead," a crucial message for both Arabs and Israelis, trapped as they are by "paralyzing features of their past." Friedman ends his book with a pitch for American exceptionalism—a belief in American innocence, in its power and diplomacy as moral force for good. He concludes with a rhapsodic, if somewhat forced, analogy between the United States and Moses: just as Moses saw the Promised Land as the future, so the United States could liberate Israelis and Arabs "from the chains of their past."[86]

If readers accepted the premises so eloquently presented by Shipler and Friedman, they would recognize that to fully understand Israel, they would need to listen to the Palestinian story as well. But the liberal insistence on two sides also created boundaries and hierarchies. In 1989, PBS broadcast a two-hour documentary based on Shipler's book *Arab and Jew: Wounded Spirits in a Promised Land.* As the narrator, Shipler interviewed many of the individuals featured in his book, and he added younger Israelis and Palestinians involved in the intifada. Reviewers praised the documentary for its balance and depth, and many commented on the chilling interviews with youths on both sides who voiced the desire to kill their enemies. The symmetrical expression of hatred, fear, and prejudice made the documentary appear realistic and balanced, and the conflict politically unsolvable.

That same year, an accomplished producer, Jo Franklin-Trout, directed a PBS documentary about the intifada from the perspective of Palestinian youth, "Days of Rage: The Young Palestinians." The documentary became controversial before it was even aired. Pro-Israel groups, including the ADL and CAMERA, obtained advance copies and pressured PBS to keep it off the air, disparaging it as biased and bigoted because it did not include the Israeli side and omitted the longer history of Jewish persecution. In addition, a smear campaign accused the director of accepting secret funding from Arab groups. PBS finally did air the ninety-minute documentary, but in a concession to its critics, the broadcast enveloped the documentary in a "wraparound" format, with a panel of speakers preceding and following the documentary to "balance the pro-Palestinian slant."[87]

A representative review in the *New York Times* contrasted "Days of Rage" unfavorably to Shipler's documentary. Walter Goodman praised *Arab and Jew* for its powerful exploration of "the emotions on both sides of a seemingly intractable issue," while he criticized "Days of Rage" as a "pure propaganda piece," which tendentiously presented

Palestinians as victims and heroic fighters for liberation. In Shipler's favor, according to Goodman, he did not link "human equivalence" to a call for political equivalence, and "did not assume to judge the claims or perils of Palestinian nationalism or the desirability of a Palestinian state." Goodman dismissed Franklin-Trout's documentary for breaching the boundaries of the genre—as advocacy rather than documentary, because it filled the entire ninety minutes with stories of Palestinians. Although the director included Israeli human rights advocates and government spokesmen alongside interviews with protesting youth and their families, Goodman criticized her for only showing Israelis as "armed soldiers pushing around defenseless villagers."[88]

The liberal framework of "human equivalence" did not guarantee that the Palestinian struggle for a homeland would be accorded either the moral or political equivalence of Israeli arguments for security or land rights. The controversy over "Days of Rage" demonstrates what the conservative backlash and liberal consensus had in common: the refusal to listen to a Palestinian narrative that was not balanced by or incorporated into a broader Israeli one. The expectation that every story about Palestinians include an Israeli counterpoint was not the norm for reporting on other international conflicts. As Franklin-Trout argued in the *New York Times,* no one would expect a documentary on protesters in Poland or South Africa to "show the other side."[89] In the case of Israel, however, showing both sides did not entail including Palestinians on the same level as Israelis in the field of representation. "Balance" served to remind viewers and readers that Israel remained vulnerable, even when it appeared indomitable, and morally exceptional even when it committed immoral acts.

The attack on "Days of Rage" was an attempt to deny Palestinians permission to narrate their own story from their point of view. By seeking symmetry in the human equivalence of two sides—unstructured by political power relations—liberals like Shipler and Friedman implicitly rejected the perspective Said called "Zionism from the standpoint of its victims." Instead, they expanded the Zionist standpoint to incorporate Palestinian perspectives—but these perspectives were dependent on Israeli-identified narratives. A few left-wing academics and journalists did try to tell a story from a Palestinian point of view, one that showed the United States as an abettor of Israeli aggression rather than as an arbiter of balance. In the 1980s, Edward Said became a public figure beyond the academy, and he started writing for the opinion pages of mainstream newspapers. In 1982, Noam Chomsky published his account of the invasion of Lebanon in *The Fateful Triangle: The United States, Israel and Palestine.* Said and Chomsky did not view the invasion of Lebanon as a break in Israel's behavior, as John Chancellor did, but rather as a continuation of a history of Israeli aggression that had been displacing Palestinians since before the founding of the state. The idea of two symmetrical stories of suffering and rage relegated their analysis, and that of other radicals, to the margins of American discourse.[90]

The conservative backlash and the new liberal consensus worked in tandem to resolve the crisis of Israel's reputation that had been precipitated by the invasion of Lebanon and was intensified by the intifada. The liberal narrative of two warring nationalisms helped restore the positive image of Israel that John Chancellor saw shattered in the bombing of Beirut. Israel might no longer fit the heroic narrative of *Exodus,* "the Israel we knew in the past," but the liberal two-sided narrative was even more effective in restoring its moral sheen than was AIPAC's effort to deny the reality of Palestinians. This narrative of "both sides" would continue to frame the idea of the two-state solution and the concept of a peace process between two groups with equivalent negotiating power.

In the aftermath of 1982, the conservative monitoring of criticism of Israel and the liberal framework of symmetry together demonstrated to Americans that Israel remained existentially insecure. They also emphasized that even when Israel exercised overwhelming military force, its citizens agonized over the damage done to the nation's soul. As criticism of Israel became more mainstream, defense of its special relationship with the United States took on heightened moral resonance and increasingly apocalyptic dimensions. Another development at the same time worked to enhance the image of Israel as both exceptionally vulnerable and distinctively humane: the growth of Holocaust consciousness in the United States.

5

THE FUTURE HOLOCAUST

FOR MANY AMERICANS, the horror of the Holocaust serves as the basis for their support of Israel. Others believe that the tragedy has been politicized in order to sustain that support. The clash between these views intensified during the 1982 Lebanon War, when advocates and opponents of the invasion argued over which combatants were acting like Nazis. The paradoxical view of Israel as an invincible victim never lost its allure in the United States, even in the face of Israel's military dominance in Lebanon and in the occupied territories during the first intifada. Israel's status as an eternal victim actually gained strength throughout the 1980s, as the Holocaust became a more prominent feature of the American cultural landscape.

Official commemorations, presidential speeches, mass culture, and school curricula taught Americans not only about the historical catastrophe that befell Jews in Europe, but also about the Holocaust as a chapter of their own history in World War II. A museum of the Holocaust was built on the National Mall in Washington, D.C. As the Holocaust was becoming part of America's national heritage, its temporal significance in relation to Israel was changing as well. The Holocaust began to represent more than the horrific suffering of the Jewish people in the past—now it also signified an imminent threat to the future of the Jewish state. A past atrocity in Europe came to foreshadow an impending apocalypse in the Middle East.

New narrative bonds were forged between America's newfound past and Israel's precarious future. Interest in Holocaust memory boomed at a time when both countries were facing crises of wars gone awry—

indeed, Israel was said to have had its own Vietnam in Lebanon. These crises had created internal divisions and international opprobrium, and challenged the belief in the moral authority of military power, a bedrock of their shared exceptionalism. The birth of Israel might be understood as the redemption of Jewish suffering, but the discovery of Holocaust memory as an American national concern also confirmed American exceptionalism and renewed the bond between the two nations.

Remembering the Future

In 1978, two events propelled the Holocaust to the center of American consciousness. An NBC television miniseries called *Holocaust* was viewed by more than 100 million Americans in April. And a month later, President Jimmy Carter initiated plans for what would ultimately become the United States Holocaust Memorial Museum.

On May 1, 1978, Carter hosted a celebration for Israel's thirtieth anniversary in the Rose Garden of the White House, where he welcomed Israeli prime minister Menachem Begin along with six hundred leaders of American Jewish organizations. For a birthday party, the tone of the ceremony was notably somber, as was the "gift" Carter presented to his guests. He announced the formation of a presidential commission charged with planning an American memorial "to the six million who were killed in the Holocaust." He soon appointed noted Holocaust survivor Elie Wiesel as chairman, and the commission embarked on the process of designing a memorial to commemorate, on American soil, the catastrophe that had befallen the Jews of Europe.[1]

Carter's commission aimed to rescue the memory of genocide victims from the oblivion of the past. But the timing addressed a more immediate controversy over his Middle East policy. In 1977, Carter became the first American president to utter the phrase "Palestinian homeland." He antagonized the Israeli government and its American supporters by proposing to include the Palestine Liberation Organization (PLO) in an international peace conference cosponsored by the Soviet Union. Begin expressed outrage at a press conference, denouncing PLO members as "Huns," its policy as "an Arab Mein Kampf," and its diplomacy as a subterfuge for its true goal: "to destroy a people; to annihilate people. The method: genocide—to kill man, woman, and child."[2] Negotiating over territory and recognition of Palestinian rights was, in Begin's terms, tantamount to exposing Israel to a second Holocaust. In less inflammatory rhetoric, American supporters of Israel also criticized Carter for putting Israel at risk by proposing to negotiate with the PLO and planning to sell fighter jets to Saudi Arabia.

In a bid to mollify Carter's critics, his aides recommended that he propose the creation of a national memorial to the Holocaust. In his Rose Garden speech, he vowed that America's "total absolute commitment to Israel's security" would "ensure for all times that the Jewish people will not be condemned to repeat the Holocaust." In response, Begin called Carter's address "one of the greatest moral statements ever."[3]

After Carter's announcement, four different presidents pledged their commitment to the project during a period that witnessed the end of the Cold War. Democrats and Republicans alike vowed that the memory of the Holocaust would remind Americans of their enduring obligation to the State of Israel. In 1993, the United States Holocaust Memorial Museum opened its doors to the public. The museum has deeply affected millions of visitors from all over the world. It serves to document the rise of Nazism and the ghastly methods of slaughter, to memorialize the dead and preserve the traumatic memories of survivors, and to transmit the profound meanings of the Holocaust to communities across generations. But when we look back at the history of the memorial, it becomes clear that this national institution of memory, dedicated to facing the ultimate evil of the past and to imparting universal values to the future, bears indelible traces of its origins in America's Middle East policies, especially its commitment to support Israel.

At the 1978 White House ceremony announcing the formation of the presidential commission, Carter related a narrative of the origins of the special relationship, claiming that it was born "out of the ashes of the Holocaust," alongside the Jewish state. Moral outrage at Nazi atrocities, he claimed, led the United States to recognize the new state in 1948—before any other nation did. Penance as well as pride drove this allegiance, for Carter acknowledged that Americans had turned their backs on Jews seeking refuge from Nazi brutality. In founding a state, Jews valiantly created for themselves a home that the world had denied them. Celebrating Israel's thirtieth anniversary, Carter focused not on its pioneering spirit or its modern accomplishments, but on its "indomitable will" to survive, and he equated Israel's survival with its capacity to avert a second Holocaust. Carter asserted that America's commitment to establishing the nation of Israel and to protecting it from future threats arose spontaneously from the encounter with the death camps at the end of World War II and had continued unbroken into the present.[4]

Carter's speech sounds so familiar today that it may be hard to believe how novel it was at the time. Carter was the first American president to place the Holocaust at the center of America's commitment to Israel and to claim culpability for past inaction as a moral guide to present policy. His predecessors in the Oval Office rarely called attention to the Holocaust. As the first U.S. president to visit Israel, Richard Nixon only reluctantly agreed to visit Yad Vashem, Israel's Holocaust memorial. He understood the rearming of Israel during the 1973 Yom Kippur War as a strategic move against the Soviet Union and did not describe it as a mission to save Israel from destruction. President Lyndon Johnson, in his warmest professions of friendship, identified Israel as a frontier state like Texas, and in the lead-up to the Six-Day War, neither he nor his advisors referred to Israel as a potential victim of genocide. Only after Carter's presidency did U.S. presidents routinely invoke the Holocaust as the ethical foundation of their relationship with Israel. This change reflected a shift that was going on in American culture about how the Holocaust was viewed, a shift that began in the 1960s and accelerated in the 1970s. In this way, American presidents have followed public discourse about the Holocaust as much as they have shaped it.[5]

"The Holocaust" as an overarching concept and a proper noun for the systematic Nazi extermination of European Jews did not come into general American circulation until the 1970s, as historian Peter Novick and others have shown. At the end of World War II, the American public did not single out the "Final Solution" as a Jewish catastrophe separate from the overall Nazi carnage that afflicted Europe. Jews mourned their dead within their own communities, while the wider public incorporated Jewish suffering into a broader conception of Nazi barbarism and the universal horrors of war. According to this narrative, the United States and its allies soundly defeated the Nazi regime, brought its crimes to justice, and consigned its atrocities to the dark ages of the past. Postwar anxiety about the future focused on the atomic bombs dropped on Hiroshima and Nagasaki, which evoked fears of imminent catastrophe—that American cities could be subject to the same inferno. Although it is a common assumption that World War II led to the universal determination to prevent future genocides, in the United States at the time, victory over Nazism was regarded as representing the end of an era; it was Hiroshima that had inaugurated a fearsome new age.[6]

Outrage at the Nazi slaughter of Jews was indeed central to postwar support for establishing a Jewish state and to the subsequent narrative about its founding, as we saw in previous chapters. But supporters of the Zionist movement and the early Israeli state did not express fear of a resurgent genocide. Liberal Zionist supporters in the 1940s did not rest their case for a state on the need to protect Jews from future extermination, nor did their accounts of the battles of 1948 raise the threat of annihilation. Leon Uris's *Exodus* was not haunted by the specter of a new Holocaust. For supporters of Israel in the 1940s and 1950s, the Nazi genocide explained the historical origins of the Jewish state but did not represent a threat to its ongoing existence.

As Nazi atrocities receded into the past, the emergence of Holocaust consciousness involved an important shift in its temporal meaning. The Holocaust entered public awareness not only as a horrific event in the past, but as an event that might be repeated in the imminent future. A related geographic shift from Europe to the Middle East made the Jewish state the locus of this threatening new catastrophe. This fear of a second Holocaust started in Israel in the 1960s after the trial of the Nazi official Adolf Eichmann in 1962 and during the lead-up to the Six-Day War in 1967.[7] The idea entered American public discourse along with the growth of Holocaust memory in the following decade. According to this way of thinking, the Nazi extermination of Jews not only explained Israel's historical origins, but also signified an impending threat to its future survival. In 1948, Americans celebrated Israel's creation as the death knell for Nazism, but three decades later, they treated the Holocaust as a timeless template for Israel's existential vulnerability, with Arabs viewed as reincarnated Nazis.

The Holocaust came to represent the precariousness of Israel's survival at a time when the new country was becoming more militarily secure in the region. Seeing Israel as the legacy of the Holocaust contributed to the sense of its vulnerability as a perpetual victim of Arab aggression. Novick contends that the Yom Kippur War awakened fears of Israel's demise among American Jews because of the surprise attack, launched on the holiest day of the year, and the unexpectedly high number of Israeli casualties—despite the fact that Egyptian and Syrian troops never advanced beyond their own territories that had been captured in 1967, and that the United States came to Israel's aid with a massive airlift of weapons. As in the aftermath of the Six-Day War, talk of annihilation increased in proportion to the decisiveness of Israel's victory. As deeply felt as these fears were, pro-Israel organizations were equally alarmed by international criticism of Israel as an oppressive occupying power, and by the international consensus that Israel should relinquish to Palestinian rule the territories it had conquered in 1967. A representative publication is *The New Anti-Semitism,* written by Arnold Forster and Benjamin Epstein of the Anti-Defamation League and published in 1974, which argued that condemnation of Israel arose not from opposition to Israeli policy in the occupied territories, but from the world's forgetting about Jewish victimization in the Holocaust. Forster and Epstein insisted that the world needed to be reminded of the Holocaust, for fear that failure to remember it would diminish support for Israel and thus threaten Jews with a new genocide in the Middle East.[8]

The idea that a second Holocaust threatened to destroy Israel did not abate with the massive increase in U.S. aid under Presidents Nixon and Reagan, or when the peace treaty with Egypt removed its military threat in 1979, or when the Israeli government annexed the Golan Heights in 1981, or when it invaded Lebanon in 1978 and 1982. On the contrary, talk of a new Holocaust increased as Israeli military power grew, and Holocaust analogies often justified the exercise of that power. When Menachem Begin became prime minister in 1977, his fiery rhetoric introduced this way of thinking to the American media. Begin's worldview had been shaped profoundly by his personal losses in the Holocaust, and he saw any threat to Israel in the present through the lens of the Nazi genocide. Begin's views of the Holocaust strongly influenced the basic doctrine of the Israeli government, and this doctrine also became central to American views of Israel.[9]

In 1979, Israel launched a surprise attack on an Iraqi nuclear reactor and received widespread condemnation for violating international law. Begin justified the attack as a preemption of future genocide. The lesson he took from the Holocaust was not only that Jews were eternal victims, but also that it was impossible to trust anyone else to protect them. Israel alone had both the moral obligation and the right to defend itself by any means necessary. In this way of thinking, if total annihilation always imperiled Israel, then no military action could ever be judged as excessive. When the Reagan administration announced that Israel might have breached an arms agreement by using American fighter jets in the raid, Begin responded by claiming that Israel had a right to guard its children, since one million children had been killed with poison gas by the Germans and "radioactivity is also poison." If Israel hadn't bombed the plant, he argued, "another Holocaust would have happened to Israel and her people."[10] Even though the association between nuclear power plants and gas chambers may have seemed dubious, this way of framing Israel's military ventures appealed to the moral clarity of a struggle against evil epitomized by the Holocaust.

Begin made his most impassioned appeals to Holocaust memory during the 1982 invasion of Lebanon, equating Palestinians with Nazis intent on committing genocide and identifying Israelis as the true victims in the war. In a widely publicized letter to President Reagan, Begin wrote, "I feel as a prime minister empowered to instruct a valiant army facing 'Berlin' where, amongst innocent civilians, Hitler and his henchmen hide in a bunker deep beneath the surface. My generation, dear Ron, swore on the altar of God that whoever proclaims his intent to destroy the Jewish state or the Jewish people seals his fate so what happened in Berlin . . . will never happen again." In this intimate public address, Begin blamed civilian causalities on the current unnamed Hitler. World War II was more than a metaphor for Begin, more even than an example of the past illuminating the present. A potential Holocaust hid beneath the surface of the present, poised to rear up at any moment if Israel failed to stop it. At a time when Israeli forces faced international criticism for brutality, Begin deemed them "valiant" because they were battling Nazis to avert another Holocaust.[11]

To claim exclusive possession of the Holocaust as a living analogy entailed policing its usage by others. In an August 1982 interview, Begin expressed outrage at Reagan for using the word "holocaust" to describe Israel's day-long bombardment of West Beirut. Although one sense of the English word does mean massive destruction especially by fire, and would be a fitting description for the conflagration caused by the bombing that day, Begin claimed that the word should only be used in its more exclusive sense, to refer to the Nazi genocide of Jews. He accused Reagan of personally hurting him by using that word and asserted that only he knew "what is a holocaust." As proof he displayed the iconic photograph of a frightened young boy, hands raised in the air, taken during the roundup of Jews in the Warsaw Ghetto. Begin explained that Israelis never intentionally targeted civilians, but that the PLO placed them in danger by hiding military installations among them. Israelis always mourned the killing of children, he asserted, in stark contrast to both Nazis and Palestinian terrorists, who celebrated the murder of Jewish children.[12]

In 1982, Begin used the high moral ground of the Holocaust to deflect widespread criticism of Israel's use of force against Palestinian and Lebanese civilians. He also drew on Nazi analogies to explain why he would not negotiate with the PLO leaders, even if they accepted Israel's right to exist: "I wouldn't believe Hitler, or Goering or Goebbels, and I will not believe Mr. Arafat, or Farouk Khaddoumi, or Abu Iyad." For Begin and his Likud Party, which had every intention of keeping the occupied territories—land that they called Greater Israel—nothing was more threatening than the Palestinians' willingness to compromise. Begin thus placed out of bounds any negotiations with a group of men who, he claimed, had no other aim than to exterminate Jews once again.[13]

Begin's righteous deployment of the Holocaust provoked a backlash. Critics of the war used their own Holocaust references to undercut his high moral ground, particularly after the massacre at Sabra and Shatila. "To a country that rose out of Hitler's death camps," wrote journalist David Shipler, "the answers 'We did not do it' and 'We did not know' are not enough." But the focus on Begin's rhetorical excess did not succeed in dislodging the narrative that Israel was threatened by a second Holocaust. It had taken hold before the invasion of Lebanon in distinctly American idioms that would continue to invest Begin's strident nationalism with universal significance. That the first American president to endorse Palestinian rights tried to assuage Israeli and Jewish objections by proposing a Holocaust memorial suggests how the Holocaust would be used in portraying a Palestinian homeland as an existential threat to the Jewish homeland.[14]

In 1978, as we saw, the presidential commission established by Carter helped to impress upon the American public the idea that the Holocaust was not only a past event of immeasurable terror, but that it also inextricably linked the United States to the birth of Israel and to current threats to the country's existence. The other major event that brought the Holocaust to the attention of Americans that year was the miniseries *Holocaust,* which tens of millions of Americans watched on TV for four consecutive nights in April 1978. For many viewers, the epic story of an upper-class, assimilated Jewish family from Berlin would have provided their first encounter with an overarching narrative of the Holocaust that tied together the different landmarks of the Nazis' mass extermination of European Jews: Kristallnacht, Babi Yar, the Warsaw Ghetto, Buchenwald, Theresienstadt, Auschwitz. Although the nine-and-a-half-hour series ends where *Exodus* begins, with the sole surviving Jewish character about to take a group of orphans to Palestine, Israel's impending creation is foreshadowed throughout the series.[15]

In the final scene, a Mossad agent—someone much like Ari Ben Canaan—recruits the only remaining member of the Weiss family, Rudi, to escort the orphaned refugees on an illegal voyage to Palestine. The agent tells Rudi that the Jewish Agency in Palestine already knows his history and has singled him out for this role. The audience has similarly viewed Rudy as a proto-Israeli throughout the film because of his actions during the war. In contrast to the rest of his family, who remain naïvely loyal to German culture and are unable to resist their fate, Rudy's independent fighting spirit spurs him to flee Germany and join a band of Ukrainian Jewish partisans, with whom he later leads an armed rebellion in Sobibór concentration camp. Rudy, however, knows little of the Zionist movement. When he teases his young Czech wife about her silly dreams of growing oranges in Palestine, viewers understand that these dreams will indeed come true. Rudi's ignorance of Zionism lends an organic quality to the idea that he is emigrating to his true homeland. That Jewish fighters in Europe would naturally become Israelis is suggested by scenes in the Warsaw Ghetto, where leaders of the uprising unfurl an Israeli flag. Although the story ends three years before the founding of the state, its conclusion gestures to the birth of the nation as the inevitable redemption of immeasurable suffering.

The miniseries linked the Holocaust to Israel's founding as a historical and moral necessity. It was accompanied by a torrent of promotional publicity, guides for schools and churches, and follow-up polls, and much of the pedagogical material included information about the significance of present-day Israel. The playwright of the miniseries, Gerald Green, wrote a novelized version, serialized by many newspapers, with over a million paperback copies sent to bookstores two weeks in advance of the broadcast. The novel emphatically connects the Holocaust to Israel's current danger. It begins in Israel with an older Rudi Weiss teaching guerrilla warfare to his sons, who are defending their kibbutz from Syrian bombardment. The American Jewish Committee commissioned a nationwide survey on the viewing experience of the miniseries. In addition to questions on what viewers had learned about history and how the series affected their attitudes toward Jews, it included questions about how the series affected viewers' attitudes toward the current situation in the Middle East. Results of the survey showed that "viewers are more sympathetic to Israel than nonviewers" and that viewers "see some sense in American Jewish support of Israel." In another informal survey, a Lutheran magazine asked its readers the question: "How has *Holocaust* affected or focused your faith?" To "many Christians and non-Christians the answer was simple": now they "understand the passion behind the Jewish sentiment behind Israel." Recognition of the Holocaust as a traumatic memory did more than explain the psychology of American Jews—why, for instance, they might fear attacks on Israel. It also explained how the Holocaust signified a living threat to Israel's existence and why non-Jews should feel obligated to support Israel.[16]

This was the message promulgated by the American Israel Public Affairs Committee (AIPAC), which sent a copy of the novel to every member of Congress as part of an intense lobbying campaign against a plan to sell aircraft to Saudi Arabia. An editorial in AIPAC's biweekly journal stated that Green's novel and the miniseries "should make all Americans more aware of the moral imperative of America's commitment to Israel's capacity to defend its citizens."[17] For AIPAC, the Holocaust was a new item in its promotional repertoire. The word first appeared in the index of its biweekly *Near East Report* in 1979. Not until 1983 did the "AIPAC Policy Statement" include a reference to the Holocaust. To earlier assertions about shared ideals and strategic assets, the 1983 statement added that "the United States recognized Israel's role in providing a safe home for victims of the Holocaust and for Jews persecuted everywhere." As popular culture was becoming more widely acquainted with the Holocaust, AIPAC mustered these associations to identify Israel with the survivors of the Holocaust, the same year it was countering pro-Palestinian views on American campuses in the wake of the Lebanon War.[18]

Never Again

Elie Wiesel was the public figure who most forcefully conveyed to the American public the living presence of the Holocaust and the continuing threat that it posed to the existence of Israel. He drew on the authority of his personal trauma as a young prisoner at Auschwitz and Buchenwald and on his life's commitment to bear witness to the unspeakable atrocities inflicted on Jews. With his numinous presence, his expression of moral angst, his haunted voice, and the anguish etched in the lines of his face, he personified the authenticity of the Holocaust survivor. His own rise to public prominence was inseparable from the rise of Holocaust memory in American public awareness. Millions of schoolchildren read his autobiographical book, *Night*; he advised American presidents and in 1985 famously chastised President Reagan for planning a state visit to a German military cemetery. He accompanied world leaders and celebrities on pilgrimages to the sites of concentration camps, and in 1986 he was awarded the Nobel Peace Prize.

Wiesel insisted on the uniquely Jewish nature of the Holocaust. He often stated that the Holocaust should transcend politics and that its representation in popular culture, such as in the TV miniseries, trivialized its significance. He spoke of the Holocaust in semireligious terms as an ineffable and timeless catastrophe that eternally threatened to recur. Wiesel related the exceptional evil of the Holocaust to Israel's exceptional morality and to the unique threats to its existence. He shared Begin's vigorous nationalism and right-wing views, but at the same time, he translated Jewish nationalism into the language of universal humanism. By attributing both uniqueness and exemplarity to the Holocaust, he turned it into a historical yardstick by which to measure other human suffering.

The first National Civil Holocaust Commemoration Ceremony was held on April 24, 1979, at the U.S. Capitol Rotunda. Both Wiesel and President Carter addressed the gathering. Wiesel's speech was entitled "The Holocaust: Beginning or End?" His questions implied the

Elie Wiesel (*right*), chairman of the President's Commission on the Holocaust, presents President Jimmy Carter (*left*) with the panel's final report, September 27, 1979.

answer: "Was it the final convulsion of demonic forces in history? A paroxysm of centuries-old bigotry and hatred? Or, on the contrary, a momentous warning of things to come?" Wiesel pointed to violence against Israel as primary evidence of the beginning of a new horror. Thirty years after the liberation of the camps, he said, we witness "more wars, new racial hostilities, and an awakening of Nazism on all five continents. Little did we know that, in our lifetime, books would appear in many languages offering so-called 'proof' that the Holocaust never occurred, that our parents, our friends did not die there. Little did we know that Jewish children would again be murdered, in cold blood, by killers in Israel." Wiesel implied that acts of terrorism against Israel, in addition to Holocaust denial, were signs that the Holocaust had not fully ended.[19]

At this same ceremony, President Carter took a more universal approach than Wiesel, who emphasized the uniqueness of Jewish suffering and the culpability of those who had abandoned the Jews to the slaughter. For Carter, the memory of this same failure taught that "human rights and human dignity are indivisible. America must, and always will, speak out in the defense of human rights not only in our own country, but around the world." Carter agreed with Wiesel about the looming risk of a new genocide—but not only to Jews in Israel. Carter urged the Senate to "take a long overdue step" and ratify the Convention on the Prevention and Punishment of Genocide, which had been adopted by the United Nations in 1948. "Without concrete action," he stated, "our words are hollow. Let us signify by deed as well as by word that the American people will never forget."[20]

In these founding speeches and documents for the national memorial, Carter and Wiesel wove together a powerful public idiom of Holocaust awareness that would resonate for years to come. They conjoined the particularity of the mass slaughter of Jews under the Nazis with the ongoing threat to Israel, and they tied the universal imperative to prevent future genocides with an American obligation to lead an international movement for human rights. As Carter declared at the presentation of the commission's final report, "Out of our memory and understanding of the Holocaust we must forge an unshakeable oath with all civilized people that never again will the world stand silent, never again will the world look the other way or fail to act in time to prevent this terrible crime of genocide."[21]

The slogan "Never Again" resounded for many who came of age in the 1980s and 1990s as a stirring ethical imperative to fight for human rights and to prevent future genocides, and young human rights activists denounced their governments' hypocrisy for failing to uphold this imperative in Rwanda and the former Yugoslavia.[22] "Never Again," however, did not originate in this universalist milieu; it was invented in 1970 by Rabbi Meir Kahane, a right-wing Jewish nationalist from Brooklyn, to serve as the motto of the militant Jewish Defense League (JDL). The phrase, which was often used by the Save Soviet Jewry movement, expressed the JDL's confrontational spirit, urging combative retaliation rather than powerless capitulation. When Kahane emigrated to Israel, his views were deemed so extreme that Israel banned the political party he founded there for its "Nazi-like," "racist," and "undemocratic positions."[23]

In the transformation of its use from advocating Jewish self-defense to preventing genocide anywhere on earth, the inspiring refrain "Never Again" made a conceptual leap that showed its ability to conform to different political meanings. What the nationalist and universalist paradigms do share is the characterization of the Holocaust both as a historical catastrophe that is never quite past, and as a portent of evil that is ever imminent. In the JDL's original nationalist meaning, the heritage of the Nazi genocide as the culmination of centuries of persecution demanded vigilance and justified violence to defend Jews everywhere and to avert the annihilation of the Jewish state. In its adaptation by human rights advocates, knowledge of the Holocaust as the universal paradigm of evil required international vigilance and intervention—diplomatic or military—to prevent the occurrence of future genocides worldwide. The nationalism that spawned this phrase, however, would never be completely purged from it, even when used in a universalist sense. This strange genealogy of "Never Again" points to certain tensions that came into play in the political mobilization of Holocaust memory as a harbinger of the future. One is the contradiction between nationalist and universalist applications; another is that between viewing Jewish victimhood as the universal standard for measuring genocide and exempting Israel from those universal standards that it deems threaten its survival.[24]

Elie Wiesel played a key role in propagating the different meanings of "Never Again" among various religious and human rights organizations and political contexts. He skillfully managed—or juggled—the tension between the universal and the particular by espousing the uniqueness of Jewish suffering and privileging Israeli vulnerability, even as he expanded the Holocaust's lessons to other human rights causes and made "Never Again" a slogan for the worldwide prevention of genocide.

As a universal symbol, the Holocaust garnered what Alan Mintz has called "moral prestige," becoming the standard for all other mass suffering. For Wiesel, this moral prestige related to his view of Israel as both exceptionally vulnerable and morally superior. For him, the exemplary evil of the Holocaust could be redeemed by the exemplary morality of the State of Israel. Wiesel made this linkage less jarring than Begin had by speaking in the idiom of universal humanism rather than aggressive nationalism. The uniqueness of Jewish victimization in the

Holocaust, Wiesel taught, had universal significance, and the redemption of humankind after the war was inseparable from the specific deliverance of the Jewish people in Israel. As he stated when he presented the report of the president's commission to President Carter in 1979, "Birkenau arouses man's most secret anguish. Jerusalem symbolizes our most fervent hope, and, therefore, we are attached to Jerusalem in such love and admiration." Avoiding the political conflict over Israel's plans to annex East Jerusalem, he implied that universal "anguish" sanctioned attachment to a particular place. Wiesel saw no contradiction between the particular and the universal, between "Never Again" as a vow to protect Israel from existential threats and as an imperative to prevent genocide around the world.[25]

Wiesel used his moral authority to support victims of contemporary atrocities: he spoke out on behalf of starving Biafrans, the millions of Cambodians murdered by the Pol Pot regime, Vietnamese refugees, the indigenous Aché people being exterminated in Paraguay, and Bosnians in the former Yugoslavia. But when it came to the situation in the Middle East, he prevaricated.

Wiesel's commitment to the paradigmatic nature of the Holocaust put him in a double bind: he would have to acknowledge Palestinian suffering, even as he disavowed it. In his 1978 essay "To a Young Palestinian Arab," Wiesel draws on his own losses in the Holocaust to express sympathy for the Palestinian tragedy of displacement and homelessness. In striving for balance, he faults Arabs for not recognizing that the Jews' suffering in the Holocaust gave them the right to a sovereign state. His essay professes an aversion to "scorekeeping" for comparative pain, but he nonetheless constructs a moral hierarchy in which Palestinian suffering has devolved into vengeful violence, while Israelis have transformed their traumatic past into a higher spiritual calling. Jewish virtue, he claims, lies in the survivors' refusing to take vengeance on their oppressors in Europe and in the special Jewish capacity to turn their own trauma into empathy for the suffering of others. Wiesel exemplifies this sentiment himself: "I do feel responsible for what happened to you, but not for what you chose to do as a result of what happened to you. I feel responsible for your sorrow, but not for the way you use it, for in its name you have massacred innocent people, slaughtered children." Ignoring Israeli violence against innocent people and Palestinian children, Wiesel claims that the Holocaust taught Israelis to respect the sanctity of life, while the Palestinians' tragedy debased them into supporting the murder of innocents.[26]

Wiesel chose not to speak out against the invasion of Lebanon or the Sabra and Shatila massacre. Instead, he mobilized the exceptionalism of the Holocaust to defend Israel as the victim of anti-Semitism. In an interview with *People* magazine in November 1982, he said that that year had been the hardest one in his life since 1945, not because of the war, but because of the global resurgence of anti-Semitism that it had unleashed. When asked how he felt about Begin using the Holocaust to justify Israeli actions, he responded that he objected to anyone using the Holocaust for political reasons, and that the word had become too "fashionable" and thus too widely available. He believed that only people who loved Israel had the right to criticize it, while all others condemned it with suspicious "relish." Wiesel never mentioned Begin; rather, he condemned the PLO observer to the UN for "speaking about 'Judeo-Nazis'—my God, the blasphemy, the obscenity of putting these words together." He did not mention that this term had first been used by an Israeli scholar, Yeshayahu Leibowitz, who created a stir by describing the war as a "Judeo-Nazi policy."[27] For Wiesel, the worst sin in using Nazi analogies was the attempt, in his words, to "demystify the Holocaust. Meaning, in a way, to take it away from the Jewish people." Indeed, the Holocaust could provide the basis for empathy with the suffering of others; but "paradoxically," as he said, "only when we tell the story of what happened to the Jewish people can we save other people." Thus, he believed that using Holocaust analogies to depict Palestinian and Lebanese suffering at the hands of the Israeli military amounted to a kind of theft and was evidence of a resurgence of anti-Semitism.[28]

Wiesel's moral authority derived from his status as a Holocaust survivor, an identity that was gaining prestige in American society with the spread of Holocaust awareness. In the *People* interview, Wiesel backed up his own observations by noting that friends of his who were also survivors were having nervous breakdowns, and even committing suicide, "all reacting to the anti-Semitism that was a reaction to Lebanon and the massacre." The image of the survivor played an important role in rehabilitating Israel's moral image in the wake of Lebanon, as the country became no longer primarily identified with its youthful pioneers, or idealistic soldiers, but with the noble survivors who had rebuilt their lives along with the country. Indeed, the *Report of the President's Commission on the Holocaust* identified the United States along with Israel as a site of rebirth for Holocaust survivors, and it cited the need to preserve their memories as a primary reason for creating an American memorial to the Holocaust.

In April 1983, at the first American meeting of the Gathering of Jewish Holocaust Survivors and Their Descendants, Vice President George H. W. Bush presented to Elie Wiesel a symbolic key to the proposed new Holocaust museum. The conveners cautiously asserted that the event was "strictly a nonpolitical affair" in relation to Israel. But they nonetheless underlined Israel's vulnerability as the key message. An organizer told the *Washington Post* that the Holocaust was "a lesson to the world that it can happen again if we will not be watchful. If we will not pay attention to small incidents." He explained that "years ago they used to call it anti-Semitism; today they call it anti-Zionism, but actually it's the same thing."[29]

In the *Jerusalem Post,* Wolf Blitzer wrote of this gathering as though the Holocaust had always formed the basis for American attachment to Israel, support that transcended all strategic and political considerations. Although he had recently called the Sabra and Shatila massacre a disaster for Israel's "high moral image in Washington," which would take years to repair, he clearly saw the rejuvenating potency of this reunion of Holocaust survivors. The organizers "did not have to use a sledgehammer to press their point for strong U.S. backing for Israel," he wrote. In the closing ceremony at the Washington Monument, President Reagan linked America and Israel as sites of redemption, promising the survivors that "the security of your safe havens, here and in Israel, will never be compromised." The mayor of New York City, Ed Koch, condemned the PLO as terrorists "attempting to finish what Hitler had started." Though thousands of attendees had other concerns—to share their traumatic stories, to locate lost friends and relatives—the public face of this "nonpolitical" event placed Israel at the top of the agenda. As the figure of the survivor gained public visibility and social esteem, the aura of the survivor amplified Israel's existential peril. Any danger faced by the country was rendered as threatening its very existence rather than as threatening the kinds of losses that any people would dread as a result of armed conflict: loss of lives and territory, damage to its army, its cities, or its economy. In Israel's case, evocation of the Holocaust transformed the fear of loss into the prospect of extinction.[30]

The equation of criticism of Israel and anti-Zionism with anti-Semitism and Nazism intensified with the temporal shift in the significance of the Holocaust. In the context of an imminent threat, anti-Semitism started to be viewed less as a prejudice that education and awareness could undo, or as a form of discrimination that could be legally challenged, and more as an ever-present genocidal urge to kill Jews and destroy their state.

In the 1980s, as Palestinians became visible to more Americans as victims of Israeli aggression and as a people struggling for human rights and a national homeland, Israel's staunchest supporters pushed back to portray them as Nazis intent on committing a second genocide. During the groundbreaking ceremony for the Holocaust Museum in 1985, for instance, Wiesel invoked the Holocaust to decry the murder of Leon Klinghoffer, a disabled Jewish American who was shot and thrown off the Mediterranean cruise ship *Achille Lauro* by members of the Palestine Liberation Front. A *Washington Post* story on Klinghoffer's funeral bore the headline "Holocaust of One." Equating terrorist acts committed by Palestinians with the Nazi Holocaust mustered great emotional power through the shared focus on innocent Jewish victims.[31]

Terrorist violence by nonstate actors, no matter how heinous, lacks the powerful state organization behind the systematic industrialized violence that characterized the Nazi slaughter of millions. Nonetheless, the repeated analogy between terrorism and the Holocaust had the powerful effect of tarring the entire Palestinian cause as a hateful reincarnation of the Nazi project to exterminate the Jews. At a time when the Carter and Reagan administrations continued Kissinger's pledge to Israel not to speak directly to the PLO, the conflation of Palestinians with terrorism and Nazism contributed to the public perception of the illegitimacy of the PLO and the cause it represented.[32]

In a universalist mode, Wiesel pulled back from this equation when he received the Nobel Peace Prize in 1986 as a "messenger to mankind," one of the world's "most important spiritual leaders and guides."[33] He interwove a plea for Israel into his most passionate appeal for universal human rights. In his acceptance speech, he stated that having endured the world's indifference to the Nazi genocide, he "swore never to be silent whenever and wherever human beings endure suffering and humiliation." His particular trauma as a Jewish survivor of the death camps made him abhor the abuse of human rights across the political spectrum, from apartheid in South Africa to the repression of dissidents in the Soviet bloc, to the situation of the Palestinians. Yet he qualified his sympathy for the Palestinians, "to whose plight I am sensitive, but whose methods I deplore when they lead to violence." Though he expressed sorrow for the losses on both sides and advocated peace between the two peoples, he condemned Palestinian terrorism alone for prolonging the conflict, and defended Israel with reference to the threat of a future Holocaust: "Let Israel be given a chance, let hatred and danger be removed from her horizons, and there will be peace in and around the Holy Land. Please understand my deep and total commitment to Israel: if you could remember what I remember, you *would* understand. Israel is the only nation in the world whose very existence is threatened." In this speech devoted to the universal message of the Jewish catastrophe, Wiesel evoked Holocaust memory as evidence of Israel's future vulnerability, and he portrayed Israel, under the eternal shadow of the Holocaust, as the exemplar of universal suffering.[34]

Two years later Wiesel found himself in a sticky moral dilemma, in the face of Israel's aggression toward Palestinians during the first intifada. Substituting "feeling" for the real danger he had insisted upon in 1986, he wrote in a *New York Times* op-ed that "Israel is the only country that feels its existence threatened." Describing his visit to Gaza during the uprising, Wiesel acknowledged the Palestinian right to fight for self-determination and criticized what he saw as the occasional excesses of Israeli violence. But his essay defends the essential morality of Israel against doubters. He writes, "Israel has not 'lost its soul.' Its soldiers are not sadists. They do not enjoy fighting stone-throwing adolescents. But confronted by them, what should a soldier do? Retreat? How far? Run away? Where?" The implication is that the soldiers are fighting for their existence. They have nowhere else to go. Although Wiesel contends that Israel should not be above criticism, he roundly criticizes its critics for describing the state as a colonial power, like France in Algeria or the United States in Vietnam. Even worse are those who compare Israeli's policies to Hitler's in Nazi Germany: "How are we to convince Israel's political adversaries that the Holocaust is beyond politics and beyond analogies?" he asks. For Wiesel, to see Israel as being under the existential threat of a new Holocaust was not a political analogy, but a truth that united feeling and reality. By disavowing the political uses of the Holocaust, he deployed the Holocaust politically to exempt Israel from censure and to police legitimate Holocaust references. Wiesel found the desire to annihilate Jews lurking in every form of Palestinian resistance, including not only terrorism and stone-throwing, but even poetry. He read Mahmoud Darwish's impassioned poem "Those Who Pass between Fleeting Words," which calls for Israelis to abandon Palestine to its people, as akin to violence and murder. Israel remained morally heroic to Wiesel because of its willingness to sue for peace despite the looming specter of the Holocaust that Palestinians represented.[35]

Many Americans saw through Wiesel's defense of Israel's policies, and some accused him of hypocrisy. On the same page of the *New York Times* on which Wiesel's editorial appeared, Anthony Lewis blamed Israel for intransigence and urged it to negotiate with the PLO. In a letter published in the *New York Review of Books,* Rabbi Arthur Hertzberg challenged Wiesel to apply to Israel the moral strictures he had gleaned from the Holocaust. The Holocaust taught Wiesel that one should never again remain silent in the face of human suffering, but Wiesel remained silent in the face of Israelis beating and shooting unarmed youth, and in the face of racist characterizations of Palestinians by a chief of staff of the IDF as "drugged cockroaches." Hertzberg implored him to break a silence that constituted a defense of Israel's right-wing policies, and to speak out against Israel's treatment of Palestinians. Where Wiesel mobilized Holocaust memory to defend Israel from its critics, Hertzberg joined other Jews who advocated that the memory of their own traumatic past should guide them toward empathy and acceptance of responsibility for the suffering of Palestinians under Israeli rule.[36]

Some American Jews went even further and called for separating the Holocaust altogether from the politics of the Middle East. In spite of the origins of the proposal for a national Holocaust memorial, some of its planners wanted to divorce its mission from overt partisanship for Israel. One proponent of this separation was Michael Berenbaum, who drafted the original report of the President's Commission on the Holocaust, served as project director from 1988 to 1993, and played a vocal role in interpreting its purpose to the public. Berenbaum had a strong attachment to Israel: he volunteered there during the Six-Day War, and he was the Jewish community representative in Washington, D.C., who observed the foreign desk of the *Washington Post* during the Lebanon War in 1982. Later in the 1980s, however, he witnessed Israel losing its mystique among American Jews and becoming a controversial issue filled with moral ambiguity. The Holocaust, he believed, could take Israel's place as the moral center that unified American Jews. The planning and construction of the Holocaust Museum, wrote Berenbaum, accompanied "the events of the 1980's [which] will slowly bring to an end the Israeli-centered period for American Jews." For his generation, those events included the Lebanon fiasco, the Palestinian uprising, and the espionage scandal of Jonathan Pollard, a Jewish American intelligence analyst who was sentenced to life in prison for spying on the United States for Israel. With Israel having become a divisive subject among American Jews, Holocaust memory appeared to supply a more secure anchor point for bringing the Jewish community together around a shared traumatic past.[37]

Liberation or Abandonment?

To raise a memorial to a European genocide on the secular but sacred space of the National Mall required enormous cultural work—nothing less than the transformation of the Holocaust into an element of American heritage. Berenbaum, for one, believed that the Holocaust could provide a center of moral unity not only for Jews, but for all Americans. He made the case that a national museum would transform the history of a uniquely Jewish catastrophe into a universal civics lesson. The story of the Holocaust, he wrote, "had to be told in such a way that it would resonate not only with the survivor in New York and his children in Houston or San Francisco, but with a black leader from Atlanta, a midwestern farmer, or a northeastern industrialist." Americans from different social spheres with diverse values could unite against a common enemy in their recognition of the Holocaust as the paradigm of ultimate evil. Instruction in the Holocaust could teach the American values of "democracy, pluralism, respect for differences, individual responsibility, freedom from prejudice, and an abhorrence of racism." It could also help recalibrate America's moral compass, fractured by the social upheavals of the 1960s and 1970s and the depredations of the powerful in the Vietnam War and Watergate.[38]

The United States Holocaust Memorial Museum is the concrete symbol of the Americanization of the Holocaust, where visitors can see enlightened American values represented in stark contrast with the evil darkness of the Nazis. The Americanization process had two strands: a national narrative framed Americanism, with its values of democracy and tolerance, as the antithesis of Nazism, and a universal narrative framed the Holocaust as a paradigm of absolute evil, bearing lessons for protecting human rights and preventing future genocides. These narratives came together in a redemptive vision of the United States as the global guarantor of human rights and the protector of the Jewish state from future Holocausts.[39]

Many of the members of the president's commission tasked with planning the memorial wanted to keep it free from overt partisanship for Israel, and some even objected to having the president of Israel speak at the opening ceremonies in 1993.[40] America's special relationship with Israel, however, was inseparable from the conception of the memorial and was woven into the framework of the exhibits. The idea of the Holocaust's unique relation to Israel—as the condition of its birth and the threat of its apocalyptic end—was not superseded by Americanization or universalization. By presenting Nazism as the antithesis of American values, the museum paired Israel and America as sites of redemption, democratic havens where survivors were reborn and memory was revered. The U.S. commitment to Israel proved essential to two basic themes of the museum: America's opposition to Nazism, and vigilance against future genocide.

At the grand opening of the museum in 1993, speakers articulated its contradictory and complementary meanings. President Clinton made explicit an organic connection between the Holocaust's nationalist and universalist implications. "The Holocaust gave rise to the Universal Declaration of Human Rights, the charter of our common humanity," he asserted; "and it contributed, indeed made certain, the long overdue creation of the nation of Israel."[41] In this double myth of origins, the birth of an individual nation was imbued with the same lofty value as the creation of a global community that transcends national boundaries.

Clinton and the other international dignitaries spoke before a backdrop of fifteen brightly colored flags representing the units of the American armed forces that had liberated the concentration camps in 1945. The flags, which would become part of the permanent exhibit, represented a central narrative in the Americanization of the Holocaust. "Our military forces," stated Clinton, "alongside the allied armies, played the decisive role in bringing the Holocaust to an end. Overcoming the shock of discovery, they walked survivors from those dark, dark places into the sweet sunlight of redemption, soldiers and survivors being forever joined in history and humanity."[42]

On the same stage, Elie Wiesel presented a darker version of America's role in the war. He castigated the U.S. government for having failed to liberate Jews by refusing to bomb the concentration camps in Poland. "Why weren't the railways leading to [Auschwitz-]Birkenau bombed by Allied bombers?" he asked. "As long as I live I will not understand that. And why was there no public outcry of indignation and outrage?" According to this equally resonant narrative, the United States was not a liberator, but a guilty bystander that abetted the Nazi genocide by abandoning the Jews. Both narratives were part of the museum's rationale from the start.[43]

Liberator or failed rescuer? Which best describes America's role in the Holocaust? These two stories describe different historical moments with different actors, and they rely on different ways of thinking about history. "Liberation" might describe what ordinary soldiers witnessed at the war's end, and it offered a coherent framework for making sense of the brutal scenes that the soldiers and journalists first encountered in the death camps.[44] The decision not to bomb Auschwitz describes a government decision made at the highest echelon during the war. Both stories contributed retrospectively to making the Holocaust central to the American memory of World War II by giving Americans major roles to play in ending the slaughter—in one case a role that they carried out, and in the other a role that they failed to fulfill. Together, both narratives convey the same message not only about the past but also about the present and future: American military might is a virtuous force for liberating the oppressed from tyranny.

For the United States as well as Israel, Holocaust memory could restore an honorable picture of military force, which was suffering from disillusionment in both countries. For Israel, its identity as a community of Holocaust victims—in the past and potential future—justified its righteous exercise of violence during the Lebanon War and the first intifada. For the United States, the role of liberator and the imperative to rescue contributed to the idealization of World War II as the "good war" and its soldiers as the "Greatest Generation," to counteract deep cynicism about the overwhelming abuse of military power in Southeast Asia and to burnish the tarnished images of both the American soldier and the nation's military command.

The commemoration of American soldiers as liberators of concentration camps was made official in 1979, just as the president's commission presented its plans for the memorial. To mark the thirty-fourth anniversary of the liberation of Dachau by American troops, Congress designated April 28 and 29 as Days of Remembrance of the Victims of the Holocaust. President Carter asked Americans to "observe this solemn anniversary of the liberation of Dachau with appropriate study, prayers and commemoration as a tribute to the spirit of freedom, justice and compassion which Americans fought to preserve."[45] Americans were being asked to remember not only the victims of the Nazis' murderous regime, but also the nobility of American opposition to that regime.

In actuality, Americans were not the only, or even the primary, liberators of the death camps, and the operation was more haphazard than the word "liberation" implies. The Soviet Army was the first to reach a major extermination camp, Madjanek, and then to enter Auschwitz and other sites in the east, months before U.S. troops reached Buchenwald and Dachau. The U.S. Army command initially had no plans to free camp inmates, and soldiers who stumbled across the death camps reported feeling overcome, dazed, and even repulsed by the survivors they found there. At first, the army continued to use some of the camps as displaced persons camps. Retrospectively, the idea of liberation allows Americans to imagine their own intimate presence in history, to touch an unspeakable but monumental reality, and it offers glorification of the nation's altruistic purpose in fighting the war.

This idealization of the American soldier had great appeal during the Reagan era. As a presidential nominee, Reagan rejected the "Vietnam syndrome" and called that war a "noble cause." In his Days of Remembrance speech, Reagan proudly referred to the liberation of the camps as evidence of America's exceptional "genius for great and unselfish deeds," and he proclaimed that "into the hands of America, God has placed an afflicted mankind."[46] Reagan never failed to link America's magnanimity to its contemporary defense of Israel from the threat of a new Holocaust. Having rescued the Jews from the horrors of Nazism, America had an ongoing obligation to "a people whose country was reborn from the ashes of the Holocaust—a country that rightfully never takes its security or its survival for granted."[47] In the rhetoric of the Cold War, Reagan tied the American liberation of Jews from Nazi concentration camps to the current movement to free Soviet Jews from communist tyranny. In his speech at the ceremony laying the cornerstone of the Holocaust Museum, he called on the Soviet Union to "let these people go!"[48]

This theme is most dramatically embodied in the monument *Liberation*, created by sculptor Natan Rapoport and dedicated in May 1985 in Liberty State Park, New Jersey. The larger-than-life bronze sculpture depicts a young American soldier trudging with his head bowed and carrying a gaunt concentration camp victim in his arms, cradling him in a pieta-like position. The soldier's youthful chest merges with the emaciated ribs of the victim, "as if sharing one heart," according to the Department of Defense's *Guide to Days of Remembrance.* With the Statue of Liberty on its cover, this guide explains that the monument is "a symbol of the strong helping the weak, not persecuting them. It is a tribute to the best of America's dreams, freedom, compassion, bravery."[49] The official state resolution dedicating the monument explains that its purpose is "to recognize that our servicemen fought, not to conquer nor to be aggressors, but rather to rescue and restore freedom to those persecuted and oppressed."[50] This monument to the liberators of Holocaust victims displaces still-vivid memories of American war-making in Southeast Asia with an idealized model of the American GI from World War II as a strong and caring savior.[51]

Celebrating the liberation of Jewish survivors enhanced the belief in the good war as the standard of American virtue. George W. Bush, campaigning for president in 1999, claimed: "No one during World War II questioned what it meant to be 'American'"—it meant that "we were liberators, not conquerors. And when American soldiers hugged the survivors of death camps, and shared their tears, and welcomed them back from a nightmare world, our country was confirmed in its calling."[52] The theme of liberation accompanied a geographic shift in the focus of

Liberation, statue by Natan Rapoport, depicting a soldier carrying a World War II concentration camp survivor, at Liberty State Park in Jersey City, NJ.

popular history and fiction about World War II from the Pacific to the European theater. At a time when the Greatest Generation was rediscovered as a national legend, one could imagine from such statements that liberating the death camps had actually provided the motivation to enter World War II.

The union of American soldiers and Jewish survivors provides an overarching framework for the United States Holocaust Memorial Museum. The permanent exhibition starts with American GIs encountering

Buchenwald and ends with concentration camp survivors rebuilding their lives in Israel and the United States. In the architecture of the building itself, the narrative of liberation offers a stable reference point for the visitor's unsettling encounter with the history of Nazi atrocities. One entrance is flanked by the flags of the liberating troops, and presidential statements about the arrival of American soldiers at the camps are engraved on the other side. The vantage point of American GIs provides the opening image: visitors encounter shocking, wall-sized photographs of charred corpses in Buchenwald through the horrified eyes and bewildered commentaries of American soldiers. The museum represents American troops as paradigmatic witnesses to history, and witnessing becomes a heroic and morally imperative act. The story of liberation concludes with the survivors' deliverance to the twin havens of America and Israel. At the end of the exhibit, the story of liberation takes on an intimate domestic dimension through a touching interview with a middle-class American couple who met when his army unit liberated the camp where his future wife was being held. A video of the interview is shown in a small amphitheater lined with Jerusalem stone. This personal story takes place against the background of historical markers that unite America and Israel as welcoming sites of redemption. The exhibit of the postwar rebirth includes artifacts related to the founding of Israel—including photographs of the SS *Exodus* and a six-foot facsimile of the Israeli Declaration of Independence. The journey through the darkened exhibit space concludes as visitors ascend into the Hall of Remembrance. There an eternal light burns over buried soil from Holocaust sites and Arlington Cemetery, comingling for eternity the memory of the victims and the American troops who liberated the camps.[53]

The Holocaust Museum does not unreservedly celebrate the American role as liberator. It also indicts the United States for failing to rescue Jews by refusing to bomb Auschwitz. The question of whether bombing the gas chambers and railroad lines in 1944 was militarily feasible or could have saved lives is controversial among historians. No one, after all, can evaluate with certainty the effects of an event that did not occur. In honor of the opening of the Holocaust Museum, the Smithsonian Institution's National Air and Space Museum cosponsored a conference on the topic, where the debates were intense and the participants divided.[54] When the museum opened, it nonetheless enshrined the counterfactual narrative that lives would have been saved if the United States had bombed Auschwitz. It displayed an enlarged copy of a U.S. Air Force intelligence photograph of Auschwitz-Birkenau from May 1944 and a letter from Assistant Secretary of War John J. McCoy rejecting a "request by the World Jewish Congress to bomb the Auschwitz concentration camp." Rather than referring to the historians' debate, the caption asserted as fact that "although bombing Auschwitz would have killed many prisoners, it would also have halted the operation of the gas chambers and, ultimately, saved the lives of many more."[55]

The belief that the Roosevelt administration knowingly abandoned Jews by refusing to bomb Auschwitz operates as a kind of folk history with great emotional power.[56] The museum exhibit also criticizes the Allies for not taking in more refugees in the 1930s and 1940s. But outrage about the failure to bomb has had greater endurance than has indignation at restrictive immigration laws. The conviction that bombing Auschwitz would have rescued Jews draws on the moral clarity of hindsight and a magical belief in the efficacy of airpower. The assumption that the United States bears responsibility for not bombing Auschwitz gives added significance to the phrase "Never Again," and it has been mobilized for different political purposes. In the opening ceremonies for the museum, Wiesel raised this failure in order to exhort Clinton to "do something" in Kosovo. And when NATO carried out its controversial air strikes in 1999, Wiesel praised the United States for taking the kind of action in Kosovo that it had failed to take during World War II.[57] In a speech before AIPAC in 2012, the prime minister of Israel, Benjamin Netanyahu, held up copies of the 1944 letters in which the War Department rebuffed the request to bomb Auschwitz, to warn of the dangers of negotiating with Iran instead of using force.[58]

Liberating the death camps and failing to bomb Auschwitz may evoke starkly conflicting emotions of pride and guilt. But these narratives worked together to create a shared vision of American military power as a force for salvation—whether cradling the weak or blasting the strong. Mobilizing the memory of inaction during the 1940s reminded Americans in later decades that the United States has the obligation to redeem its past failure by wielding military power to protect the innocent and to defy tyrants. This argument has appealed to people across a range of political positions, from neoconservatives dedicated to restoring American imperial might to humanitarian interventionists committed to the "responsibility to protect."

American presidents have ritually accepted guilt for not doing more to rescue Jews during World War II. They have, however, refused to accept guilt for destruction caused by U.S. military action. President Carter, as we have seen, was the first president to express a sense of guilt for abandoning the Jews. He presented Wiesel with copies of the aerial photographs of Auschwitz-Birkenau when asking him to serve as chair of the commission. Yet Carter rejected American culpability for the devastating bombing of Vietnam and neighboring countries. He not only opposed monetary reparations, but rejected any moral obligation. "The destruction was mutual," he avowed. "We went to Vietnam without any desire to capture territory or impose American will on other people. . . . I don't feel we ought to apologize or castigate ourselves or assume the status of culpability." George McGovern and his supporters opposed Carter's position during the campaign for the Democratic presidential nomination, but their willingness to accept guilt about Vietnam was criticized as a symptom of national weakness and divisiveness. Carter claimed to represent a party seeking national renewal and unity.[59]

Why would Carter, and many Americans, reject guilt for the damage inflicted by American power in Southeast Asia but accept guilt for not wielding that power to stop the Holocaust? An obvious answer is that the latter is cost-free, though it has morally underwritten costly obligations to Israel. Historian Barbara Keys has argued that some Americans in the Carter era championed the cause of human rights abroad to revive a sense of national virtue that had been tarnished in the Vietnam War.[60] The American embrace of the Holocaust as their own history, with both guilt and pride, may have had a similar effect, allowing Americans to oppose atrocities that others committed in the past. A Holocaust Museum on the National Mall provided a painless way to both acknowledge American guilt and redeem American virtue.

The tension between failure and liberation in the story of the Holocaust was part of a bigger controversy about American history during the "culture wars" of the 1990s. The United States Holocaust Memorial Museum opened to mostly reverent reviews at a time when other major exhibits of American history were generating fierce controversy. The museum was not free from criticism—some questioned the priority of memorializing a European genocide when there were no national memorials to the genocide of Native Americans or the enslavement of African Americans. Others raised questions about whether the museum was turning the Holocaust into a spectacle. But these questions were mild compared with the criticism that erupted around the same time about two Smithsonian exhibitions, one on the western United States, and one on the use of the atomic bomb in World War II.

In 1991, the Smithsonian's National Museum of American Art mounted an exhibit titled *The West as America, Reinterpreting Images of the Frontier, 1820–1920*. Conservative critics blasted the exhibit for undercutting the noble myth of Manifest Destiny, and, instead, pointing to the way traditional images veiled the violence and dispossession of Native Americans in the march of westward expansion. The suggestion that familiar frontier images included racist depictions and glorified a history of displacement, pillage, and atrocity was an anathema to conservatives, who had no trouble accepting a national museum memorializing the victims of genocide committed by Nazis in Europe.[61]

The same year the Holocaust Museum opened, a greater controversy enveloped a Smithsonian announcement to organize an exhibit around the display of the *Enola Gay*, the plane that dropped the atomic bomb on Hiroshima. The curators planned an exhibit that would have explored the multiple causes and ramifications of the bomb, including the political and military reasons for using it, the unprecedented destruction it caused, and its role in ending the war. Veterans' groups and politicians raised such an outcry that they succeeded in shutting down the exhibit before it opened. Their argument, too, relied on a narrative of rescue with a speculative dimension asserted as fact: that bombing Hiroshima had saved the lives of thousands, perhaps even a million, American servicemen from dying in what would have been a bloody land invasion. These critics believed that to explore the damage wrought by the bomb and raise the question of its morality would be an affront to veterans and would desecrate the memory of all those American soldiers who had sacrificed their lives during the war.[62]

These exhibits generated outrage because they challenged a core belief of American exceptionalism, that the country exercises military force only for righteous ends. No public outcries were raised against exhibits at the Holocaust Museum that criticized the United States for failing to bomb Auschwitz or to rescue Jews. On the contrary, this failure became an item of received wisdom about the war, and public officials ritually admitted American culpability at Holocaust commemorations. Guilt for not bombing Auschwitz did not detract from the mythic narrative about American virtue; instead, it contributed to the idea that America has the power and the moral obligation to exercise force for humanitarian ends. The United States ought to behave as its better self— to act out its essential identity as liberator. Since the Holocaust was not only a catastrophe from the past, but an ever-threatening possibility in the future, this narrative implied that the United States could get it right this time—by supporting Israel and deploying its firepower to save innocents and prevent new Holocausts.

In American popular culture, the best-known savior of Jews from the Nazis is not an American GI but a German businessman, Oskar Schindler. Based on a historical novel about a real German entrepreneur and Nazi party member, *Schindler's List* (1993), directed by Steven Spielberg, tells the story of Schindler's change of heart and his successful effort to protect the Jewish workers at his factory in Krakow, Poland, from being taken to the death camps.[63] Two months after the Holocaust Museum opened its doors to the public, Spielberg's film was released to reverential critical acclaim. The media treated the film, the first big-budget Hollywood film about the Holocaust, as more of an event than a movie, a "document of witnessing," as Spielberg told *Newsweek*. Public officials, including President Clinton, personally attested to its impact and implored the public to see it. Free public screenings were offered to high school students all over the country, and it has remained a centerpiece of school curricula ever since. As James Young noted, "There are a couple of gigantic institutions now, Spielberg being one and the U.S. Holocaust Memorial Museum being another, which are defining a kind of public consciousness of the Holocaust."[64] Both institutions contributed to a view of the Holocaust as bonding the United States to Israel.

The film presents both sides of the American liberation narrative: pride for what was done, and guilt for what was not. The plot revolves around Schindler's rescue of 1,100 Jews on his celebrated list. As the character that viewers most identity with, Schindler is recognizable as a Hollywood protagonist: a heroic individual, a lusty can-do capitalist with a mind of his own, who, upon witnessing the suffering of others, rises above political ideology to do the right thing. Viewers also witness his moral growth and awakening, as he painfully begins to realize the limits of his efforts to oppose the evil power of the Nazis. Although Schindler saves "his Jews," he comes to recognize his failure to rescue more. In a moving scene at the war's end, Schindler sinks to his knees under the weight of overpowering guilt, and he repeats the words expressing his terrible remorse: "I could have saved more. I could have saved more."

The film's narrative of liberation requires Israel as a haven for deliverance. *Schindler's List* concludes in Jerusalem as the site of redemption for both Schindler and his Jews. Like the ending of the 1978 miniseries *Holocaust*, Spielberg's film culminates in the memory of Israel's rebirth out of the ashes of the Holocaust. Yet it ends in a Jerusalem cemetery where the real Schindler is buried.

Israel may be a conventional destination for popular Holocaust narratives, but Spielberg arrives there by breaking from the documentary quality of the rest of the film to transport his characters to Jerusalem through a cinematic feat of magical realism. Unlike the end of the *Holocaust* miniseries, or the beginning of *Exodus,* no Mossad agent from Palestine leads the survivors to the Promised Land. Instead, as they sit listlessly along the railroad tracks, a Russian soldier on horseback tells them that they are not wanted in the East or the West, and he points over a hill where they can find food. The group then links arms and marches as a phalanx up the hill, with the Israeli song "Jerusalem of Gold" playing in the background, making a contrast with the plaintive violin theme played throughout the film. The camera focuses on the weathered yet hopeful faces until they reach the crest of the hill, and then everything changes in one frozen shot. The film switches from black and white to color, from past to present, from fiction to reality. The young actors are replaced by the actual, now elderly Jews whom Schindler saved, and at the same time, the landscape changes under their feet from the grass-covered hill of Poland to the dry stony ground of Jerusalem. The scene then shifts to Schindler's gravesite in a Christian cemetery on a Jerusalem hillside, bathed in bright Mediterranean light. The aging survivors walk haltingly down an incline to place a stone on Schindler's tombstone, which is engraved with a cross and Hebrew writing. They are accompanied by the actors who have played their younger selves.

Israeli previews of the film criticized Spielberg's choice of "Jerusalem of Gold," for its historical anachronism and political implications.[65] The song became hugely popular during the Six-Day War and has endured as a national anthem celebrating military conquest and messianic longing. The question of anachronism, however, is moot. The film's ending posits an ahistorical timeless connection between the Holocaust and Israel, with Jerusalem as its mystical uncontested center. The history of 1948 disappears, and the victory song magically transports survivors from Poland to Jerusalem. Even though the individuals actually saved by Schindler dispersed to many countries, the film brings them all to Jerusalem to memorialize their liberator, as though it were their final destination. What links the Holocaust and Israel in the movie is the timeless obligation to honor the dead. The universal message of the film, about Schindler overcoming indifference to rescue the weak, merges with the nationalist message, epitomized by "Jerusalem of Gold." The only part of Israel shown in the film is the graveyard visited by elderly survivors. No nation of refugees, pioneers, or fighters appears— only a memorial site that unites the liberator and the liberated in a ritual of commemoration. Spielberg's cinematic magic projects a timeless bond between the liberator, the survivor, and the land of Israel.

6

APOCALYPSE SOON

LONG BEFORE the State of Israel was founded in 1948, American Christians of all denominations had identified its territory with the biblical geography of the Holy Land. Puritan settlers in colonial America cast themselves as the chosen people of the Old Testament and imagined the New World as the Promised Land. Colonists engraved this identity on the North American landscape with biblical names—Salem, Jericho, Canaan. Manifest Destiny draped national expansion in biblical garb, as Herman Melville observed: "We are the peculiar chosen people, the Israel of our time. We bear the ark of the liberties of the world." The rise of historical criticism in the nineteenth century spawned a popular obsession with the Holy Land. Archeologists unearthed material evidence of the biblical past, and tourists thrilled to walk in Jesus's footsteps. To experience these lands vicariously, one could read the historical novel *Ben-Hur: A Tale of the Christ,* the most popular book of the late nineteenth century—or watch it performed on stage and later on film. One could visit Palestine Park, built in Chautauqua, New York, in 1874, the first of many Holy Land models throughout the United States, or wander through a replica of Jerusalem's Old City at the 1904 St. Louis World's Fair. In Sunday school, children pored over colorful atlases, memorized strange place names, and charted Bible stories as geographical journeys. Through all these different media, millions of American Christians were prepared to form images of modern Israel from their familiarity with the mythic landscape of the Holy Land.[1]

Israel has come to embody Holy Time as well as the Holy Land. Since the rise of the Christian Right in the late 1970s, evangelical Christians have become fervent political supporters of Israel, and many of them have looked to Israel both as the setting for the Second Coming of Jesus Christ, and as the primary actor in hastening that event. For evangelicals who believe in biblical prophecy, the Bible not only literally records divine history, it also accurately foretells the divine future. Since Israel's founding, evangelicals have combed its political landscape for forecasts of the end times. This temporal geography relies less on the New Testament chronicles of Jesus's life and death than on the book of Revelation and the Old Testament prophets to map a landscape of impending apocalypse.[2]

The establishment of the State of Israel in 1948 proved to believers the accuracy of the ancient prophecy that God would restore the Jews to Zion and that this ingathering would trigger a chain of events culminating in the end of days. This restoration of the Jews to Zion meant something very different from secular Zionism. The significance of Israel was not in realizing the political goal of Jewish sovereignty, but in manifesting God's sovereignty and making it possible for some Jews to convert to Christianity to correct the fatal mistake they had made in rejecting Christ two millennia ago. In this prophetic narrative, Israel is the epicenter of the apocalypse, where Christ will launch the final battle of Armageddon and vanquish the Antichrist to inaugurate God's kingdom on earth. Conjoining eschatology and geopolitics, this old belief system energized the movement called Christian Zionism, which has become one of the most powerful sources of American support for Israel's right-wing politics from the 1980s into the new millennium.[3]

Christian Zionism did not evolve in a world apart from mainstream American culture. As we have seen, it was the popular crooner and born-again Christian Pat Boone who wrote and recorded the famous lyrics to the film *Exodus*, "This land is mine, God gave this land to me." His evangelical audience would have taken the lyrics literally, as God's promise to Abraham in Genesis (13:15): "For all the land you see I will give to you and to your offspring forever." They understood this decree not as a metaphor or a past event, but as an enduring promise for Abraham's future descendants. Throughout his career, Boone worked to promote Israel to American Christians, including in his 1972 musical production *The Pat Boone Family in the Holy Land,* and in his official position as spokesman for Israel's tourism ministry in the 1990s. At the end of the Yom Kippur War in 1973, he entertained Israeli troops camped on the Golan Heights with rock-and-roll hits and a rousing rendition of *Exodus*. Some years later, after Israel had annexed the Golan Heights, Boone mentioned this visit to Prime Minister Yitzhak Rabin. According to Boone, Rabin consulted a map and responded: "You sang a prophecy. . . . Where you were singing, 'God gave this land to me' is now part of the map of Israel."[4] In Boone's belief system, the knowledge that "God gave this land to me" transcends history and geography, but is verified by current events and geopolitics. In prophetic time, Israel's wars look backward to fulfill ancient prophecy, and look forward to the final cosmic war on the horizon.

Pat Boone's lifelong involvement with Israel exemplifies the potent mix of popular culture, masculine militarism, and belief in biblical prophecy that bonds conservative American evangelicals to the modern nation of Israel. In the right-wing turn in both countries, evangelicals equated support for Israel's expansionist policies with the revival of military power in the United States. Israel, they believed, had a special role to play both at the end of times and in the present, by combatting America's decline and renewing belief in American exceptionalism.

Boone contributed to the emergence of the Christian Right as a political force on the national scene. His was a well-known public face on cable television's evangelical circuit, where he appeared with celebrity preachers such as Pat Robertson and Jimmy Swaggart. Boone also worked behind the scenes in California with a coterie of businessmen, politicians, and evangelical leaders to help elect his good friend Ronald Reagan as governor of California in 1967 and president of the United States in 1980. In the presidential election, the influence of Reverend Jerry Falwell's Moral Majority helped a group of neoconservatives make Israel central to Reagan's foreign policy.

In 2013, Boone donated the Christmas card on which he had composed the original lyrics of *Exodus* to Israel's Holocaust memorial, Yad Vashem.[5] The symbolism of this donation is not hard to decipher. The evangelical anticipation of the end times parallels the apocalyptic fear that Israel is facing the existential threat of a second Holocaust. Both ways of thinking interpret the past—whether the Bible or twentieth-century history—as a sign of Israel's future. And both see catastrophe on the horizon. Memory of the Holocaust solidifies Israel's status as history's ultimate victim. Evangelicals, in contrast, view Israel as ultimately invincible, in accordance with God's plan to end history. Holocaust memory evokes the dread of recurring atrocities, while biblical prophecy welcomes the hastening of Armageddon's gory end. Both apocalyptic narratives assume an uncompromising conflict between good and evil. Apocalypse begets redemption. In the Holocaust narrative, protecting Israel from the threat of annihilation can redeem America from its past failures. In the prophecy narrative, recognizing Israel's divine status can redeem America from moral and military decay.

Apocalypse Now

Christian Zionism became a phenomenon in popular culture a decade before the Christian Right became a force in American politics. The evangelical leader Hal Lindsey was the most influential proponent of the movement. In his book *The Late Great Planet Earth* (1970), Lindsey transformed an arcane belief in biblical prophecy into a diagnosis of the crises besetting modern society. Lindsey placed the State of Israel at the center of an esoteric eschatology called premillennial dispensationalism, and he exhorted Americans to watch the end times unfold in the escalating crises between Israel and its Arab neighbors.[6]

The first blockbuster about Israel since *Exodus, The Late Great Planet Earth* focuses not on the country's heroic founding but on its apocalyptic future. Lindsey identifies the birth of Israel and the decline of America as the two major signs that the end is near. Catastrophe and salvation loom together on the horizon. While America careens toward World War III, Israel is gearing up for the final cosmic conflict, in which a militant Christ will defeat the Antichrist and establish his kingdom on earth.

Hal Lindsey was an unlikely candidate to write a mega-bestseller. A veteran of the Korean War, he had a Mark Twain–like start as a Mississippi River tugboat captain and then studied at the Dallas Theological Seminary. In the late 1960s, he lectured on California campuses, recruiting alienated students to evangelical youth groups. *The Late Great Planet Earth,* which is written in the colloquial idiom of the counterculture and stocked with historical and scientific evidence, offers the Bible as "history written in advance," the authoritative guide to humanity's future. Issued by a small Christian publishing house, the book appealed far beyond the intended audience of Christian youth, selling a million copies in a month and ten million over the course of the decade, to become the bestselling work of nonfiction in the 1970s. Lindsey became a star on the evangelical circuit and an outspoken booster for Israel, leading many trips to the Holy Land. He produced a film version of *The Late Great Planet Earth* with Orson Welles as the narrator, and he has written at least twenty more books that update biblical prophecy to match geopolitical change. Israel never veers far from the center of his books.[7]

The Late Great Planet Earth addresses contemporary fears of the atomic bomb and civilization's collapse. Nuclear weapons, environmental degradation, and overpopulation promise to destroy the earth. Third World nations and revolutionary movements threaten the West, just as crime menaces the streets of America. Global threats are matched by social decay at home: the disaffection of youth, the deluge of drugs, pornography, and mental illness, with no moral authority to stem this tide. All of these events are predicted in the Bible, an infallible guide that makes "future events that were predicted hundreds of years ago read like today's newspaper."[8]

For prophecy believers, if you read the Bible literally, you have no need to fear impending disasters. Instead, you welcome them as omens of a cosmic drama carefully scripted by God. In this divine script, the rise of Israel is the bright spot that counters the gloom and doom of the coming end times. If decline results from humanity's abandonment of God, the restoration of Jews to Zion is evidence of God's presence. Old-time Bible scholars, Lindsey claims, misinterpreted earlier upheavals as heralding the return of Christ. They missed the "paramount prophetic sign: Israel had to be a nation again in the land of its forefathers."[9] Only when Jews were restored to Zion could the "countdown" to Armageddon begin. Israel's establishment was the temporal precondition, and its land the geographical setting, for the apocalypse.

The belief in the restoration of Jews to Zion as a precondition for the millennium had roots in the nineteenth century, before the rise of the secular Jewish Zionist movement. Irish evangelical John Nelson Darby popularized the idea of premillennial dispensationalism on both sides of the Atlantic. He claimed that God had never transferred his favor and promises from the Jews to the Christian Church—the traditional narrative of the Catholic Church and most Protestant sects. Jews would thus have a crucial role in the final "dispensation," when their return to Zion marked the beginning of the end. Darby introduced the idea of the Rapture that Lindsey adopted. Christians would be swept up to Heaven without dying before the Tribulation and the rule of the Antichrist, when immense devastation, foretold in the book of Revelation, would bring human society close to annihilation. At this time, Jews would have their last chance to convert. A significant remnant would accept Christ as their Messiah, but the rest would be destroyed along with other unbelievers. Christ would then return to defeat the Antichrist at Armageddon and inaugurate the thousand-year reign of God's kingdom on earth, ending with the Last Judgment.[10]

Prophecy belief had an impact on the development of political Zionism at the turn of the twentieth century. In the United States, William Blackstone, a Chicago businessman and author of the popular prophecy book *Jesus Is Coming,* worked to convince American Protestants to help Jewish people emigrate to Palestine. In 1891, drawing on humanitarian outrage at Russian pogroms, Blackstone collected signatures from over four hundred prominent men for a petition, known as the Blackstone Memorial, which called for returning Jews to Palestine. This document, which was presented to President Benjamin Harrison, combined aspects of biblical prophecy with concern for Jewish persecution, attention to developments in the Ottoman Empire, and unease over the possibility of increased Jewish immigration to America. Blackstone was one of the first to publish a statement that would later become a Zionist slogan: he described Palestine under Ottoman rule as an "astonishing anomaly—a land without a people for a people without a land!"[11] Premillennial dispensationalism also had a profound influence on the British circle of leaders who came together behind the Balfour Declaration in 1917, which set out the aim to establish a Jewish homeland in Palestine. Their belief in biblical prophecy bolstered their political interest in establishing a foothold in the region for the British Empire.[12]

By 1948, dispensationalism had primed millions of evangelicals to welcome the founding of Israel as a great piece of prophetic news. At that time, however, some were concerned about Israel's origins in "unbelief," that is, its founding by secular Zionists. When Israel conquered the Old City of Jerusalem in 1967, they saw world history taking a gigantic leap forward. L. Nelson Bell, Billy Graham's father-in-law, exclaimed in *Christianity Today*: "That for the first time in more than

2,000 years Jerusalem is now completely in the hands of the Jews gives a student of the Bible a thrill and a renewed faith in the accuracy and the validity of the Bible."[13] For Lindsey, the conquest of Jerusalem paved the way for one more event that would "completely set the stage for Israel's part in the last great act of her historical drama. This is to rebuild the ancient Temple of worship upon its old site." There was one obstacle, however, standing in the way. "That obstacle," wrote Lindsey, "is the second holiest place of the Moslem faith, the Dome of the Rock." According to prophecy, however, God would remove the obstacle, perhaps by earthquake. Some prophecy believers have since argued that the Dome of the Rock and neighboring mosque could remain while the new temple was rebuilt on a nearby site, while others have applauded Jewish extremists' plots to blow up the mosque.[14]

The Six-Day War galvanized evangelicals, who believed that Israel's miraculous triumph was a literal miracle. They believed that God had intervened to save his chosen people and hasten the world's end. Secular Americans may have welcomed Israel's victory as a psychological lift out of the Vietnam quagmire, but prophecy believers hailed it as proof of God's agency in the world. The conjunction of American decline and Israeli restoration corresponded to the signs predicted in the Bible of impending catastrophe for most of humanity and the ultimate victory for God and his believers.

The Late Great Planet Earth addressed contemporary concerns about global challenges to American power. Lindsey's interpretation of biblical conflicts reproduced a Cold War interpretation of the free world as being threatened by communists and their Third World allies. The Bible, in his view, predicted an assault on Israel by a Russian-led confederation that included "the Egyptian plan to unite the Arabs and the black Africans into a 'third world force.'"[15] God would intervene to destroy the attackers, leaving Israel totally unscathed. In a chapter called "The Yellow Peril," Lindsey ingeniously mines the Bible to predict that hordes from communist China, two hundred million in force, will cross the Euphrates to attack Israel during the battle of Armageddon. In these apocalyptic projections, American readers could imagine Christ defeating the same enemies that appeared to be besting them in Southeast Asia: the Soviet Union, China, and Third World nations. In this scenario, Israel becomes a proxy for America, as the target of its enemies and the recipient of divine salvation.

Although known for his countercultural cadences, Lindsey in fact reveled in militarism, and his book reads like an anti-antiwar book. It presents war as the engine of human history and as part of God's design for ending human history. Lindsey welcomes each new thermonuclear weapon as evidence of the unearthly plagues predicted in the Bible. He avidly describes the blood flowing for miles in the valley of Megiddo, site of the battle of Armageddon, and he heralds global nuclear destruction as the ultimate proof of God's power as described in the book of Revelation: "Imagine Cities like London, Paris, Tokyo, New York, Los Angeles, Chicago—obliterated!" Lindsey indulges his readers in an orgy of violence inflicted on others, offering them a ringside seat where they remain unscathed while watching the apocalypse unfold. Anyone who accepted Christ would have been spared the horror of the Tribulation, having been spirited away during the Rapture—"the ultimate trip," an experience akin to walking on the moon, better than "mind expansion drugs!"[16] From this vantage point, the destruction of nonbelievers becomes a spectacle of divine intervention, where Israel provides the stage setting and plays the starring role.

As the "fuse of Armageddon," Israel's escalating conflicts will lead to World War III. The Arabs' implacable "unwillingness to accept the Israeli occupation of what they consider to be their land," together with Israel's iron determination to resist them, make the conflict inevitable. According to Lindsey, the Bible predicts that "the Middle East crisis will continue to escalate until it threatens the peace of the whole world. The focus of all nations will be upon this unsolvable and complex problem which keeps bringing the world to the precipice of a thermonuclear holocaust." Not until mankind is "on the brink of self-annihilation" will Christ return "to put an end to the war of wars called Armageddon." In the final global battle, the Jews "will be on the verge of annihilation when God gives them supernatural strength to fight."[17] Lindsey transforms the peril of Israel's earthly vulnerability into the Christian promise of divine invincibility, casting Jewish warriors for Christ in the image of the Israel Defense Forces (IDF).

Jews also have another warrior role, as militant proselytizers for Christ. God will "reveal Himself in a special way to 144,000 physical, literal Jews," writes Lindsey, "who are going to believe with a vengeance that Jesus is the Messiah. They are going to be 144,000 Jewish Billy Grahams turned loose on this earth—the earth will never know a period of evangelism like this period. These Jewish people are going to make up for lost time."[18] Those Jews who refuse to convert—a predicted two-thirds—will perish in gruesome plagues and massacres along with all nonbelievers.

War unites Christians with a militarized Israel through the figure of the militant Christ. The Bible, Lindsey claims, paints pictures of two Messiahs: the suffering Messiah of the First Coming is the "humble servant" who was sacrificed on the Cross. Prophecies of the Second Coming refer to the "reigning Messiah" or the "political deliverer," the Messiah as "conquering king with unlimited power, who comes suddenly to earth at the height of a global war and saves men from self-destruction." It is this militant Christ who favors the "Israelites who believe in Him"—those who had converted to Christianity—and makes them "the spiritual and secular leaders of the world."[19]

The identification of the militant Christ with the Israeli military was connected with the movement to invigorate a masculine Christianity. In *Tender Warrior: God's Intention for a Man*, Pastor Stu Weber critiqued the curly-haired, feminine images of Christ found everywhere from Renaissance paintings to Hollywood films. His first visit to Israel in 1974 radically changed this portrait when he met an Israeli driver, David, who inspired his vision of a muscular Christ. A "Jewish male in his prime," David was a "native born *sabra*" recovering from wounds received in the Yom Kippur War. With dark skin, black hair, and piercing, dark eyes "hard as black steel," he reminded Stu of the biblical David, the "great warrior." After Weber encountered David, "the pale, limp-wristed Galilean faded like a bad dream and the laughing, dark-skinned Son of David took over the picture in my mind. The Greater *Sabra*. The real Tender Warrior." For this former Green Beret, the modern Israeli soldier, an incarnation of biblical Israelite warriors, rescued Christ's image from centuries of feminization.[20]

Many conservative evangelical leaders admired the IDF and prided themselves on access to its inner circle.[21] In the prophetic landscape, the Israeli military is often represented as the sole part of modern Israel worthy of note, as in Lindsey's illustrated book *A Prophetical Walk through the Holy Land* (1983). The only people appearing in the photographs are Orthodox Jews and Palestinian shepherds, elements of the picturesque past. Modern photographs exclude urban scenes and portray only military scenes, including fighter jets over Masada, a tank on the Golan Heights, and Haifa Bay, described as the location where "the Soviets will make an amphibious invasion of Israel as part of the all-out War of Armageddon." The title page shows an Israeli fighter jet in camouflage colors flying directly above the Dome of the Rock, which glistens beneath like a golden bull's eye. Lindsey notes that he received this picture from a personal friend, "one of the greatest jet fighter pilots in history," and the caption reassures readers that "modern Israeli warriors guard their ancient capital."[22]

"America's Key to Survival"

Many prophecy believers were concerned that America did not appear in the Bible, and that the holy text did not reveal a divine agenda for reversing the nation's worrisome moral and military decline. Indeed, *The Late Great Planet Earth* interpreted America's deterioration as a major sign that the end was near. By 1980, however, Lindsey cast Americans in the more active role of helping to redeem their nation. In his next bestseller, *The 1980s: Countdown to Armageddon,* he argued that the Bible advocated political action to "ensure our nation's survival" against the twin threats of social decay and military impotence. In a world hell-bent on self-destruction, America could still regain its preeminence in time for the Second Coming; it could do this by restoring Christian morality and "creating the world's strongest military."[23]

This vision of renewal informed the worldview of the Moral Majority, a political organization of the Christian Right that was founded in 1979 to advance a conservative social agenda at home and restore American military power abroad. Its leaders and grassroots supporters had a hand in electing President Ronald Reagan, who fluently spoke their language, with references to the "evil empire" and nuclear Armageddon. Many of the founders of the Moral Majority, including Jerry Falwell, Tim LaHaye, and Pat Robertson, were premillennial dispensationalists. They claimed a special dispensation for the United States, a window of time that had opened for activism just before the end. During this period, which LaHaye dubbed the "pre-tribulation tribulation," Christians would perform a kind of dress rehearsal for Armageddon. They would fight the same battle against the dark forces of secularism and disarmament that the Antichrist would lead during the final Tribulation.[24]

Staunch support for Israel formed the lynchpin of the Moral Majority's foreign policy. "You can't belong to Moral Majority without being a Zionist," Falwell told ABC TV.[25] To these committed Cold Warriors, Israel represented the best line of defense against Soviet aggression in the Middle East and Arab power as displayed by the OPEC boycott in 1973. Israel's divine status elevated it above other anticommunist regimes supported by the Christian Right, such as Guatemala, Taiwan, and apartheid South Africa. "Whoever stands against Israel, stands against God," Falwell declared.[26] In an influential book, *Israel—America's Key to Survival,* Christian Zionist Mike Evans called on Christians to recognize not only what America could do for Israel, but what Israel could do for America.[27] Christians had an obligation to arm Israel in its battle for survival, while Israel in turn played a crucial role in saving America as it struggled for survival against secularists at home and communists abroad.

Cold War politics met eschatology in the belief that standing up for Israel could revive America's status as an exceptional nation. A foundational prophecy for Christian Zionists is God's promise to Abraham in Genesis 12:3: "And I will bless them that bless thee, and curse him that curseth thee." As proof of the Bible's success in predicting the future, they point to the eventual decline of every empire that has mistreated Jews, from Babylon and Rome to the Third Reich. The eclipse of the British Empire also serves as a cautionary tale, its decline attributed to its failure to uphold the Balfour Declaration. America, in contrast, has flourished because it has treated Jews well both at home and abroad. Tim LaHaye went so far as to claim that the United States had rescued Jews from the Holocaust.[28] The United States could avoid the fate of all other empires in history if it continued to "bless Israel," but, warned Falwell, if the country abandoned Israel, it would lose its position of world leadership "for a place in history books alongside of Rome."[29]

The Christian Right envisioned the United States in Israel's image, as both vulnerable and invincible. "National survival is the issue," exhorted Falwell in his 1980 jeremiad *Listen, America!* Faltering military defense and moral corruption had led America to the "threshold of destruction or surrender."[30] Falwell's narrative of decline, shared by many conservatives, started at the end of World War II, when Roosevelt negotiated with Stalin. It was downhill from there: the abandonment of China to the communists, the failure to follow Douglas MacArthur to victory in Korea, and the debacle of Vietnam, when a weak government prevented the generals from deploying full military force.

The nadir of this trajectory occurred in the 1960s, when military weakness met moral decay. The counterculture, liberal media, Black Power, and the antiwar movement induced a failure of nerve on every front, from helping Fidel Castro to flourish, to relinquishing the Panama Canal, to allowing the Shah of Iran to be toppled. Failure to rescue the American hostages who had been taken during the Islamic Revolution was the crowning blow. On the nuclear front, "disarmament" was seen as synonymous with "suicide." Anything short of victory over the Soviets—including nuclear treaties and détente—would lead to America's total capitulation. "The Miracle called Israel," in Falwell's words, offered salvation in two ways. It showed that the United States was not in total decline, since its foreign policy had gotten it right in supporting Israel. And Israel's robust militarism provided a model to emulate, since it had proven that pursuit of invincibility was the only alternative to the threat of extinction.[31]

On the domestic front, "blessing Israel" could also save America from moral decline. In a foundational text for Christian conservatives, *Battle for the Mind*, Tim LaHaye sounded a clarion call to redeem America from the sinfulness and permissiveness that the false religion of secular humanism had promulgated. He and his colleagues blamed this ideology for all forms of moral decay: "drugs, crime, pornography, children's rights over parents, homosexuality rites, prostitution, gambling and the equal rights amendment for women."[32] Evidence of such degradation led to the conundrum of why God would continue to favor America. In *The Coming Peace in the Middle East*, LaHaye addressed this problem and related it to the absence of America in the Bible. He explained that America could maintain its favored status in God's eyes only as long as it upheld its historical commitment to God's original chosen people. He warned Americans that "if we ever change our policy toward the Jews, we will become like Sodom and Gomorrah."[33] Defending Israel protected America from descent into moral perdition.

Conservative evangelicals often compared their own precarious status in America with Israel's vulnerable position internationally. Feeling besieged by the liberal institutions that had been undermining

American society since the 1960s, they saw themselves as righteous underdogs fighting the Goliath of secular humanism. They often described themselves as persecuted outcasts; John Hagee claimed that "Christians are the only group in America that it is politically correct to hate, discriminate against and lampoon." Pat Robertson controversially described the Holocaust as "the work of Satan prefiguring the coming holocaust of American Christians at the hands of diabolical liberals, including liberal Jews." According to Robertson, the Nazis' methods for isolating Jews were "being used already against Christian people" in the United States.[34] Many people were offended by such claims. Yet Robertson was voicing a common notion: conservative Christians saw themselves as a persecuted minority who had to battle the courts, the education system, and the media to keep from being wiped out, just as Israel had to defend itself from hostile surrounding nations. American Christians, just like Israel, would ultimately triumph through their own militant rebellion and the miraculous intervention of God.

Identification with Israel did not mean identification with actual Jews, however—either in America or in Israel. LaHaye warned that Jews as a group "have often yielded to secularistic, even atheistic spirit. Brilliant minds have all too frequently been dedicated to philosophies that have proved harmful to mankind. Consider for example, Karl Marx, Leon Trotsky, Sigmund Freud." This apostasy, LaHaye claimed, explained why God had punished the Jews over the ages, in addition to the more traditional explanation that they had crucified Christ. Once Jews had been restored to Zion, they would have a second chance to redeem themselves from the sin of "choosing Caesar over Jesus Christ."[35]

Just as Israel enabled God to fulfill his promise to the Jews, so could America become the Promised Land for Christians. "America is tied by a spiritual umbilical cord to Israel," Jimmy Swaggart preached on television. "The Judeo-Christian concept goes all the way back to Abraham and God's promise to Abraham. The Jewish people represent Judaism. The American people represent Christianity."[36] Swaggart viewed "the American people" as white evangelical Christians, while Israel alone represented Jews and Judaism.

Many conservative evangelicals understood their movement as bringing America back to its Christian roots, just as Zionism represented the restoration of Jews to their biblical birthright. The reign of secular humanism was to the Christian Right what the Diaspora was to Zionists—a time of powerlessness, persecution, and marginality that could only be overturned by a militant struggle for redemption. While evangelicals projected the prophetic future onto Israel, they imagined returning America to a harmonious past of security and social order. The restoration of Christian values was their Zion.

Reviving America as a Christian nation meant freeing it from the shackles of domination by a cabal of secular elites. Conspiracy theories are common among conservative evangelicals, who have implicated vast networks of institutions, including the Trilateral Commission, the Council on Foreign Relations, the World Council of Churches, and the American Civil Liberties Union. While particular conspiracies can get quite elaborate, they all assume the existence of a shadow state ruled by, in LaHaye's words, "a small but very influential cadre of committed humanists . . . determined to turn America into an amoral, humanist country ripe for merger into a one-world, socialist state."[37]

For Christian Zionists who believe in these dark networks that are strangling America, Israel offers a shining counterforce. Prophecy and conspiracy both offer the certitude of a controlling center in a world spinning out of control. The satanic cabal governing America finds its counterpart in the divine designs for Israel's future. The infernal plot bringing down America finds its inversion in the divine plot elevating Israel. "The Nation of Destiny," wrote LaHaye, is the only one in the world that God chose to manipulate directly, so "unlike other nations, Israel has a guaranteed future." While evil forces may drag America into historical oblivion, "all human history began with Israel, and it will also end with Israel."[38]

Prophecy and conspiracy, the Rapture and Armageddon, the restoration of the Jews, and the revival of America all came alive in the hugely popular Left Behind series, a set of sixteen novels authored by Tim LaHaye and Jerry B. Jenkins and published between 1995 and 2007. Like *The Late Great Planet Earth,* these novels have had an astonishing appeal beyond the ranks of the prophecy believers. They ascended the bestseller lists and spawned a cottage industry of websites, tie-in products, and spinoffs, including films, video games, and specialized series for teens and for military personnel. More than 65 million copies have sold to date. Rivaling the international publication success of the Harry

Cover of the novel *Assassins,* by Tim Lahaye and Jerry B. Jenkins, part of the Left Behind series.

Potter books, the Left Behind series has flourished primarily in the American market.[39]

The concept of the Left Behind phenomenon is simple: Hal Lindsey meets Leon Uris. American and Israeli characters unite as natural allies in these futuristic action-thrillers about the seven years of Tribulation between the Rapture and the Second Coming. Arcane biblical prophecies play out in a high-tech setting, and formulaic romantic plots and family dramas unfold with apocalyptic gore. A small band of heroic Christians deploys faith and technological know-how to outwit the devious machinations of a global evil empire. White Americans and converted Israelis are the major protagonists, although the series includes a wide cast of minor characters of different races, ethnicities, and nationalities. The Israeli characters become the most pious proselytizing Christians, while the Americans behave like ace Israeli commandos. Together they form a mighty guerrilla group bent on saving souls for Christ and thwarting the tyranny of the Antichrist on the road to Armageddon. Where Puritan settlers once conceived of America as the new Israel, at the turn of the twenty-first century, the Left Behind novels reimagine Israel as the new America.

The novels take place in a post-apocalyptic future that features the major dilemmas of the post–Cold War 1990s. Refurbishing the prophetic narrative that Lindsey had modernized for the 1970s, LaHaye and Jenkins address a diffuse set of threats identified with globalization and an increasingly interconnected world. The novels imagine a secular dystopia where America has forfeited its sovereignty to the seductive conspiracy of the Antichrist, a young Romanian diplomat, Nicholae Carpathia, who heads the United Nations. Carpathia institutes a one-world government with a single currency and an ecumenical embrace of all religions. In a world colonized by secular forces and ravaged by physical calamities, only the State of Israel remains intact as God's special nation and a bulwark against the nefarious networks of globalization.

The miraculous survival of Israel serves as a counterweight to the awful destruction of the United States. The first novel opens aboard an airplane, where a number of passengers mysteriously vaporize into thin air. It is the Rapture, and true Christians have been taken directly to heaven. The characters remaining on earth return to an America decimated by the disappearance of ordinary people who kept the wheels of everyday life turning and maintained social order: drivers, pilots, traffic controllers, police officers, nurses, and doctors have suddenly disappeared from their jobs, and disasters ensue. As soon as the main characters realize that they were "left behind," they become believers and form the Tribulation Force to fight against the Antichrist. An American journalist comes to Christ after witnessing a prophecy fulfilled in Israel: the entire Russian air force was on its way to attack the unprepared nation, but the fighter jets fell out of the sky and left Israel unscathed.

As the characters travel back and forth between America and Israel, the contrasting landscapes are striking. Nuclear bombs level American cities, and crime becomes rampant in burnt-out urban zones. Earthquakes destroy whatever infrastructure remains, as plagues spread. The Holy Land, in contrast, "had been spared damage from the wrath of the Lamb," leaving Israel "the one place that looked normal . . . since the earthquake and the subsequent judgments."[40] Israel is to other nations what believers are to unbelievers. When demonic locusts swarm over the earth gnawing at human flesh, they miraculously pass over anyone who has become a believer, just as when rivers turn to blood all over the world, water runs clear in the Holy Land.

The novels describe Israel as a familiar landscape, placing modern landmarks in a biblical topography. American pilots fly in and out of Ben Gurion Airport, Israeli soldiers guard the Western Wall, the proclamation of the Messiah takes place before a huge crowd at Teddy Kollek stadium in Jerusalem, and the protagonists stage a daring escape on a boat up the Jordan River to the Sea of Galilee. Israel's territory extends into the Sinai Peninsula and Jordan. In accordance with prophecy, the Antichrist tries to rebuild the Temple in Jerusalem as a site of idolatry after he persuades all Muslims to move away. In a possible allusion to Palestinian resistance, an unidentified terrorist yelling "Allah" starts shooting indiscriminately near the Western Wall and is promptly incinerated by two fire-breathing prophets. The novels magically fulfill the Zionist fantasy of a land without Palestinians.[41]

The Left Behind novels display a relationship to modern Israel that is ambivalent at best. The authors glorify Israel's exceptional place in biblical prophecy and appropriate Zionist myths, while solidly rejecting secular Zionism. LaHaye had warned in 1984 that Israeli Jews were "still in a state of disbelief," and that "we Christians must remember that many of Israel's leaders are Zionists: consequently, some of them are as secular as America's humanists."[42] By showing Israeli Jews converting to Christianity, the novels redeem them from Israel's secular past and present. Among the main characters, Jewish converts to Christianity are the most devout proselytizers. An Israeli Orthodox rabbi, Tsion Ben-Judah, becomes the spiritual guide of a worldwide rebel community of believers. A renowned scholar of world religion, he publicly proclaims Jesus to be the true Messiah. Incurring the wrath of the Antichrist, he goes underground with his American comrades and then converts millions of unbelievers via the worldwide web. The technical ingenuity of another converted Israeli keeps these stealth broadcasts under the radar of the Antichrist's extensive media empire.

Throughout the novels, the authors adapt secular Zionist tropes, imbuing them with Christian meaning. Consider the central character, Chaim Rosenzweig, an internationally revered Israeli scientist. Rosenzweig invents a chemical that makes crops grow when applied directly to barren soil. His discovery literally makes the desert bloom. Nations around the world covet his formula as the solution to world hunger, and because he is an idealist, he makes it freely available in order to secure an international peace treaty.

An intellectual committed to nuclear disarmament, Rosenzweig unwittingly abets the rise of the Antichrist. The Antichrist, Carpathia, is a cosmopolitan celebrity and mesmerizing orator who speaks multiple languages and is hailed by popular magazines as the sexiest man on the planet. Backed by a shadowy cabal of financiers, he rapidly ascends to power as the head of the United Nations with his promise to establish a one-world government based on one currency and one religion that preaches tolerance for all beliefs. Espousing every tenet of secular humanism, a conservative Christian nightmare, Carpathia rules the world as a welfare state writ large, one that encourages free abortions, among other abominations.

Conservatives have long reviled the United Nations as a threat both to America sovereignty and to Israel's existence. These fears come to fruition in the novels, as Carpathia's humanitarian mask falls away and he becomes the leader of the most tyrannical regime in human history. He deploys nuclear weapons against the nations that had surrendered them under the lure of disarmament, controls the world population through terror and surveillance, forces his subjects to have computer chips implanted as a measure of loyalty, and insists on being worshipped as the Messiah.

In the meantime, after maintaining his faith in ʻscience rather than religion throughout the first five novels, Rosenzweig finally converts to Christianity and assassinates Carpathia (who comes back to life after three days). The tale of Rosenzweig's subsequent actions turns the traditional Zionist narrative into a Christian one. As a new Moses, he presides over an Exodus in reverse and leads thousands of converted Jews, known as "the Remnant," out of Israel, which is being ruled by the Pharaoh-like Antichrist. He takes them to the ancient Jordanian city of Petra—a staple of prophecy since the late nineteenth century—where they feast on manna from heaven, their clothing never gets dirty, and the earth parts to protect them from relentless bombing by Carpathia's Global Forces. In the Petra scenes, returning to "days of old," converted Jews dress in flowing robes and speak in the cadences of biblical characters. When Christ appears on earth to command the final battle, they accompany him on a journey likened to the original Exodus, re-entering the Promised Land as Christian conquerors.[43]

Transforming the secular landscape of Zionist iconography, the authors turn the ancient hilltop fortress of Masada into a staging ground for the conversion of Jews to Christianity. Masada is a celebrated Israeli historical site, where Jewish rebels committed mass suicide rather than surrender to the legions of the Roman Empire. In Israel's national mythology, this story symbolizes Zionist fortitude, and the self-sacrifice of the rebels represents a heroic act of national liberation. In the Left Behind novels, a recalcitrant group of Orthodox Jews refuse to bow to the Antichrist but also resist accepting Christ as the Messiah. At Masada they have their last chance to convert, and rather than commit suicide, this time they are born again as Christians.

As more Israelis convert, the authors use Holocaust references to describe the Christian martyrdom of these converts under the Antichrist's dictatorship. In persecuting those who defy him, the Antichrist displays special animus toward Jewish converts, for whom he plans a "final solution."[44] His police force rounds up converted Jews to take them to concentration camps, and he plans to starve out the refugees in Petra, led by the now Christian Rosenzweig, and turn it into "the largest Jewish concentration camp in history."[45] References to the Holocaust not only signal the Antichrist's absolute evil, but also bestow on the newly converted Christian martyrs the respect typically accorded to Jewish Holocaust victims.

While Jews recover their spiritual identity in Christ as a result of the violent upheavals of the Tribulation, American characters reclaim their rugged frontier identity and behave like tough Israeli soldiers. In the first novel, the president of the United States blindly submits to Carpathia's humanitarian blandishments, leading to the destruction of most of the country. When the president belatedly realizes that he has sacrificed

American sovereignty to the United Nations, he joins forces with independent militia groups to stage an insurrection. Carpathia brutally crushes the rebellion with nuclear weapons. The remaining members of the underground Tribulation Force, which takes on characteristics of the modern militia movement, live off the grid in secret communities and continue the battle. Many are veterans, who stage daring rescue missions and escape from captivity by smashing guards to death with their body weight. As Armageddon approaches, they blend characteristics of American cowboys and Israeli commandos, brandishing Uzis and speaking the lingo of Westerns, saying things like "Howdy" and "Let's get out of Dodge." One character even prefaces a remark with, "I know this is gonna sound like a cowboy movie."[46] Finally at the end of days, American men will be able to regain their mettle.

As the armed forces of the world amass for the climactic battle of Armageddon, Israel's wars against its Arab enemies are reenacted on a cosmic scale. The "rebels" defending Jerusalem are "outnumbered a thousand to one," and at Petra, a "ragtag bunch of earnest impassioned believers" faces "the largest fighting force in the history of mankind."[47] At Megiddo, believers confront "the greatest military power ever assembled on the face of the earth."[48] Despite the military might of their antagonists, they feel confident that they are fighting "on the right side" of the "battle between good and evil."[49] This time, the Christian David bests the unbelieving Goliath, and Christ's arrival on a white horse (literally) transforms any traces of vulnerability into indomitability. During the battle, Christ's words became swords that ripped open the bodies of millions, who "dropped in heaps of bones"; "even as they struggled, their own flesh dissolved, their eyes melted, and their tongues disintegrated."[50] This bloody battle ushers a gathering of Christian believers into the New Jerusalem, the seat of God's kingdom on earth.

Although the United States never recovers, the New Jerusalem is reborn, and it looks much like small-town America. Throughout the novels, the language of American exceptionalism fuses with the language of Christian redemption in which it was first formulated. Rosenzweig and Ben-Judah translate their own conversions into a classic American idiom of westward expansion while hiding out in an Illinois safe house. "The history of this country carries much discussion of a manifest destiny," proclaims Ben-Judah. "Well, my brother," he continues, "if ever a people had a manifest destiny, it is our people! Yours and mine! And now we include our Gentile brothers who are grafted into the branch because of their belief in Messiah and his work of grace and sacrifice and forgiveness on the cross."[51] In the prophetic plot of the Left Behind novels, America disappears as a modern nation, but its destiny is indeed manifest at the end of time in the New Jerusalem. As the main characters reunite in Jerusalem at the dawn of the millennium, Israel becomes the new America.

"Israel's Only Safety Belt"

Otherworldly narratives about the end of time have real-world consequences. When the Christian Right started to flex its muscles in American politics, the dispensationalists in the movement did not sit back passively to watch for signs of the impending apocalypse in the Middle East. They started working to hasten God's design through political organizing on behalf of Israel's most far-right policies. Their map of the Holy Land had never stopped at the borders designated in 1948, and, since 1967, they have fervently opposed Israel's relinquishing any territory, viewing it as God's original gift to Abraham and as the final setting for the battle of Armageddon. As the Left Behind series dramatized, the peace process itself smacked of the Antichrist's machinations.

In 1983, Jerry Falwell announced that "the best friends Israel has in the world today are Evangelical and Fundamentalist Christians." He stated this in a book of interviews directed toward American Jews, many of whom opposed the Christian Right's conservative social agenda. Falwell was responding to a question about what the interviewer, Merrill Simon, called the "hysterical reaction by the Free World press" to the Sabra and Shatila massacre. Israel was desperate for new friends at the time, as Falwell well recognized, after the invasion of Lebanon had tarnished its image in the eyes of so many Americans.[52]

Over a decade earlier, the Israeli government had already been seeking out new friends in the evangelical community. Their apocalyptic fervor for Israel's conquests contrasted starkly with international calls for Israel to withdraw from those territories that were captured during the Six-Day War. In 1971, Israel hosted the Jerusalem Conference on Biblical Prophecy, a gathering of 1,500 evangelical Christians who were addressed by Israeli leaders and evangelical notables. The tourism ministry eagerly solicited Christian visitors to visit major biblical sites that were now in Israel rather than Jordan. The ministry also enlisted well-known evangelicals like Pat Boone and Billy Graham, who produced a feature film called *His Land,* a love letter to Israel.[53]

When Jimmy Carter, a born-again Christian, was running for president in 1976, the cover of *Newsweek* declared it the "Year of the Evangelical" and claimed that one-third of Americans had been "born again" and 38 percent believed the Bible should be taken literally.[54] The following year, Menachem Begin became prime minister, and the Israeli government began to cultivate the Christian Right as a political ally in a serious way. Like members of the Christian Right, however, Begin was disappointed that President Carter did not see the Israeli-Arab conflict through the same prism that he did. When Begin talked to him of the divine right to the Holy Land, Carter responded with the biblical injunction to make peace. And when Carter referred to the "Palestinian right to a homeland," conservative Christians were as aghast as American Jews, whose antagonism galvanized Carter's proposal for a national Holocaust memorial.

In reaction to Carter's support for Palestinian rights, Christian Zionists launched an advertising campaign in major U.S. newspapers, placing a full-page ad stating that "the time has come for evangelical Christians to affirm their belief in biblical prophecy and Israel's divine right to the land." The advertisement was signed by leading dispensationalist theologians and public figures like Pat Boone. Financing and publicity for the campaign brought together a Jerusalem-based Christian Zionist organization and American supporters of Begin's Likud Party. An American Jewish coordinator of the campaign was quoted in *Newsweek* as saying that Carter had better listen to his constituency of evangelicals, and that "the real source of strength the Jews have in this country is from the evangelicals."[55]

Begin did meet a kindred spirit in Jerry Falwell, who was thrilled to see Israeli soldiers capture Jerusalem's Temple Mount in 1967. Actively courting Falwell as the "man who represents 20 million Americans," the Likud government paid for Falwell to visit Israel dozens of times and helped him conduct "Friendship Tours" for hundreds of ministers and laypeople. The IDF flew Falwell by helicopter over the Golan Heights, where he planted saplings for a forest in his honor. He visited new settlements in the occupied territories, where he endorsed Israel's right to Judea and Samaria, the biblical names for the West Bank. Falwell received a gift of a Lear jet from the Israeli government, and in 1981, he became the first non-Jew to win the Jabotinsky Award, in honor of the founder of right-wing Zionism.[56]

Falwell reciprocated with unfaltering support. When Begin launched the controversial strike on Iraq's nuclear reactor in 1981, Falwell was one of the few public figures to congratulate him. Identifying the raid as a victory for America, he lauded Begin "for a mission that made us very proud that we manufacture those F-16s. In my opinion, you must've put it right down the smokestack." On a broadcast that Sunday, Falwell urged eighty thousand pastors in the Moral Majority to preach favorable sermons in defiance of the condemnation of Israel's attack by both President Reagan and the United Nations.[57]

Christian Zionists offered crucial support during Israel's invasion of Lebanon in 1982. In *Israel—America's Key to Survival,* Evans called the invasion a "miracle" and a "dress rehearsal for Armageddon," and he applauded Israel's mighty blow against heavily armed Soviet proxies in its defense of oppressed Lebanese Christians.[58] In 1979, Pat Robertson had started a radio station in southern Lebanon for a right-wing Christian militia, and during the invasion, he and Falwell visited Lebanon as guests of the IDF. When the news broke of the massacres at Sabra and Shatila, Falwell protested that the "Israelis were not involved" and dismissed reports as "media bias."[59] On his *Old Time Gospel Hour* show, he compared the massacre to My Lai, with a strange twist: since people didn't call for Nixon's resignation after My Lai, he argued, only anti-Semites would call for Begin to resign.[60]

Christian Zionists have consistently opposed any Israeli efforts to trade land for peace, for they share with the Israeli religious right the belief that "Greater Israel" was divinely deeded to the Jews. Some also believe that peace efforts are the work of the Antichrist, a theme in the Left Behind novels. When the Israeli parliament approved a bill in 1980 declaring Jerusalem to be the nation's undivided capital, in defiance of international law, the few foreign embassies remaining in that city protested by joining the majority in Tel Aviv. To support Israel's declaration, a Dutch evangelical established the International Christian Embassy in Jerusalem, with financial contributions from Americans, who still use the thriving institution as the umbrella organization for Christian Zionist activities in Israel. Officially committed to "comforting" Israel, restoring Jews to Zion, and spreading the prophetic word, the "embassy" has also provided a meeting ground for evangelicals committed to conservative causes throughout the world. A 1987 Bill Moyers documentary showed footage of supplies labeled ICEJ crossing at the Honduras border en route to the right-wing contras in Nicaragua.[61]

On the home front, Christian Zionists led the battle to convince the U.S. government to recognize Jerusalem as Israel's eternal capital. Testifying before a congressional hearing in 1984, Falwell attested that "there are hundreds of references to Jerusalem" in the Bible, but God "made no reference to Tel Aviv." While that city is the "brainchild of man; Jerusalem is the heartthrob of God." Adept at combining political and religious language, he concluded that "moving our embassy from exile in Tel Aviv to its rightful home in Jerusalem would tell the world that our commitment to this single democracy in the Middle East is irrevocable."[62] At the end of 2017, evangelicals found a champion for this cause in the White House. President Donald Trump, with Vice President Mike Pence, a Christian Zionist, by his side, formally recognized Jerusalem as Israel's capital and ordered the U.S. embassy moved there, reversing nearly seven decades of American foreign policy.

Christian Zionists have continuously opposed relinquishing any territory as part of a peace agreement with the Palestinians. They objected to the Oslo Accords of 1993 and criticized Prime Minister Rabin for negotiating with Yasser Arafat. After Rabin's assassination in 1995, John Hagee published a book detailing how the Bible predicted the assassination, which would trigger the end times. Hagee described Rabin's killer, Yigal Amir, a right-wing Israeli settler, as a man of faith who was committed to keeping the land God had promised to his people.[63] When Likud's Benjamin Netanyahu became prime minister in 1996, he revived the close relationship with conservative evangelicals that Begin had initiated. As ambassador to the United Nations, Netanyahu had been a popular guest speaker at the National Prayer Breakfast for Israel, an annual event held in Washington, D.C., where he highlighted the "impact of Christian Zionism on western statesmen that helped modern Jewish Zionism achieve the rebirth of Israel." Within months of taking power, Netanyahu flew Christian Zionist leaders to Israel; when they returned, they took out full-page ads supporting the settlements and Israel's claim to Jerusalem. On a visit to Washington in 1998, he snubbed President Clinton in order to attend a gala celebration of Christian Zionists. There Falwell declared that asking Israel to withdraw from the occupied territories would be like "asking America to give Texas to Mexico." Netanyahu told the group that Israel had "no greater friends and allies than the people sitting in this room."[64]

Netanyahu spoke prophetically—in a sense. Organized Christian Zionism would grow tremendously in the new millennium, in terms of membership, finances, and political clout. In addition to giving moral and political support to Israel, Christian Zionists supplied the country with ample financial aid and boosted its tourism industry with prophecy-oriented tours. To hasten the restoration of Jews to Zion, Christian organizations with names like Exobus have helped transport immigrants from Russia, Ethiopia, India, and anywhere they can find hidden Jewish communities. American churches have also adopted and provided aid to individual settlements in the occupied territories. In 2006, John Hagee founded Christians United for Israel, which has developed significant lobbying power in the United States. Christian Zionist organizations have routinely endorsed the Israeli government's perspective on its use of force and have approved of all military incursions, often seeing them as part of the divine plan. They have also opposed all efforts at diplomatic negotiations, including the 2015 nuclear deal with Iran.

American Jewish organizations have been more ambivalent than the Israeli government about allying with the Christian Right. In the 1980s and 1990s, they swung back and forth between opposing the Right's conservative domestic agenda and welcoming a pragmatic alliance with it as a way to strengthen Israel's security. In 1982, the head of the American Jewish Congress warned that the Moral Majority "threatens the freedoms that make Jews safe in America," freedoms that include the separation of church and state, keeping prayer out of public schools, and supporting pro-choice policies and women's rights. At the same time, Nathan Perlmutter, director of the Anti-Defamation League of B'nai B'rith (ADL), wrote that allegiance to Israel trumps domestic politics and theological beliefs: "We need all the friends we have to support Israel. . . . If the Messiah comes, on that day we'll consider our options. Meanwhile, let's praise the Lord and pass the ammunition." In an influential article in *Commentary* in 1984, Irving Kristol urged American Jews to set aside their political reservations and welcome the Moral Majority's support for Israel, which "could, in the near future, turn out to be decisive for the very existence of the Jewish state."[65]

This alliance between American Jewish Zionists and Christian Zionists stemmed from more than political expediency. The rise of the Christian Right dovetailed with the emergence of the neoconservative movement. Both groups launched a crusade to rebuild America's military power and prestige around the world, and both found a champion in Ronald Reagan. Neoconservatives, like Kristol, made the strongest intellectual case for American Jews to align with Christian conservatives, as part of a broader appeal to Jews to break away from liberalism.

Despite deep differences in background and belief, neoconservatives shared with Christian conservatives a remarkably similar narrative about the decline of American power and morality. They both blamed the counterculture and social movements of the 1960s for the breakdown of moral authority at home, and they held liberals responsible for undercutting American military power abroad. These two crises had converged in the failure of Vietnam. In the 1980s, both groups imagined a vital role for Israel in reversing this crisis.

Neoconservatives also shared with evangelicals an apocalyptic sensibility. Ultimately attuned to national rather than divine triumph, neoconservatives viewed American military might as the singular force for good in a world beset by evil, and as the only power standing between the survival of democracy and worldwide anarchy. They also saw annihilation looming as the world lurched from one crisis to the next—from Soviet military expansion in the 1980s to Islamic terrorism in the aftermath of the Cold War. Just as dispensationalists interpreted contemporary events as a biblical sign of the approaching apocalypse, neoconservatives read most conflicts, whether political, military, or cultural, as potential threats to the survival of Western civilization.

Granted, different blueprints underlay the construction of these parallel worldviews. For neoconservatives, the historical lessons of the 1938 Munich Agreement, which permitted Hitler to annex part of Czechoslovakia, provided an indispensable guide to future action that was as fully revealed as Scripture was for prophecy believers. By appeasing Hitler, they argued, England and France failed to combat absolute evil and thus enabled the Holocaust, which could have been averted had the West, including the United States, had the foresight and courage to use force. Wielding this blueprint, neoconservatives have interpreted most choices to pursue diplomatic negotiation over military force as acts of appeasement—particularly the policy of détente with the Soviet Union and nuclear disarmament treaties, and more recently the 2015 nuclear deal with Iran. They feared that diplomatic concessions to evil forces could have catastrophic consequences, just as dispensationalists viewed such diplomatic efforts as the work of the Antichrist.[66]

The imperative to avert a second Holocaust in Israel epitomizes this neoconservative way of thinking. Kristol, after all, advocated allying with the Moral Majority not merely as a pragmatic coalition for particular political aims, but as "decisive for the very existence of the Jewish state." In the same article nudging Jews closer to conservative Christians, he urged them to abandon their allegiance to international law and to the Enlightenment ideal of a "community of nations," as represented by the United Nations. If support for Israel was the paramount value, this meant endorsing Israel's flouting of international law, and by extension unshackling America from international restrictions to its sovereignty. If American Jews expected the United States to shore up Israel's military security, argued Kristol, they had to support full-throated American militarism, just like Christian conservatives, and get over their moralistic squeamishness against anticommunist interventions in Central America and other places. American Jews had to support "the indispensable precondition for the exercise of American influence on behalf of Jewish interests in the world: a large and powerful military establishment that can, if necessary, fight and win dirty, little (or not so little) wars in faraway places." Kristol concluded that it was time for American Jews to leave behind their traditional commitment to liberal allies and internationalist ideals and to seek a "new home, however uncomfortable, in the conservative and neoconservative politics that, in reaction to liberalism's leftward drift, seems to be gaining momentum." That meant forging an alliance with Christian conservatives, for whom Israel and America were inseparably bound together in military might and divine favor.[67]

The Jewish American alliance with Christian conservatives hit some rocky spots during the 1990s, when the culture wars at home and negotiations toward a two-state solution found liberal Jews and Christian Zionists on opposite sides. In 1994, the ADL became alarmed by the crude anti-Semitic conspiracy theories of Pat Robertson, who founded the Christian Coalition to succeed the Moral Majority in 1989. Abraham Foxman, director of the ADL, warned of the imposition of a "Christian nation" on America's democracy in his book *The Religious*

Right: The Assault on Tolerance and Pluralism in America. While Norman Podhoretz defended Robertson, and AIPAC held meetings with him, Foxman refused his demand for an apology.[68]

After September 11, 2001, however, when President George W. Bush declared a "war on terror," mainstream Jewish organizations overcame their suspicions of the Christian Right. In the American geopolitical imagination, the al-Qaeda operatives who attacked the World Trade Center merged with Palestinian suicide bombers attacking Israelis during the second intifada. Once the front line against Soviet communism, Israel now became the front line against Islamic terrorism. When Israel faced worldwide condemnation for its disproportionate punitive attacks on Palestinian civilians during the second intifada, Christian Zionists went into action. In 2002, President Bush criticized Israel's invasion of the West Bank and its bombardment of Yasser Arafat's headquarters in Ramallah. Jerry Falwell immediately rallied his base to protest Bush's condemnation. That year, Foxman changed his view on the Christian Right, writing an article titled "Why Evangelical Support for Israel Is a Good Thing."[69]

On a 2003 *60 Minutes* broadcast, Falwell branded Mohammed a "terrorist," and said that "Jesus set the example for love, as did Moses. And I think that Mohammed set an opposite example." The war on terror, for some Christians and Jews, redefined the meaning of the Judeo-Christian tradition as a war against Islam. On the same broadcast, Falwell warned that "the Bible Belt in America is Israel's only safety belt right now." Foxman agreed with him that "on this specific issue on this day we come together. And what is the issue? The issue is fighting terrorism."[70]

7

HOMELAND INSECURITIES

SEPTEMBER 11, 2001, is known to millions of Americans as the day that changed everything. "Ground Zero" represented not only a site of carnage in Lower Manhattan, but also a rupture in time, the moment Americans lost their innocence and no longer felt invulnerable. On that day, al-Qaeda terrorists flew airplanes into the World Trade Center in New York City and the Pentagon, killing almost three thousand. At day's end, "night fell on another world," observed President George W. Bush, when he announced before a joint session of Congress a week later that he was declaring a "war on terror" and establishing a new Office of Homeland Security.[1] Unique and unprecedented, al-Qaeda's terrorist attacks on the United States appeared to defy both comparison and historical analysis. Any attempt to put the event in context—likening American losses to the suffering of others, or explaining acts of terrorism as reactions to political policies—raised the specter of moral relativism and blurred the clear line between "our way of life" and "evildoers."

Israel stood out as an exception to the unwritten rule about the incomparability of American suffering. "Now we are all Israelis" was a common refrain, but it did not undermine the exceptional quality of America's calamity or becloud its moral clarity.[2] On the contrary, identification with Israel sharpened the sense that the two countries shared a unique position in the world. The familiar image of Israelis as long-suffering victims of terrorism offered an emotional touchstone for comprehending incomprehensible losses, and Israel's vaunted military vigilance provided a guide to action. In the rhetoric of President Bush and his advisors, the United States took on Israel's paradoxical role as an invincible victim. In this view, America was confronting, on a global scale, murderous enemies who threatened nothing less than total annihilation. Terrorism would force the United States to fight a never-ending battle for national survival, even as the country was providentially destined to vanquish all evil.

For Americans to place themselves in Israeli shoes was to imagine the nation in a new way, as a homeland—a nation one needed to fight for against the threat of total loss. In the decade following 2001, Israel increasingly appealed as a model to emulate in defending America at home and abroad from existential threats, both real and imagined. The military and the media, think tanks and popular culture, all enjoined Americans to study Israel as the gold standard for fighting terrorism in foreign lands, at the borders, in cyberspace, in urban centers, in the homeland, and in private homes. Israel's permanently imperiled state exemplified the new concept of homeland security. This concept entailed, on the one hand, erecting impregnable barriers between inside and outside, the citizen and the alien, the self and the other. On the other hand, it meant effacing boundaries between home and abroad, domestic and foreign affairs, civilian and military control.

The history and language of America's close identification with Israel offered a ready-made narrative of innocence and danger that helped some Americans understand what at first seemed incomprehensible. Americans could believe that, like Israeli Jews, they were hated for who they were, not for what they did. This hatred, even by a small cadre of non-state actors, seemed so dangerous that it threatened to "destroy our way of life." The rhetoric of the existential threat, associated primarily with Israel since the 1980s, entered the lexicon of the war on terror, which Vice President Dick Cheney would refer to as an "existential conflict."[3] Since retaliation alone could not guarantee security against such an all-encompassing menace, the only option was to preemptively eradicate this shadowy but omnipresent enemy.

In the post-9/11 model of homeland security, perceptions of vulnerability and invincibility fed on each other. With imminent extermination on the horizon, any available means can be used to destroy impending threats before they strike. Military advantage alone, however, never suffices in the face of existential peril. Fears of omnipresent danger continually stoke the call for vigilance in the name of total security. These views perpetuate and rely on the continuous production of radical insecurity. In this apocalyptic way of thinking, the only imaginable outcomes are absolute supremacy or utter annihilation; negotiation or compromise can lead only to appeasement and capitulation. David Frum and Richard Perle, neoconservative advisors to President Bush, expressed this idea succinctly in their book *An End to Evil: How to Win the War on Terror:* "There is no middle way for Americans: it is either victory or holocaust."[4]

"Now We Are All Israelis"

In the days following 9/11, journalists likened the devastation in New York to the tragic routine of terrorist attacks in Tel Aviv and Jerusalem. "The acrid and unexpungeable odor of terrorism, which has hung over Israel for many years," wrote George Will in the *Washington Post* on September 12, "is now a fact of American life. Yesterday morning Americans were drawn into the world that Israelis live in every day." On the same day, the *New York Times* published no less than three pieces on Israel, all solemnly acknowledging that "we" now understand what "they" have bravely endured for so long, that our overwhelming catastrophe is their everyday norm. Clyde Haberman noted that the most recent suicide bombing in Tel Aviv had taken place at an American pizza chain, linking Americans and Israelis in a shared fragile landscape, where everyday life becomes vulnerable to destruction. In the following years, journalists would return to this theme. "With every new threat, . . . our everyday life becomes more like Israel's," wrote Bruce Hoffman in the *Atlantic.*[5]

Some journalists acknowledged that people in many other countries—Northern Ireland, Rwanda, Sri Lanka—also lived with the horrific effects of terrorism. But most were quick to assert a more intimate identification with Israelis. In his editorial in the *New York Times* the day after the attacks, Bill Keller repeated the phrases "like Israelis" and "like Israel" as a sober but reassuring refrain, remarking that the bombings of the U.S. embassies in Kenya and Tanzania felt "too far way," and the bombing of the federal building in Oklahoma City by a domestic terrorist too "freakish." When Dexter Filkins rushed to the smoldering scene of the collapsed Twin Towers, it occurred to him that many of the street vendors from Third World countries would have encountered comparable disasters—whether natural or manmade—that destroyed thousands of innocent lives in their own homelands. But then he noticed a surreal object lying on the street, a human intestine, and he flashed back to a scene in Tel Aviv, where Orthodox Jews had been collecting fragments of body parts in the aftermath of a suicide bombing. Comparisons to Israel offered psychic ballast and a cognitive chart to navigate by in the chaotic wake of the attacks, which had made home seem frighteningly foreign. Some Americans easily saw themselves, like the Israelis, as virtuous victims of inexplicably evil forces, and they could then rally to emulate Israeli resilience. The language of that day resonated in newspapers from around the country. In the words of a *Philadelphia Inquirer* editorial, "We've lost our old invulnerability, and must learn the art of survival in the presence of peril."[6]

Americans turned to Israel for education in the art of survival. Israeli leaders were eager to edify, though not without a note of schadenfreude. When Benjamin Netanyahu, former (and future) prime minister, was asked how the attacks would affect relations between Israel and the United States, he answered, "It's very good," before correcting himself: "Well, not very good, but it will generate immediate sympathy." The attacks, Netanyahu explained, would "strengthen the bond between our two peoples, because we've experienced terror over so many decades, but the United States has now experienced a massive hemorrhaging of terror." Prime Minister Ariel Sharon decried the assault on "our common values" and declared that "together we can defeat these forces of evil." Israel's minister for public security accused Yasser Arafat, president of the Palestinian Authority, of having laid "the foundation for modern terrorism," and officials repeatedly equated Osama bin Laden, mastermind of the 9/11 attack, with Arafat, and al-Qaeda with the Palestinian Authority.[7]

In the decade before the 9/11 attacks, the Likud government of Israel and its conservative supporters in the United States had laid the conceptual foundation for American and Israeli partnership in a global war on terror. Throughout the 1990s, experts and politicians at think tanks and conferences had worked to define Islamic-inspired terrorism as the primary threat to Western democracies after the fall of Soviet communism.[8] In 1996, Netanyahu published a well-received book, *Fighting Terrorism: How Democracies Can Defeat Domestic and International Terrorists*, in which he articulated ideas that would later be

taken up by President Bush. Terrorists have no political goals, no grievances or aspirations, but are driven by irrational hatred, he claimed.
Although they belong to a hydra-headed network of disparate groups,
they are united in their aim of destroying the West. Netanyahu did not
refer to the clash of civilizations that Samuel Huntington had made famous in his 1993 essay and book, but rather to a battle of civilization
against barbarism. Published on the heels of the bombing of the federal building in Oklahoma, Netanyahu's book distinguished domestic
terrorism, represented by the Irish Republican Army (IRA) and the
white supremacist militias in the United States, as destined to wither
away in democratic societies, which by nature would not tolerate them.
Islamic terrorism, on the other hand, would remain dangerous because
of its death-driven theology and its political support from authoritarian
states. Netanyahu made no distinctions among the myriad groups that
employed terror as a tactic, whether al-Qaeda, Chechen rebels, Hez-
bollah, Hamas, or the mujahideen. He labeled Yasser Arafat as the pro-
genitor of contemporary terrorism, and he placed Israel at the vanguard
of the global struggle.[9]

Netanyahu's narrative helped frame American perceptions of the
second intifada, which received more media coverage in the United
States than any other foreign event in the year before 9/11. The uprising
was triggered by Ariel Sharon's visit to the Temple Mount in Jerusalem,
site of the al-Aqsa Mosque, in September 2000. Its roots lay in Palestinian
disappointment with the failure to achieve statehood in the U.S.-led peace
process, and mounting frustration with growing Israeli settlements
and with the Israeli occupation, which had become even more draconian since the Oslo Accords of 1993. In the fall of 2000, most of the
world looked on with horror at the overwhelming firepower that Israeli forces unleashed on Palestinian protesters, followed by the military reoccupation of cities and refugee camps in the West Bank and the
Gaza Strip. Some Palestinian militias responded with deadly suicide
bombings that killed and maimed Israeli civilians in buses and cafes, at
street corners and weddings. The bombings wreaked havoc on the daily
life of most Israelis.[10]

The U.S. media focused almost entirely on the suffering of Israelis.
News reports told of Israel defending innocent civilians against death-
loving Arabs, who were willing to sacrifice their youth just to foment
violence aimed at eradicating Israel from the face of the earth. The

American media rarely mentioned the context of the occupation or acknowledged what many observers and international human rights groups saw as Israel's disproportionate assaults on civilians. At most, the media bemoaned the terrible cycle of violence on both sides.[11]

After 9/11, America's war on terror merged with Israel's war against the Palestinians in both rhetoric and practice, with each legitimating the other. Israeli officials were concerned that the U.S. government would be distracted by its own war, but they also believed it would look sympathetically at the assault by the Israel Defense Forces (IDF) on the occupied territories, as an attack on terrorists. On September 13, 2001, the *Washington Post* reported that Israeli tanks had entered Jericho, a city controlled by the Palestinian Authority, with little international notice. A few days later, the paper noted that Sharon believed the "shell-shocked West" had become receptive to his argument that Yasser Arafat was not a national leader, but a terrorist like Osama bin Laden.[12] Sharon visited ground zero in November in order to highlight the bond between the two countries, united in fighting against terrorists and mourning the losses they inflicted. The next month, Mayor Rudy Giuliani of New York City and mayor-elect Michael Bloomberg went to Jerusalem, where they visited the site of a suicide bombing. Giuliani proclaimed that "the people of Jerusalem and the people of New York City are shoulder-to-shoulder, and the people of America and the people of Israel are shoulder-to-shoulder in the fight against terrorism," and that the experience of terrorism had made the kinship between the two nations closer than ever.[13]

On March 27, 2002, a Palestinian suicide bomber attacked a Passover Seder at a hotel in Netanya, murdering 28 Israelis and injuring 140. Israel launched a massive military offensive in retaliation, an operation that had been planned well in advance. In Operation Defensive Shield, the IDF invaded cities and refugee camps on the West Bank and besieged Ramallah, where it pummeled Arafat's presidential headquarters, targeting not only security installations but also civilian ministries and municipal buildings. In justifying the assaults, Sharon drew analogies between the Taliban's infrastructural support for al-Qaeda and the Palestinian Authority's enabling of suicide bombers in Israel. Columnist Charles Krauthammer compared the Passover massacre to both the Holocaust and the World Trade Center attack, referring to it as "Kristallnacht transposed to Israel," and "Israel's Sept. 11, a time when spo-

Israeli prime minister Ariel Sharon (*left*) and New York mayor Rudy Giuliani (*right*) inspect the site of the destroyed World Trade Center, November 30, 2001.

radic terrorism reaches a critical mass of malevolence such that war is the only possible response." Krauthammer argued that Israel's military raids and America's attacks on Afghanistan were essential, not merely to kill individual terrorists, but to destroy the regimes that sponsored them and the groundwork that facilitated them. America's war in Afghanistan may have distracted attention from Israel's attacks on the West Bank and Gaza. But it also provided support for Israel's bombardment of Palestinian social institutions in an attempt to destroy the rudiments of any future state.[14]

The United States benefited, in turn, from Israel's military campaigns in Operation Defensive Shield. In preparation for the invasion of Iraq, U.S. military observers visited the West Bank in 2002 to watch the Israeli army bulldoze a 40,000-square-meter area in the center of the Jenin refugee camp, an operation that killed an estimated fifty-two Palestinians. Marines showed a special interest in learning about urban warfare and about how to undertake search-and-destroy missions against insurgents. Israeli advisors visited Fort Bragg to train Special Forces. After the initial invasion of Iraq, when the U.S. military faced numerous uprisings throughout the country, especially in densely packed cities, American forces adopted counterinsurgency tactics that the Israeli military used in the occupied territories. These techniques included searching house to house, razing buildings, erecting walls to seal off areas within and between neighborhoods, making mass arrests, setting up checkpoints, and monitoring people's movements using biometric identity cards and surveillance systems. Americans also adopted the Israeli practice of extra-judicial executions by helicopters or drones as part of the broader doctrine of what Israelis called "urban area domination." American troops trained in mock "Arab" towns built on Israeli bases and paid for in part with U.S. funds. Interrogators in Iraq used a torture technique called the Palestinian chair, in which the prisoner is secured in a painful crouching position. These convergences were not lost on Iraqis, who named an opening between barriers in Baghdad "Rafah," after the crossing point between Gaza and Egypt. One Iraqi protester complained, "This wall makes us feel as if we were in Palestine."[15]

The American military was certainly not learning for the first time about methods of counterinsurgency, assassination, torture, or attacks on civilians; it had its own long history of interventions, from Southeast Asia to Latin America. But the Bush administration represented the war on terror as an exceptional response to an unprecedented threat rather than as a continuation of this history. With the country at risk from what Bush called a "new and changing threat unlike any we have faced before," Israel appeared to be far ahead of the game. Think tanks and military research centers churned out papers about lessons the United States could learn from Israel about "fighting terrorists," "irregular warfare," "homeland security," and "urban military operations." Most addressed preemptive strikes and targeted assassinations. Although these studies focused on Israel's most advanced strategies and technologies, they started from the premise of its uniquely vulnerable position. "No political entity since medieval times," began one influential report by Thomas Henriksen, a senior fellow with the Joint Special Operations University, "has been more constant [*sic*] under military siege—whether conventional, terrorist, or even existential—than Israel."[16]

Israel offered a moral framework, not only a strategic one, for the belief that was fundamental to the American war on terror: in the face of extraordinary peril, the old rules do not apply. "The civilized world faces unprecedented dangers," said Bush in his State of the Union address in January 2002. Viewed as a nation born out of the cauldron of absolute evil, whose survival was continuously endangered, Israel was understood to have developed the will and expertise to avert a second Holocaust by any means necessary. The United States now shared a similar moral imperative to defend itself by extraordinary means.

The war on terror was oriented to the future, with the goal of defeating a known enemy as well as preventing any potential impending catastrophes. With this orientation, important security doctrines of the Bush administration drew on Israel's practice and theory, particularly the commitment to preemption. The Six-Day War had long been viewed as a model for preemptive war, the sole exception to the injunction against preemptive strikes according to the just war theory, as articulated most influentially by Michael Walzer in 1977. The U.S. deployment of targeted assassinations, or extra-judicial killings, also followed Israel's practices, using the same logic of anticipatory security based on eradicating perceived threats in advance. The United States had banned targeted assassinations in 1976 but reintroduced them in November 2002. Based on his research on the new militarization of modern cities, urban geographer Stephen Graham claims that "the Bush administration's justification of its reliance on extra-judicial and pre-emptive assassination in its global war on terror clearly was heavily influenced by Israel's practices." As the decade progressed, notes military historian Andrew Bacevich, "Targeted assassination has eclipsed conventional military methods as the hallmark of the Israeli way of war."[17]

Key to the justification of preemption in attacking nations and targeting individuals is the idea that the war on terror is exceptional, and that it lacks any legal precedents. This notion informed the U.S. government's reformulation of rules about torture, detainment, prisoners of war, and the applicability of the Geneva Convention. Legal scholar Lisa Hajjar contends that the claim that the war on terror constituted a legal no-man's-land had a recent Israeli precedent: "the Israeli military at the start of the second intifada had already characterized its war on terror in the West Bank and Gaza as a legal *terra nulla*." Although the two governments were operating in very different political, historical, and legal contexts, the United States claimed that the Guantánamo Bay detention camp was a space outside of national sovereignty, and Israel redefined the occupied territories as "disputed" territories, based on the contention that no nation has sovereignty over them. Both nations constructed gray zones of productive ambiguity for the exercise of power: between occupied and disputed territory, between detainees and prisoners of war; between torture and enhanced interrogations; between military and civil jurisdiction; between soldiers, terrorists, and unlawful combatants; between legitimate and illegitimate violence.[18]

In addition to military and legal precedents, Israel offered Americans a powerful myth of origins for the war on terror, in the terrorist attack at the 1972 Munich Olympics that killed eleven Israeli athletes. In retaliation, Israel launched a clandestine campaign called Operation Wrath of God to assassinate those who had perpetrated the massacre. Thirty years later, Americans showed an acute interest in this historical incident, demonstrated in journalism and popular culture. One month after 9/11, the CBS news show *60 Minutes* broadcast "An Eye for an Eye," a documentary about this operation, which was offered as an object lesson that the CIA was studying now that Bush had directed the agency to "take its gloves off." The former head of Mossad, who directed the operation, explained that it went beyond targeting the gunmen who had carried out the attack; the objective was to "wipe out the entire terror network" in Europe and Lebanon, including anyone who had been even indirectly involved. CBS presented the Israeli mission as an exemplar, and an adventurous one at that. To imitate the Israelis, it was suggested, Americans must prepare to get their hands just as dirty—to use illegal methods, violate the laws of other nations, and accept the death of innocent bystanders as a necessary cost. As Ehud Barak, one of the Israeli participants and a future prime minister, exclaimed, "What the hell is wrong about hitting someone who did not hesitate to use hijacked planes with 150 tons of fuel, as a living cruise missile to kill 5,000 people?" A CIA agent agreed that this is "no tea party," and the head of Mossad had the last word, expressing his belief that the world will come around to the Israeli way, because "we have no alternative. This is the coming war. It's here." Operation Wrath of God came across as a mix of biblical retribution and frontier justice that was of urgent relevance.[19]

A model for heroic violence can easily be recast as a cautionary tale. That was the point of Steven Spielberg's *Munich*, a controversial film about the band of Israeli assassins who took "God's wrath" into their own hands. The film, released in 2006, turns the genre of international thriller into a moral drama about the psychic damage afflicting those who kill for righteous ends. The main Israeli characters come to doubt the justice and efficacy of a mission that threatens to dehumanize them, with no guarantee that the terrorists they kill won't be replaced by new ones. Like some of the liberal criticism of the Lebanon War, the movie focuses, in Michelle Goldberg's words, on "the effect of retaliatory Jewish violence on the Jewish soul and not the Palestinian flesh." As one character exclaims after a particularly bloody scene, "This isn't how Jews are supposed to act." Spielberg portrays civilized Israeli Jews as victims of the barbarism that forces them, against their better nature, to become murders. His cinematic portrayal of their anguished soul-searching ultimately redeems the humanity they are afraid of losing.[20]

Munich is an allegory for the American war on terror. The film ends with the Israeli protagonist wandering along the postindustrial Brooklyn waterfront. The recently opened Twin Towers loom on the horizon. His traumatic experience has made it impossible for him to return to his home in Israel, which his mission was meant to protect. He ends up in exile. From this vantage, it looks as though the homelessness and self-doubt that resulted from Operation Wrath of God may be the legacy for the United States, as well. Spielberg's film raises ethical and psychological questions about the impact that the war on terror may have on the warriors of both nations. Spielberg presents Israelis as models, too, but unlike the bellicose heroes shown in "An Eye for an Eye," here they are guilt-ridden moral guides for Americans who are navigating their own self-doubts.[21]

By superimposing questions about the U.S. war on terror onto an iconic episode of Israeli history, Spielberg breached a double taboo for neoconservatives, for whom Israel and America both exemplified the righteous use of military power against absolute evil. Viciously attacking the film, they accused Spielberg and screenwriter Tony Kushner of committing the sin of positing moral equivalence between Palestinian terrorists and Israeli agents, and between their respective causes. David Brooks criticized Spielberg for distorting reality because "he will not admit the existence of evil, as it really exists." In portraying ambivalence about Operation Wrath of God, Spielberg undercut Israel's lessons for the present: that in the face of real evil, "the only way to achieve peace is through military victory over the fanatics." For Brooks, the film undermined the binary logic of the war on terror, where the apprehension of moral ambiguity can only abet evil—and violence cannot corrupt those who wield it against fanatics. To his neoconservative critics, Spielberg muddied the moral clarity that Israel had always embodied, and that Americans finally rediscovered after the 9/11 attacks.[22]

Another fictional response to terrorism displayed no such ambiguity. Moral qualms about killing terrorists do not disturb Gabriel Allon, the formidable spymaster of Daniel Silva's bestselling espionage thrillers. The most popular fictional Israeli hero since Ari Ben Canaan in *Exodus*, Allon gets his start as the leader of Operation Wrath of God. The first novel of the series, *The Kill Artist* (2000), describes Allon's backstory. The head of Mossad—who had himself captured Adolf Eichmann in Argentina—had plucked Allon out of his promising art studies to lead the squad of assassins at the age of eighteen. In three years of hunting down the members of the Black September Organization that had carried out the Munich attack, Allon personally shot six of the targeted terrorists, pumping eleven bullets into each victim in memory of the eleven murdered Israelis. Allon's background story is recounted in every one of the sixteen novels in the series, which all take place when Allon is well into his fifties. His 1972 pedigree compensates for his aging body, and his history reminds readers that only an Israeli forged by these mythic origins has the resolve, know-how, and moral authority to fight a global war against the hydra-headed terrorist enemy in Europe, America, and the Middle East. Only two of the novels focus on Israel and Palestine. The rest are international and depict Allon making use of his connections to the highest echelons of power, including the pope, the British prime minister, and the American president. As an Israeli, born to Holocaust survivors, with his multigenerational experience of fighting for survival, he is called on to accomplish what the intelligence agencies of other nations cannot because they are hampered by legalities, bureaucracy, international diplomacy, reliance on Arab oil, or their own lack of willpower. As a model warrior in a shifting global conflict, Allon adapts his skills to each new terrorist group that rears its head, including, in the most recent books, ISIS, which threatens the existence not only of Israel and America but of civilization itself.[23]

Despite this lifelong calling, which eventually leads him to the directorship of Mossad, Allon has no passion for violence. In the tradition of the reluctant warrior, he retires whenever possible to his studio in Italy, where he works as a renowned restorer of classical European paintings. Only an Israeli could play this double role as both spy/assassin and expert restorer of Old Masters—defending the civilized world from catastrophic assaults while refurbishing the most highly valued objects of Western culture.

Silva's novels dramatize in fiction a belief, widespread since 2001, that Americans and Israelis were battling the same enemy, Islamic radicalism, despite the fact that the PLO was a secular organization that included Christians, that Hamas did not target the United States, and that neither group had ties to al-Qaeda. The rhetorical power of the war on terror as a battle against evil writ large, rather than against any particular organization or state, reinforced this generalized sense of a common foe. So, too, did the long-term identification of Palestinians with terrorists in the popular and political imagination, as the revived interest in Munich 1972 shows. Furthermore, as we have seen, both Israelis and Americans had long portrayed Arabs as Nazis with a genocidal desire to exterminate Jews by destroying their state. The 9/11 attacks proved to some that Nazified Muslims had expanded their murderous aims from Israel to the United States.

In President Bush's address to Congress on September 20, 2001, he answered the question "Who attacked us?" by identifying the then unfamiliar group al-Qaeda as "the heirs of all the "murderous ideologies of the 20th century," that is, "fascism, and Nazism, and totalitarianism." The focus on radical Islam as the source of terrorism never strayed far from its association with the Holocaust as the primary and universal symbol of evil.[24]

After 9/11, three linked stereotypes supported the ideology that construed Islam as the common enemy of Israel and the United States: Islam's cultural resistance to modernity, its inherent violence as a religion, and its political connection to fascism. In an article published in *Newsweek* a month after the attacks, "The Politics of Rage: Why Do They Hate Us?" the journalist Fareed Zakaria asserts that although Islam is not inherently opposed to modernity, Arab nations (as well as Iran) have dismally botched the project of modernization. The attacks, he avers, erupted from simmering resentment and humiliation at their own failure. Although he mentions anger at U.S. support of Israel's "iron-fisted rule," ultimately he deems that Israel's proximity as a success story has exacerbated Arab jealousy and rage. Zakaria's implicit answer: they hate us for their own failure to become like us.[25]

Some conservative evangelical leaders saw the 9/11 terrorist attacks as part of Islam's diabolical scheme for global dominion. They viewed Islam as an inherently violent religion that fostered murderous hatred toward both Christians and Jews. Jerry Falwell immediately declared that Mohammed was a terrorist, though public pressure later forced him to apologize. The leader of Christians United for Israel, John Hagee, wrote that "the first step in fulfilling Mohammed's dream is the destruction of Israel." With apocalyptic urgency, he warned that "America is at the crossroads!" It can obey God's word and "bless" Israel with absolute support, or face even greater disasters than 9/11. Another evangelical preacher wrote that the "legacy of hate that focuses on the Jews—and includes the Christians—has always been the obsession of Islam, and this clearly identifies it as *satanic*." Christian Zionism's most vociferous preachers attributed genocidal motivations to Islam as a religion, and they merged America together with Israel as potential Judeo-Christian victims of a new Holocaust perpetrated by Muslims.[26]

Another supposed common danger to the United States and Israel was "Islamofascism," a controversial concept propounded largely by secular intellectuals. Christopher Hitchens, one of the popularizers of the term, contended that although no form of Islam actually "preaches

racial superiority or proposes a master race," in practice, "Islamic fanatics operate a fascistic concept of the 'pure' and the 'exclusive' over
the unclean and the . . . profane." This attitude, he claimed, views Jews
as "an inferior or unclean race," and he generalized from an 1948 ca-
nard about Amin al-Husseini that this fanaticism explains "why many
Muslim extremists like the grand mufti of Jerusalem gravitated to Hitler's side." According to those who defended the validity of this term,
the political fusion of Islam and totalitarianism imperiled both Israel
and America, as Western democracies. In 2006, President Bush announced that "this nation is at war with Islamic fascists." Without
naming Israel, the word "fascist" conjures images of the Holocaust. "Islamic fascists," in popular understanding, look like Nazis reincarnated
in Middle Eastern garb, this time bent on exterminating freedom-loving
Americans alongside Jews in Israel. All three narratives of the Islamic
threat—as antimodern resentment, religious domination, and fascism—
united America and Israel as potential victims of horrendous violence,
but also as inevitable victors over the forces of evil.[27]

The United States and Israel faced another common foe according
to some neoconservative intellectuals, this one in Europe rather than
the Middle East. The anti-American sentiment being expressed by some
Europeans—in anti-globalization protests and marches against the invasion of Iraq—was coming to sound an awful lot like anti-Semitism,
and was, they claimed, indistinguishable in these discussions from anti-
Israel attitudes. The common answer to the post-9/11 question about
terrorists, "Why do they hate us?" already had that ring of eternal
bigotry: they hate us for who we are. "They" would now include those
Europeans who opposed the United States' 2003 invasion of Iraq at
the United Nations and in the streets. International criticism of the
United States mounted when the invasion yielded neither weapons of
mass destruction nor regime change, but instead scenes of mass destruction and photographs of abuse of Iraqis by American soldiers at
Abu Ghraib prison.

To those who championed America and Israel as allies in the war on
terror, criticism of America sounded more like irrational hatred than
reasoned critique, more like bigotry than political analysis. As Rabbi
Shmuley Boteach wrote from London in 2004, "For 2,000 years, Jews
have asked themselves the question an increasing number of Americans
are now asking: Why do they hate us? Is it possible that the underlying

causes are similar to the underlying causes of anti-Americanism?" Yes, wrote Nathan Sharansky in *Commentary:* "Anti-Americanism was a continuation of anti-Semitism by other means." Like anti-Semitism, according to this equation, anti-Americanism relies on standard conspiracy theories: hyperbolic fantasies of financial power and world domination. When European protesters yoked George Bush with Ariel Sharon as oppressors and warmongers, criticism of Israel, anti-Semitism, and anti-Americanism appeared to converge. "Rambo Jew has largely supplanted Shylock in the anti-Semitic imagination," wrote Daniel Goldhagen.[28]

Those who sought to explain this fusion of anti-Semitism and anti-Americanism as "twin brothers" identified resentment and envy at its heart. They argued that, in contrast to the Arab resentment of modernity, Europeans resented America and Israel for not being modern enough, for embracing a retrograde nationalism that relied on a belief in divine providence and was buttressed by their eagerness to use force. In a 2004 article in *Commentary,* Josef Joffe, editor of the German weekly *Die Zeit,* wrote that to "postnational" Europeans, who saw themselves in the moral avant-garde, America and Israel were "outriggers of the Occident"; they were "different from the rest of the West—different in the same way." From a cosmopolitan European outlook, both America and Israel appeared too nationalistic—they lustily revived those barbaric traits that Europeans had abandoned after the devastating lessons they had learned about nationalism from two world wars.[29]

Nonetheless, Europeans, Joffe contended, unconsciously envied the loss of those fierce warrior qualities they had come to reject—hence their irrational antagonism toward the power and exceptionalism expressed by Israel and America. This contorted mix of envy and hatred was widespread and could have destructive consequences. It motivated al-Qaeda members to kill Jews and Americans, and, in Europe, it led to "elimination lite," that is, pushing back against "the hyperpower-turned-empire" by "containing and defanging the American behemoth." In this article Joffe applies the idea articulated by neoconservative defenders of Israel in the late 1970s, and deployed forcefully after 1982, that verbal attacks can be as dangerous as military assaults.

In overreacting to the power of America and Israel, claims Joffe, Europeans refused to acknowledge the actual vulnerability of both nations. They ignored the fact that Israel's existence is still uniquely threatened, and that America is the only Western nation to have been attacked since 1945, leaving it precariously clinging to its perch as the "last remaining superpower." Given the irrational hatred directed toward them, both countries have no choice but to exercise more power against the threat of elimination—whether physical or verbal. In response to the twin threats of anti-Semitism and anti-Americanism, wrote Joffe, "America and Israel will remain both targets and warriors," ever victimized and fighting to retain their invincibility.

Although fear of Islamic terrorism was clearly more widespread among Americans than concern about European anti-Americanism, the latter, when equated with anti-Semitism, expressed anxiety that the whole world had turned against the United States. This in turn enhanced the belief in the moral innocence of Americans as victims of irrational hatred, and created an implicit connection between the attacks of 9/11 and the Holocaust. Americans could imagine themselves as persecuted by overcivilized Europeans, who, while claiming superiority to Bush's cowboy mentality, were reaching into their own dark past to vilify Americans, now as vulnerable as Jews and as primed as Israelis to battle a hostile world.

"The Harvard of Antiterrorism"

Americans turned to Israelis for guidance in defending their nation from threats at home as well as identifying common enemies abroad. As a 2006 U.S. Air Force study put it, "The United States is decades behind Israel in coming to terms with terrorism, and accepting the need for enhanced security measures on a day to day basis." Because the Israeli people "have faced daily attacks from Palestinian terrorists for decades," the study claimed, "Israel is, sadly, much more experienced, much more practical, and more willing to sacrifice some individual liberty for the sake of security in the face of a known and immediate threat." Lessons in sacrificing civil liberties were only part of what Israel had to offer when American police, soon after 9/11, started training with Israeli counterterrorism experts. Merging foreign and domestic spheres into a single battlespace epitomized the new concept of homeland security, and Israel offered the experience, technology, and language to tutor Americans in this new way of conceiving the nation as the homeland.[30]

When President Bush first used the word "homeland" on September 20, 2001, in his announcement launching the war on terror, the locution struck many as jarring and even un-American. Although "homeland" has the ring of ancient loyalties, no American president had used it before to rally the nation for war, and it had never been part of the political lexicon. "Homeland" had Old World associations, like the place immigrants left behind with sentimental attachments. But it also evoked darker meanings, like "fatherland" and the German *Heimat,* as appropriated by Nazi ideologies of racial purity.[31]

"Homeland" implies an ethnocentric foundation of national identity, a connection to a land embedded in the past, a sense of native origins, birthplace, and birthright. It appeals to common bloodlines, ancient ancestry, and ethnic or racial homogeneity. Although American national identity has always been linked to geography, "homeland" has connotations that depart from the image of a boundless American identity, a nation in motion, that has long characterized its exceptional nature, as in "Manifest Destiny," or a "nation of immigrants." These visions of nationhood also rely on racial exclusions and the appropriation of native land. "Homeland," though, makes mobility look suspicious, and the term appeals to the xenophobic fears raised after 9/11, when "aliens," immigrants, and foreigners, even naturalized citizens, began to be regarded as threatening outsiders and potential terrorists.

"Homeland" refers to the aspirations of a people to realize their sense of nationhood in a sovereign state, but also to the opposite: exile or foreign domination. In 2001, the Zionist idea of the Jewish homeland was arguably the best known usage of this term to Americans, who were also becoming aware of the contesting Palestinian claim to a homeland in same territory. Bush's reference to the "American homeland" did not borrow directly from this context, but given the strong American identification with Israel, the Jewish homeland had a striking resonance after 9/11. "Homeland" tied a people to a territory and birthright, and it also evoked the threat of catastrophic loss.

When Bush first used the word in 2002, no one could tell whether it would catch on in vernacular usage, outside the bureaucracy of the new Department of Homeland Security. Its use remains limited and has not supplanted "our country" or "America" as a common rallying cry for patriotic pride. "Homeland" rarely appeared in the nationalist slogans popularized by Donald Trump as candidate and president—"America First," "Make America Great Again," "American Carnage"—but these expressions incorporate many of the connotations of the word.

"Homeland," rather than becoming just another word for the American nation, came to signify American insecurity: the nation as victim, as existentially endangered, vulnerable to protean threats that include terrorists, "illegal aliens," drug smugglers, refugees, and immigrants, all merged together in a racialized sense of foreignness. The concept of homeland makes little sense apart from security, and homeland security relates to making all aspects of domestic life secure, both in the narrow sense of a domicile and in the broader sense of the nation. This all-encompassing approach to security is what Americans have sought to learn from Israelis since 2001.

Commentators after 9/11 claimed that the attack on the World Trade Center exposed the permeability of national borders, which had been eroded by the very forces of globalization that the trade center represented. The word "homeland" performed the cultural work of shoring up those borders, while at the same time keeping alive a sense of pervasive insecurity. Although homeland security may strive to wall off the nation from foreign threats, it has worked both bureaucratically and conceptually to break down boundaries between inside and outside, between civil and military jurisdictions, and between policing and war-making, while strengthening divisions between citizens and aliens. Building walls and high-tech security systems to monitor foreigners at the borders, homeland security also redraws those boundaries throughout the nation, between Americans who can claim the United States as their native land and their birthright, and immigrants and those who look to homelands elsewhere, who can be rendered as inexorably foreign.

The concept of homeland security did not emerge suddenly from the wreckage of the Twin Towers; it draws on a long history of affective emotional associations between the home and the nation, and its landscape includes institutions in place before 2001, such as prisons and gated communities. Homeland security focuses on securing every area of social life by means of home security systems, border security, cyber security, urban surveillance, and systems that monitor communication and intrude into the private lives of citizens and noncitizens alike. Every public and private space is seen as susceptible to foreign intrusion. In the 2004 election, "security moms" replaced "soccer moms" as the key voters to court, both referring to a similar population of white suburban women. A columnist for *USA Today,* who identified herself as a security mom, said that the two figures she feared most were "Islamic terrorists" and "criminal illegal aliens." In 2007, Attorney General Alberto Gonzales defended his embattled Justice Department by contending that during the previous two years, the department had made "great strides in securing our country from terrorism, protecting our neighborhoods from gangs and drugs, shielding our children from predators and pedophiles and protecting the public trust by prosecuting public corruption." He yoked terrorism and crime to the intimate violation of children, portraying the nation as both vulnerable and innocent.[32]

Paradoxically, homeland security is inseparable from an expansionist agenda, with the acceptance of a never-ending war against terrorism and the embrace of empire as a way of life. If every crevice of the home requires constant vigilance from intruders, the borders of the homeland are not strong enough when thought of as conterminous with the geographic boundaries of the nation-state. The 2001 attack revealed that threats to the homeland from small stateless groups are omnipresent, and so, according the 2004 *9/11 Commission Report*, "9/11 has taught us that terrorism against American interests 'over there' should be regarded just as we regard terrorism against America 'over here.' In this same sense, the American homeland is the planet."[33]

This idea is not connected with a sense of feeling at home in the world. On the contrary, with no distinction between "over there" and "over here," the planet permeates the homeland with the threat of foreign infiltration. For Americans, to understand their nation as a homeland beset by existential threats is to see themselves like Israelis, who inhabit a land they regard as their inalienable birthright, but one vulnerable to annihilation, and secured only by proactive and mobile intelligence and military capacities beyond the borders of the nation.

A popular Israeli television drama helped Americans imagine their country as "homeland." While the word rarely stands alone without its partner "security," an exception is the title of the acclaimed Showtime series *Homeland,* which premiered in 2011. Alex Gansa, who developed the show with Howard Gordon, explained that he came up with the title when he was seeking a word that would convey "creepy subversion," or, as James Traub describes it, "something sinister, xenophobic, un-American."[34]

It is possible to binge-watch every season of *Homeland* without ever realizing that it was an adaptation of a popular Israeli television show, *Prisoners of War.* Though different in style and substance, *Homeland* adopted the premise of the Israeli original, in which an Israeli soldier held as a prison of war in Lebanon converts to Islam and turns against his country. He becomes a double traitor, against both his religion and his nation. *Homeland* dramatizes the deep fear at the heart of the concept of homeland security—that there are no stable boundaries between us and them. Neither bombing terrorist bases abroad nor infiltrating sleeper cells at home can totally block the porous borders between the domestic and the foreign. *Homeland* explores terrors more frightening than the machinations of a terrorist mastermind whose minions masquerade as worldly reporters, or tailor-spies sewing Confederate costumes for Gettysburg reenactments—both plot points in the show. The horror driving the plot is that the most American of Americans—a white marine, Sergeant Nicholas Brody, a war hero running for office with a photogenic suburban family—can be transformed into the enemy: a Muslim and a suicide bomber. Uncertainty about his real allegiance—and the catastrophic potential of this uncertainty—created the frantic suspense that characterizes the first season. The uncertainty about the white marine's patriotism stands out against the situation of a black marine captured with him, who has clearly gone over to the other side. What's more, the advanced surveillance technology meant to secure the homeland only makes things worse. The protagonist of *Homeland,* CIA agent Carrie Mathison, illegally installs sophisticated equipment to monitor the inner domestic recesses of Brody's life. Her round-the-clock surveillance does yield the truth; it makes her the only official who knows that he is a terrorist. Yet the intimacy of surveillance also leads her to fall in love with him, which further blurs the boundaries between us and them. *Homeland* reveals that the terror at the heart of homeland security is not about the foreigner next door or the imam at the local mosque, but about the American war hero you elect for public office, the lover in your bed, or the suburban dad in his garage workshop—the idea that everything truly American could turn into its opposite and implode.

Homeland, with its Israeli roots, remapped America as the homeland. When the first season came out, critics praised it as a more subtle alternative to the first popular television series of the war on terror, the spy thriller *24*, also created by Gansa and Gordon. Commentators had criticized *24* for its overt xenophobia, and public officials accused it of normalizing torture. Though *Homeland* was also castigated for its stereotypes of bloodthirsty Arabs and Muslims, critics applauded it for displaying a moral conscience lacking in *24*. In *Homeland*, Brody becomes a turncoat only after witnessing the murder of Iraqi children in an American bombing attack. The ethical ballast of the series is the character Saul Berenson, a high-ranking CIA operative who is Carrie's mentor and protector. He is a secular American Jew with a sense of Jewish traditions, and he combines steely resolve with moral contemplativeness. He occasionally struggles with his ambivalent relationship to Israel, which ranges from illegally supplying intelligence to his Mossad counterpart to fending off a Mossad plot against him, and he has a tense visit with his sister, a settler on the West Bank, whose militant views repel him. Though Israel is not featured in any of the main plots, scenes that take place in Arab countries were often filmed there. The Israeli underpinnings are never far from the American *Homeland*.

Before *Homeland* Americanized its Israeli precursor, one of the longest-running and most popular network television series, *NCIS*, featured the collaboration between American and Israeli intelligence agents. Ziva David, a female Mossad agent, moves fluidly between Israeli and American intelligence agencies as though no national borders separated them. This tough and gorgeous assassin, played by the Chilean American actress Cote de Pablo, was rated one of the most popular characters on television for a decade, from 2003 to 2013. The show's huge viewing audience had critics comparing it to staples of the 1980s like *Dallas* and *ER*, and it spawned several popular spin-offs. *NCIS*, which stands for Navy Criminal Investigation Service, epitomizes the general understanding of homeland security as a combination of thwarting terrorist plots and solving crimes. The series shows the nation in terrible jeopardy on a regular basis, and its expert but playful agents fight terrorists and other criminals with high-tech gadgets—but without warrants—from their base in a Washington, D.C., office. In this serious milieu, a lovable, family-like team with a gruff father-figure act as though they were in an office comedy, in which scenes of Ziva's integration into American ways of espionage and life are often part of the joke.[35]

The Israeli characters in *NCIS* are introduced in the third season. At first it is difficult to distinguish between good guys and bad guys, but, unlike in *Homeland*, the ambiguity is quickly and clearly resolved. A Palestinian terrorist, Ari Ashwari, who is working for both al-Qaeda and Hamas, kills a beloved female American member of the intelligence team, and antiterrorism becomes a family affair for both the Americans and the Israelis. When Ziva shows up to represent Mossad in the investigation, we learn that Ari is her half brother. Their father is the head of Mossad, and his mother was a Palestinian doctor. The father raised his bicultural and bilingual son to become a double agent for Israel, and Ziva at first thinks he still works for Mossad. Ari, however, rebelled against his father, adopted his mother's side, and became a terrorist at large. When Ziva realizes what Ari has done, she shoots him in order to save her new boss, a rite of passage that integrates her into the American team. Ziva is like a female Ari Ben Canaan: she's a sharpshooter, a hardened assassin, a martial-arts expert, and a bit emotionally gruff. Over time, Ziva shifts her affections from her father and her Israeli lover to American counterparts, becomes a naturalized U.S. citizen, and has a child with her American colleague/lover. Although Ziva becomes Americanized and appears somewhat less aggressive than her male Israeli colleagues, she never loses the essential Israeli qualities she contributes to the team. What's key about her popular role in *NCIS* is that she makes her Israeli identity—whether in a dangerous undercover operation in Morocco or in the Jewish mourning ritual for her father—both natural and fundamental to the work of securing the American homeland.

In the realm of popular entertainment, *NCIS*, with its captivating Israeli agent, served to domesticate and normalize the actual cooperation between the United States and Israel in the work of counterterrorism, policing, and homeland security. That cooperation runs very deep. Soon after 9/11, delegations of law enforcement officials from all over the United States started traveling to Israel for training in counterterrorism. Two major pro-Israel groups sponsored them: the Anti-Defamation League of B'nai B'rith (ADL), and the Jewish Institute for National Security of America (JINSA), a neoconservative think tank with strong ties to the Likud Party and the Bush administration. JINSA also held Israeli-led seminars and conferences throughout the United States and claimed to have trained over nine thousand American law enforcement officials at the federal, state, and municipal levels in its Law Enforcement Exchange Program (LEEP) between 2002, when it was established, and 2011.[36]

The American police officers in these exchanges studied a variety of topics, such as "New Security Technology," "Border Security," and "Suicide Bombings: Methodology and Responses." They were given the opportunity to identify with Israel and to see America in its image. A brochure on the LEEP program quotes an FBI official who participated in the program: "Understanding terrorism from an Israeli perspective gave me a renewed sense of urgency relative to the war we are waging against terrorism here in the United States."[37] Promotional materials, newspaper articles, and testimonials tell a poignant tale of tiny Israel coming to the rescue of a sleeping giant who has just awoken to a perilous reality. As one Israeli sponsor told a reporter, "We are a little nation that has paid with blood for our experience. We don't want the American people or the American police to pay as we have." Israel's perilous past foretold what was in store for America, and its experience in combating terrorism made it a trailblazer for Americans to follow. Participants saw Israel on the front line of a global war on terror; most would likely have agreed with the assessment of the chief of the U.S. Capitol Police that "Israel is the Harvard of antiterrorism."[38]

That the United States and Israel faced the same enemy was a key message of these programs. The LEEP brochure quotes a sheriff from Louisiana stating, "There are countries out there and religious leaders and political leaders that wake up every day trying to kill Americans and trying to kill Israelis and others to be sure, so from that standpoint you carry that passion and reality back home." After a visit to Israel, the head of the New Jersey State Police claimed to have restructured his organization to defend his state against the "worldwide threats by Hamas and Al Qaeda," even though Hamas did not operate globally. Delegates carried home the conviction that Israel was the vanguard for a battle America had yet to face. One of the initiators of the program, Louis Anemone, director of security for the New York Metropolitan Transit Authority, contended that "today's terrorists appear to be using Israel as a testing ground to prepare for a sustained attack against the U.S."[39]

LEEP emphasized the monolithic nature of this global enemy. One of its sessions examined "The Mindset of the Suicide Bomber," as though an essential psychology could be divorced from any political context. That psychology fit the stereotype of an Islamic radical. Illustrating a description of that session in the LEEP brochure is a photograph of a young man encased in a suicide vest, his face veiled in black, holding a rocket launcher in one hand and a Koran in the other. LEEP's thirty-eight-page glossy brochure has only one page of photographs without captions. At the top, Osama bin Laden stands with an outstretched arm as though blessing the terrorists in the other photos, identifiable as members of Hamas by their green flags and insignia. Anyone could recognize their evil intentions, represented by marching male fighters, a mother defiantly holding a rifle with her baby on her hip, and a little boy wearing a belt of bombs around his waist. The message is an old one associated with Palestinians, not only about the danger these unnamed figures pose toward their potential victims, but also about their disregard for the sanctity of life, even of their own children.[40]

The delegations to Israel included travel to sites of suicide bombings, border patrols, and checkpoints in the West Bank—as well as tourist sites. None of the accounts mention the occupied territories, and they make no distinction between the military control of an occupied population and civilian policing in the United States. American police express envy at the extraordinary cooperation among Israeli agencies: "You can't tell the difference between the military, the border guards, and the police," stated one participant. None acknowledge the merging of these agencies as the hallmark of the occupation and what has been called the "matrix of control" over every aspect of Palestinian lives.[41] None note, either, how such cooperation would violate the traditional American law that separates the military from civil law enforcement, a separation that homeland security—both in theory and in practice—had a hand in eroding after 9/11.

The pedagogy of homeland security united America and Israel as allies in the war on terror by blurring other boundaries—between military occupation and urban policing, between different Arab and Islamic organizations, and, most important, between terrorists and criminals. "Terrorism" became a capacious term for many different forms of criminality. In 2006, Israel's minister of internal security, Avi Dichter, spoke at the annual convention of the International Association of Chiefs of Police in Boston. With FBI chief Robert Mueller and Attorney General Alberto Gonzales by his side, Dichter told the audience of ten thousand that there was an intimate connection between crime and terror—that they were "two sides of the same coin." The war on drugs, he declared, should be fought in the same way as the interconnected war on terror, and he applauded U.S. plans to construct a security fence along the entire Mexican border. He claimed that because there is a limited pool of deeply committed religious fanatics, terrorists enlist new recruits from the ranks of criminals, who are easily seduced to "decorate their shallow criminal values with nationalism, religion and pseudo-fanaticism." He coined a new term to describe this melding of the terrorist and the criminal: "crimiterrorist."[42]

The basic assumption of these programs is that the conditions of Israeli counterterrorism can be transferred to policing the cities and borders of the United States. The question is never raised (in public accounts of these training sessions) of the propriety of policing American cities as though they were occupied territory, and of treating citizens as though they were potential terrorists. If anything, these identifications are reinforced, especially in New York City, where, according to a *New York Times* article from 2005, "the New York City Police Department has worked with the Israelis since soon after the Sept. 11 terrorist attacks and has permanently stationed a Hebrew-speaking detective in Israel, who returns to the city often to train other officers." In 2003, a secret Demographics Unit was established in New York to spy on and monitor Muslim communities in the city; it was not abandoned until 2014. A former police official told the Associated Press that the goal of the Demographics Unit was to "map the city's human terrain" through a program that was partially modeled on Israeli operations in the West Bank.[43]

Civil rights and civil liberties groups objected to American police being trained in using the Israeli antiterrorist tactic of profiling. One police chief denied that this was racial profiling because the Israelis taught them how to focus on the "behavior of potential bombers, not on race or religion." Most of the police officials interviewed by the press praised their Israeli trainers for their "technical skills," such as how to spot suicide bomber "handlers" in a crowd, or how to aim for a suspect's head so as not to detonate any explosives that might be strapped to his torso.[44]

The synergy between Israeli training and American policing influenced a wide array of connections. In 2005, the *Los Angeles Times* ran a feature about a JINSA alumnus from the Los Angeles Police Department bomb squad whose extensive Israeli training helped him become an expert in dealing with suicide bombs and improvised explosive devices (IEDs). He then became a military advisor who taught Marines fighting in Iraq to protect themselves from both. He explained some of the parallels between the streets of LA, Israeli counterterrorist training, and Fallujah, Iraq: "You've got to go door to door to dig these guys out. . . . The more you stay in your vehicle, the more you're going to pay—just like in police work. You're not going to find the dope dealers or bank robbers by sitting in the police station." His international itinerary connected the dots between Los Angeles and Fallujah via Gaza, to map a political landscape in which criminals, insurgents, and terrorists blend into a single threat.[45]

The militarization of the police in the United States and around the globe started long before 9/11 and cannot be attributed solely to Israeli initiatives. But the reframing of criminals as potential terrorists and the use of tactics transferred from a military occupation to the streets of American cities had the effect of casting the American police as an occupying force, and it may have contributed to the increased tendency to treat people of color and people engaged in political protest as foreign threats. Israeli training also emphasized police officers' perception of their own vulnerability and the need to exert aggressive force to defend themselves.

Reports of the encounters between American and Israeli police played up their strong emotional appeal, showing the Americans as identifying with the potent Israeli mix of vulnerability and invincibility. The first JINSA delegation, for instance, included "an emotionally charged meeting" in which the chief of the Port Authority of New York and New Jersey presented the Israeli police commissioner with a "Star of David crafted from steel salvaged from the destroyed World Trade Center." According to a JINSA account of the meeting, American police came away with "respect for Israel's efficiency and advanced tactics, coupled by its ability to enforce the law in a humane manner, despite dealing with countless depraved terrorists." Newspaper accounts of American police training in Israel include tragic personal stories of Israeli police running to the site of a suicide bombing only to find a family member in the wreckage. The Americans in one story are described as "particularly moved by the candor and openness of the Israeli police," and after a description of one harrowing tale, "there was not a police chief in the room not in tears."[46]

The perception of the morality and vulnerability of the Israeli police was reinforced by the visit each delegation took to the Yad Vashem Holocaust memorial in Jerusalem. Within the United States, the ADL and the United States Holocaust Memorial Museum created a joint program to train law enforcement officials, including police cadets and FBI agents, in the lessons of the Holocaust. The lesson is a cautionary one: it teaches that German police enforced the racist policies of the Nazis and urges American police to respect the civil rights of the people they serve. Israeli police provide a countermodel, one based on their own heritage of Jewish persecution in the Holocaust and its legacy of an ever-present threat.[47]

The Laboratory and the Start-Up

After 9/11, Israel's reputation as a leader in the methods and ethics of counterterrorism was enhanced by its booming new homeland security industry, which produced advanced surveillance systems, high-tech weapons and devices, and military drones, along with expertise in deploying these technologies. With funding from the Department of Homeland Security, law enforcement agencies joined U.S. public and private institutions to purchase from Israel cutting-edge systems for airports, border control, urban surveillance, intruder detection, cybersecurity, and data mining. In 2004, the United States signed an agreement with Israel to fund research for jointly developing new homeland security technologies. Two years later, Boeing formed a consortium with the Israeli firm Elbit Systems, which was largely responsible for construction of the separation barrier along the Gaza and West Bank borders. The consortium worked on a project to install a high-tech surveillance system along the U.S.–Mexico border. The Department of Homeland Security had already used drones manufactured by Elbit to test the first unmanned aerial patrols of the southern border. In 2014, Elbit alone was awarded the contract for the U.S. Customs Border Protection Integrated Fixed Towers project, which was renewed and expanded in 2018. Promotional material for the initial consortium explained that "the talent and expertise that Elbit Systems . . . has employed for years in protecting Israel's border will now be put to use on US borders to keep Americans safe."[48]

Observers have described Israel's towering achievements in the homeland security industry in two radically different ways. Critics of the occupation have used the metaphor of the laboratory to explain how Israel has profited from its draconian and highly specialized control over the lives of Palestinians in the occupied territories. Boosters of Israel's economic accomplishments, in contrast, have emphasized the start-up, not only to refer to the large number of new high-tech companies in the country, but also as a metaphor for the nation as a whole.

In a 2007 article in *The Nation,* "Laboratory for a Fortressed World," Naomi Klein wrote that Israel's bestselling products, such as "high-tech fences, unmanned drones, biometric IDs, video and audio surveillance gear, air passenger profiling and prisoner interrogation systems" were developed from "precisely the tools and technologies Israel has used to lock-in the occupied territories." In the *New York Times,* in "Israel Discovers Oil," Thomas Friedman explained the same economic boom as stemming from Israel's advanced modern culture, which nurtured an "ecosystem of young innovators and venture capitalists." In Friedman's view, rather than a laboratory of domination, Israel is itself an experiment where the innovative imagination can roam free in pursuit of creative ventures.[49]

In the idea of the occupied territories as a laboratory, Palestinians are understood as being treated like guinea pigs, over whose land and livelihood Israelis seek to exert maximum control while accepting minimal responsibility for human life. According to this view, Israel's lucrative business in homeland security took off because sealed and controlled spaces were available close at hand for experimenting with all forms of securitization. Based on his research in Gaza, human rights organizer Darryl Li contends that the Israeli disengagement from the Gaza Strip in 2005 did not remove the territory from Israeli control as much as allow for more experimentation in the use of buffer zones, closure of certain areas, and air power. Cutting off Palestinian areas with barriers and checkpoints, mostly in Gaza but also in enclaves throughout the West Bank, created conditions for testing a wide variety of techniques that monitored and restricted the movement of people, including systems of incarceration and interrogation.[50] For some, this view of the occupied territories as a vast security laboratory provides an explanation for why the Israeli government has refused to relinquish land for a political agreement with the Palestinians. Rather than representing a security threat or a humanitarian disaster, they argue, the occupied territories—including their threats and disasters—have offered opportunities for researching, implementing, and marketing equipment, services, and systems that armies and police from the United States and other countries can purchase and deploy both at home and abroad.

In 2013, the Israeli filmmaker Yotam Feldman made a documentary, *The Lab,* about the Israeli defense industry. He explains in an essay that "the product [Israeli salesmen and executives] are selling is unique. Rather than rifles, rockets or bombs, the Israeli companies sell their experience. The long-running conflict with the Palestinians has created a unique and unrivalled laboratory for testing technologies and ideas relating to 'asymmetric warfare'—a conflict between a state and civil or irregular resistance. In this manner the Israeli conflict with the Palestinians may be seen as a national asset—rather than a burden." The documentary dates this trend to 2002, when Israel re-invaded the West Bank and the Gaza Strip during Operation Defensive Shield, reversing the process of Israeli territorial withdrawals that had been initiated by the Oslo Accords. Many army officers went into private business after that, and Israel's arms industry began bringing in record amounts of money.[51]

Feldman's documentary shows that Israel's weapons and security systems appeal to a broad international market. Jeff Halper, an Israeli anthropologist and activist, explains this widespread appeal based on the credibility of Israel's experimentation, which turns the conduct of real life into a laboratory of control:

> The Occupied Palestinian Territory has been transformed into probably the most monitored, controlled and militarized place on earth. It epitomizes the dream of every general, security expert and police officer to be able to exercise total biopolitical control. In a situation where the local population enjoys no effective legal protections or privacy, they and their lands become a laboratory where the latest technologies of surveillance, control and suppression are perfected and showcased, giving Israel an edge in the highly competitive global market. Labels such as "Combat Proven," "Tested

in Gaza" and "Approved by the IDF" on Israeli or foreign products greatly improves their marketability.[52]

Israelis have marketed their weapons and systems of homeland security to Americans not only based on testing in the occupied territories, but also through a broader perception of Israel as an invincible victim. According to this image, Israel has confronted terror throughout a long, tragic history of Jewish persecution, Arab aggression, and Palestinian suicide bombing. It has applied itself to developing weapons and security systems out of the urgent need to protect its population from extermination, all the while maintaining belief in its integrity as a Western-style democracy.

In this narrative of the laboratory, Israelis have little incentive to negotiate a real peace with the Palestinians, because the lucrative security market has too much potential. What the Israelis are selling to the rest of the world is not weaponry to defeat an enemy once and for all, but systems for pacification and management, which match the approach that many governments have come to take toward their increasingly urbanized and heterogenous populations. Naftali Bennett, the far-right Israeli economy minister, was quoted as saying, after a trip to China in 2013, "No one on earth is interested in the Palestinian issue. What interests the world from Beijing to Washington to Brussels is Israeli high-tech."[53] As Naomi Klein writes, "The chaos in Gaza and the rest of the region doesn't threaten the bottom line in Tel Aviv, and may actually boost it. Israel has learned to turn endless war into a brand asset, pitching its uprooting, occupation and containment of the Palestinian people as a half-century head start in the 'global war on terror.'"[54]

The occupation as laboratory is not the narrative of Israel's economic achievements that is featured in publications like *Forbes* and the *Wall Street Journal*. The story found there is more often the one told by Dan Senor and Saul Singer in *Start-Up Nation: The Story of Israel's Economic Miracle* (2009).[55] Dan Senor had served as spokesperson for the U.S. Coalition Provisional Authority in Iraq in 2003–2004, where he became known for his positive media spin as Baghdad spun out of control, especially for his portrayal of Iraqi leaders as happy with the occupation.[56] He had more success with his work on Israel. *Start-Up Nation* was widely reviewed in both the business and the mainstream press, and the title has stuck as a kind of nickname for Israel.

Senor and Singer try to explain the same phenomenon as do those who focus on the laboratory: how Israel wrested lucrative economic gains from terribly unstable political conditions of war and terrorism, during a decade of global economic downturn. The authors repudiate the narrative of Israel experimenting in a laboratory of occupation by revivifying a heroic narrative of triumph over adversity, one that repeats many of the major Zionist tropes through which Americans came to know Israel.

Start-Up Nation reads like the business edition of *Exodus,* with brains substituting for brawn. The book reanimates earlier popular narratives about Israel's modernity and revamps them for the neoliberal economy. Even the kibbutz, the symbol of Israel's socialist origins, becomes the prototype for modern entrepreneurship. The "barren wasteland" of Palestine spurred the agricultural ingenuity of the kibbutz, and twenty-first-century Israelis inherited this penchant for taking problems and turning them into assets. The proliferation of start-ups is the modern incarnation of "making the desert bloom." Senor and Singer also use the metaphor of the laboratory, but in a different way from left-leaning critics. In their preface, they quote a young software executive saying that by isolating Israel, its "adversaries had actually created the perfect laboratory to test ideas." The authors later ask the rhetorical question, "What is the value of the attributes that Israelis have developed as a result of the constant efforts to crush their nation's development?" Bringing curiosity and creativity to the brutal fight for survival, claim Senor and Singer, was what turned Israel into a laboratory, not domination over others.[57]

Senor and Singer claim that Israel's history, society, and culture made it uniquely suited to the entrepreneurial spirit of the high-tech start-up economy, and they identify military service as the major factor. The incubator for innovation is Israel's unique military structure, with its universal service and frequent reserve duty. The military, they claim, has an unusually egalitarian, anti-hierarchical culture, where, in contrast to traditional armies with top-down discipline, middle-level commanders have the leeway to improvise and are even expected to question their superiors. In addition, army service levels class differences, because recruits come from all walks of life and backgrounds and make lifelong connections. These descriptions resemble the romantic images of Israeli soldiers from 1967, when American reporters delighted in their ragtag appearance, and a militarized nation gave the appearance of being antimilitaristic. To emphasize the anti-elitist and communal nature of military service, the authors quote Michael Oren, an American-born historian who was formerly Israeli ambassador to the United States, saying that the Israeli army is more similar to "George Washington's 1776 Continental Army than it is to the American army of 2008," thus rendering Israeli soldiers more American than the post-Vietnam members of the United States Armed Forces.[58]

While praising the egalitarianism of the military, the authors make it clear that there is a hierarchy of elite intelligence units, which they liken to Ivy League universities. Promising students are selected and groomed from high school for special research units, and those coming from one particular elite army intelligence group launch the majority of high-tech start-ups. It is not just that these graduates are well connected, claim the authors. Their experience in the unit provides them with all the qualities of successful entrepreneurship: fluidity, creativity, assertiveness, anti-authoritarianism, self-reliance, and a competitive team spirit.

As an example of the ingenuity of Israeli middle-level commanders, *Start-Up Nation* offers a "typical" story of a young commander in the West Bank city of Nablus who is faced with rescuing an injured soldier being held by a terrorist. With only his troops, a bulldozer, and an attack dog, he must figure out how to save the soldier and kill the terrorist, while protecting Palestinian schoolchildren next door and staying cognizant of international journalists on the rooftop. With no time to get instructions from higher-ups, he improvises—and within four hours, he has smoke-bombed the school, bulldozed the house, shot a new terrorist on the scene, and used the dog to "neutralize the terrorist" who is holding the injured soldier. For the authors, this story exemplifies the innovativeness and multitasking required of a commander who is "responsible for the lives of a lot of people: his soldiers, Palestinian schoolchildren, journalists."[59] The context of the second intifada does not come into play, nor is any explanation offered for the situation the soldier faces in Nablus.

The idea that Israel is an invincible victim constantly besting the challenges of a perpetual war contributes to its value in the eyes of international business. The authors explain that Google, Microsoft, and other companies initially hesitated to invest in Israel because of their fear that violence and terrorism would disrupt business. But Israelis, responding with characteristic grit, were not afraid to go to their offices as shells exploded during the 2006 Lebanon War, and they demonstrate on a daily basis that violence does not interrupt the flow of business. This determination, write Senor and Singer, "transformed the very dangers that may make Israel seem risky into evidence of inviolable assets."[60] Vulnerability to constant risk turns Israel into a lucrative investment.

The narrative of *Start-Up Nation* reproduces the paradox of exceptionalism, presenting Israel as both unique and exemplary. Its entrepreneurial culture is superior to that of other countries, even advanced ones like Singapore, and certainly to Arab countries, whose business models are described as "bazaars." Yet "the whole world has much to learn from Israel," especially the United States. Americans should imitate the Israelis, for instance, in making better use of their own experience in fighting the war on terror. The authors recommend that Silicon Valley recognize the value of U.S. veterans, who have become more like Israelis. After many tours in Iraq and Afghanistan, junior commanders have developed an "interdisciplinary" range, just like Israelis, in counterinsurgency multitasking: they have played the role of "small-town mayor, economic-reconstruction czar, diplomat, tribal negotiator, manager of millions of dollars' worth of assets, and security chief, depending on the day."[61] Following the model of Israel could turn America's long and costly wars into a more profitable venture, and its overstretched veterans into multitasking entrepreneurs.

Ultimately the authors present the start-up nation as a unique combination of cutting-edge modernity and a return to Zionist origins in the land. As one entrepreneur puts it, "You're doing something for humanity. You are inventing a new drug or a new chip. You feel like a *falah* ["farmer" in Arabic], a farmer of high tech. You dress down. You're with your buddies from the army unit. You talk about a way of life—not necessarily about how much money you're going to make, though it's obviously also about that."[62] The authors trace the theme of Israel as the original start-up nation to its mythic founding: "a conscious effort to build from scratch a modern reincarnation of an ancient nation-state." This unique past also makes it a model for the future, a light to other nations: "Israel is one of the world's foremost idea factories, and provides clues for the meta-ideas of the future."[63]

Those who view the occupied Palestinian territories as a laboratory of state control also see Israel as an idea factory, manufacturing the "meta-ideas of the future." But it will be a dystopian future: all around the world, people will inhabit cities that look like military zones, occupied by police indistinguishable from soldiers, and monitored by sophisticated systems of homeland security.

CONCLUSION

In his 2009 speech in Cairo, President Barack Obama spoke of the unbreakable bond between the United States and Israel. The meaning and strength of that bond have fluctuated over the decades since Israel became a state in 1948, but it remains as powerful as ever today. At the same time, it is also more contested than ever before.

While campaigning for office the year before he gave this speech, Obama had evoked a nostalgic view of Israel as a paragon of progressive values. He honored "the idea of returning to a homeland and what that meant for people who had suffered from the Holocaust," and he spoke of his "great affinity for the idea of social justice that was embodied in the early Zionist movement and the kibbutz." Israel's story resonated with Obama's personal "history of being uprooted" and with "the African-American story of exodus," through the example of "overcoming great odds and a courage and a commitment to carving out a democracy and prosperity in the midst of hardscrabble land." What Obama loved about Israel when he visited was that "the land itself is a metaphor for rebirth."[1]

On the campaign trail eight years later, Donald Trump evoked another Israel, one which is successfully fighting present dangers—an example of rigorous homeland security. After a bomb went off in New York City, Trump called on local law enforcement to follow the Israelis' lead on racial profiling. If a person even looks suspicious, he said, the Israelis "will take that person in and check [him or her] out," while he lamented that Americans, in contrast, were hobbled by "trying to be so politically correct." Trump promised to build a wall on the Mexican border and argued that "all you have to do is ask Israel whether walls work." His analogy to the separation barrier on the West Bank implicitly associated Mexican immigrants with the threatening image of Palestinian terrorists.[2]

Each presidential candidate related his image of Israel to his own idea of American exceptionalism. For Obama, Israel's origins had a multiethnic appeal that reflected America's noble commitment to social amelioration and renewal. For Trump, Israel's vigilant devotion to security offered a robust model for "making America great again." Trump's praise of walls and profiling in Israel validated racial paranoia at home.

In a speech before the American Israel Public Affairs Committee when he was campaigning, Trump used language similar to Obama's, declaring that "the bond between the United States and Israel is absolutely and totally unbreakable."[3] Once in office, despite their different rhetorical cadences, both presidents took unprecedented steps to fortify the alliance for the future. Although President Obama garnered a reputation for bringing the bond nearer to a breaking point, he presided over an agreement that provided a record military aid package to Israel. A year after this deal, President Trump, breaking with U.S. precedent and international consensus, recognized Jerusalem as the capital of Israel and ordered that the U.S. embassy be moved there from Tel Aviv.

Campaign rhetoric and presidential policy obscured the mounting tensions around the special relationship in the United States. By the second decade of the twenty-first century, Israel had become a more contentious topic than at any time since the 1982 Lebanon War. On the eve of Obama's first inauguration, when many Americans were disaffected with their own endless wars in Iraq and Afghanistan, Israel's military invaded the Gaza Strip, and it did so again in 2012 and 2014. Many Americans supported these attacks as acts of self-defense to protect civilians from rockets launched into Israel by Hamas. Others decried Israel's overwhelming use of force—the killing of civilians and the widespread destruction of homes and infrastructure—as disproportionate to the threat posed by Palestinians in Gaza.

Reactions to events in Gaza brought to the surface long-simmering unease with Israel's treatment of Palestinians. The harshness of life under occupation had become more visible in mainstream American media, as had the stridency of Jewish settlers, whose numbers had doubled to eight hundred thousand during the Obama years. Younger generations of Americans, Jews and non-Jews alike, hadn't read or seen *Exodus,* nor did they recall the thrill of David defeating Goliath in the Six-Day War. They were not nostalgic for images of "the Israel we have seen in the past," which John Chancellor's generation venerated. Israel has been occupying Palestinian territories throughout their lifetime, and many have grown up with the tragic narrative about two peoples warring over one land, both with valid aspirations and grievances. Many Jewish youth no longer identify with Israel the way their parents and grandparents did, because they refuse to set aside their liberal values when it comes to Israel's illiberal treatment of Palestinians. Within the organized community, a number of rabbis avoid speaking of Israel to their congregants.[4]

The American liberal consensus about Israel has also broken down. It was a consensus formulated in the 1940s by New Deal liberals who were committed to antifascism, internationalism, and modernization, and reinforced by enthusiasm about Israel's humane and mighty army in 1967. But the consensus was shaken by the invasion of Lebanon in 1982, and a new liberal consensus then formed in response to the first intifada, expressing the belief that acknowledging the Palestinian side of the story would help end the occupation and restore Israel to its idealistic Zionist roots.

This liberal consensus has now been replaced by a conservative one, whose origins date back to neoconservative arguments of the 1970s and 1980s, the backlash against the media portrayal of the 1982 war, and the political ascension of the religious Right during the Reagan administration. When President Trump endorsed a long-standing conservative agenda item for Jerusalem, he appealed not only to his pro-Likud Republican Jewish backers, but also to white Christian evangelicals, who overwhelmingly supported him in the election. Israel has become a defining cause for Republicans, Orthodox Jews, and Christian evangelicals.

A generation gap is surfacing, however, not just among American Jews. Young evangelicals are beginning to question their elders' allegiance to the biblical image of Israel as they see real Palestinians suffering under Israeli rule.[5] Tensions within the Democratic Party also reflect generational fissures, with an old guard asserting its staunch allegiance to Israel—although criticizing its right-wing government—while a younger, multiracial, progressive alliance criticizes Israeli policies and supports Palestinian rights. In November 2017, for the first time, Democratic congressional representatives introduced a bill promoting Palestinian human rights.[6]

Radical activism on behalf of Palestinian rights has also increased, and some of the arguments hark back to the transnational connections made by the Black Power movement, the antiwar movement, and the struggle against apartheid in South Africa. Some Americans have endorsed the international Boycott, Divestment, Sanctions (BDS) movement, started in 2005 by Palestinian nongovernmental organizations. The movement has been extremely controversial in the United States. Supporters see BDS as a nonviolent campaign for equality and human rights, while detractors view it as the latest attempt to destroy the Jewish state and accuse its supporters of anti-Semitism. The organization has faced a backlash on campuses and in government. Critics of BDS have expended great effort to defeat it, claiming that the movement is mortally dangerous to Israel and yet, at the same time, that it has been ineffectual in shaking the fundamental attachment of Americans to Israel.

This paradox of extreme vulnerability and fundamental indomitability has been at the heart of the story of "our American Israel." Despite generational and political changes, the image of the invincible victim continues to underlie a broad cultural consensus about Israel in the United States. It has framed what liberals and conservatives alike talk about when they talk about Israel, and its pliability has given it remarkable staying power. It has not only crossed party lines but has also spanned historical eras, providing continuity when fear of "radical Islam" replaced that of the "communist menace," and the war on terror followed the Cold War. Israel fought at the front lines of these American wars. Veneration of Israel's military relies on the perception that it defends the nation from unique exposure to the threat of annihilation. Concern for Israel's vulnerability casts its exercise of power in a humane light because of the idea that it is wielded to protect a historically persecuted people from extermination, and not from any desire for domination or expansion. In this way, Israel mirrors a widespread image of America as anti-imperial.

The paradox of power and weakness also informs Americans' view of their own place in the world. Despite living in a country that has a global military presence, hundreds of bases around the world, and drone technology that penetrates faraway spaces from above, many Americans perceive their borders as remarkably violable—by terrorists, illegal immigrants, drug dealers, and criminals. President Trump's motto, "Make America Great Again," means reinforcing the indomitable essence of national identity, perceived to be undermined by hostile forces abroad and enfeebled by political correctness at home. As in Israel's case, vulnerability and invincibility are inextricably intertwined.

With the announcement that the U.S. embassy would move to Jerusalem, President Trump reinforced the ties binding the two nations and signaled his imperviousness to the rest of the world. Siding with Israel meant asserting American power against the world of nations. In Ambassador Nikki Haley's speech before the United Nations General Assembly announcing this decision, she was not defending Israel against a vote that condemned it, as the United States had done so often in the past. This time, the resolution was against the U.S. decision, and the ambassador was standing up for America against the world. Israel's violation of international law—in annexing Jerusalem—became the occasion for the United States to assert its own sovereignty against the opprobrium of world opinion and the pressure to adhere to international norms.[7]

America and Israel make their stand, in Jerusalem, opposing the hostile world around them. That's also the plot of a popular zombie apocalypse film from 2013, *World War Z*. The undead are rising and overrunning the planet, turning living human beings into zombies. An American hero and his Israeli sidekick, a female soldier, save the remnants of civilization from the zombies, who represent an amalgam of Western fears: terrorism, refugees, pandemics, and climate change, infused with echoes of slavery and miscegenation. What unites all these threats is their overrunning of borders, ultimately that between the living and the dead. In *World War Z*, Left Behind meets *Exodus*. The final apocalypse arrives in the form of loathsome creatures worthy of the Book of Revelation, with Jerusalem at ground zero.[8]

Jerusalem first appears on the screen as the only place of order and beauty remaining on the planet. The American hero, a world-weary international health expert played by Brad Pitt, arrives from South Korea in search of solutions to the zombie plague. The Israelis have succeeded in keeping out the zombies by building a huge wall, ancient in appearance but with state-of-the-art surveillance technology. In the 2006 book on which the movie is based, only Israel, South Africa, and Cuba have the know-how and political willpower to quarantine their citizens from the zombie invasion. The Israelis are the first to comprehend the nature of the threat because of the acute vigilance they already exercise to secure their precarious survival. In the book, the Israeli intelligence agents have impeccable credentials from having led heroic exploits in the past. One headed Mossad's assassination team, Operation Wrath of God, tracking down the terrorists who committed the Munich Olympics murders. His comrade directed the famous operation that rescued hostages in Entebbe.

In the movie, Israeli soldiers welcome both Arabs and Jews into their walled haven. The people inside resemble the "remnant" in prophecy stories, who survived the Tribulation and are awaiting the Second Coming. Jews and Arabs hold hands in a circle, dancing and singing together to celebrate their salvation. Music, however, arouses the zombies, who stampede over the walls by the thousands. While escaping by helicopter, Brad Pitt meets his match, a buff Israeli woman soldier who is a symbol of Israeli feminism and modernity. She proves her mettle by stoically enduring the amputation of her forearm after being bitten by a zombie. Through her sacrifice, the young, vibrant Israeli infuses the worn-out American with new fighting resolve. Together, with scientific knowledge and military skills, they halt the zombie invasion and save what remains of the sorry world.

Standing alone in defiance of the world, or fighting together to save it, many Americans tend to see idealized visions of their nation in Israel. This practice has great appeal but is also perilous. To disentangle the bonds tying together the two nations requires more than separating national interest from the influence of domestic politics and lobbying. It means reckoning with the image in the looking glass, recognizing how we have projected images of American exceptionalism onto our visions of Israel, as exceptionally modern, humane, powerful, and threatened.

Americans do share with Israel a foundational narrative, in which national liberation from colonial rule rests on the history of colonial conquest, and stories of exodus from tyranny rely on the dispossession of indigenous people. Looking beyond romantic reflections of the

past—promised lands, chosen peoples, frontier pioneers, wars of independence—would enable us to see the darker shadows of shared exceptionalism: the fusion of moral value with military force, the defiance of
international law, the rejection of refugees and immigrants in countries
that were once known as havens.

The "eternal bond" between Israel and America is not timeless. Its
history has been entangled both in political alliances and in the stories
Americans have told about their own national identity, the nature of
their society, and the role they play in the world. To stop seeing Israel
as a mirror of America means more than to shed myths for realism. No
relationship or alliance is free of fantasies and fears projected onto the
other as friend or foe. But by examining the mirror itself in order to
reckon with the image we are seeing there, we can break free from the
fantasy of accepting that image as reality. Not seeing ourselves in the
mirror—but seeing the mirror itself—would allow us to understand
ourselves as actors and not observers, and to take responsibility for the
tragic consequences of our actions.

"No daylight between the United States and Israel" is a phrase that
has recently joined "special relationship" and "unbreakable bond" in
the lexicon of U.S.-Israel relations. The metaphor of "no daylight" implies that the two nations' interests are so closely knit together that
nothing and no one can come between them. To see daylight between
the two countries would suggest separation and betrayal. But "no daylight" also means darkness, a fitting metaphor for the blindness that
has characterized the special relationship between the United States and
Israel. We must let in daylight if Americans are to understand why and
how this bond has come to be seen as unbreakable.

NOTES

ACKNOWLEDGMENTS

ILLUSTRATION CREDITS

INDEX

NOTES

Introduction

1. Barack Obama, "On a New Beginning," Remarks by the President at Cairo University, June 4, 2009, https://obamawhitehouse.archives.gov/the-press-office/remarks-president-cairo-university-6-04-09.

2. Ibid.

3. For an overview of U.S. aid to Israel through 2016, see the Congressional Research Service report prepared by Jeremy M. Sharp, "U.S. Foreign Aid to Israel," Congressional Research Service, December 22, 2016, https://fas.org/sgp/crs/mideast/RL33222.pdf. On the 2016 aid package, see Peter Baker and Julie Hirschfeld Davis, "U.S. Finalizes Deal to Give Israel $38 Billion in Military Aid," *New York Times*, September 13, 2016, A6.

4. Major works that take a cultural approach to the relationship between the United States and Israel include Michelle Mart, *Eye on Israel: How America Came to View Israel as an Ally* (Albany: State University of New York Press, 2006), and Melani McAlister, *Epic Encounters: Culture, Media, and U.S. Interests in the Middle East since 1945* (Berkeley: University of California Press, 2005). Mart focuses on the 1940s and 1950s, while McAlister discusses Israel as part of the wider relationship of the United States to the Middle East. I am indebted to both.

5. On the Puritan connection, see Todd Gitlin and Liel Leibovitz, *The Chosen Peoples: America, Israel, and the Ordeals of Divine Election* (New York: Simon and Schuster, 2010); Shalom Goldman, *God's Sacred Tongue: Hebrew and the American Imagination* (Chapel Hill: University of North Carolina Press, 2004); and Peter Gross, *Israel in the Mind of America* (New York: Knopf, 1983). Gross concludes: "Even as they go their own way, in pursuit of their own national interests, Americans and Israelis are bonded together like no two other sovereign peoples. As the Judaic heritage flowed through the minds of America's early settlers and helped to shape the new

American republic, so Israel restored the vision and values of the American dream. Each, the United States and Israel, grafted the heritage of the other onto itself" (p. 316).

6. On settler colonialism, see Lorenzo Veracini, *Settler Colonialism: A Theoretical Overview* (New York: Palgrave Macmillan, 2010); Patrick Wolfe, *Traces of History: Elementary Structures of Race* (New York: Verso, 2016); Steven Salaita, *The Holy Land in Transit: Colonialism and the Quest for Canaan* (Syracuse, NY: Syracuse University Press, 2006). For an analysis of the U.S. relationship with Israel that brings together Puritan origins and settler colonialism, see Anatol Lieven, *America Right or Wrong: An Anatomy of American Nationalism* (Oxford: Oxford University Press, 2004), 173–216.

7. Abiel Abbot, *Traits of Resemblance in the People of the United States of America to Ancient Israel: In a Sermon, Delivered at Haverhill, on the Twenty-eighth of November, 1799, the Day of Anniversary Thanksgiving* (Haverhill, MA: Moore & Stebbins, 1799), 6. On the significance of this passage, see Lieven, *America,* 188.

8. Benedict Anderson, *Imagined Communities: Reflections on the Origin and Spread of Nationalism* (New York: Verso, 1991).

9. Quoted in Michelle Mart, "Eleanor Roosevelt, Liberalism, and Israel," *Shofar: An Interdisciplinary Journal of Jewish Studies* 24 (2006): 78.

10. Leon Uris, *Exodus* (1958; repr., New York: Bantam Books, 1959), 572, 517.

1. Lands of Refuge

1. *Gentleman's Agreement,* directed by Elia Kazan (Los Angeles: 20th Century Fox, 1947).

2. Michael Cohen, *Truman and Israel* (Berkeley: University of California Press, 1990); Michael Cohen, *Palestine and the Great Powers: 1945–1948* (Princeton, NJ: Princeton University Press, 1982); Irene Gendzier, *Dying to Forget: Oil, Power, Palestine, and the Foundations of U.S. Policy in the Middle East* (New York: Columbia University Press, 2015); John Judis, *Genesis: Truman, American Jews, and the Origins of the Arab/Israeli Conflict* (New York: Farrar, Straus and Giroux, 2014); Allison Radosh and Ronald Radosh, *A Safe Haven: Harry S. Truman and the Founding of Israel* (New York: Harper, 2009); Dan Tschirgi, *The Politics of Indecision: Origins and Implications of American Involvement with the Palestine Problem* (New York: Praeger, 1983).

3. Quoted in Ben Shepard, *The Long Road Home: The Aftermath of the Second World War* (New York: Knopf, 2011), 112.

4. Anglo-American Committee of Inquiry, "Report to the United States Government and His Majesty's Government in the United Kingdom, 20 April 1946," http://

avalon.law.yale.edu/subject_menus/angtoc.asp. On the committee, see Cohen, *Palestine and the Great Powers*, 96–115; Leonard Dinnerstein, *America and the Survivors of the Holocaust* (New York: Columbia University Press, 1982), 73–100; William Roger Louis, *The British Empire in the Middle East, 1945–1951* (New York: Oxford University Press, 1984), 397–419; Amikam Nachmani, *Great Power Discord in Palestine: The Anglo-American Committee of Inquiry into the Problems of European Jewry and Palestine, 1945–1946* (London: Frank Cass, 1987).

5. Anglo-American Committee of Inquiry, "Report."

6. William H. Stringer, "Many Palestine Alternatives Offered," *Christian Science Monitor,* January 19, 1946, 16.

7. Ruth Gruber, *Exodus 1947: The Ship That Launched a Nation* (1948; repr., New York: Random House, 1999), 12; R. H. S. Crossman, *Palestine Mission: A Personal Record* (New York: Harper Brothers, 1947), 22; Nachmani, *Great Power Discord,* 74–75. On Crum's life, see his daughter's memoir: Patricia Bosworth, *Anything Your Little Heart Desires: An American Family Story* (New York: Simon and Schuster, 1998).

8. Crossman, *Palestine Mission,* 100.

9. "The Biltmore Program: Towards a Jewish State (May 11, 1942)," in *The Israel-Arab Reader: A Documentary History of the Middle East Conflict,* ed. Walter Laqueur and Barry Rubin, 7th ed. (New York: Penguin, 2008), 57.

10. Nachmani, *Great Power Discord,* 56; Ofer Shiff, *The Downfall of Abba Hillel Silver and the Foundation of Israel* (Syracuse, NY: Syracuse University Press, 2014), 94–95.

11. Crossman, *Palestine Mission,* 38, Allen Howard Podet, *The Success and Failure of the Anglo-American Committee of Inquiry, 1945–1946: Last Chance in Palestine* (Lewiston, NY: Mellen Press, 1986), 149–153.

12. "Leaders of Major Zionist Organizations Testify before Anglo-American Committee," *Jewish Telegraphic Agency,* January 9, 1946, 1; Bartley C. Crum, *Behind the Silken Curtain: A Personal Account of Anglo-American Diplomacy in Palestine and the Middle East* (New York: Simon and Schuster, 1947), 15.

13. Crossman, *Palestine Mission,* 39; Thomas A. Kolsky, *Jews against Zionism: The American Council for Judaism, 1942–1948* (Philadelphia: Temple University Press, 1990), 130–133.

14. Harold A. Hinton, "Einstein Condemns Rule in Palestine: Calls Britain Unfit but Bars Jewish State and Favors UNO—Compromise Is Studied," *New York Times,* January 12, 1946, 7; Crum, *Behind the Silken Curtain,* 15, 23–24; Crossman, *Palestine Mission,* 39.

15. Podet, *Success and Failure,* 184–186; Nachmani, *Great Power Discord,* 126–128.

16. Podet, *Success and Failure*, 172–173; Crum, *Behind the Silken Curtain*, 21–23.

17. Crum, *Behind the Silken Curtain*, 23; Crossman, *Palestine Mission*, 39.

18. Crossman, *Palestine Mission*, 33.

19. Quoted in Dinnerstein, *America and the Survivors*, 96–97.

20. Crossman, *Palestine Mission*, 33–34.

21. Ibid., 75.

22. Ibid., 79; Crum, *Behind the Silken Curtain*, 90.

23. For the vote, see Yosef Grodzinsky, *In the Shadow of the Holocaust* (Monroe, ME: Common Courage Press, 2004), 139. On Zionist organizing in DP camps, see Yehuda Bauer, *Flight and Rescue: Brichah* (New York: Random House, 1970); Dinnerstein, *America and the Survivors*, 63–96; Atina Grossman, *Jews, Germans, and Allies: Close Encounters in Occupied Germany* (Princeton, NJ: Princeton University Press, 2007), 178–182; Arieh J. Kochavi, *Post-Holocaust Politics: Britain, the United States, and Jewish Refugees, 1945–1948* (Chapel Hill: University of North Carolina Press, 2001), 33–62; Peter Novick, *The Holocaust in American Life* (Boston: Houghton Mifflin, 1999), 63–84; Shepard, *Long Road Home*, 105–112, 180–202.

24. Crum, *Behind the Silken Curtain*, 102; Crossman, *Palestine Mission*, 79–81.

25. Crum, *Behind the Silken Curtain*, 134.

26. Crossman, *Palestine Mission*, 19, 79, 38, 46.

27. Quotations from Dinnerstein, *America and the Survivors*, 97.

28. Quotations from ibid., 132–134.

29. Congressman quoted in Dinnerstein, *America and the Survivors*, 158; American Legion quoted in "Opposition to DPs Relaxed by Legion," *New York Times*, November 1, 1947, 5.

30. Henry Wallace, "Palestine, Food and Chiang Kai-shek," *New Republic*, November 24, 1947, 12.

31. Crum, *Behind the Silken Curtain*, 149.

32. Crossman, *Palestine Mission*, 109–110, including quote from Azzam Pasha.

33. Ibid., 110, 111.

34. Crum, *Behind the Silken Curtain*, 152.

35. Ibid., 153, 155.

36. Ibid., 159.

37. Ibid., 160; Crossman, *Palestine Mission*, 119.

38. Crum, *Behind the Silken Curtain*, 195, 197 (emphasis in original).

39. Ibid., 198, 203, 213.

40. Ibid., 213.

41. Ibid., 192.

42. James G. McDonald, *My Mission in Israel, 1948–1951* (New York: Simon and Schuster, 1951), 73; Kenneth Bilby, *New Star in the Near East* (New York: Doubleday, 1950), 265.

43. Crum, *Behind the Silken Curtain*, 203–204, 228, 230 (emphasis in original). For the population of Palestine, see Gudrun Krämer, *A History of Palestine: From the Ottoman Conquest to the Founding of the State of Israel* (Princeton, NJ: Princeton University Press, 2008), 305–306.

44. Crossman, *Palestine Mission*, 118, 134–135, 138.

45. Clifton Daniel, "Jewish Majority in Palestine Asked: Zionists Link State Claim to Million Influx in Ten Years," *New York Times*, March 9, 1946, 5.

46. Crossman, *Palestine Mission*, 123; Crum, *Behind the Silken Curtain*, 170.

47. Crum, *Behind the Silken Curtain*, 66, 227.

48. Anglo-American Committee of Inquiry, "Report," chap. 8.

49. Clifton Daniel, "Palestine Group Approves Magnes: Advocate of Bi-national State Evokes Tribute for Fair Play and Moderation," *New York Times*, March 15, 1946, 12.

50. Crossman, *Palestine Mission*, 130; Nachmani, *Great Power Discord*, 169. Historians have since debated the extent of the mufti's influence in the Nazi hierarchy and the prevalence of his views among Palestinians. For historical assessments of Haj Amin al-Husseini and the relation between Arab nationalists and Nazism, see Gilbert Achcar, *The Arabs and the Holocaust: The Arab-Israeli War of Narratives* (New York: Metropolitan Books, 2009); Jeffrey Herf, *Nazi Propaganda for the Arab World* (New Haven, CT: Yale University Press, 2009); and Philip Mattar, *The Mufti of Jerusalem: Al-Hajj Amin Al-Husayni and the Palestinian National Movement* (New York: Columbia University Press, 1988).

51. Albert Hourani, "The Case against a Jewish State in Palestine: Albert Hourani's Statement to the Anglo-American Committee of Enquiry of 1946," *Journal of Palestine Studies* 35 (Autumn 2005): 80–90; Crum, *Behind the Silken Curtain*, 254–255.

52. Hourani, "The Case against a Jewish State," 85, 81. For a condemnation of "refugeeism as a substitute for Zionism," see "World Zionist Conference Warned against 'Backdoor Diplomacy' in Fight for Palestine," *Jewish Telegraphic Agency*, August 5, 1945, 2. Ben-Gurion's diary quoted in Nachmani, *Great Power Discord*, 211.

53. Hourani, "The Case against a Jewish State," 88–89.

54. David Horowitz, *State in the Making* (New York: Knopf, 1953), 50; Crossman, *Palestine Mission*, 63; Nachmani, *Great Power Discord*, 191.

55. Anglo-American Committee of Inquiry, "Report," chap. 1.

56. Crossman, *Palestine Mission*, 167–168.

288 NOTES TO PAGES 38–43

57. Crum, *Behind the Silken Curtain*, 288, 260–261.

58. Ibid., vii, x. Crum's book was more overtly partisan and less sophisticated than Crossman's. Indeed, one committee member, Evan Wilson, later accused Crum of having had it ghostwritten by the pro-Zionist journalist Gerold Frank, who is thanked profusely in the acknowledgments. No matter how much prose Frank may have penned, the book was clearly a collaborative work. See Evan Wilson, *A Calculated Risk: The U.S. Decision to Recognize Israel* (1979; repr., Cincinnati, OH: Clerisy Press, 2008), 333. Wilson served as a State Department staff member of the Anglo-American Committee. Gerold Frank later became a famous ghostwriter for Hollywood stars, including Judy Garland.

59. I. F. Stone, *Underground to Palestine* (New York: Boni and Gaer, 1946); Stone, *This Is Israel* (New York: Boni and Gaer, 1948); Ruth Gruber, *Destination Palestine: The Story of the Haganah Ship Exodus 1947* (New York: A. A. Wyn, 1948); Henry Wallace, "The Problem of Palestine," *New Republic,* April 21, 1947, 12. Dorothy Thompson shifted her sympathies to the Arab cause after 1948, at great expense to her career.

60. Giora Goodman, "'Palestine's Best': The Jewish Agency's Press Relations, 1946–1947," *Israel Studies* 16, no. 3 (2011): 16; Freda Kirchwey et al., *The Palestine Problem and Proposals for Its Solution,* Memorandum submitted to the General Assembly of the United Nations (New York: Nation Associates, 1947). Lilli Shultz, director of the Nation Associates, insisted that the Jewish Agency's support for *The Nation* be confidential and that it be paid in installments by individuals without appearing in the Jewish Agency's books. Both Kirchwey and Shultz continued to advocate for Israel after 1948. In 1951 Kirchwey organized a memorandum signed by "nineteen religious, labor, education, and liberal leaders submitted to the General Assembly of the United Nations" calling for the "permanent resettlement of the Arab-refugee population in the Arab States." "The Arab-Refugee Problem: A Plan for Its Solution," *The Nation,* December 29, 1951, 563–566. In 1956, Shultz opened her own public relations firm, Kenmore Associates, whose main client was Israel.

61. Kirchwey, quoted in Sara Alpern, *Freda Kirchwey: A Woman of "The Nation"* (Cambridge, MA: Harvard University Press, 1987), 139–140, 197.

62. Kirchwey et al., *The Palestine Problem,* 47, 52. For an analysis of how this exaggerated accusation against Haj Amin al-Husseini developed in the 1940s and its subsequent political consequences, see Achcar, *Arabs and the Holocaust,* 150–173.

63. I. F. Stone, "Palestine Pilgrimage," *The Nation,* December 8, 1945, 616–617; Stone, "Jewry in a Blind Alley," *The Nation,* November 24, 1945, 543–544.

64. Walter C. Lowdermilk, *Palestine: Land of Promise* (New York: Harper, 1944).

65. Ibid., 66, 14, epigraph. See also Rory Miller, "Bible and Soil: Walter Clay Lowdermilk, the Jordan Valley Project and the Palestine Debate," *Middle Eastern Studies* 39, no. 2 (April 2003): 60.

66. Quoted in Miller, "Bible and Soil," 61; Lowdermilk, *Palestine,* 14–15.

67. Wallace, "The Problem of Palestine," 12–13; I. F. Stone, "The Palestine Report," *The Nation,* May 11, 1946, 564; Crum, *Behind the Silken Curtain,* 236–237; Kirchwey et al., *The Palestine Problem,* 130–133.

68. Quoted in Michelle Mart, "Eleanor Roosevelt, Liberalism, and Israel," *Shofar: An Interdisciplinary Journal of Jewish Studies* 24 (Spring 2006): 78.

69. Kirchwey et al., *The Palestine Problem,* 1.

70. Michelle Mart, *Eye on Israel: How America Came to View Israel as an Ally* (Albany: State University of New York Press, 2006), 30–33; Henry Wallace, "In Rome, as in Palestine," *New Republic,* November 17, 1947, 13; "The Partition of Palestine," *New York Times,* November 30, 1947, E10.

71. Sumner Welles, *We Need Not Fail* (Boston: Houghton Mifflin, 1948), 53.

72. Lillie Shultz, "Who Wrote the Bernadotte Plan?" *The Nation,* October 23, 1948.

73. Wallace, "The Problem of Palestine," 12; I. F. Stone, "Gangsters or Patriots?" *The Nation,* January 12, 1946, 34–35. Right-wing supporters of the Irgun used the phrase "It's 1776 in Palestine" throughout their publicity; see Rafael Medoff, *Militant Zionism in America: The Rise and Impact of the Jabotinsky Movement in the U.S., 1926–1948* (Tuscaloosa: University of Alabama Press, 2002), 171–200. On the effect of terrorism on public opinion, see Bruce J. Evensen, *Truman, Palestine, and the Press: Shaping the Conventional Wisdom at the Beginning of the Cold War* (New York: Greenwood Press, 1992), 71–98.

74. Stone, *Underground to Palestine,* xiii.

75. Ibid., 162, 186, 240.

76. Bartley Crum, "Escape from Europe," *The Nation,* January 27, 1947, 104–105.

77. I. F. Stone, "Confessions of a Jewish Dissident," *New York Review of Books,* March 9, 1978. The essay criticized the contemporary American Jewish community for suppressing dissent about Israel and sympathy for the Palestinians. The essay was reprinted in I. F. Stone, *Underground to Palestine: And Other Writing on Israel, Palestine, and the Middle East* (New York: Open Road Media, 2015), loc. 3037–3047 of 6015, Kindle.

78. Stone, *This Is Israel,* 27, 30.

79. Ibid., 28, 29, 91.

80. Ibid., 7, 26.

81. Ibid., 127.

82. "Palestine Strife Creates DP Issue," *New York Times,* May 4, 1948, 20; "Refugees: The New D.P.s," *Time,* October 25, 1948, 31; journalist quoted in Benny Morris, *The Birth of the Palestinian Refugee Problem, 1947–1949* (Cambridge: Cambridge University Press, 1987), 278. For Israel's decision against repatriation and subsequent steps to block the refugees' return, see Morris, *Birth of the Palestinian Refugee Problem,* 132–196. For articles and editorials that compare the Jewish and Arab refugees, see "The Dispossessed," *New York Times,* March 28, 1949, 20; Nasri Khattar, "Problem of Arab Refugees," *New York Times,* May 5, 1948, 24; Clifton Daniel, "Diplomatic and Military Defeat in Palestine Followed by Acute Refugee Problem," *New York Times,* July 26, 1948, 6; "The Arab Refugees," *New York Times,* August 12, 1948, 20; Sam Pope Brewer, "Arab Refugee Problem Threatens a New Crisis," *New York Times,* August 15, 1948, E5; Clifton Daniel, "Refugee Plight Shown," *New York Times,* October 13, 1948, 3; George Barret, "The Star of Bethlehem Looks Down on 750,000 Refugees in Holy Land," *New York Times,* December 25, 1948, 2; Kermit Roosevelt, "Aiding Arab Refugees: Peace in Middle East Held Dependent on Solution to Problem," *New York Times,* February 11, 1949, 22; "Arab Refugee Camps Pitiful, Democrats Told," *Washington Post,* May 25, 1949, B5; "U.S. Urged to Admit 10,000 Arabs as DPs," *Washington Post,* September 10, 1949, 2. For an objection to this analogy, see "Jewish DPs—Arab Refugees," *Jewish Exponent,* August 20, 1948, 4. On the congressional debate, see Milton Friedman, "Congress and the DP's," *Jewish Exponent,* August 1, 1949, 16; "Celler Discounts Value of Any Arab DP Testimony," *Washington Post,* September 1, 1949, 9; "Arab Issue 'Fogs' DP Case-Celler," *Washington Post,* September 2, 1949, 21; William Conklin, "Arab DP Hearings Fought by Celler," *New York Times,* September 2, 1949, 10; Bess Furman, "Inclusion of Arabs in DP Groups Urged: Witnesses at a Senate Hearing Stress Problems of Palestinian Refugees Displaced by Jews," *New York Times,* September 10, 1949, 7.

83. Freda Kirchwey, "Israel at First Glance," *The Nation,* November 27, 1948, 599, 600.

84. Freda Kirchwey, "Israel at First Glance: Why Did the Arabs Run?" *The Nation,* December 4, 1948, 624–626.

85. Ibid., 625.

86. Ibid., 625–626.

87. Freda Kirchwey, "Israel at First Glance: Jerusalem under Fire," *The Nation,* December 25, 1948, 718–720.

88. One might assume that in 1948–1949, Kirchwey and Stone could not have been aware of Israeli troops expelling Arabs from their homes since historians, such as Benny Morris, did not document the expulsion until the 1980s. But in 1948–1949, other journalists in the same political circle, such as Kenneth Bilby, a self-identified

pro-Zionist journalist for the *New York Herald,* wrote about the terror inflicted by violent acts of Jewish soldiers, along with tales of violence, which impelled Arabs to flee: Bilby, *New Star in the Near East,* 30, 43–44. Similarly, Hal Lehrman expressed regret about what he reported: "Now that I've traveled every corner of this country, it has become clear that the Israeli troops must have been decidedly tough even with non-combatant Arabs during the war. There are, for instance, too many dynamited, desolated native villages where little or no fighting ever occurred. The Jews simply came in and smashed the place, often sparing only the mosques." He received some of this information from veterans: "'The Israeli soldier has looted, burned, and slaughtered,' I have been told, 'and it is no comfort for us that soldiers of every other army do likewise.' It is even hinted that certain officers actually ordered their troops to let themselves go. The best evidence that there were atrocities—and, I suppose, the best apology for them, if such things can be apologized for—came to me from a high-ranking veteran of the Jerusalem siege." Hal Lehrman, "The Arabs of Israel: Pages from a Correspondent's Notebook," *Commentary* 8, no. 6 (1949): 523–533.

89. Dana Adams Schmidt, "200 Arabs Killed; Stronghold Taken," *New York Times,* April 10, 1948, 6. Newspapers at the time originally reported that 240 people had been killed. For a recent historical account, see Matthew Hogan, "The Massacre at Deir Yassin Revisted," *The Historian* 63, no. 2 (2001): 309–334.

90. William O. Douglas, *Strange Lands and Friendly People* (New York: Harper and Brothers, 1951), 264–265. Douglas also noted that "the villagers were told by the Arab leaders to leave. It apparently was a strategy of mass evacuation whether or not necessary as a military or public safety measure."

91. Isidore Abramowitz, "New Palestine Party," *New York Times,* December 4, 1948, 12.

92. Bilby, *New Star in the Near East,* 238.

2. Founding Israel in America

1. Dan Wakefield, "Israel's Need for Fiction," *The Nation,* April 11, 1959, 318–319.

2. Ibid.; Victor Haas, "Rich Novel of Israel's Birth," review of *Exodus,* by Leon Uris, *Chicago Daily Tribune,* September 28, 1958, C3.

3. Ira B. Nadel, *Leon Uris: Life of a Best Seller* (Austin: University of Texas Press, 2010), 104.

4. Ibid., 1–2.

5. "The Best Pictures of 1960," *Time,* January 2, 1961, 49; "The New Pictures," *Time,* December 19, 1960, 71; Bosley Crowther, "A Long 'Exodus,'" *New York Times,* December 16, 1960, 44; Philip K. Scheuer, "'Exodus' Stirring but Uneven Epic," *Los*

Angeles Times, December 22, 1960, B9; Stanley Kauffmann, "Double Feature," *New Republic,* December 19, 1960, 22.

6. Edward Tivnan, *The Lobby: Jewish Political Power and American Foreign Policy* (New York: Simon and Schuster, 1987), 51. In a 2001 essay lamenting the lack of empathy for Palestinians in the American media, Edward Said wrote that "the main narrative model that dominates American thinking still seems to be Leon Uris's 1950 [sic] novel." Said, "Propaganda and War," *Al-Ahram Weekly Online,* no. 55, September 6–12, 2001, http://weekly.ahram.org.eg/Archive/2001/550/op2.htm. In 2010, Alan Dershowitz bemoaned Israel's waning reputation: "Israel needs to be portrayed in the twenty-first century the way it was portrayed years ago by Leon Uris." "Alan Dershowitz: Hollywood Actors Jumping on Lubavitch Bandwagon," Matzav.com, November 18, 2010, http://matzav.com/alan-dershowitz-hollywood-actors-jumping-on-lubavitch-bandwagon/.

7. Aviva Halamish, *The Exodus Affair: Holocaust Survivors and the Struggle for Palestine* (Syracuse, NY: Syracuse University Press, 1998), 141–143.

8. Leon Uris, *Exodus* (1958; repr., New York: Bantam Books, 1959), 182.

9. Leon Uris to William Uris, March 4, 1958, box 137, folder 8, Leon Uris Archive, Harry Ransom Humanities Research Center, University of Texas, Austin (hereafter cited as Uris Archive).

10. Ibid.

11. Ruth Gruber, *Destination Palestine: The Story of the Haganah Ship Exodus 1947* (New York: Current Books, 1948), 35.

12. D. D. Guttenplan, *American Radical: The Life and Times of I. F. Stone* (New York: Farrar, Straus and Giroux, 2009), 228.

13. Uris, *Exodus,* 4.

14. Rachel Simon, "Zionism," in *The Jews of the Middle East and North Africa in Modern Times,* ed. Reeva Spector Simon, Michael Menachem Laskier, and Sara Reguer (New York: Columbia University Press, 2003), 165–179.

15. On the Judeo-Christian tradition in the 1950s, see Deborah Dash Moore, "Jewish GIs and the Creation of the Judeo-Christian Tradition," *Religion and American Culture: A Journal of Interpretation* 8, no. 1 (1998): 31–53; Mark Silk, "Notes on the Judeo-Christian Tradition in America," *American Quarterly* 36, no. 1 (1984): 65–85; Kevin M. Schultz, *Tri-Faith America: How Catholics and Jews Held Postwar America to Its Protestant Promise* (New York: Oxford University Press, 2011).

16. Leon Uris to William Uris, February 20, 1956, box 137, folder 7, Uris Archive; Nadel, *Leon Uris,* 95–97.

17. On the Israeli government's efforts to influence U.S. public opinion and policy makers, see Peter Hahn, "The View from Jerusalem: Revelations about U.S. Diplomacy from the Archives of Israel," *Diplomatic History* 22, no. 4 (1998): 509–532.

On the cross-border raids, Dan Wakefield (who reviewed *Exodus* for *The Nation*) wrote: "The reprisal raids have discouraged infiltration and shooting on the border, but have also seriously damaged Israel in outside opinion. Even in Jewish communities, Zionist fund-raising regularly drops after one of the Israeli raids." Dan Wakefield, "Israel's 'Direct' Policy: First Talk with Golda Myerson," *The Nation*, August 4, 1956, 93–96. On Uris's friendship with the Israeli ambassador in Los Angeles, see Nadel, *Leon Uris*, 95.

18. Leon Uris to William Uris, March 8, 1956, box 137, folder 7, Uris Archive; Nadel, *Leon Uris*, 97–104.

19. On the making of the film, see Chris Fujiwara, *The World and Its Double: The Life and Work of Otto Preminger* (New York: Faber and Faber, 2008), 256–271. To secure contacts in the Israeli government, Preminger enlisted an old friend from Vienna, veteran Zionist Meyer Weisgal, a former impresario in America who had become president of the Weizmann Institute of Science. In exchange, Preminger promised to donate the Israeli royalties from the film to the institute. For funding, Preminger called on Arthur Krim of United Artists, a known supporter of Israel, who would later become an intimate advisor to President Lyndon B. Johnson. Weisgal applauded *Exodus* for clearing the Zionist record from the taint of terrorism. In the 1940s, he had been infuriated that "political violence in other parts of the world" was called "patriotism, resistance, revolt," while in Palestine it was reduced to a "very simple thing: terror." For information on the government's aid and the quotation from Weisgal's diary, see Tony Shaw, *Cinematic Terror: A Global History of Terrorism on Film* (London: Bloomsbury Academic, 2014), 64–66.

20. Leon Uris to William Uris, May 14, 1956, box 137, folder 7, Uris Archive.

21. Ibid.

22. Leon Uris to William Uris, September 17, 1956, box 137, folder 8, Uris Archive.

23. Leon Uris, "Author in Search of a Novel," promotional essay for Doubleday, box 25, folder 7, Uris Archive.

24. Edward Murrow, "Egypt-Israel," *See It Now*, season 5, episode 5, CBS, March 13, 1956. The article Uris wired to the *Philadelphia Inquirer* is available in box 25, folder 3, Uris Archive.

25. After the 1949 armistice, according to historian Benny Morris, Palestinian refugees stole across the new borders primarily for social and economic reasons—to recover property, reunite with families, shepherd their flocks, or harvest their fields. In the mid-1950s, politically motivated groups of fedayeen (Arabic for "those who sacrifice themselves") started conducting raids into Israeli territory to attack soldiers and civilians and to gather intelligence. Israel reacted by mounting larger and fiercer reprisals, which culminated in the shelling of Gaza City on April 5, 1956. Benny

Morris, *Israel's Border Wars, 1949–1956: Arab Infiltration, Israeli Retaliation, and the Countdown to the Suez War* (Oxford, Oxford University Press, 1993), 382–389. On Roi Rothberg and the text of Dayan's eulogy, see Idith Zertal, *Israel's Holocaust and the Politics of Nationhood* (Cambridge: Cambridge University Press, 2005), 178–182.

26. "We Must Not Be Lulled by Peace Talk—Dayan," *Jerusalem Post*, May 2, 1956, 1; quotations from Zertal, *Israel's Holocaust*, 180–181.

27. Leon Uris to William Uris, May 4, 1956, box 137, folder 7, Uris Archive. On Uris's response to Rothberg's funeral, see M. M. Silver, *Our Exodus: Leon Uris and the Americanization of Israel's Founding Story* (Detroit: Wayne State University Press, 2010), 172–174. Uris mentioned the *See It Now* episode in an unpublished article on the funeral that he wrote for the *Philadelphia Inquirer*.

28. Lewis W. Gillenson, "Young Kids on a Tense Border," *Coronet*, October 1956, 44–53. Uris had a copy of Gillenson's article with his research material.

29. Paul Breines, *Tough Jews: Political Fantasies and the Moral Dilemma of American Jewry* (New York: Basic Books, 1990), 54–59.

30. Yael Zerubavel, *Recovered Roots: Collective Memory and the Making of Israeli National Tradition* (Chicago: University of Chicago Press, 1995), 39–47, 43, 44.

31. Uris, *Exodus*, 52, 177, 443, 44, 25, 41, 56.

32. David Boroff, "Exodus: Another Look," *New York Post*, May 17, 1959; "When Men Were Men—and Killers," *World-Telegram and Sun*, May 3, 1957, in Leon Uris scrapbook, box 168, Uris Archive; "westerns" quote from Nadel, *Leon Uris*, 87.

33. Richard Slotkin, *Regeneration through Violence: The Mythology of the American Frontier, 1600–1860* (Norman: University of Oklahoma Press, 1973); Slotkin, *Gunfighter Nation: The Myth of the Frontier in Twentieth-Century America* (New York: Atheneum, 1992).

34. Uris, *Exodus*, 264.

35. Ibid., 264, 379.

36. Ibid., 265.

37. Ibid., 551, 281.

38. Ibid., 271.

39. Interview quoted in Nadel, *Leon Uris*, 316n16; Leon Uris to William Uris, September 17, 1956, box 137, folder 7, Uris Archive; Leon Uris to William Uris, June 25, 1957, box 137, folder 8, Uris Archive. Marjorie Morningstar is the main female character in a popular novel (1955) of the same name by Herman Wouk, which deals with Jewish assimilation, and whose main male character is an artist.

40. On the "crisis of masculinity," see K. A. Cuordileone, *Manhood and American Political Culture in the Cold War* (New York: Routledge, 2005); Robert D. Dean,

Imperial Brotherhood: Gender and the Making of Cold War Foreign Policy (Amherst: University of Massachusetts Press, 2001); James Gilbert, *Men in the Middle: Searching for Masculinity in the 1950s* (Chicago: University of Chicago Press, 2005).

41. Schlesinger quoted in Dean, *Imperial Brotherhood,* 172; Arthur M. Schlesinger Jr., *The Vital Center: The Politics of Freedom* (Boston: Houghton Mifflin, 1949), 13–15, 25, 36–44; John F. Kennedy, "The New Frontier," Speech, Democratic National Convention, Los Angeles, July 15, 1960.

42. Uris, *Exodus,* 448, 551.

43. Rudolf Flesch, "Conversation Piece: A Book with Universal Appeal," *Los Angeles Times,* February 8, 1960, B5.

44. Editorial reprinted in 1956 *Congressional Record,* Uris scrapbook, box 168, Uris Archive.

45. Bosley Crowther, "The Screen in Review: Movie Study of Jewish-British Strife in Palestine, 'Sword in the Desert,'" *New York Times,* August 25, 1949, 20.

46. Robert Friedman, "'Israeli Minutemen,' review of *Exodus,* by Leon Uris," *St. Louis Post-Dispatch,* in Uris scrapbook, box 168, Uris Archive.

47. Uris, *Exodus,* 25.

48. Ibid., 257, 268.

49. Leon Uris, "A Summary of the Outstanding Actions of the Jewish Underground," box 25, folder 1, Uris Archive.

50. Quoted in Fujiwara, *World and Its Double,* 256–277.

51. Quoted in ibid., 263 (emphasis in original).

52. Uris, *Exodus,* 518, 572.

53. Ibid., 588, 589.

54. Ibid., 348.

55. Ibid., 458.

56. Ibid., 523, 553, 554.

57. Ibid., 550.

58. Ibid., 19.

59. Salim Yaqub, *Containing Arab Nationalism: The Eisenhower Doctrine and the Middle East* (Chapel Hill: University of North Carolina Press, 2004); Carroll Kilpatrick, "Vice President Calls It Declaration of Independence from Colonialism," *Washington Post,* November 3, 1956, 1.

60. Roger Cohen, "A Crass and Consequent Error," review of *Patriot of Persia: Muhammad Mossadegh and a Tragic Anglo-American Coup,* by Christopher de Bellaigue, *New York Review of Books,* August 16, 2012.

61. "Ghana: A People Reaching for the Light," *Life,* January 18, 1960, 82.

62. Jason Parker, "The Eisenhower Administration and the Bandung Conference," in *The Eisenhower Administration, the Third World and the Globalization of the Cold*

War, ed. Kathryn Statler and Andrew Johns (Lanham, MD: Rowman and Littlefield, 2006), 168.

63. Douglass Little, *American Orientalism: The United States and the Middle East since 1945* (Chapel Hill: University of North Carolina Press, 2008), 178.

64. Quoted in ibid., 175.

65. Dana Adams Schmidt, "Israel Relaxed and Confident after a Decade of Hardships: Nation's Mood Found to Contrast Sharply with Crises of Its Early Statehood—Shops Full of Goods and Buyers," *New York Times,* December 20, 1959, 17.

66. Agnes E. Meyer, "Israel's Labor Movement Is Its Backbone," *Washington Post,* January 22, 1961, E1. See also "Israel in Africa," *New Republic,* October 5, 1959, 6–7; Kalman Seigel, "Israel to Step Up Aid to Neighbors: Official Tells Zionists of Plan to Turn Nation into Pilot Plant for Progress," *New York Times,* November 20, 1960, 27; "Israel is Democracy's Classroom for Africans," *Washington Post/Times Herald,* March 23, 1961, D1.

67. From Herzl's *The Jewish State,* as quoted in Arthur Hertzberg, *The Zionist Idea: A Historical Analysis and Reader* (Philadelphia: Jewish Publication Society, 1997), 222.

68. Uris, *Exodus,* 589, 596.

69. Seth King, "'Exodus' and Israel," *New York Times,* October 4, 1959, 21; Arthur Hertzberg, *The Jews in America: Four Centuries of an Uneasy Encounter* (New York: Simon and Schuster, 1989), 319.

70. Philip Roth, "Some New Jewish Stereotypes," in *Reading Myself and Others* (New York: Farrar, Straus and Giroux, 1975), 145–146.

71. Ibid., 146 (emphasis in original).

72. Aziz S. Sahwell, "*Exodus:* A Distortion of Truth" (New York: Arab Information Center, 1960). A few reviews in the United States did note the bias of the novel and film. *Time* named *Exodus* one of the ten best films of 1960, but a review in the magazine had objected that "the film unequivocally blames the Arabs, absolutely absolves the Jews. Then, in chauvinistic frenzy, the picture goes on to sanctify the Jewish terror." "The Best Pictures of 1960," *Time,* January 2, 1961, 49; "The New Pictures," *Time,* December 19, 1960, 71. A *Cosmopolitan* article on Preminger's filming in Israel reported that four men in Nazareth were arrested for distributing circulars protesting the novel's "degradation of Arabs" and that "Egypt radio urged a boycott of the film." It also mentioned a critique of the film by Palestinian poet Rashad Husein in the Arab-language newspaper *Al Mirsad.* "Saga of Exodus," *Cosmopolitan,* November 1960, 12–15.

73. For three very different responses, see Jeffrey Goldberg, *Prisoners: A Story of Friendship and Terror* (New York: Vintage Books, 2006); Karen Brodkin, *How Jews Became White Folks: And What That Says about Race in America* (New Brunswick,

NJ: Rutgers University Press, 2000), loc. 1603 of 2887, Kindle; Julius Lester, *Lovesong: Becoming a Jew* (New York: Arcade, 1988), 30. Goldberg wrote of discovering, as an adolescent, a new hero in Ari Ben Canaan, a "Hebrew (not, somehow, Jewish) warrior, brave and cold-eyed, who defended Jewish honor." Goldberg was inspired to enlist in the IDF, where he served as a prison guard during the first intifada.

74. Albert Hazbun, email message to the author, March 16, 2010.

75. L. R. S., "Exodus—Unhistorical Novel," *Issues* 13, no. 5 (Fall 1959): 31–35; Irwin M. Hermann, "An Historical Appraisal," *Issues* 13, no. 5 (1959): 35–41.

3. Invincible Victim

1. "Hero of the Israelis: Itzhak Rabin," *New York Times*, June 8, 1967, 16; Theodore H. White, "Mideast War," *Life*, June 23, 1967, 24.

2. "Hero of the Israelis."

3. Jack Pitman, "6-Day War: $6 Mil TV 'Event,'" *Variety*, June 14, 1967, 40.

4. "Israel Forswears War of Conquest: Premier Declares Nation Has No Territorial Aims," *New York Times*, June 6, 1967, 16.

5. James Reston, "Washington: Nasser's Reckless Maneuvers," *New York Times*, May 24, 1967, 46; Reston, "The Issue in Cairo: Israel a U.S. 'Base,'" *New York Times*, June 4, 1967, 1; Reston, "Tel Aviv: The Irony of Israel's Success," *New York Times*, June 7, 1967, 46.

6. "The Israeli Thrust—The Astounding Sixty Hours," *Life*, June 16, 1967, 33; "In 60 Hours a New Middle East," *Life*, June 16, 1967, 4.

7. "Law and the Middle East," editorial, *Christian Science Monitor*, May 27, 1967, 16; "Testing the Aqaba Blockade," editorial, *Washington Post*, June 2, 1967, A20.

8. David Pela, "Mobilization Motivates Israel's Moves and Moods," *Jewish Chronicle* (Pittsburgh, PA), June 2, 1967, 14, http://doi.library.cmu.edu/10.1184/pmc /CHR/CHR_1967_006_014_06021967; Alfred W. Bloom, "Israel Will Wait—How Long?" *Jewish Chronicle* (Pittsburgh, PA), June 2, 1967, 26, http://doi.library.cmu .edu/10.1184/pmc/CHR/CHR_1967_006_014_06021967.

9. Don Cook and Tom Lambert, "Odds in Battle Favor Israel, Experts Declare," *Los Angeles Times*, May 24, 1967, 6; James Feron, "Dayan Says Israel Needs No Aid by Foreign Troops," *New York Times*, June 4, 1967, 1; William Beecher, "U.S. Military Analysts Expect Short War, with Israel Winning," *New York Times*, June 6, 1967, 1; "U.S. Believes Israel Can Hold Its Own: Congressmen Report McNamara View," *Chicago Tribune*, June 6, 1967, 8. For the "turkey shoot" memo, see Michael Oren, *Six Days of War: June 1967 and the Making of the Modern Middle East* (New York: Rosetta Books, 2004), 210.

10. Theodore White, "After the Last Campaign, the Hazards of Victory," in "Israel's Swift Victory," special edition of *Life,* June 1967, 83.

11. J. J. Goldberg, *Jewish Power: Inside the American Jewish Establishment* (New York: Basic Books, 1997), 137. See also Lucy Dawidowicz, "American Public Opinion," *American Jewish Yearbook* 69 (1968): 198–229, and Arthur Hertzberg, "Israel and American Jewry," *Commentary* 44, no. 2 (1967): 69–73.

12. "Israel's Chief Orator: Abba Eban," *New York Times,* June 21, 1967, 15; "Text of Kosygin Address to General Assembly and Excerpts from Eban Speech: Russian and Israeli Talks Give Sharply Opposing Views of Conflict in the Mideast," *New York Times,* June 20, 1967, 16; "Major Points of Speech by Eban," *Los Angeles Times,* June 20, 1967, 16.

13. According to Michael Oren (*Six Days of War,* 306), "between 175,000 (Israeli estimates) and 250,000 (Jordanian estimates) Palestinians fled the West Bank."

14. Alfred Friendly, "Israel's Image: Agreement on Refugees," *Washington Post,* August 8, 1967, A11; James Feron, "Israel Has the Image Problem of a Tough Victor," *New York Times,* July 20, 1969, E4. See also "Israel's Opportunity," editorial, *New York Times,* June 19, 1967, 34.

15. Carl T. Rowan, "Why the Danger Is So Great," *Los Angeles Times,* May 28, 1967, D7. See also C. L. Sulzberger, "Foreign Affairs: The Edge of Infinity," *New York Times,* May 24, 1967, 46.

16. See Michael Sherry, *In the Shadow of War: The United States since the 1930s* (New Haven, CT: Yale University Press, 1995), 158.

17. Bill Mauldin, "Not a Litterbug among Them, Those Israeli Troops," *New Republic,* June 24, 1967, 6.

18. "Israel's Swift Victory"; Associated Press, *Lightning out of Israel: The Six-Day War in the Middle East* (New York, 1967); S. L. A. Marshall and United Press International, *Swift Sword: The Historical Record of Israel's Victory, June 1967* (New York: American Heritage Publishing, 1967); Mike Wallace and S. L. A. Marshall, "How Israel Won the War," CBS News Special, July 18, 1967, produced by Burton Benjamin, Gene Deporis, and Palmer Williams (National Archives and Records Administration: Washington, D.C., 2009). When fighting broke out, Egypt expelled foreign journalists, while Israel welcomed them. The Associated Press opened its first bureau office there, and the number of foreign journalists registered in Tel Aviv soared to nearly four hundred (rivaling the numbers in Washington, D.C., and Moscow). See Giovanna Dell'Orto, *American Journalism and International Relations: Foreign Correspondence from the Early Republic to the Digital Era* (Cambridge: Cambridge University Press, 2013), 127–133.

19. "Israel's Swift Victory," 3, 17–19.

20. Ibid., 25, 20, 36, 74, 82, 80.

21. Edmund Stillman, "The Short War and the Long War," *New York Times,* June 18, 1967; "Defoliating Viet Nam," *Time,* February 23, 1968, 84.

22. "Israel's Swift Victory," 8.

23. Ibid., 4–5, 8.

24. Ibid., 44–45.

25. "Wrap Up of the Astounding War," *Life,* June 23, 1967.

26. "Israel's Swift Victory," 48–49.

27. Wallace and Marshall, "How Israel Won the War"; Mike Wallace, "The Ordeal of Con Thien," CBS News Special, October 1, 1967, Archive.org, uploaded by National Archives, http://archive.org/details/gov.archives.arc.653071.

28. Wallace and Marshall, "How Israel Won the War."

29. James Reston, "A War's First Hours: Propaganda of All Sides Can Be Heard in Israel, and Determination Can Be Felt," *New York Times,* June 6, 1967, 16.

30. Marshall Frady, "In Israel: An American Innocent in the Middle East: Part III," *Harper's Magazine,* January 1971, 71.

31. Alfred Kazin, "In Israel: After the Triumph," *Harper's Magazine,* November 1967, 84, 74, 73.

32. "A Nation under Siege," *Time,* June 9, 1967, 46–55.

33. White, "After the Last Campaign, the Hazards of Victory," 84.

34. "Blintzkrieg," *Time,* June 16, 1967, 35.

35. Curtis G. Pepper, "Hawk of Israel," *New York Times,* July 9, 1969, 169; Yael Dayan, "General Dayan: Father and Hero," *Look,* August 22, 1967.

36. C. W. Gonick, "Israel: The Stagnation of War," *The Nation,* November 18, 1968, 526; "Israel's Swift Victory," 10; Mauldin, "Not a Litterbug among Them," 5.

37. Kazin, "In Israel: After the Triumph," 83, 73–74.

38. Barbara Tuchman, "Israel's Swift Sword," *Atlantic Monthly,* September 1967, 62.

39. "Israel's Swift Victory," 57; "Israeli Thrust—The Astounding 60 Hours," *Life,* June 16, 1967, 38A.

40. "Israel's Swift Victory," 60–61.

41. This image was reproduced on the back cover of Marshall and United Press International, *Swift Sword.*

42. Stanley Wolpert, "Today in Tel Aviv," *The Nation,* July 3, 1967, 7.

43. Amos Perlmutter, "Israel's Tough Stand on Captured Territories," *New Republic,* January 13, 1968, 13.

44. Louis Walinsky, "'Now We Must Fear Our Friends': Victorious Israel's Look and Mood," *New Republic,* July 8, 1967, 10.

45. Michael Walzer and Martin Peretz, "Israel Is Not Vietnam," *Ramparts,* July 1967, 11–14.

46. Ibid.

47. I. F. Stone, "The Future of Israel," *Ramparts,* July 1967, 41–44.

48. I. F. Stone, "Holy War," review of *Le conflit israélo-arabe,* ed. Claude Lanzmann, *New York Review of Books* 9, no. 2 (August 3, 1967), http://www.nybooks.com/articles/archives/1967/aug/03/holy-war/?pagination=false.

49. Kwame Ture (formerly known as Stokely Carmichael) and Charles V. Hamilton, *Black Power: The Politics of Liberation* (New York: Vintage Books, 1992), 1, 5. The epigraph is from I. F. Stone, "People without a Country," review of *The Negro American,* ed. Talcott Parsons and Kenneth B. Clark, *New York Review of Books* 7, no. 2 (August 18, 1966), http://www.nybooks.com/articles/archives/1966/aug/18/people-without-a-country/.

50. On the relationship of the Black Power movement to Israel and Palestine, see Keith Feldman, *A Shadow over Palestine: The Imperial Life of Race in America* (Minneapolis: University of Minnesota Press, 2015), 59–102; Alex Lubin, *Geographies of Liberation: The Making of an Afro-Arab Political Imaginary* (Chapel Hill: University of North Carolina Press, 2014), 111–141; Lewis Young, "American Blacks and the Arab-Israeli Conflict," *Journal of Palestine Studies* 2, no. 1 (1972): 70–85; Salim Yaqub, "'Our Declaration of Independence': African Americans, Arab Americans, and the Arab-Israeli Conflict, 1967–1979," *Mashriq and Mahjar* 3, no. 1 (2015): 12–29; Eric Sundquist, *Strangers in the Land: Blacks, Jews, and Post-Holocaust America* (Cambridge, MA: Harvard University Press, 2005), 310–380; Cheryl Lynn Greenberg, *Troubling the Waters: Black-Jewish Relations in the American Century* (Princeton, NJ: Princeton University Press, 2006), 205–250.

51. Quoted in Feldman, *Shadow over Palestine,* 59–60.

52. Quoted in Melani McAlister, *Epic Encounters: Culture, Media, and U.S. Interests in the Middle East since 1945* (Berkeley: University of California Press, 2005), 113.

53. Gene Roberts, "S.N.C.C. Charges Israel Atrocities," *New York Times,* August 15, 1967, 1; Kathleen Teltsch, "S.N.C.C. Criticized for Israel Stand," *New York Times,* August 16, 1967, 28. For analysis of the SNCC newsletter and ensuing controversy, see Clayborne Carson, *In Struggle: SNCC and the Black Awakening of the 1960s* (Cambridge, MA: Harvard University Press, 1995), 265–269; Feldman, *Shadow over Palestine,* 71–80.

54. "SNCC and the Arab-Israeli Conflict," editorial, *The Movement* 3, no. 9 (September 1967): 2.

55. Quotations from Lubin, *Geographies of Liberation,* 122–123; Young, "American Blacks," 80.

56. "An Appeal by Black Americans for United States Support for Israel," *New York Times,* June 28, 1970, 5. See also Lubin, *Geographies of Liberation,* 118.

57. "An Appeal by Black Americans against United States Support for the Zionist Government of Israel," *New York Times,* November 1, 1970, 172. See also Marjorie Feld, *Nations Divided: American Jews and the Struggle over Apartheid* (New York: Palgrave Macmillan, 2014), 63–86; Sasha Polakow-Suransky, *The Unspoken Alliance: Israel's Secret Relationship with Apartheid South Africa* (New York: Pantheon, 2010).

58. Dick Edwards, "Black Man in Israel: Reason for Trip—II," *New York Amsterdam News,* January 31, 1970, 1; Edwards, "Black Man in Israel: Abba Eban on Arabs," *New York Amsterdam News,* February 28, 1970, 2.

59. Stanley Meisler, "S. Africa Jews Caught between Two Cultures," *Los Angeles Times,* November 25, 1968, 1; C. L. Sulzberger, "Strange Nonalliance," *New York Times,* April 30, 1971, 39; Martin Peretz, "Israel, South Africa and a 'Preposterous Analogy,'" letter to editor, *New York Times,* May 17, 1971, 34.

60. "Let There Be Peace," editorial, *New York Times,* June 11, 1967, 206; "The Ugly Face of War," editorial, *Washington Post,* June 13, 1967, A18; "The Guerrilla Threat in the Middle East," *Time,* December 14, 1968, 29.

61. Joseph Kraft, "Israel Considers a Homeland for Its Palestinian Arabs," *Washington Post,* September 14, 1967, A21; "Bitter Pill," editorial, *Washington Post,* October 22, 1967, B6; Flora Lewis, "Arabs' Own Efforts Forced Israel into Expansionism," *Washington Post,* September 15, 1967, A21.

62. Joseph Alsop, "'No Problems, No Trouble' on West Bank, but for How Long?," *Los Angeles Times,* September 19, 1967, A5.

63. Joseph Alsop, "Hussein Visit to U.S. Indicates Hard Choice Ahead for Israel," *Washington Post,* November 13, 1967, A17; Alsop, "Israel Joy in Victory Dimmed by Schism in Soul over Future," *Washington Post,* September 8, 1967, A21; Alsop, "Moshe Dayan Faces Issue of Israel's Million Arabs," *Washington Post,* September 11, 1967, A21; Alsop, "No Problems, No Trouble," A5.

64. Joseph Alsop, "Eshkol Insists Jorrdan [*sic*] Bank Is Israel's Security Border," *Washington Post,* September 13, 1967, A21; Alsop, "Israel Joy in Victory," A21; Alsop, "Failure to Face Facts Has Blunted Negro Aid Plans," *Los Angeles Times,* August 1, 1967, A5; Alsop, "Matter of Fact . . . For God's Sake (and Ours)," *Washington Post,* August 4, 1967, A19.

65. Joseph Alsop, "The Non-Modernism of Israel," *Los Angeles Times,* September 21, 1967, B5; Alsop, "Eshkol Insists Jorrdan [*sic*] Bank Is Israel's Security Border." Alsop's critique of Israel's occupation lasted only as long as it fulfilled a Cold War imperative. As the upheavals of the late 1960s abated at home, and Nixon armed Israel as a regional proxy, Alsop discarded the link from southern Africa to Israel and America and replaced it with a rigid dichotomy between superpowers. He also advocated selling Israel the most advanced weapons to protect it from destruction—by Soviet proxies. He came to see America's global power as

necessary for maintaining Israel's military might and protecting it from genocide. Alsop therefore attacked antiwar liberals (especially I. F. Stone) who criticized Israel, on the grounds that they were abetting an assault on "American power and will." Joseph Alsop, "Now Is Time for Plain Talk on Israel and American Jews," *Washington Post*, February 11, 1970, A21.

66. "The Guerrilla Threat in the Middle East," 35; Paul Thomas Chamberlin, *The Global Offensive: The United States, the Palestine Liberation Organization, and the Making of the Post–Cold War Order* (New York: Oxford University Press, 2012).

67. "The Guerrilla Threat in the Middle East," 36.

68. Ibid., 29.

69. William Tuohy, "Poverty, Hope Fill Palestinian Camp," *Washington Post*, March 13, 1969, F1.

70. "Train Black Panthers, Arab Commandos Say," *Los Angeles Times*, February 1, 1970, F12.

71. "The Guerrilla Threat in the Middle East," 35.

72. Gavin Young, "Commandos Who Raid the Borders of Israel Are New Heroes of the Arab World," *Washington Post*, November 7, 1968, F6.

73. William Tuohy, "Lebanese Camps Spawn Commandos," *Los Angeles Times*, December 14, 1969, F4; Tuohy, "Poverty, Hope Fill Palestinian Camp," F1.

74. Dana Adams Schmidt, "Commandos Are Now the Heroes of the Arab World," *New York Times*, December 27, 1968, 3; "The Guerrilla Threat in the Middle East," 32; Marshall Frady, "On Jordan's Banks: An American Innocent in the Middle East, Part II," *Harper's Magazine*, November 1970, 109.

75. Dana Adams Schmidt, "Sensational Claims Win Recruits for Palestinian Commando Unit," *New York Times*, September 17, 1969, 12. In his book *Armageddon in the Middle East* (New York: New York Times Co., 1974), Schmidt attributed this "philosophy" to "Dr. George Habash, the PFLP founder, and his most brilliant ideologist, Ghassan Kanafani, editor until his assassination in 1972 of *al-Hadaf*" (163).

76. Georgie Anne Geyer, "The Palestinian Refugees: A New Breed: Smart, Skilled, Fanatical," *New Republic*, November 21, 1970, 14, 15, 16, 18.

77. Schmidt, *Armageddon*, 152, 18.

78. Zalin B. Grant, "Commando Revolution: A Hundred Years War in the Middle East?" *New Republic*, January 24, 1970, 11.

79. Walter Laqueur, "The Middle East Is Potentially More Dangerous than Vietnam," *New York Times Magazine*, June 5, 1968, SM40.

80. Dana Adams Schmidt, "An Arab Guerrilla Chief Emerges," *New York Times*, March 4, 1969, 6.

81. Peter Jennings, "Palestine—New State of Mind," *ABC News*, New York, 1970.

82. "Palestine: A Case of Right v. Right," *Time,* December 21, 1970, 30–31; Stone, "Holy War."

83. James Feron, "Israel Concerned over Guerrillas," *New York Times,* March 9, 1969, 9.

84. Interview with Frank Giles of the *Sunday Times,* reprinted as "Golda Meir Scorns Soviets," *Washington Post,* June 16, 1969, 2.

85. "The Guerrilla Threat in the Middle East," 35.

86. Alfred Friendly, "Anti-Israeli Guerrillas Are Mostly a Nuisance," *Washington Post,* March 16, 1969, 35.

87. Philip Ben, "Americans, Not Arabs, Worry Israelis," *New Republic,* April 6, 1968, 12.

88. "The U.S. and the Skyjackers: Where Power Is Vulnerable," *Time,* September 21, 1970, 29–30.

89. Ibid.

90. "Murder in Munich," editorial, *New York Times,* September 6, 1972, 44; Stephen Rosenfeld, "Terror a Tactic of Many Aspects," *Washington Post,* September 8, 1972, A22; David S. Broder, "Munich and Vietnam," *Washington Post,* September 10, 1972, B7.

91. "Israel's New War," *Time,* September 25, 1972, 28.

92. Ibid.

93. Robert Alden, "Policy Shift by U.S. at U.N.," *New York Times,* September 12, 1972, 10. The first veto, which Great Britain joined, was in 1970, against a resolution calling for the isolation of Rhodesia and condemning Britain for not using force against Rhodesia's white government.

94. James Naughton, "Ford Pledges to Resist the Third World in the U.N.," *New York Times,* July 1, 1975, 3.

95. "Speech to the United Nations General Assembly, by U.S. Ambassador to the UN Daniel Patrick Moynihan, November 10, 1975," in Gil Troy, *Moynihan's Moment: America's Fight against Zionism as Racism* (New York: Oxford University Press, 2012), 275–280. See also Feldman, *Shadow over Palestine,* 23–43.

96. Moynihan, "Speech to the United Nations General Assembly."

97. Quoted in Troy, *Moynihan's Moment,* 102.

98. Quoted in Feldman, *Shadow over Palestine,* 54.

99. Responses to Moynihan quoted in Troy, *Moynihan's Moment,* 176, 8, 103.

100. "Response to Terror," editorial, *New York Times,* July 5, 1976, 10; "A Victory over Terrorism," editorial, *Washington Post,* July 6, 1976, A16; William Stevenson, *90 Minutes at Entebbe* (New York: Bantam Books, 1976); "Entebbe Derby," *Time,* July 26, 1976, 86; see also McAlister, *Epic Encounters,* 183–186.

101. Stevenson, *90 Minutes at Entebbe,* ix. For the image of soldiers singing, see *Raid on Entebbe,* directed by Irving Kershner, 1977.

102. William F. Buckley Jr., "Israel to the Rescue—of the U.S., That Is!" *Los Angeles Times,* June 12, 1967; "Israel Acting like U.S. Used to Act, Reagan Says," *Los Angeles Times,* July 6, 1976, A16; "Comment: Thirty-Six Minutes," *New Republic,* July 17, 1976, 7; "A Legend Is Born," *New York Times,* July 6, 1967, 23.

103. "Response to Terror," 10; "The Israeli Commando Force: Faceless, Swift, and Deadly," *Washington Post,* July 5, 1976, A4.

104. Stevenson, *90 Minutes at Entebbe,* i; "Comment: Thirty-Six Minutes"; "Vindication for the Israelis," *Time,* July 26, 1976, 46; "Response to Terror."

4. "Not the Israel We Have Seen in the Past"

1. *NBC Nightly News,* August 2, 1982.

2. Martin Peretz, "Lebanon Eyewitness," *New Republic,* August 2, 1982, 15–23.

3. Edward Said, "Permission to Narrate," review of *Israel in Lebanon: The Report of the International Commission,* by Sean MacBride [etc.], *London Review of Books* 6, no. 3 (1984): 13–17.

4. For historical accounts of the war, see Ze'ev Schiff and Ehud Ya'ari, *Israel's Lebanon War* (New York: Simon and Schuster, 1984); Rashid Khalidi, *Under Siege: PLO Decisionmaking during the 1982 War* (1985; repr., New York: Columbia University Press, 2014); Robert Fisk, *Pity the Nation: The Abduction of Lebanon* (New York: Nation Books, 2002), 199–442; Avi Shlaim, *The Iron Wall: Israel and the Arab World* (New York: Norton, 2001), 384–423.

5. On the first week of the invasion, see Roger Morris, "Beirut—and the Press—under Siege," *Columbia Journalism Review,* November/December 1982, 24–25; William A. Dorman and Mansour Farhang, "The U.S. Press and Lebanon," *SAIS Review* 3, no. 1 (1983): 65–81; Edmund Ghareeb, ed., *Split Vision: The Portrayal of Arabs in the American Media* (Washington, D.C.: American–Arab Affairs Council, 1983), 169–175, 299–319.

6. ABC report as quoted in Trudy Rubin, "Lebanon: The (Censored) Price of War," *Christian Science Monitor,* June 16, 1982, 23; James LeMoyne et al., "Suffer the Children," *Newsweek,* June 28, 1982, 26. For sample press reports from Sidon, see Edward Cody, "Once Lively and Lawless, Sidon Now Is Occupied and Hungry: Sidon Is a Ghostly Captive," *Washington Post,* June 11, 1982, A17; David K. Shipler, "In Lebanon, White Flags Fly amid the Misery and Rubble," *New York Times,* June 15, 1982, A1; Eric Pace, "In Sidon, 80 More Bodies for a Vast Bulldozed Pit," *New York Times,* June 17, 1982, A21.

7. Dorman and Farhang, "The U.S. Press and Lebanon," 70–73; David K. Shipler, "Israelis Say Siege Will Not Drag On," *New York Times,* June 29, 1982, A8.

8. David K. Shipler, "Piles of Rubble Were the Homes of Palestinians," *New York Times,* July 3, 1982, 1.

9. "Israelis Are Censoring Accounts of Invasion," *New York Times,* June 9, 1982, A19. For sample of censorship notice, see David K. Shipler, "At School in Tyre, Guns and Rockets," *New York Times,* June 17, 1982, A20; Sally Bedell, "3 Networks in Dispute with Israel," *New York Times,* June 25, 1982, C8; *NBC Nightly News,* June 26, 1986. On the Arafat interview, see "Israel Says ABC Violated Military Censorship Ban," *Washington Post,* June 23, 1982, A20; "Israel Bars ABC-TV from Using Satellite after Arafat Interview," *Los Angeles Times,* June 23, 1982, B12.

10. On the accessibility of Beirut, see Dorman and Farhang, "The U.S. Press and Lebanon," 74; Edward Cody and Pnina Ramati, "Covering the Invasion of Lebanon," *Washington Journalism Review* (September 1982): 19; Fisk, *Pity the Nation,* 407–408.

11. *NBC Nightly News,* July 2, 1982.

12. Thomas Friedman, "Palestinians Say Invaders Are Seeking to Destroy P.L.O. and Idea of a State," *New York Times,* June 9, 1982, A18.

13. Jonathan Randal, "Getting Stuck in Lebanon: Begin May Become as Trapped as the PLO he's surrounded," *Washington Post,* July 18, 1982, p. B5; *NBC Nightly News,* August 11, 1982.

14. John Chancellor, *NBC Nightly News,* August 2; William E. Farrell, "Dazed Refugees Deluge a Graceful Park in Beirut," *New York Times,* June 30, 1982, A1; Morris, "Beirut—and the Press—under Siege," 29; John Brecher et al., "Beirut: A City in Agony," *Newsweek,* August 16, 1982, 10–11.

15. *NBC Nightly News,* July 9, 1982.

16. Quoted in Morris, "Beirut—and the Press—under Siege," 30.

17. Angus Deming et al., "Special Report: Where Do They Go From Here?" *Newsweek,* August 16, 1982, 16–22.

18. Morris, "Beirut—and the Press—under Siege," 30.

19. Dorman and Farhang, "The U.S. Press and Lebanon," 73.

20. CBS example in Joshua Muravchik, "Misreporting Lebanon," *Policy Review* 23 (Winter 1983): 11–66, at 44; *NBC Nightly News,* August 13, 1982.

21. Philip Geyelin, "Lebanon—1958 and Now," *Washington Post,* August 3, 1982, A17.

22. David Lamb, "War Has Cost Israel Its Underdog Image," *Los Angeles Times,* June 30, 1982, 6; Edward Cody, "Palestinian Captives Are Problem for Israel, *Washington Post,* June 22, 1982, A14; Glenn Frankel, "'Battle over the Truth' Rages,"

Washington Post, July 18, 1982, A1; Alfred Friendly, "Israel: Recollections and Regrets," *Washington Post*, June 29, 1982, A17.

23. Lamb, "War Has Cost Israel Its Underdog Image."

24. David K. Shipler, "Some Israelis Fear Their Vietnam Is Lebanon," *New York Times*, June 27, 1982, 149.

25. Nat Hentoff, "The Silence of American Jews," *Village Voice*, June 29, 1982, 7–8; Paul L. Montgomery, "Discord among U.S. Jews over Israel Seems to Grow," *New York Times*, July 15, 1982, A16.

26. Stone quoted in Montgomery, "Discord among U.S. Jews," A16; Nathan Glazer and Seymour Martin Lipset, "Israel Isn't Threatened: The War's Ill-Advised," *New York Times*, June 30, 1982, A23. The ad, entitled "A Call to Peace," is quoted in Steven T. Rosenthal, *Irreconcilable Differences? The Waning of the American Jewish Love Affair with Israel* (Hanover, NH: University Press of New England, 2001), 67.

27. Richard Cohen, "Israel," *Washington Post*, June 27, 1982, B1.

28. Cohen, "Israel"; Hentoff, "Silence of American Jews," 8. At the height of the bombing of Beirut, the *New York Times* reminded its readers of an older Zionist dream of a progressive social experiment by publishing a long magazine article by the Israeli writer Amos Oz: "Has Israel Altered Its Vision?" *New York Times Magazine*, July 11, 1982, SM1.

29. For contemporary accounts, see Thomas L. Friedman, "The Beirut Massacre: The Four Days," *New York Times*, September 26, 1982, 1, 19–22; William Smith, Harry Kelly, and Robert Slater, "The Verdict Is Guilty," *Time*, February 21, 1983, 36–45. For a comprehensive history, see Bayan Nuwayhed al-Hout, *Sabra and Shatila: September 1982* (London: Pluto Press, 2004).

30. George F. Will, "Israel Should Show 'a Decent Respect,'" *Washington Post*, September 23, 1982, A27.

31. *Time*, September 27, 1982; *Newsweek*, October 4, 1982.

32. "Newsweek Poll: Israel Loses Ground," *Newsweek*, October 4, 1982.

33. Wolf Blitzer, "Distraught Friends," *Jerusalem Post*, September 24, 1982, 18, reprinted in *The Beirut Massacre: Press Profile*, 2nd ed. (New York: Claremont Research and Publications, 1984), 51. See also Barry Sussman, "Beirut Massacre Sours American Views on Israel," *Washington Post*, September 29, 1982, A1.

34. David K. Shipler, "Post Mortem: The Massacre Brings on a Crisis of Faith for Israelis," *New York Times*, September 26, 1982, E1; Anthony Lewis, "The End of a Policy," *New York Times*, September 20, 1982, A15; "The Horror in Beirut," *New Republic*, October 11, 1982, 7–8.

35. Arthur Hertzberg, "Begin Must Go," *New York Times*, September 26, 1982, E19. See also "The Horror, and the Shame," *New York Times*, September 21, 1982, A26.

36. Meg Greenfield, "How to Defend Israel," *Washington Post,* September 29, 1982, A23; "The Conscience of Israel," *Christian Science Monitor,* September 28, 1982, 24; "Israel's Soul, and Security," *New York Times,* September 26, 1982, E18.

37. Richard Cohen, "Proportion," *Washington Post,* June 10, 1982, B1; Greenfield, "How to Defend Israel."

38. "Israel Finds Its Voice," *New York Times,* September 29, 1982, A26; "All the Facts and Factors," *Washington Post,* September 30, 1982, A22.

39. Morris, "Beirut—and the Press—under Siege," 23.

40. For criticism of media coverage, see Peretz, "Lebanon Eyewitness"; Norman Podhoretz, "J'Accuse," *Commentary,* September 1982, 21–31; Pear Sheffy Gefen, "Behind the Lie in Lebanon," *Jerusalem Post,* October 29, 1982, 5; Marvin Maurer and Peter E. Goldman, "Lessons of the Lebanese Campaign," *Midstream,* April 1983, 44–52; Muravchik, "Misreporting Lebanon"; Frank Gervasi, "Media Coverage: The War in Lebanon," *Center for International Studies,* 1983, 1–29; Dan Bavly and Eliahu Salpeter, *Fire in Beirut: Israel's War in Lebanon with the PLO* (New York: Stein and Day, 1984), 135–150; Ze'ev Chafets, *Double Vision: How the Press Distorts America's View of the Middle East* (New York: William Morrow, 1985). On the *Washington Post*'s invitation to the director of the Jewish Community Council of Greater Washington, see R. J. McCloskey, "Open to Criticism," *Washington Post,* October 6, 1982. Quotation from ADL study (Anti-Defamation League of B'nai B'rith, "Television Network Coverage of the War in Lebanon," unpublished study prepared by Garth-Furth International, New York, October, 1982) is from Noam Chomsky, *The Fateful Triangle: The United States, Israel and the Palestinians* (Boston: South End Press, 1983), 285. For excerpts of this study, see Landrum R. Bolling, ed., *Reporters under Fire: U.S. Media Coverage of Conflicts in Lebanon and Central America* (Boulder, CO: Westview Press, 1985). See also Tony Schwartz, "A.D.L. Criticizes TV over Coverage of Lebanon," *New York Times,* October 21, 1982, C30.

41. "America-Israel Dialogue—*Hasbara:* Israel's Public Image: Problems and Remedies," *American Jewish Congress Monthly,* 51, no. 2–3 (1984): 3.

42. Ibid., 7.

43. Peretz, "Lebanon Eyewitness"; Arnold Foster, "The Media's Most Disgraceful Hour," *Penthouse* 15, no. 6 (February 1984): 116–120; Chafets, *Double Vision,* 127–154.

44. Podhoretz, "J'Accuse." The essay was also printed on October 24, 1982, in the *New York Times* and the *Los Angeles Times.* For influential formulations of the new anti-Semitism from the Anti-Defamation League, see Arnold Foster and Benjamin R. Epstein, *The New Anti-Semitism* (New York: McGraw-Hill, 1974), and Nathan Perlmutter and Ruth Ann Perlmutter, *The Real Anti-Semitism in America* (New York: Arbor House, 1982). On the trope of the "Jew among nations," see

Norman Finkelstein, *Beyond Chutzpah: On the Misuse of Anti-Semitism and the Abuse of History* (Berkeley: University of California Press, 2005), 32–65.

45. Podhoretz, "J'Accuse," 23.

46. Ibid., 22, 25. Podhoretz did find one suitable analogy: "But if we are looking for analogies, a better one than any fished up in recent weeks would be the invasion of France by allied troops in World War II. The purpose was not to conquer France but to liberate it from its German conquerors, just as the purpose of the Israelis in 1982 was to liberate Lebanon from the PLO" (25).

47. Ibid., 22, 25, 26.

48. Ibid., 28, 29

49. Ibid., 29–30 (emphasis in original).

50. Norman Podhoretz, *Why We Were in Vietnam* (New York: Simon and Schuster, 1982), 210; Podhoretz, "J'Accuse," 30 (emphasis in original).

51. Podhoretz, "J'Accuse," 30, 31.

52. On CAMERA's history and activities since 1982 see its website, http://www.camera.org/.

53. On comparative critiques of media coverage in Lebanon and Central America see Bolling, *Reporters under Fire*; Mike Hoyt, "The Mozote Massacre," *Columbia Journalism Review* 31, no. 5 (January 1993): 31–34.

54. Edward Tivnan, *The Lobby: Jewish Political Power and American Foreign Policy* (New York: Simon and Schuster, 1987), 178. The need to control the public narrative and produce knowledge about Israel that serves its interests was seen as too important by key members of AIPAC to be left to their overt advocacy role. In 1984, a group of AIPAC leaders started a new think tank, the Washington Institute for Near East Policy (WINEP), naming as its executive director Martyn Indyk, who had previously worked in the AIPAC research department. Its purpose was not to sell Israel's policy but to "define the agenda in a way that's conducive to Israeli interests" (quoted in Jonathan J. Goldberg, *Jewish Power: Inside the American Jewish Establishment* [New York: Basic Books, 1996], 221). On the founding of WINEP, see M. J. Rosenberg, "Does PBS Know That 'The Washington Institute' Was Founded by AIPAC?" *Huffpost*, May 25, 2011, https://www.huffingtonpost.com/mj-rosenberg/does-pbs-know-that-washin_b_533808.html. In 1982, AIPAC started publishing a series of papers that documented this case for Israeli power, with titles like "Strategic Value of Israel," "Israel and the U.S. Airforce," "Israeli Medical Support for the U.S. Armed Forces," and "U.S. Procurement of Israeli Defense Goods and Services."

55. Amy Kaufman Goott et al., *The Campaign to Discredit Israel* (Washington, D.C.: American Israel Public Affairs Committee, 1983); Jonathan Kessler and Jeff

Schwaber, *The AIPAC College Guide: Exposing the Anti-Israel Campaign on Campus* (Washington, D.C.: American Israel Public Affairs Committee, 1984); *Pro-Arab Propaganda in America: Vehicles and Voices: A Handbook* (New York: Anti-Defamation League of B'nai B'rith, 1983).

56. *Pro-Arab Propaganda in America,* 1.

57. Goott et al., *Campaign to Discredit Israel,* 14–15.

58. Ibid., viii, 14–16.

59. Kessler and Schwaber, *AIPAC College Guide,* v, 22, 55 (emphasis in original).

60. Zachary Lockman, *Contending Visions of the Middle East: The History and Politics of Orientalism* (Cambridge: Cambridge University Press, 2010), 254–255; David K. Shipler, "On Middle East Policy, a Major Influence," *New York Times,* January 30, 1985, 1; Anthony Lewis, "No Moderates Allowed," *New York Times,* December 22, 1983, A21; Kenneth Bialkin, "A Palestinian Professor Unqualified to Be Called a Moderate," letter to the editor, *New York Times,* January 12, 1984, A30; Anthony Lewis, "Protocols of Palestine," *New York Times,* January 16, 1985, A15; Kenneth Bialkin, "Of Khalidi and the Anti-Defamation League," letter to the editor, *New York Times,* January 23, 1984, A20.

61. Joan Peters, *From Time Immemorial: The Origins of the Arab-Jewish Conflict over Palestine* (New York: Harper and Row, 1984).

62. Avi Shlaim, "The Debate about 1948," *International Journal of Middle East Studies* 27, no. 3 (1995): 287–304.

63. Peters, *From Time Immemorial,* 173.

64. The universal rejection of Peters's scholarship by professional historians has never fully buried her book, which remains alive on the right today. On CAMERA's website, the book appears in a bibliography for its "Adopt a Library Project," which advocates donating to libraries "solid works presenting reliable information" to counteract the more readily available "volumes by Edward Said, Noam Chomsky and other extreme detractors of Israel." See http://www.camera.org/index.asp?x_context =2&x_article=704#list; http://www.camera.org/index.asp?x_context=53.

65. Sidney Zion, "Scoop!" review of *From Time Immemorial,* by Joan Peters, *National Review,* October 5, 1984, 47.

66. Norman G. Finkelstein, "Disinformation and the Palestine Question: The Not-So-Strange Case of Joan Peters's *From Time Immemorial,*" in *Blaming the Victims: Spurious Scholarship and the Palestinian Question,* ed. Edward W. Said and Christopher Hitchens (New York: Verso, 1988), 33–69; Porath quoted in Colin Campbell, "Dispute Flares over Book on Claims to Palestine," *New York Times,* November 28, 1985, C16; Yehoshua Porath, "Mrs. Peters's Palestine," review of *From Time Immemorial,* by Joan Peters, *New York Review of Books* 32, nos. 21 and

22 (January 16, 1986); Edward Said, "Conspiracy of Praise," in Said and Hitchens, *Blaming the Victims,* 30; Anthony Lewis, "There Were No Indians," *New York Times,* January 13, 1986, A15.

67. Leon Uris, *The Haj* (New York: Bantam, 1984). Uris did not invent these stereotypes. He credited his "knowledge" to meetings with the distinguished Princeton historian Bernard Lewis, whom Peters also acknowledged, and to the "huge influence" of Raphael Patai's book *The Arab Mind.* Lewis espoused an influential view of Islam as a monolithic and unchanging civilization inherently antagonistic to modernity, as embodied in the "Judeo-Christian" West. Patai's book was based on ideas of the supposed essential irrationality of Arab culture and displayed a prurient interest in sexuality. See Ira B. Nadel, *Leon Uris: Life of a Best Seller* (Austin: University of Texas Press, 2010), 245–256.

68. Quoted in Mark A. Tessler, *A History of the Israeli-Palestinian Conflict,* 2nd ed. (Bloomington: Indiana University Press, 2009), 701.

69. David K. Shipler, *Arab and Jew: Wounded Spirits in a Promised Land* (New York: Random House, 1986); Thomas L. Friedman, *From Beirut to Jerusalem* (New York: Anchor, 1989).

70. Shipler, *Arab and Jew,* 77, 16.

71. Friedman, *From Beirut to Jerusalem,* 73, 164.

72. Ibid., 159; Shipler, *Arab and Jew,* 74–75.

73. Friedman, *From Beirut to Jerusalem,* 163.

74. Shipler, *Arab and Jew,* 378–380.

75. Ibid., 254–255.

76. Friedman, *From Beirut to Jerusalem,* 361–363.

77. Ibid., 360, 391, 345. On the casualty figures for the intifada, see https://www .btselem.org/statistics/first_intifada_tables.

78. Thomas L. Friedman, "How Long Can Israel Deny Its Civil War?" *New York Times,* December 27, 1987, E3.

79. Friedman, *From Beirut to Jerusalem,* 391, 392.

80. Quoted in Friedman, *From Beirut to Jerusalem,* 403.

81. Friedman, *From Beirut to Jerusalem,* 421.

82. Ibid., 488, 450.

83. Shipler, *Arab and Jew,* 111, 159–160, 33, 63, 332–333.

84. Ibid., 500–502, 511.

85. Ronald Sanders, "What Strangers, Whose Gates," review of *Arab and Jew,* by David K. Shipler, *New York Times,* September 28, 1986, BR1; Gary Abrams, "Pulitzer Winner Shipler Reflects on 'Arab and Jew,'" *Los Angeles Times,* April 20, 1987, F1.

86. Friedman, *From Beirut to Jerusalem,* 499, 509.

87. "PBS Producing Program to Offset Criticism of 'Days of Rage' Film," *Jewish Telegraphic Agency,* August 3, 1989, https://www.jta.org/1989/08/03/archive/pbs-producing-program-to-offset-criticism-of-days-of-rage-film. On the controversy, see B. J. Bullert, *Public Television: Politics and the Battle over Documentary Film* (Brunswick, NJ: Rutgers University Press, 1997), 63–90.

88. Walter Goodman, "Two Views of Mideast Conflict: A Delicate Balance for PBS," *New York Times,* May 29, 1989, 40.

89. Jo Franklin-Trout, "It's a Fair Honest Film," *New York Times,* September 6, 1989, A25.

90. Edward Said, *The Question of Palestine* (1979; New York: Vintage, 1992); Noam Chomsky, *The Fateful Triangle: The United States, Israel and the Palestinians* (Boston: South End Press, 1983).

5. The Future Holocaust

1. On the development of the United States Holocaust Memorial Museum, see Edward Linenthal, *Preserving Memory: The Struggle to Create America's Holocaust Museum* (New York: Columbia University Press, 1995); Judith Miller, *One, by One, by One: Facing the Holocaust* (New York: Simon and Schuster, 1990), 220–275. For Carter's speech and Begin's response, see "30th Anniversary of the State of Israel Remarks of the President and Prime Minister Menachem Begin at a White House Reception," May 1, 1978, in Gerhard Peters and John T. Woolley, *The American Presidency Project,* http://www.presidency.ucsb.edu/ws/?pid=30730.

2. Oswald Johnston, "Israeli Denounces Group as 'Huns,'" *Los Angeles Times,* August 10, 1977, B1.

3. On the political context of Carter's announcement see Linenthal, *Preserving Memory,* 17–20. On the first time an American president used the phrase "Palestinian homeland," see William Quandt, *Peace Process: American Diplomacy and the Arab-Israeli Conflict since 1967* (Berkeley: University of California Press, 2005), 182. On American Jewish discontent with Carter, see James Perry, "American Jews and Jimmy Carter," *Wall Street Journal,* March 2, 1978, 20; Judith Miller, "Holocaust Museum: A Troubled Start," *New York Times,* April 22, 1990, 34; Edward Tivnan, *The Lobby: Jewish Political Power and American Foreign Policy* (New York: Simon and Schuster, 1987), 98–134.

4. "30th Anniversary of the State of Israel Remarks of the President and Prime Minister Begin."

5. On Nixon's reluctance to visit Yad Vashem, see Noam Kochavi, *Nixon and Israel: Forging a Conservative Partnership* (Albany: State University of New York

Press, 2010), 71. On Johnson, see Steven Spiegel, *The Other Arab-Israeli Conflict: Making America's Middle East Policy from Truman to Reagan* (Chicago: University of Chicago Press, 1985), 123–124.

6. Peter Novick, *The Holocaust in American Life* (Boston: Houghton Mifflin, 1999); Linenthal, *Preserving Memory,* 5–11. Hasia Diner argues against the claim that American Jews did not address the Holocaust until the 1970s but does acknowledge that Holocaust memorialization shifted from local Jewish communities to a national scale at that time, in *We Remember with Reverence and Love: American Jews and the Myth of Silence after the Holocaust, 1945–1962* (New York: New York University Press, 2009). On American fear of nuclear attacks, see Paul Boyer, *By the Bomb's Early Light: American Thought and Culture at the Dawn of the Atomic Age* (New York: Pantheon, 1985). My argument is indebted to Novick's seminal study, but the major shift I see in the 1970s is not only that Jewish organizations evoked the Holocaust to support Israel, as he argues, but that the temporal significance of the Holocaust changes from past event to future threat.

7. On Israel's national uses of the Holocaust, see Tom Segev, *The Seventh Million: The Israelis and the Holocaust,* trans. Haim Watzman (New York: Holt, 1991); Idith Zertal, *Israel's Holocaust and the Politics of Nationhood* (Cambridge: Cambridge University Press, 2005). On the fear in the weeks before the Six-Day War, see Tom Segev, *1967: Israel, the War, and the Year That Transformed the Middle East* (New York: Metropolitan Books, 2007), 283–387.

8. Novick, *The Holocaust in American Life,* 146–160; Arnold Forster and Benjamin Epstein, *The New Anti-Semitism* (New York: McGraw-Hill, 1974). Some scholars regard 1967 as the turning point in Holocaust consciousness among American Jews: see Norman Finkelstein, *The Holocaust Industry: Reflections on the Exploitation of Jewish Suffering* (London: Verso, 2000), 16–32; J. J. Goldberg, *Jewish Power: Inside the American Jewish Establishment* (New York: Basic Books, 1996), 144–147; Michael Berenbaum, "Is the Holocaust Being Exploited?" *Midstream* 50, no. 3 (2004): 2–9.

9. Segev, *The Seventh Million,* 396–400.

10. David K. Shipler, "Begin Defends Raid, Pledges to Thwart a New 'Holocaust,'" *New York Times,* June 10, 1981, 1.

11. For letter to Reagan, see Yoram Kessel, "Israel Isn't Ready to Cope with the Issue of Palestinians, Even if PLO Alters Tack," *Wall Street Journal,* August 6, 1982, 6. Some Israeli Holocaust survivors and intellectuals objected to Begin's use of these Holocaust analogies; see Benny Morris, *Righteous Victims: A History of the Zionist-Arab Conflict, 1881–1998* (New York: Knopf, 2001), 514–516.

12. David K. Shipler, "Begin Is Optimistic All Foreign Units Will Quit Lebanon," *New York Times,* August 29, 1982, 1.

13. "Begin on Begin: Soon I'll Retire to Write My Book," *Wall Street Journal,* July 9, 1982, 1.

14. David K. Shipler, "In Israel, Anguish over the Moral Questions," *New York Times,* September 24, 1982, A1. Peter Novick argued that Begin's "promiscuous" use of Holocaust imagery discredited that usage, and that in the 1980s, particularly after the intifada, the Holocaust frame became implausible, except for the far right (*The Holocaust in American Life,* 162–165). I contend, on the contrary, that the Holocaust became more important as a means to convey Israel's vulnerability precisely at the time that its military power was increasing.

15. *Holocaust,* produced by Robert Berger and Herbert Brodkin, broadcast April 16–19, 1978, National Broadcasting Company. On this miniseries, see Judith Doneson, *The Holocaust in American Film* (Syracuse, NY: Syracuse University Press, 2002), 141–196; Jeffrey Shandler, *While America Watches: Televising the Holocaust* (New York: Oxford University Press, 1999), 155–181; John De Vito and Fran Tropea, *Epic Television Miniseries: A Critical History* (Jefferson, NC: McFarland, 2010), 42–52.

16. Gerald Green, *Holocaust* (New York: Bantam Books, 1978), 3; American Jewish Committee, "NBC's 'Holocaust' Program: A Nationwide Survey among Viewers and Nonviewers" (1978), 42. For an overview of the publicity and the responses to the miniseries, see Sander A. Diamond, "'Holocaust' Film's Impact on Americans," *Patterns of Prejudice* 12, no. 4 (1978): 1–19; "Human Relations Catalogue Printed," *American Israelite,* September 7, 1978, 16. Quotations from Lutheran magazine in Diamond, "'Holocaust' Film's Impact," 9.

17. "Lesson of the Holocaust," *Near East Report,* April 19, 1978, 65.

18. "AIPAC Policy Statement," *Near East Report,* June 17, 1983, 98.

19. Elie Wiesel, "The Holocaust: Beginning or End?" April 24, 1979, in *Report to the President, President's Commission on the Holocaust,* September 27, 1979, 30–31, reprinted by United States Holocaust Memorial Museum, June 2005, https://www.ushmm.org/m/pdfs/20050707-presidents-commission-holocaust.pdf.

20. "Address by President Jimmy Carter," April 24, 1979, in *Report to the President, President's Commission,* 26–27. The Senate had long dragged its feet on ratifying this UN Convention, drafted in 1948, because of fear that it would be used against segregation and lynching in the United States. See Barbara J. Keys, *Reclaiming American Virtue: The Human Rights Revolution of the 1970s* (Cambridge, MA: Harvard University Press, 2014), 23–26; Mark Philip Bradley, *The World Reimagined: Americans and Human Rights in the Twentieth Century* (Cambridge: Cambridge University Press, 2016), 110–112.

21. "Remarks of the President at the Presentation of the Final Report of the President's Commission on the Holocaust," in *Report to the President, President's Commission,* 35.

22. See, for example, Samantha Powers, *A Problem from Hell: America and the Age of Genocide* (New York: Harper Collins, 2002), xxi. Powers refers to the Holocaust Museum and the vows of four presidents to prevent the recurrence of genocide, and concludes that "the forward-looking, consoling refrain of 'never again,' a testament to America's can-do spirit, never grappled with the fact that the country had done nothing, practically or politically, to prepare itself to respond to genocide. The commitment proved hollow in the face of actual slaughter."

23. Meir Kahane, *Never Again! A Program for Survival* (New York: Pyramid Books, 1972); John Kifner, "Meir Kahane, 58, Israeli Militant and Founder of the Jewish Defense League," *New York Times,* November 6, 1990, B13. On the invention of the slogan, see Gal Beckerman, *When They Come for Us, We'll Be Gone: The Epic Struggle to Save Soviet Jewry* (New York: Houghton Mifflin, 2010), loc. 3551 of 11879, Kindle.

24. Robert Meister, *After Evil: A Politics of Human Rights* (New York: Columbia University Press, 2011), 192–206.

25. Alan Mintz, *Popular Culture and the Shaping of Holocaust Memory in America* (Seattle: University of Washington Press, 2012), 10, 21, 161; Elie Wiesel, "Presentation of the Report of the President's Commission on the Holocaust to the President of the United States," in *Report to the President, President's Commission,* 34.

26. Elie Wiesel, "To a Young Palestinian Arab," in *A Jew Today* (New York: Vintage, 1979), 122–127. On Wiesel's attitude toward Israel and the Palestinians, see Mark Chmiel, *Elie Wiesel and the Politics of Moral Leadership* (Philadelphia: Temple University Press, 2001), 79–114.

27. Segev, *The Seventh Million,* 401.

28. Eric Levin, "Holocaust Survivor Elie Wiesel Decries a Rising Tide of Anti-Semitism at Home and Abroad," *People,* November 29, 1982. Wiesel was one of the authors whose responses were collected in the *New York Times* after the massacre at Sabra and Shatila ("Prominent U.S. Jews Support Israel, but Some Criticize Begin and Sharon," September 22, 1982, A16), but his statement is hard to decipher. He acknowledged feeling darkness and sadness, said that he did not blame the Israelis, and stated enigmatically: "Perhaps if we had told the story more convincingly, if we had prevented the cheapening and trivialization of what was and remains a unique catastrophe, things would not have happened his way."

29. Caryle Murphy, "The Holocaust: A Gathering of Survivors; Holocaust Survivors to Rally Here," *Washington Post,* April 9, 1983, 1.

30. Wolf Blitzer, *Between Washington and Jerusalem: A Reporter's Notebook* (New York: Oxford University Press, 1985), 9–10.

31. Dody Tsiantar, "'A Holocaust of One': 800 Hear Klinghoffer Eulogized in N.Y.," *Washington Post,* October 22, 1985, A25.

32. Mark A. Tessler, *A History of the Israeli-Palestinian Conflict,* 2nd ed. (Bloomington: Indiana University Press, 2009), 481.

33. "Press Release—Peace 1986," Nobelprize.org, Nobel Media, October 14, 1986, http://www.nobelprize.org/nobel_prizes/peace/laureates/1986/press.html.

34. Elie Wiesel, "The Nobel Address," in Wiesel, *From Kingdom of Memory: Reminiscences* (New York: Summit, 1990), 233. This version of the speech differs slightly from the written transcript available on the Nobel website ("Elie Wiesel—Acceptance Speech," http://www.nobelprize.org/nobel_prizes/peace/laureates/1986/wiesel-acceptance_en.html). The version in the book is closer to the actual speech delivered at the ceremony (https://www.nobelprize.org/mediaplayer/index.php?id=2028).

35. Elie Wiesel, "A Mideast Peace—Is It Impossible?" *New York Times,* June 23, 1988, 23. See also Chmiel, *Elie Wiesel,* 105–108; "Palestinian's Poem Unnerves Israelis," *New York Times,* April 5, 1988, A18.

36. Anthony Lewis, "A Chance to Talk," *New York Times,* June 23, 1988, 23; Arthur Hertzberg, "An Open Letter to Elie Wiesel," *New York Review of Books,* August 18, 1988, 14.

37. Berenbaum quoted in Edward Norden, "Yes and No to the Holocaust Museums," *Commentary,* August 1, 1993, 23–32. See also Michael Berenbaum, "High Intensity Jewishness or We Wither Away," *Sh'ma,* October 19, 1990, 146–148; Michael Berenbaum, "Will Israel Divide Where It Once United?" *Sh'ma,* May 1, 1987, 102–104.

38. Michael Berenbaum, *After Tragedy and Triumph: Essays in Modern Jewish Thought and the American Experience* (Cambridge: Cambridge University Press, 2009), 20, 11.

39. On the Americanization of the Holocaust, see, e.g., Alvin H. Rosenfeld, "The Americanization of the Holocaust," *Commentary,* June 1, 1995, 35–40; Hilene Flanzbaum, ed., *Americanization of the Holocaust* (Baltimore: Johns Hopkins University Press, 1999); Tim Cole, *Selling the Holocaust: From Auschwitz to Schindler: How History Is Bought, Packaged, and Sold* (New York: Routledge, 2000); James Young, *The Texture of Memory: Holocaust Memorials and Meaning* (New Haven, CT: Yale University Press, 1993); David B. MacDonald, *Identity Politics in the Age of Genocide: The Holocaust and Historical Representation* (London: Routledge, 2008), 13–58; Novick, *The Holocaust in American Life,* 207–238. See also the influential article by sociologist Jeffrey Alexander, "The Social Construction of Moral Universals"

and the responses to it, in Jeffrey Alexander, *Remembering the Holocaust: A Debate* (New York: Oxford University Press, 2009).

40. Controversies continued about the relation of the Holocaust Museum to the politics of Israel and Palestine. See Linenthal, *Preserving Memory*, 258; Marilyn Henry, "A House Divided," *Jerusalem Post*, July 17, 1998, 8. Holocaust scholar John Roth wrote about the controversy that involved him in *Holocaust Politics* (Louisville, KY: Westminster John Knox, 2001).

41. William J. Clinton, "Remarks at the Dedication of the United States Holocaust Memorial Museum," April 22, 1993, in Peters and Woolley, *The American Presidency Project*, http://www.presidency.ucsb.edu/ws/?pid=46468.

42. Ibid.

43. The Holocaust Museum dedication on April 23, 1993, can be viewed at https://www.c-span.org/video/?39949-1/holocaust-memorial-museum-dedication.

44. On "chronicles of liberation" as a framework for journalists in 1945, see Barbie Zelizer, *Remembering to Forget: Holocaust Memory through the Camera's Eye* (Chicago: University of Chicago Press, 1998), 63–68. On the disorienting encounter of soldiers with the death camps, see Robert Abzug, *Inside the Vicious Heart: Americans and the Liberation of Nazi Concentration Camps* (New York: Oxford University Press, 1987), 21–44.

45. Jimmy Carter, "Proclamation 4652: Days of Remembrance of Victims of the Holocaust, April 28 and 29, 1979," April 2, 1979, in Peters and Woolley, *The American Presidency Project*, http://www.presidency.ucsb.edu/ws/index.php?pid=32137.

46. Ronald Reagan, "Remarks at the First Annual Commemoration of the Days of Remembrance of Victims of the Holocaust," April 30, 1981, in Peters and Woolley, *The American Presidency Project*, http://www.presidency.ucsb.edu/ws/?pid=43761.

47. Ronald Reagan, "Remarks at a White House Ceremony Commemorating the Day of Remembrance of Victims of the Holocaust," April 20, 1982, in Peters and Woolley, *The American Presidency Project*, http://www.presidency.ucsb.edu/ws/?pid=42425.

48. Ronald Reagan, "Remarks at the Site of the Future Holocaust Memorial Museum," October 5, 1988, in Peters and Woolley, *The American Presidency Project*, http://www.presidency.ucsb.edu/ws/?pid=34970. Reagan's relationship to the Holocaust is best remembered for the controversy that erupted when he agreed to lay a wreath at a German military cemetery in Bitburg. Elie Wiesel exhorted Reagan to change his plans during a televised ceremony conferring on Wiesel the Congressional Gold Medal. For an overview of the controversy and commentaries see Geoffrey Hartman, ed., *Bitburg in Moral and Political Perspective* (Bloomington: Indiana University Press, 2000); on Wiesel's involvement, see Chmiel, *Elie Wiesel*, 131–137. For

Wiesel's televised exhortation, see "Elie Wiesel Receives Congressional Gold Medal," 131 Cong. Rec .S4431, April 22, 1985; for Wiesel's remarks after the controversy, see Michael Elkin, "Elie Wiesel's Frame of Mind," *Jewish Exponent,* November 8, 1985, 89.

49. *Days of Remembrance: A Department of Defense Guide for Annual Commemorative Observances* (Washington, D.C.: Department of Defense, 1989), inside cover.

50. Quoted in Young, *Texture of Memory,* 321.

51. In "The Social Construction of Moral Universals," Jeffrey Alexander argues that a historical transformation occurred in Holocaust memory in which a postwar progressive narrative about America's triumph over Nazism was supplanted by a tragic universal narrative, in which everyone has come to acknowledge complicity in the evil that the Holocaust epitomizes. He sees this development as a growth in moral consciousness, which reflects the post-Vietnam disillusionment with American power. Alexander's sequential narrative ignores the fact that the progressive narrative of America as liberator actually grew in importance in the 1980s and 1990s, at the same time that the universal narrative came into its own.

52. Quoted in David Hoogland Noon, "Operation Enduring Analogy: World War II, the War on Terror, and the Uses of Historical Memory," *Rhetoric and Public Affairs* 7, no. 3 (2004): 345.

53. This description relies on my own visits and the guides to the exhibit on the museum's website: https://www.ushmm.org/. See also Greig Crysler and Abidin Kusno, "Angels in the Temple: The Aesthetic Construction of Citizenship at the United States Holocaust Memorial Museum," *Art Journal,* 56, no. 1 (1997): 52–64; Jennifer Hansen-Glucklich, *Holocaust Memory Reframed: Museums and the Challenges of Representation* (New Brunswick, NJ: Rutgers University Press, 2014), locs. 1586–1774 of 6823, Kindle. Specifics of the exhibition have been altered at times.

54. For the different positions in this debate, see Michael J. Neufeld and Michael Berenbaum, eds., *The Bombing of Auschwitz: Should the Allies Have Attempted It?* (New York: St. Martin's Press, 2000). The contention that the Allies should have bombed Auschwitz first achieved public notice with David Wyman's 1978 essay in *Commentary,* "Why Auschwitz Was Never Bombed," which he followed with *The Abandonment of the Jews* (New York: New Press, 2007). William D. Rubinstein rejects this thesis in *The Myth of Refuge: Why the Democracies Could Not Have Saved More Jews from the Nazis* (New York: Routledge, 1997).

55. Quoted in Linenthal, *Preserving Memory,* 218, who writes that the "definite word 'would' instead of 'might' keeps visitors from appreciating an ongoing controversy, and makes an interpretive stance a statement of fact." The Museum's online encyclopedia offers a more nuanced interpretation, mentioning the intense debate,

and changing the wording to indicate more tentative speculation: https://www.ushmm .org/wlc/en/article.php?ModuleId=10008041.

56. Deborah Lipstadt, "The Failure to Rescue and Contemporary American Jewish Historiography of the Holocaust, Judging from a Distance," in Neufeld and Berenbaum, *Bombing of Auschwitz,* 227–236.

57. "'This Time the World Acted': Wiesel Hails Action in Kosovo," *Jewish Telegraphic Agency,* April 14, 1999, http://www.jta.org/1999/04/14/archive/this-time-the -world-acted-wiesel-hails-action-in-kosovo-2.

58. Jackie Calmes and Mark Lander, "Obama Scolds G.O.P. Critics of Iran Policy: Backs Diplomatic Path over 'Drums of War,'" *New York Times,* March 7, 2012, A1.

59. Carter quoted in Keys, *Reclaiming American Virtue,* 268.

60. Keys, *Reclaiming American Virtue.*

61. Byron Price, "'Cutting for Sign': Museums and Western Revisionism," *Western Historical Quarterly* 24.2 (May 1993): 229–234.

62. Edward T. Linenthal and Tom Engelhardt, eds., *History Wars: The "Enola Gay" and Other Battles for the American Past* (New York: Macmillan, 1996).

63. *Schindler's List,* directed by Steven Spielberg (Universal Pictures, 1993).

64. Spielberg quoted in David Ansen, "Spielberg's Obsession," *Newsweek,* December 19, 1993; James Young, "Schindler's List: Myth, Movie, and Memory," *Village Voice,* March 24, 1994, 24.

65. Omer Bartov, "Spielberg's Oskar, Hollywood Tries Evil," in *Spielberg's Holocaust: Critical Perspectives on "Schindler's List,"* ed. Yosefa Loshitzky (Bloomington: Indiana University Press, 1997), 45; Haim Bresheeth, "The Great Taboo Broken: Reflections on the Israeli Reception of *Schindler's List,*" in ibid., 205.

6. Apocalypse Soon

1. For overviews of Christian attitudes toward the Holy Land, see John Davis, *The Landscape of Belief: Encountering the Holy Land in Nineteenth-Century American Art and Culture* (Princeton, NJ: Princeton University Press, 1996); Shalom L. Goldman, *Zeal for Zion: Christians, Jews, and the Idea of the Promised Land* (Chapel Hill: University of North Carolina Press, 2009); Melani McAlister, *Epic Encounters: Culture, Media, and U.S. Interests in the Middle East, 1945–2000,* rev. ed. (Berkeley: University of California Press, 2005), 13–20; Hilton Obenzinger, *American Palestine: Melville, Twain, and the Holy Land Mania* (Princeton, NJ: Princeton University Press, 1999).

2. On the history of prophecy belief in America, see Paul Boyer, *When Time Shall Be No More: Prophecy Belief in Modern American Culture* (Cambridge, MA: Har-

vard University Press, 1992). On the contemporary belief in the end of days, see Nicholas Guyatt, *Have a Nice Doomsday: Why Millions of Americans Are Looking Forward to the End of the World* (New York: Harper Perennial, 2007).

3. On Christian Zionism, see Yaakov Ariel, *An Unusual Relationship: Evangelical Christians and Jews* (New York: New York University Press, 2013); Caitlin Carenen, *The Fervent Embrace: Liberal Protestants, Evangelicals, and Israel* (New York: New York University Press, 2012); Victoria Clark, *Allies for Armageddon: The Rise of Christian Zionism* (New Haven, CT: Yale University Press, 2007); Samuel Goldman, *God's Country: Christian Zionism in America* (Philadelphia: University of Pennsylvania Press, 2018); Goldman, *Zeal for Zion*; Gershom Gorenberg, *The End of Days: Fundamentalism and the Struggle for the Temple Mount* (New York: Free Press, 2000); Grace Halsell, *Prophecy and Politics: The Secret Alliance between Israel and the U.S. Christian Right* (Chicago: Lawrence Hill, 1986); Robert O. Smith, *More Desired Than Our Owne Salvation: The Roots of Christian Zionism* (New York: Oxford University Press, 2013); Stephen Spector, *Evangelicals and Israel: The Story of American Christian Zionism* (New York: Oxford University Press, 2009); Timothy P. Weber, *On the Road to Armageddon: How Evangelicals Became Israel's Best Friend* (Grand Rapids, MI: Baker Academic, 2004).

4. David Brinn, "Pat Boone's Christmas Present to the Jews," *Jerusalem Post,* February 9, 2010, http://www.jpost.com/Arts-and-Culture/Music/Pat-Boones-Christmas -present-to-the-Jews.

5. Sam Sokol, "Pat Boone Sells Land in Galilee to Evangelicals," *Jerusalem Post,* February 13, 2013, http://www.jpost.com/Features/In-Thespotlight/Pat-Boone-sells -land-in-Galilee-to-evangelicals.

6. Hal Lindsey with C. C. Carson, *The Late Great Planet Earth* (Grand Rapids, MI: Zondervan, 1970).

7. Boyer, *When Time Shall Be No More*, 5–7, 126–128; Weber, *On the Road to Armageddon*, locs. 2572–2623 of 4795, Kindle.

8. Lindsey, *The Late Great Planet Earth*, 20.

9. Ibid., 43.

10. Premillennialism refers to the idea that Christ must come to earth before the dawning of one thousand years of peace (as opposed to postmillennialism—which holds that man's good works would progressively lead to this utopian stage of human history). Dispensationalism refers to the division of human history into biblical eras, in which Church history and the biblical history of the Jews are on separate trajectories, both of which will culminate in the final Messianic Age. Dispensationalist beliefs were codified in the enormously popular Scofield Reference Bible (1909), in which prophecy interpretations were printed alongside the biblical text, merging the two as a single whole. On Darby, Scofield, and premillennial dispensationalism, see

Boyer, *When Time Shall Be No More*, 80–112, Clark, *Allies for Armageddon*, 73–92, Weber, *On the Road to Armageddon*, locs. 163–509 of 4795, Kindle.

11. Quoted in Goldman, *God's Country*, loc. 1267 of 5604, Kindle.

12. On the Blackstone Memorial, see ibid., locs. 1236–3108; Clark, *Allies for Armageddon*, 92–97; Weber, *On the Road to Armageddon*, locs. 1358–1381 of 4795, Kindle; Hilton Obenzinger, "In the Shadow of 'God's Sun-Dial': The Construction of American Christian Zionism and the Blackstone Memorial," *Stanford Electronic Humanities Review* 5, no. 1 (Spring 1996), n.p., https://www.stanford.edu/group/SHR /5-1/text/obenzinger.html. On Christian Zionism and British imperial politics, see Clark, *Allies for Armageddon*, 92–97; Donald M. Lewis, *The Origins of Christian Zionism: Lord Shaftesbury and Evangelical Support for a Jewish Homeland* (New York: Cambridge University Press, 2010).

13. Quoted in Smith, *More Desired Than Our Owne Salvation*, 11.

14. Lindsey, *The Late Great Planet Earth*, 55–56; Gorenberg, *The End of Days*, 175–179.

15. Lindsey, *The Late Great Planet Earth*, 79.

16. Ibid., 166, 135, 144.

17. Ibid., 150, 44, 174.

18. Ibid., 111.

19. Ibid., 29.

20. Stu Weber, *Tender Warrior: God's Intention for Man* (Colorado Springs, CO: Multnomah Books, 1993), 208–209.

21. Halsell, *Prophecy and Politics*, 122.

22. Hal Lindsey, *A Prophetical Walk through the Holy Land* (Eugene, OR: Harvest House, 1983), 190.

23. Hal Lindsey, *The 1980s: Countdown to Armageddon* (New York: Bantam Books, 1981), 157.

24. Tim LaHaye, *The Battle for the Mind* (Old Tappan, NJ: Fleming H. Revell, 1980), 217. On the Religious Right, see Darren Dochuk, *From Bible Belt to Sun Belt: Plain-folk Religion, Grassroots Politics, and the Rise of Evangelical Conservatism* (New York: Norton, 2010); Susan Friend Harding, *The Book of Jerry Falwell: Fundamentalist Language and Politics* (Princeton, NJ: Princeton University Press, 2000); Michael Lienesch, *Redeeming America: Piety and Politics in the New Christian Right* (Chapel Hill: University of North Carolina Press, 1993).

25. Quoted in Clark, *Allies for Armageddon*, 187.

26. Quoted in William Martin, "The Christian Right and American Foreign Policy," *Foreign Policy* 114 (Spring 1999): 72.

27. Mike Evans, *Israel—America's Key to Survival*, rev ed. (Bedford, TX: Bedford Books, 1983). On Evans's influence, see Daniel K. Eisenbud, "The Bridge Builder,"

Jerusalem Post, June 14, 2012, http://www.jpost.com/Magazine/Features/The-bridge -builder; Bill Berkowitz, "The Most Influential (and Self-Promotional) Christian Zionist You've Never Heard Of," *Alternet,* February 23, 2009, http://www.alternet.org /story/128353/the_most_influential_%28and_self-promotional%29_christian _zionist_you%27ve_never_heard_of.

28. Tim LaHaye, *The Coming Peace in the Middle East* (Grand Rapids, MI: Zondervan, 1984), 169.

29. Jerry Falwell, *Listen, America!* (New York: Bantam, 1980), 98.

30. Ibid., 84.

31. This narrative underwrote Reagan's "Star Wars" agenda of creating an impenetrable shield of nuclear defense missiles, which would protect America in fighting and winning a nuclear war. "Blessing Israel," to Falwell and the Christian right, also meant blessing America with Reagan's massive military buildup of nuclear and conventional arms.

32. LaHaye, *The Battle for the Mind,* 138.

33. LaHaye, *The Coming Peace,* 170.

34. John Hagee, *Beginning of the End: The Assassination of Yitzhak Rabin and the Coming Antichrist* (Nashville, TN: Thomas Nelson, 1996), 124; Robertson quoted in Michael Lind, "Rev. Robertson's Grand International Conspiracy Theory," *New York Review of Books,* February 2, 1995, http://www .nybooks.com/articles/archives/1995/feb/02/rev-robertsons-grand-international -conspiracy-theo/.

35. LaHaye, *The Coming Peace,* 60, 61.

36. Quoted in Evans, *Israel,* 120.

37. Tim LaHaye, quoted in Michelle Goldberg, *Kingdom Coming: The Rise of Christian Nationalism* (New York: Norton, 2006), 161.

38. LaHaye, *The Coming Peace,* 13.

39. Michael Standaert, *Skipping towards Armageddon: The Politics and Propaganda of the Left Behind Novels and the LaHaye Empire* (New York: Soft Skull Press, 2006), 13–14. On the popularity of the novels, see Craig Unger, "American Rapture," *Vanity Fair,* December 2005, 204.

40. Tim LaHaye and Jerry B. Jenkins, *Apollyon: The Destroyer Is Unleashed* (Colorado Springs, CO: Tyndale, 1999), 2.

41. Melani McAlister, "Prophecy, Politics, and the Popular: The *Left Behind* Series and Christian Fundamentalism's New World Order," *South Atlantic Quarterly* 102 (2003): 773–798.

42. LaHaye, *The Coming Peace,* 16, 170.

43. Tim LaHaye and Jerry B. Jenkins, *The Mark: The Beast Rules the World* (Colorado Springs, CO: Tyndale, 2000), 235.

44. Tim LaHaye and Jerry B. Jenkins, *Desecration: Antichrist Takes the Throne* (Colorado Springs, CO: Tyndale, 2001), 339.

45. Tim LaHaye and Jerry B. Jenkins, *The Remnant: On the Brink of Armageddon* (Colorado Springs, CO: Tyndale, 2002), 264, 225.

46. Ibid., 169, 174, 100.

47. Tim LaHaye and Jerry B. Jenkins, *Armageddon: The Cosmic Battle of the Ages* (Colorado Springs, CO: Tyndale, 2003), 339; Tim LaHaye and Jerry B. Jenkins, *Glorious Appearing: The End of Days* (Colorado Springs, CO: Tyndale, 2004), 28.

48. LaHaye and Jenkins, *Glorious Appearing,* 200.

49. LaHaye and Jenkins, *Armageddon,* 251.

50. LaHaye and Jenkins, *Glorious Appearing,* 273.

51. LaHaye and Jenkins, *The Mark,* 234.

52. Merrill Simon, *Jerry Falwell and the Jews* (Middle Village, NY: Jonathan David, 1984), 87–88.

53. Clark, *Allies for Armageddon,* 189.

54. Kenneth L. Woodward, "Born Again!" *Newsweek,* October 25, 1976, 68.

55. Quoted in Donald Wagner, "Evangelicals and Israel: Theological Roots of a Political Alliance," *The Christian Century,* November 4, 1998, 1020–1026.

56. Clark, *Allies for Armageddon,* 189–192; Halsell, *Prophecy and Politics,* 73–74, 118–122.

57. Clark, *Allies for Armageddon,* 192. Falwell was fond of telling the story (which journalists and historians have repeated) that Begin called him with the news before letting Reagan know. Though Begin in fact only called him a few days later, the story indicates the pride that Falwell and other evangelical leaders expressed at being insiders with access to the highest echelons of government in Israel.

58. Evans, *Israel,* 9–11.

59. On Robertson and Falwell in Lebanon, see Clark, *Allies for Armageddon,* 193.

60. Falwell, *Old Time Gospel Hour,* November 7, 1982; transcript at http://crwsarchive.berkeley.edu/sites/default/files/shared/sourcedocs/1982-11.pdf, p. 13.

61. Sara Diamond, *Spiritual Warfare: The Politics of the Christian Right* (Boston: South End Press, 1989), 203.

62. Quoted in Irvine H. Anderson, *Biblical Prophecy and Middle East Policy: The Promised Land, America and Israel, 1917–2002* (Gainesville: University Press of Florida, 2005), 123.

63. Hagee, *Beginning of the End,* 16.

64. Quotations from Clark, *Allies for Armageddon,* 192–193.

65. Quoted in Caitlin Stewart, "Patriotism, National Identity, and Foreign Policy: The US–Israeli Alliance in the Twenty-First Century," in *United States Foreign Policy and National Identity in the 21st Century,* ed. Kenneth Christie (New York: Rout-

ledge, 2009), 58; Nate Perlmutter and Ruth Ann Perlmutter, *The Real Anti-Semitism in America* (New York: Arbor House, 1982), 156; Irving Kristol, "The Political Dilemma of America's Jews," *Commentary*, July 1984, 23–29.

66. These observations on parallels between conservative evangelicals and neoconservatives rely on Andrew J. Bacevich, *The New American Militarism: How Americans Are Seduced by War* (New York: Oxford University Press, 2005); Justin Vaïsse, *Neoconservatism: The Biography of a Movement*, trans. Arthur Goldhammer (Cambridge, MA: Harvard University Press, 2010); David Bruce MacDonald, *Thinking History, Fighting Evil: Neoconservatives and the Perils of Analogy* (Lanham, MD: Lexington Books, 2009); John Ehrman, *The Rise of Neoconservativism: Intellectuals and Foreign Affairs, 1945–1994* (New Haven, CT: Yale University Press, 1996); Gary Dorrien, *The Neoconservative Mind: Politics, Culture, and the War of Ideology* (Philadelphia: Temple University Press, 1993); and Jacob Heilbrunn, *They Knew They Were Right: The Rise of the Neocons* (New York: Doubleday, 2008).

67. Kristol, "Political Dilemma of America's Jews."

68. Lind, "Rev. Robertson's Grand International Conspiracy Theory"; Clark, *Allies for Armageddon*, 195–196.

69. Clark, *Allies for Armageddon*, 217; Abraham H. Foxman, "Why Evangelical Support for Israel Is a Good Thing," Jewish Telegraphic Agency, *Daily News Bulletin*, July 16, 2002. Ze'ev Chafets describes this post–9/11 alliance based on a common Islamic foe in *A Match Made in Heaven: American Jews, Christian Zionists, and One Man's Exploration of the Weird and Wonderful Judeo-Evangelical Alliance* (New York: Harper Collins, 2007).

70. "Falwell Brands Mohammed a 'Terrorist,'" *60 Minutes*, CBS News, June 5, 2003, http://www.cbsnews.com/news/falwell-brands-mohammed-a-terrorist/.

7. Homeland Insecurities

1. George W. Bush, "Address to the Joint Session of the 107th Congress," September 20, 2001, 65–73, https://georgewbush-whitehouse.archives.gov/infocus/bush record/documents/Selected_Speeches_George_W_Bush.pdf.

2. Gary Gerson quoted in Nancy Gibbs, "If You Want to Humble an Empire," *Time*, September 14, 2001. For other examples, see Samuel G. Freedman, "We're All on the Front Lines Now," *USA Today*, September 13, 2001; Martin Peretz, "Israel, the United States, and Evil," *New Republic*, September 24, 2001.

3. Jan Freeman, "Existentially Speaking," *Boston Globe*, February 4, 2007.

4. David Frum and Richard Perle, *An End to Evil: How to Win the War on Terror* (New York: Random House, 2003), 7.

5. George F. Will, "The End of Our Holiday from History," *Washington Post,* September 12, 2001, A31; Clyde Haberman, "When the Unimaginable Happens and It's Right Outside Your Window," *New York Times,* September 12, 2001, A10; James Bennet, "The Israelis: Spilled Blood Is Seen as Bond That Draws Two Nations Closer," *New York Times,* September 12, 2001, A22; Bill Keller, "America's Emergency Line: 9/11," *New York Times,* September 12, 2001, A27; Bruce Hoffman, "The Logic of Suicide Terrorism," *Atlantic,* June 2003, 40–47.

6. Keller, "America's Emergency Line"; Dexter Filkins, *The Forever War* (New York: Knopf, 2008), 45; Carolyn Davis, "This Day We Joined the Dangerous World," *Philadelphia Inquirer,* September 12, 2001, A27.

7. Quotations from Bennet, "The Israelis." See also Brian Whitaker, "Sharon Likens Arafat to Bin Laden," *Guardian,* September 14, 2001. For agreement with Sharon, see Alan Dershowitz, "Bin Laden's Inspiration," *Jerusalem Post,* November 10, 2005. For Arafat's refutation, see Ian Fisher, "Arafat Disavows Bin Laden, Saying 'He Never Helped Us,'" *New York Times,* December 16, 2002. For a rejection of the connection between the two men on pragmatic grounds, see Gerald Seib, "Arafat Can't Be Dealt with Like bin Laden Because There Isn't Any Viable Alternative," *Wall Street Journal,* December 5, 2001.

8. Lisa Stampnitzky, *Disciplining Terror: How Experts Invented "Terrorism"* (Cambridge: Cambridge University Press, 2013), 139–164.

9. Benjamin Netanyahu, *Fighting Terrorism: How Democracies Can Defeat Domestic and International Terrorists* (New York: Farrar, Straus and Giroux, 1996). Peretz takes the same position in "Israel, the United States, and Evil."

10. On the second intifada, see Mark A. Tessler, *A History of the Israeli-Palestinian Conflict,* 2nd ed. (Bloomington: Indiana University Press, 2009), 807–827.

11. Seth Ackerman, "Al-Aqsa Intifada and the U.S. Media," *Journal of Palestine Studies* 30, no. 2 (2000–2001): 61–74; Barbie Zelizer, David Park, and David Gudelunas, "How Bias Shapes the News: Challenging *The New York Times'* Status as a Newspaper of Record on the Middle East," *Journalism* 3 (2002): 283–307.

12. Lee Hockstader, "Israelis Say U.S. Could Learn from Their Tactics," *Washington Post,* September 13, 2001, 13; Hockstader, "Sharon Defies Bush's Request for Peace Talks," *Washington Post,* September 16, 2001, 16.

13. "Giuliani: Israel, U.S. Shoulder-to-Shoulder in Fight against Terror," *Haaretz* (via the Associated Press), December 9, 2001, http://www.haaretz.com/news/giuliani -israel-u-s-shoulder-to-shoulder-in-fight-against-terror-1.76912.

14. Charles Krauthammer, "Banish Arafat Now," *Washington Post,* April 5, 2002, A23. On the convergence of the war on terror with the second intifada, see Derek Gregory, *The Colonial Present: Afghanistan, Palestine, Iraq* (Malden, MA: Blackwell, 2004), 107–143.

15. Stephen Graham, "Laboratories of War: United States–Israeli Collaboration in Urban War and Securitization," *Brown Journal of World Affairs* 17, no. 1 (2010): 31–51 (marine quoted on 36); Seymour Hersh, *Chain of Command: The Road from 9/11 to Abu Ghraib* (New York: HarperCollins, 2004), 279–280; Chris McGreal, "Send In the Bulldozers: What Israel Told Marines about Urban Battles," *Guardian,* April 2, 2003, https://www.theguardian.com/world/2003/apr/02/iraq.israel; Eric Fair, *Consequence: A Memoir* (New York: Henry Holt, 2016), 106 (reference to "Palestinian chair"); Steve Niva, "Walling Off Iraq: Israel's Imprint on U.S. Counterinsurgency Doctrine," *Middle East Policy* 15, no. 3 (2008): 67–79 (Iraqi protester quoted on 68).

16. President George W. Bush, "Message to the Congress Transmitting Proposed Legislation to Create the Department of Homeland Security," June 18, 2002, http://www.presidency.ucsb.edu/ws/index.php?pid=64050&st=&st1; Avi Dichter and Daniel Byman, "Israel's Lessons for Fighting Terrorists and Their Implications for the United States," Saban Center for Middle East Policy at the Brookings Institute, Analysis Paper no. 8, March 2006; Jeffrey A. Larsen and Tasha L. Pravecek, *Comparative U.S.-Israeli Homeland Security,* Maxwell Air Force Base, Alabama, USAF Counterproliferation Center, Air University, 2006, http://purl.access.gpo.gov/GPO/LPS105341; Thomas Henriksen, "The Israeli Approach to Irregular Warfare and Implications for the United States," Joint Special Operations University Report 07-3 (Hurlburt Field, FL: JSOU Press, 2007), https://jsoupublic.socom.mil/publications/jsoupubs_2007.php, p. 1.

17. Michael Walzer, *Just and Unjust Wars: A Moral Argument with Historical Illustrations* (1977; repr., New York: Basic Books, 2015), 81–85; Stephen Graham, *Cities under Siege: The New Military Urbanism* (London: Verso, 2010), loc. 5583 of 10754, Kindle; Andrew Bacevich, "How We Became Israel: Peace Means Dominion for Netanyahu—and Now for Us," *American Conservative,* September 10, 2012, 16.

18. Lisa Hajjar, "International Humanitarian Law and 'Wars On Terror': A Comparative Analysis of Israeli and American Doctrines and Policies," *Journal of Palestine Studies* 36, no. 1 (2006): 32.

19. "An Eye for an Eye," *60 Minutes,* CBS News, November 20, 2001, https://www.cbsnews.com/news/an-eye-for-an-eye-20-11-2001/.

20. *Munich,* directed by Steven Spielberg (Universal Pictures, 2005); Michelle Goldberg, "Steven Spielberg's Controversial New Film: The War on 'Munich,'" *Spiegel Online,* December 20, 2005, http://www.spiegel.de/international/steven-spielberg-s-controversial-new-film-the-war-on-munich-a-391525-druck.html.

21. Yosefa Loshitzky, "The Post-Holocaust Jew in the Age of 'The War on Terror': Steven Spielberg's *Munich,*" *Journal of Palestine Studies* 40, no. 2 (2011): 77–87.

22. David Brooks, "What 'Munich' Left Out," *New York Times,* December 11, 2005, C13.

23. The book was written before 9/11. In *The Kill Artist* (New York: Random House, 2000), Allon does express remorse after an assassination, saying that it only felt good until "you start to think you're as bad as the people you're killing" (p. 82). However, by the fifth novel, *The Prince of Fire* (New York: Signet, 2005), Allon proudly describes filling a body with eleven bullets for every Jew murdered (pp. 88, 289), an item repeated in the novels that followed.

24. Bush, "Address to the Joint Session of the 107th Congress," 68–69.

25. Fareed Zakaria, "The Politics of Rage: Why Do They Hate Us?" *Newsweek,* October 15, 2001, 22.

26. Mary-Jayne McKay, "Falwell Brands Mohammed a 'Terrorist': Conservative Christian Says Founder of Islam Set a Bad Example," *60 Minutes,* CBS News, June 5, 2003, http://www.cbsnews.com/news/falwell-brands-mohammed-a-terrorist/; John Hagee, *Jerusalem Countdown: A Warning to the World* (Lake Mary, FL: FrontLine, 2006), 42, 193; Chuck Missler, *Prophecy 20/20: Profiling the Future through the Lens of Scripture* (Nashville, TN: Nelson Books, 2006), 148 (emphasis in original). See also Stephen Fink, "Fear under Construction: Islamophobia within American Christian Zionism," *Islamophobia Studies Journal* 2, no. 1 (2014): 26–43.

27. Christopher Hitchens, "Defending Islamofascism: It's a Valid Term," *Slate,* October 22, 2007, http://www.slate.com/articles/news_and_politics/fighting_words /2007/10/defending_islamofascism.html; "Bush: U.S. at War with 'Islamic Fascists,'" CNN.com, August 10, 2006, http://www.cnn.com/2006/POLITICS/08/10/washington .terror.plot/. For a discussion of the term "Islamofascism," see Katha Pollitt, "Wrong War, Wrong Word," *Nation,* August 24, 2006, https://www.thenation.com/article /wrong-war-wrong-word/; Fred Halliday, *Shocked and Awed: A Dictionary of the War on Terror* (Berkeley: University of California Press, 2010), 185–187.

28. Boteach quoted in Brian Klug, *Being Jewish and Doing Justice: Bringing Argument to Life* (London: Vallentine Mitchell, 2012), 69; Natan Sharansky, "On Hating the Jews," *Commentary,* November 1, 2003, 26–34; Daniel Goldhagen, "Globalization of Antisemitism," *Forward,* May 2, 2003, http://forward.com/opinion /8736/the-globalization-of-antisemitism/; Andrei Markovits, *Uncouth Nation: Why Europe Dislikes America* (Princeton, NJ: Princeton University Press, 2007). The link between anti-Semitism and anti-Americanism became part of the U.S. State Department's 2005 *Report on Global Anti-Semitism.* The first section of the executive summary ends with the statement that "Global anti-Semitism in recent years has had four main sources." The fourth source is described as "Criticism of both the United States and globalization that spills over to Israel, and to Jews in general who are identified

with both." See *Anti-Semitism in the United States: Report on Global Anti-Semitism,* U.S. Department of State, January 5, 2005, executive summary, part 1, https://2009 -2017.state.gov/j/drl/rls/40258.htm.

29. Josef Joffe, "The Demons of Europe," *Commentary,* January 1, 2004, 29–34. Markovits repurposes the phrase "twin brothers" from André Glucksmann: see *Uncouth Nation,* 150–200. For further discussion of the relationship between anti-Americanism and anti-Semitism, see Alvin Rosenfeld, *Anti-Americanism and Anti-Semitism: A New Frontier of Bigotry,* American Jewish Committee, July 1, 2003, http://www.ajc.org/site/apps/nlnet/content3.aspx?c=7oJILSPwFfJSG&b =8449851&ct=12484851.

30. Larsen and Pravecek, *Comparative U.S.-Israeli Homeland Security,* 43, 67, 69.

31. James Traub, "The Dark History of Defending 'The Homeland,'" *New York Times Magazine,* April 5, 2016, https://nyti.ms/2pCAuCX. For more on the meanings of "homeland," see my article "Homeland Insecurities: Reflections on Language and Space," *Radical History Review* 85 (2003): 82–93.

32. Michelle Malkin, "Candidates Ignore 'Security Moms,' at Their Peril," op-ed, *USA Today,* July 20, 2004, https://usatoday30.usatoday.com/news/opinion/editorials /2004-07-20-malkin_x.htm; Inderpal Grewal, "'Security Moms' in the Early Twentieth-Century United States: The Gender of Security in Neo-liberalism," *Women's Studies Quarterly,* 34, nos. 1–2 (2006): 25–39; Alberto Gonzales, "Nothing Improper," *Washington Post,* April 15, 2007, B07.

33. National Commission on Terrorist Attacks upon the United States, *The 9/11 Commission Report* (New York: Norton, 2004), 362.

34. *Homeland,* Showtime Networks, http://www.sho.com/homeland; Traub, "The Dark History of Defending 'The Homeland.'"

35. *NCIS,* CBS, https://www.cbs.com/shows/ncis/. On the popularity of the character Ziva David, see Mike Hale, "Sugar and Spice and Vicious Beatings," *New York Times,* March 10, 2011, 6.

36. For JINSA, see the brochure *Empowering Law Enforcement Protecting America,* which discusses the Homeland Security Program (formerly known as the Law Enforcement Exchange Program [LEEP]), at http://www.jinsa.org/files /LEEPbookletforweb.pdf. For ADL, see website for National Counter-Terrorism Seminar in Israel, https://www.adl.org/who-we-are/our-organization/signature-programs /law-enforcement-training/counter-terrorism-seminar. See also Max Blumenthal, "From Occupation to 'Occupy': The Israelification of American Domestic Security," *Al-Akhbar English,* December 2, 2011, https://english.al-akhbar.com/node/2178.

37. LEEP, "Empowering Law Enforcement Protecting America."

38. Sari Horwitz, "Israeli Experts Teach Police on Terrorism," *Washington Post,* June 12, 2005, C01.

39. LEEP, "Empowering Law Enforcement Protecting America"; Anemone quoted in Hoffman, "The Logic of Suicide Terrorism."

40. LEEP, "Empowering Law Enforcement Protecting America."

41. Andrea Adelson, "Lessons from Israel," *Jewish Journal,* October 3, 2002. For "matrix of control," see Jeff Halper, "The 94 Percent Solution: A Matrix of Control," *Middle East Report* 216 (Fall 2000): 14–19.

42. Rebecca Anna Stoil, "Dichter's Tour Fosters Bonds with US Marshals," *Jerusalem Post,* October 18, 2006, 4.

43. Sarah Kershaw, "Suicide Bombings Bring Urgency to Police in U.S.," *New York Times,* July 25, 2005, A14; Travis Hudson, "AP Investigation: With CIA Help, NYPD Moves Covertly in Muslim Areas Post-9/11," *Dallas News,* August 24, 2011. On the Israeli inspiration for the Demographics Unit, see Matt Apuzzo and Adam Goldman, *Enemies Within: Inside the NYPD's Secret Spying Unit and bin Laden's Final Plot against America* (New York: Simon and Schuster, 2013), 73. See also Horwitz, "Israeli Experts Teach Police on Terrorism"; Blumenthal, "From Occupation to 'Occupy.'"

44. Kershaw, "Suicide Bombings Bring Urgency"; Horwitz, "Israeli Experts Teach Police on Terrorism."

45. H. J. Reza, "Arming Marines with Know-How for Staying Alive," *Los Angeles Times,* October 24, 2005.

46. Daniel K. Eisenbud, "U.S. Police Delegation Visits Israel to Learn Counterterrorism Techniques," *Jerusalem Post,* September 9, 2016, 4; for the "Star of David," see "JINSA Launches Law Enforcement Exchange," *JINSA Online,* September 6, 2002, http://www.jinsa.org/events-programs/law-enforcement-exchange-program-leep/jinsa-launches-law-enforcement-exchange; for the emotional force experienced by American law enforcement, see Horwitz, "Israeli Experts Teach Police on Terrorism."

47. ADL, "Law Enforcement and Society: Lessons on the Holocaust," http://dc.adl.org/law-enforcement-and-society/; United States Holocaust Memorial Museum, "Law Enforcement," https://www.ushmm.org/professionals-and-student-leaders/law-enforcement.

48. On the consortium between Boeing and Elbit, and quotation, see "Israeli Technology to Keep US Borders Safe," Israel21c, October 15, 2008, https://www.israel21c.org/israeli-technology-to-keep-us-borders-safe/. On the southern border drones, see "Elbit UAVs patrolling Arizona-Mexico Border," Globes, June 28, 2004, http://www.globes.co.il/en/article-809421. On Elbit Systems's 2014 and 2018 contracts, see Kathleen Miller, "Israel's Elbit Wins U.S. Border Work after Boeing Dumped," Bloomberg Technology, February 27, 2014, https://www.bloomberg.com/news/articles/2014-02-27/israel-s-elbit-wins-u-s-border-surveillance-contract; "U.S. Customs and Border

Protection Certifies Elbit Systems of America's In-fill Radar and Tower System," PR Newswire, February 1, 2018, https://www.prnewswire.com/news-releases/us-customs -and-border-protection-certifies-elbit-systems-of-americas-in-fill-radar-and-tower -system-300591799.html.

49. Naomi Klein, "Laboratory for a Fortressed World," *The Nation,* July 2, 2007, 9; Thomas Friedman, "Israel Discovers Oil," *New York Times,* June 10, 2007, C15.

50. Darryl Li, "The Gaza Strip as Laboratory: Notes in the Wake of Disengagement," *Journal of Palestine Studies* 35, no. 2 (2006): 38–55.

51. Yotam Feldman, "The Lab: Filmmaker's View," *Al-Jazeera,* May 8, 2014, https://www.aljazeera.com/programmes/witness/2014/05/lab-20145475423526313 .html; Jonathan Cook, "'The Lab': Israel Tests Weapons, Tactics on Captive Palestinian Population," *Washington Report on Middle Eastern Affairs,* September 2013, 16–17.

52. Jeff Halper, *War against the People: Israel, The Palestinians and Global Pacification* (London: Pluto Press, 2015), loc. 2855 of 9372, Kindle.

53. Quoted in Cook, "The Lab," 17.

54. Klein, "Laboratory for a Fortressed World."

55. Dan Senor and Saul Singer, *Start-Up Nation: The Story of Israel's Economic Miracle* (New York: Hachette, 2009).

56. Rajiv Chandrasekaran, *Imperial Life in the Emerald City: Inside Iraq's Green Zone* (New York: Knopf, 2006), 144–147.

57. Senor and Singer, *Start-Up Nation,* 8, 61.

58. Ibid., 53.

59. Ibid., 48.

60. Ibid., 150.

61. Ibid., 81.

62. Ibid., 228 (bracketed phrase in original).

63. Ibid., 229, 235.

Conclusion

1. Jeffrey Goldberg, "Obama on Zionism and Hamas," *Atlantic,* May 12, 2008.

2. Tessa Stuart, "Why Trump Calls for Racial Profiling after Attacks," *Rolling Stone,* September 19, 2016; Tracy Wilkinson, "Trump Says Walls Work: 'Just ask Israel,'" *Los Angeles Times,* February 8, 2017.

3. Alan Rappeport, "Donald Trump Calls Himself 'Lifelong Supporter' of Israel," First Draft newsletter, *New York Times,* March 21, 2016, https://www.nytimes .com/politics/first-draft/2016/03/21/donald-trump-calls-himself-lifelong-supporter -of-israel/.

4. Peter Beinart, *The Crisis of Zionism* (New York: Macmillan, 2012).

5. Christina Maza, "Support for Israel among Young Evangelicals Drops Despite Biblical Teachings on Jewish Homeland," *Newsweek,* December 5, 2017.

6. *Promoting Human Rights by Ending Israeli Military Detention of Palestinian Children Act, H.R. 4391,* 115th Congress, 1st Session (2017).

7. "Nikki Haley's Jerusalem Speech at UN—Full Speech," UN Watch, December 10, 2017, https://www.unwatch.org/nikki-haleys-jerusalem-speech-un-full-text/.

8. *World War Z,* directed by Marc Foster (Paramount Pictures, 2013). The film is based on the book *World War Z: An Oral History of the Zombie War,* by Max Brooks (New York: Random House, 2006).

ACKNOWLEDGMENTS

This book could not have been written without the help of so many people and institutions that I fear I may not thank them all.

The Institute for Advanced Study in Princeton, New Jersey, provided me with a fellowship for starting my research. A Dean's Leave from the School of Arts and Sciences at the University of Pennsylvania allowed me to finish writing the book.

I appreciated the opportunity to explore ideas in conversation with scholars at many institutions: the Center for American Studies and Research at the American University of Beirut, the Clinton Institute at University College Dublin, George Washington University, the John F. Kennedy Institute at Freie Universität Berlin, the Rothermere American Institute at the University of Oxford, Stockton University, Temple University, the University of California at Los Angeles, the University of Illinois Urbana-Champaign, the University of Lisbon, the University of Pennsylvania, and the University of Warsaw.

I am grateful to Tim Marr, Hilton Obenzinger, and Basem Ra'ad for inviting me to a conference on Herman Melville in Jerusalem, where I got a glimpse of the nineteenth-century Holy Land through Melville's eyes. I also benefited from a fellowship from the Palestinian American Research Center that allowed me to participate in the first Faculty Development Seminar in Palestine.

My talented research assistant, Aaron Steinberg-Madow, ingeniously found everything I asked for, and more—his findings were always most interesting. He synthesized vast amounts of material in beautifully written summaries that could have been chapters on their own. I look forward to reading the book that I know he will write one day.

Phillip Maciak and Danielle Holtz contributed vital research at an early stage, and Mark Firmani assisted in preparing the final manuscript with great care.

Chapter 2 builds on ideas first presented in "Zionism as Anti-Colonialism: The Case of Exodus," *American Literary History* 25, no. 4 (Winter 2013): 870–895. I first explored the ideas about homeland security that are developed in Chapter 7 in "Homeland Insecurities: Transformations of Language and Space," in *September 11 in History: A Watershed Moment?*, edited by Mary Dudziak (Durham, NC: Duke University Press, 2003), 55–69, and "In the Name of Security," *Review of International American Studies* 3, no. 3–4, no. 1 (Winter 2008/Spring 2009): 15–24.

Many colleagues contributed valuable readings and useful knowledge for different parts of the book: John Bodnar, Paul Breines, Anna Brickhouse, Thomas Dichter, Jed Esty, Nava Et-Shalom, Marjorie Feld, Keith Feldman, Israel Gershoni, Sylvia Gillet, Åsmund Borgen Gjerde, Pamela Haag, Waleed Hazbun, Ed Linenthal, Alex Lubin, Ian Lustick, Saree Makdisi, Samuel Moyn, Mounira Soliman, Michael Staub, Bob Vitalis, and Barbie Zelizer. I thank them all.

Six people read the entire manuscript and made invaluable contributions, including two readers for Harvard University Press. I am especially grateful to Melani McAlister, the first person I turned to with my idea for the book. She generously shared her expertise and friendship at every stage, reading and commenting on each chapter, sometimes more than once. At Princeton I had the privilege to meet Joan Wallach Scott, who, from start to finish, shared her belief in the project and her wisdom about its contents. Martha Hodes helped me to see many of the issues anew and to think about a diverse readership. Doug Rossinow was an enthusiastic interlocutor on email, engaging deeply with many aspects of the book and sharing his own extensive knowledge. Paul Kramer brought to the final draft ideas about the broader American context, and his comments about the writing sharpened my presentation of the issues. Rashid Khalidi generously answered questions about the Middle East context, and his response to the final draft made me hopeful that other readers would also "get it" as thoroughly as he did.

When I decided to write this book, I knew I wanted to work with Joyce Seltzer of Harvard University Press, and I have remained grateful ever since that she agreed to be my editor. She has been supportive and demanding, open minded and questioning in just the right proportions. She accompanied me on a journey of grappling with the issues that this book raises. For the final preparation of the manuscript, Louise Robbins did a magnificent job editing to unite style and substance.

I am grateful to many dear friends who, in addition to reading parts of the book, have supported me in more ways than I can say. Judy Frank has been involved in every aspect of living this book. She has shared stories of her own special relationship between Israel and America, and lovingly included me in her wonderful family with Liz, Abby, and Claire. Sherri Grasmuck and John Landreau have nurtured me—intellect, body, and soul—especially with gracious hospitality at their forest retreat. Nina Gerassi-Navarro has long accompanied me on the roller coaster of writing books and raising families with a warm heart and cheerful spirit. No one knows how to talk about writing like Carla Kaplan, and I appreciate our many conversations. Peter Agree generously provided professional and personal advice, always in his calm and knowing way.

My father, Solomon Kaplan, passed away while I was writing this book. He would have disagreed with much of it, but he would have fiercely defended my right to have my say.

I have been blessed with the love and support of two amazing women— my mother, Eunice Kaplan, and my daughter, Rose Weiss. While I was writing this book, they were each going through major changes in their own lives with grace and determination that continues to inspire me.

I dedicate this book to Paul Statt, my life partner and daily companion. He once quoted Martin Amis to me: "you know you're dealing with experience, with main-event experience, when a cliché grips you with all its original power." Paul, I couldn't have done this without you.

ILLUSTRATION CREDITS

INDEX

Note: Page numbers in *italics* indicate figures.